Praise for *1968*

"For a generation of baby-boomers Mark Kurlansky's eminently readable book will bring a flood of memories of an exceptional year in the exceptional 1960s."

—*The Economist*

"Mark Kurlansky writes history as verbal collage. He begins with a grand subject, creates or borrows shards of narrative and character and dramatic occasion, then arranges the pieces so they touch and merge with one another in innovative ways. The resulting pastiche delights and informs.... Kurlansky is splendid at clipping key moments and telling remarks from an exhaustively documented era."

—*The Chicago Tribune*

"In this highly opinionated and highly readable history, Kurlansky makes a case for why 1968 has lasting relevance in the United States and around the world. Whether you agree or disagree with its points, you'll find it makes for fascinating reading."

—Dan Rather, CBS News

"Mark Kurlansky brings [this] watershed year to life . . . [he] re-creates that amazing year . . . in a sweeping popular history . . . [a] fascinating account."

—*Seattle Post-Intelligencer*

"Whether celebrating the significance of the mundane, as in his recent histories of such prosaic topics as salt and cod, or illuminating a slice of time, Kurlansky finds the universe in a grain of sand. The result here is a bracing retrospective of a terrible, pivotal moment in our history, one that many of us who were there can recall only with an almost guilty nostalgia."

—*Portland Oregonian*

"Many of 1968's events are so firmly lodged into our institutional memory that they've ossified into little more than familiar touchstones.... But Mark Kurlansky's *1968* breathes a new life into those moments and others. In novelistic prose, he uncovers how small collections of people and direction-changing incidents formed a perfect storm of geopolitical neurosis."

—*Chicago Sun-Times*

Praise for
Cod: A Biography of the Fish that Changed the World

(Winner of the 1998 James Beard Award for Food Writing)

"This eminently readable book is a new tool for scanning world history."
— *The New York Times Book Review*

"An elegant brief history . . . related with vast brio and wit."
— *The Los Angeles Times*

"[A] naturalist triumph, a smoothly written, beautifully designed book . . . Kurlansky's steady tone, somewhere between *Captains Courageous* and the mourner's Kaddish, is perfect."
— *Boston magazine*

Praise for *A Chosen Few:*
The Resurrection of European Jewry

"In this valuable book, Kurlansky brings alive the missing years of European Jewry."
— *The Washington Post Book World*

"Consistently absorbing . . . *A Chosen Few* investigates the relatively uncharted territory of an encouraging phenomena."
— *Los Angeles Times*

"A richly descriptive and insightful survey . . . With a novelist's eye for irony and description, [Kurlansky] offers many moments of transcendence and humor; entertaining culture clashes between communists and capitalists, religious and secular, Zionists and diasporists. . . . A lively, penetrating follow-up to Holocaust readings that speaks volumes about the resiliency of the Jewish people."
— *Kirkus Reviews*

MARK KURLANSKY is the award-winning and *New York Times* bestselling author of *Nonviolence: 25 Lessons from the History of a Dangerous Idea, The Big Oyster: History on the Half Shell, Salt: A World History, The Basque History of the World, Cod: A Biography of the Fish That Changed the World*, and several other books. He lives in New York City.

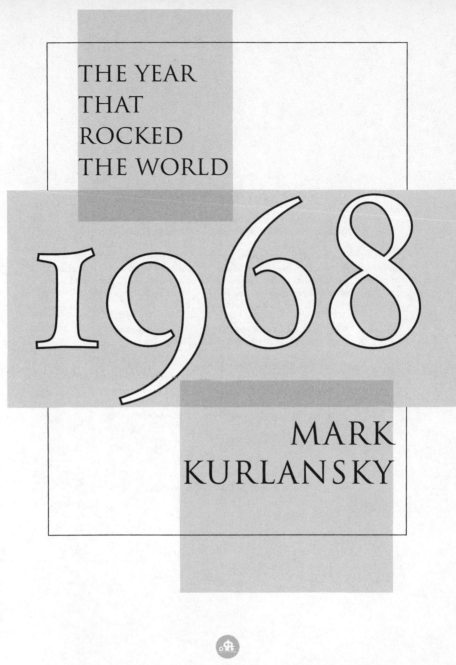

THE YEAR
THAT
ROCKED
THE WORLD

1968

MARK
KURLANSKY

RANDOM HOUSE TRADE PAPERBACKS
NEW YORK

2005 Random House Trade Paperback Edition

Copyright © 2004 by Mark Kurlansky
Questions for discussion © 2005 by Random House, Inc.

All rights reserved under International and Pan-American Copyright
Conventions. Published in the United States by Random House Trade Paperbacks,
an imprint of The Random House Publishing Group, a division of Random House,
Inc., New York, and simultaneously in Canada by Random House
of Canada Limited, Toronto.

RANDOM HOUSE TRADE PAPERBACKS and colophon
are trademarks of Random House, Inc.

Library of Congress Control Number: 2004095998

ISBN 0-345-45582-7

Random House website address: www.atrandom.com

Printed in the United States of America

4 6 8 9 7 5

Book design by Carole Lowenstein

To my beautiful Talia Feiga;
so that she will know truth from lies, love life, hate war,
and always believe that she can change the world

ACKNOWLEDGMENTS

I want to express my deep admiration and profound gratitude to Walter Cronkite, Gene Roberts, and Daniel Schorr, who informed this book with countless invaluable insights and the wisdom they so generously shared from three most remarkable careers.

I also owe a great debt to Nancy Miller, my patient editor, who has been dreaming and thinking with me about this book for ten years; to Deirdre Lanning, who helped me through a cybernightmare; and to my absolutely incomparable agent, Charlotte Sheedy, who is the kind of sixties person I am proud to have as a friend.

Thanks to Alice Dowd of the New York Public Library for her help and cooperation, to Mary Haskell for generously sharing her poster collection, and to my friend Hanna Kordowicz for her help in Poland, Elzbieta Wirpsza for her Polish translation, my friend Krystyna Skalski and Andrzej Dudzinski for help in Warsaw, Mark Segall for his assistance, and Dariusz Stola for his insights into Polish history. Thanks to Peter Katel, Fernando Moreno, and Tito Ramirez Morales for help in Mexico City, and Chantal Siri and Chantal Regnault in Paris. Thanks to Marlene Adler for her help at CBS, Jane Klain at the Museum of Broadcasting, Sarah Shannon for help in research, and Deborah Kroplick, without whose help and enthusiasm I am not sure how I would have finished.

Thanks to my wife, Marian Mass, who helped me in a hundred ways and whose great heart renews my faith in the world, and to the memory of her sister, Janet Phibbs, who I think would have liked this book.

I am also deeply appreciative of the help given to me by Adolfo Aguilar Zinser, Raúl Álvarez Garín, Eleanor Bakhtadze, François Cerutti, Evelyn Cohen, Dany Cohn-Bendit, Lewis Cole, Roberto

Escudero, Konstanty Gebert, Alain Geismar, Radith Geismar, Suzanne Goldberg, Myrthokleia González Gallardo, Tom Hayden, Alain Krivine, Jacek Kuroń, Ifigenia Martínez, Pino Martínez de la Roca, Lorenzo Meyer, Adam Michnik, François Pignet, Roberto Rodríguez Baños, Nina and Eugeniusz Smolar, Joanna Szczesna, and especially Mark Rudd for his time, hospitality, the use of his unpublished manuscript, and for his honesty.

And to everyone who said "No!" and most especially all those who are still saying it.

CONTENTS

I think that the people want peace so much that one of these days governments had better get out of the way and let them have it.

—DWIGHT DAVID EISENHOWER, *1959*

There is a time when the operation of the machine becomes so odious, makes you so sick at heart, that you can't take part . . . and you've got to put your bodies upon the gears . . . and you've got to make it stop.

—MARIO SAVIO, *Berkeley, 1964*

The road is strewn with many dangers. . . . First is the danger of futility; the belief there is nothing one man or one woman can do against the enormous array of the world's ills. . . . Yet . . . each time a man stands up for an ideal, or acts to improve the lot of others, or strikes out against injustice, he sends forth a tiny ripple of hope, and crossing each other from a million different centers of energy and daring, those ripples build a current which can sweep down the mightiest walls of oppression and resistance.

—ROBERT F. KENNEDY, *Cape Town, South Africa, 1966*

Our program is based on the conviction that man and mankind are capable not only of learning about the world, but also of changing it.

—ALEXANDER DUBČEK, *speech in Bohemia, May 16, 1968*

We criticize all society where people are passive.

—DANIEL COHN-BENDIT, *visiting London, June 1968*

Silence is sometimes a disgrace.

—YEVGENY YEVTUSHENKO, *August 22, 1968*

The youth rebellion is a worldwide phenomenon that has not been seen before in history. I do not believe they will calm down and be ad execs at thirty as the Establishment would like us to believe. Millions of young people all over the world are fed up with shallow unworthy authority running on a platform of bullshit.

—WILLIAM BURROUGHS, *"The Coming of the Purple Better One,"* Esquire, *November 1968*

The magic words are: Up against the wall motherfucker this is a stick-up!

—LEROI JONES (AMIRI BARAKA), *"Black People!," 1967*

INTRODUCTION
THE YEAR THAT
ROCKED THE WORLD

> One of the pleasures of middle age is to find out that one *was* right, and that one was much righter than one knew at say 17 or 23.
>
> —EZRA POUND, ABC of Reading, *1934*

There has never been a year like 1968, and it is unlikely that there will ever be one again. At a time when nations and cultures were still separate and very different—and in 1968 Poland, France, the United States, and Mexico were far more different from one another than they are today—there occurred a spontaneous combustion of rebellious spirits around the world.

There had been other years of revolution. 1848 had been such a year, but in contrast to 1968 its events were confined to Europe, its rebellions confined to similar issues. There had been other global events, the result of global empire building. And there was that huge, tragic global event, World War II. What was unique about 1968 was that people were rebelling over disparate issues and had in common only that desire to rebel, ideas about how to do it, a sense of alienation from the established order, and a profound distaste for authoritarianism in any form. Where there was communism they rebelled against communism, where there was capitalism they turned against that. The rebels rejected most institutions, political leaders, and political parties.

It was not planned and it was not organized. Rebellions were directed through hastily called meetings; some of the most important decisions were made on a moment's whim. The movements were anti-authoritarian and so were leaderless or had leaders who denied being leaders. Ideologies were seldom clear, and there was widespread agreement on very few issues. In 1969, when a federal grand jury indicted eight activists in connection with the demonstrations in Chicago in 1968, Abbie Hoffman, one of the eight, said about the group, "We couldn't agree on lunch." And though rebellion was everywhere, rarely did these forces come together, or when they did, as with the civil rights, antiwar, and feminist movements in the United States, or the labor and student movements in France and Italy, it was an alliance of temporary convenience, quickly dissolved.

Four historic factors merged to create 1968: the example of the civil rights movement, which at the time was so new and original; a generation that felt so different and so alienated that it rejected all forms of authority; a war that was hated so universally around the world that it provided a cause for all the rebels seeking one; and all of this occurring at the moment that television was coming of age but was still new enough not to have yet become controlled, distilled, and packaged the way it is today. In 1968 the phenomenon of a same-day broadcast from another part of the world was in itself a gripping new technological wonder.

The American war in Vietnam was not unique and certainly no more reprehensible than numerous other wars, including the earlier French war in Vietnam. But this time it was being pursued by a nation with unprecedented global power. At a time when colonies were struggling to re-create themselves as nations, when the "anticolonial struggle" had touched the idealism of people all over the world, here was a weak and fragile land struggling for independence while this new type of entity known as a "superpower" dropped more non-nuclear bombs on its small territory than had been dropped on all of Asia and Europe in World War II. At the height of 1968 fighting, the U.S. military was killing every week the same number of people or more as died in the September 11, 2001, World Trade Center attack. While within the movements in the United States, France, Germany, and Mexico there was tremendous splintering and factionalism, everyone could agree— because of the power and prestige of the United States and the brutal and clearly unfair nature of the American war in Vietnam—that they opposed the Vietnam War. When the American civil rights movement became split in 1968 between the advocates of nonviolence and the advocates of Black Power, the two sides could come together in agreement on opposition to the Vietnam War. Dissident movements around the world could be built up simply by coming out against the war.

When they wanted to protest, they knew how to do it; they knew about marches and sit-ins because of the American civil rights movement. They had seen it all on television from Mississippi, and they were eager to be freedom marchers themselves.

Those born in the aftermath of World War II, when "Holocaust" was a new word and the atom bomb had just been exploded, were born into a world that had little in common with everything before. The generation that grew up after World War II was so completely different from the World War II generation and the ones before it that the struggle for common ground was constant. They didn't even laugh at the same jokes. Comedians popular with the World War II generation such as Bob Hope and Jack Benny were not remotely funny to the new generation.

1968 was a time of shocking modernism, and modernism always fascinates the young and perplexes the old, yet in retrospect it was a time of an almost quaint innocence. Imagine Columbia students in New York and University of Paris students discovering from a distance that their experiences were similar and then meeting, gingerly approaching one another to find out what, if anything, they had in common. With amazement and excitement, people learned that they were using the same tactics in Prague, in Paris, in Rome, in Mexico, in New York. With new tools such as communication satellites and inexpensive erasable videotape, television was making everyone very aware of what everyone else was doing, and it was thrilling because for the first time in human experience the important, distant events of the day were immediate.

It will never be new again. "Global village" is a sixties term invented by Marshall McLuhan. The shrinking of the globe will never be so shocking in the same way that we will never again feel the thrill of the first moon shots or the first broadcasts from outer space. We now live in a world in which we await a new breakthrough every day. If another 1968 generation is ever produced, its movements will all have Web sites, carefully monitored by law enforcement, while they are e-mailing one another for updates. And no doubt other tools will be invented. But even the idea of new inventions has become banal.

Born in 1948, I was of the generation that hated the Vietnam War, protested against it, and has a vision of authority shaped by the memory of the peppery taste of tear gas and the way the police would slowly surround in casual flanking maneuvers before moving in, club first, for the kill. I am stating my prejudices at the outset because even now, more than three decades later, an attempt at objectivity on the subject of 1968 would be dishonest. Having read *The New York*

Times, Time, Life, Playboy, Le Monde, Le Figaro, a Polish daily and a weekly, and several Mexican papers from the year 1968—some claiming objectivity and others stating their prejudices—I am convinced that fairness is possible but true objectivity is not. The objective American press of 1968 was far more subjective than it realized.

Working on this book reminded me that there was a time when people spoke their minds and were not afraid to offend—and that since then, too many truths have been buried.

Mexican student movement silk-screen poster with the
SDS peace sign and a Cuban Che Guevara slogan "We shall win!"
(Amigos de la Unidad de Postgrado de la Escuela de Diseño A.C.)

PART I

THE WINTER OF OUR DISCONTENT

The things of the eye are done.
On the illuminated black dial,
green ciphers of a new moon—
one, two, three, four, five, six!
I breathe and cannot sleep.
Then morning comes,
saying, "This was night."

—ROBERT LOWELL, *"Myopia: a Night,"*
from For the Union Dead, 1964

CHAPTER 1

THE WEEK IT BEGAN

THE YEAR 1968 BEGAN the way any well-ordered year should—on a Monday morning. It was a leap year. February would have an extra day. The headline on the front page of *The New York Times* read, WORLD BIDS ADIEU TO A VIOLENT YEAR; CITY GETS SNOWFALL.

In Vietnam, 1968 had a quiet start. Pope Paul VI had declared January 1 a day of peace. For his day of peace, the pope had persuaded the South Vietnamese and their American allies to give a twelve-hour extension to their twenty-four-hour truce. The People's Liberation Armed Forces in South Vietnam, a pro–North Vietnamese guerrilla force popularly known as the Viet Cong, announced a seventy-two-hour cease-fire. In Saigon, the South Vietnamese government had forced shop owners to display banners that predicted, "1968 Will See the Success of Allied Arms."

At the stroke of midnight in South Vietnam's Mekong Delta, the church bells in the town of Mytho rang in the new year. Ten minutes later, while the bells were still ringing, a unit of Viet Cong appeared on the edge of a rice paddy and caught the South Vietnamese 2nd Marine Battalion by surprise, killing nineteen South Vietnamese marines and wounding another seventeen.

A *New York Times* editorial said that although the resumption of fighting had shattered hopes for peace, another chance would come with a cease-fire in February for Tet, the Vietnamese New Year.

"*L'année 1968, je la salue avec sérénité,*" pronounced Charles de Gaulle, the tall and regal seventy-eight-year-old president of France, on New Year's Eve. "I greet the year 1968 with serenity," he said from his ornate palace where he had been governing France since 1958. He had rewritten the constitution to make the president of France the most powerful head of state of any Western democracy. He was now three years into his second seven-year term and saw few problems on the horizon. From a gilded palace room, addressing French television—whose only two channels were entirely state controlled—he said that soon other nations would be turning to him and that he would be able to broker peace in not only Vietnam but also the Middle East. "All signs indicate, therefore, that we shall be in a position to contribute most effectively to international solutions." In recent years he had taken to referring to himself as "we."

As he gave his annual televised message to the French people, the man the French called the General or Le Grand Charles seemed "unusually mellow, almost avuncular," sparing harsh adjectives even for the United States, which of late he had been calling "odious." His tone contrasted with that of his 1967 New Year's message, when he had spoken of "the detestable unjust war" in Vietnam in which a "big nation" was destroying a small one. The French government had grown concerned at the level of animosity that France's allies had been directing at it.

France was enjoying a quiet and prosperous moment. After World War II, the Republic had fought its own Vietnam war, a fact that de Gaulle seemed to have forgotten. Ho Chi Minh, America's enemy, had been born under French colonial rule the same year as de Gaulle and had spent most of his life fighting the French. He had once lived in Paris under the pseudonym Nguyen O Phap, which means "Nguyen who hates the French." During World War II, Franklin Roosevelt had warned de Gaulle that after the war France should give Indochina its independence. But de Gaulle told Ho, even as he was enlisting his people in the fight against the Japanese, that after the war he intended to reestablish the French colony. Roosevelt argued, "The people of Indochina are entitled to something better than that." De Gaulle was determined that his Free French troops participate in any action in Indochina, saying, "French bloodshed on the soil of Indochina would constitute an impressive territorial claim."

After World War II, the French fought Ho for Vietnam and suffered bitter defeat. Then they fought and lost in Algeria. But since 1962 France had been at peace. The economy was growing, despite de Gaulle's notorious lack of interest in the fine points of economics. Between the end of the Algerian war and 1967, real wages in France rose 3.6 percent each year. There was a rapid increase in the acquisition of consumer goods—especially cars and televisions. And there was a dramatic increase in the number of young people attending universities.

De Gaulle's prime minister, Georges Pompidou, anticipated few problems for the year ahead. He predicted that the Left would be more successful in unifying than they would in actually taking power. "The opposition will harass the government this year," the prime minister announced, "but they will not succeed in provoking a crisis."

The popular weekly *Paris Match* placed Pompidou on a short list of politicians who would maneuver in 1968 to try to replace the General. Yet the editors predicted there would be more to watch abroad than in France. "The United States will unleash one of the fiercest electoral battles ever imagined," they announced. In addition to Vietnam, they saw the potential hot spots as a fight over gold and the dollar, growing freedom in the Soviet Union's Eastern satellite countries, and the launching of a Soviet space weapons system.

"It is impossible to see how France today could be paralyzed by crisis as she has been in the past," said de Gaulle in his New Year's message.

Paris had never looked brighter, thanks to Culture Minister André Malraux's building-cleaning campaign. The Madeleine, the Arc de Triomphe, the Pantheon, and other landmark buildings were no longer gray and charcoal but beige and buff, and this month cold-water sprays were going to remove seven hundred years of grime from Notre Dame Cathedral. It was one of the great controversies of the moment in the French capital. Would the water spray damage the building? Would it look oddly patchwork, revealing that not all the stones were originally of matching color?

De Gaulle, seated in his palace moments before midnight on the eve of 1968, was serene and optimistic. "In the midst of so many countries shaken by confusion," he promised, "ours will continue to give an example of order." France's "primordial aim" in the world is peace, the General said. "We have no enemies."

Perhaps this new Gaullian tone was influenced by dreams of a Nobel Peace Prize. *Paris Match* asked Pompidou if he agreed with some of the General's inner circle who had expressed outrage that de Gaulle had not already received the prize. But Pompidou answered, "Do you really think that the Nobel Prize could be meaningful to the General? The General is only concerned about history, and no jury can dictate the judgment of history."

Aside from de Gaulle, the American computer industry struck one of the new year's rare notes of optimism, predicting a record year for 1968. In the 1950s computer manufacturers had estimated that six computers could serve the needs of the entire United States. By January 1968 fifty thousand computers were operating in the country, of which fifteen thousand had been installed in the past year. The cigarette industry was also optimistic that its 2 percent growth in sales in 1967 would be repeated in 1968. The executive of one of the leading cigarette manufacturers boasted, "The more they attack us the higher our sales go."

But by most measurements, 1967 had not been a good year in the United States. A record number of violent, destructive riots had erupted in black inner cities across the country, including Boston, Kansas City, Newark, and Detroit.

1968 would be the year in which "Negroes" became "blacks." In 1965, Stokely Carmichael, an organizer for the remarkably energetic and creative civil rights group the Student Nonviolent Coordinating Committee, or SNCC, invented the name Black Panthers, soon followed by the phrase Black Power. At the time, *black*, in this sense, was a rarely used poetic turn of phrase. The word started out in 1968 as a term for black militants, and by the end of the year it became the preferred term for the people. *Negro* had become a pejorative applied to those who would not stand up for themselves.

On the second day of 1968, Robert Clark, a thirty-seven-year-old schoolteacher, took his seat in the Mississippi House of Representatives without a challenge, the first black to gain a seat in the Mississippi State Legislature since 1894.

But in the civil rights struggle, action was shifting from the soft-spoken rural South to the hard-edged urban North. Northern blacks were different from blacks in the South. While the mostly southern followers of Martin Luther King, Jr., studied Mohandas Gandhi and his nonviolent anti-British campaign, Stokely Carmichael, who had grown up in New York City, became interested in violent rebels such as the Mau Mau, who had risen up against the British in Kenya. Carmichael, a good-humored man with a biting wit and a sense of theater that he brought from his native Trinidad, had been for years regularly jailed, threatened, and abused in the South, as had all the SNCC workers. And during those years there were always moments when the concept of nonviolence was questioned. Carmichael began hurling back abuse verbally and sometimes physically, confronting segregationists who harassed him. The King people chanted, "Freedom now!" The Carmichael people chanted, "Black Power!" King tried to persuade Carmichael to use the slogan "Black Equality" rather than "Black Power," but Carmichael kept his slogan.

Increasing numbers of black leaders wanted to fight segregation

1967 poster designed by Tomi Ungerer
(Collection of Mary Haskell, copyright © 1994 Diogenes Verlag)

with segregation, imposing a black-only social order that at least paid lip service to excluding even white reporters from press briefings. In 1966 Carmichael became head of SNCC, replacing John Lewis, a soft-spoken southerner who advocated nonviolence. Carmichael turned SNCC into an aggressive Black Power organization, and in so doing Black Power became a national movement. In May 1967 Hubert "Rap" Brown, who had not been a well-known figure in the civil rights movement, replaced Carmichael as the head of SNCC, which by now was nonviolent in name only. In that summer of bloody riots, Brown said at a press conference, "I say you better get a gun. Violence is neces-sary—it is as American as cherry pie."

King was losing control over a badly divided civil rights movement in which many believed nonviolence had outlived its usefulness. 1968 seemed certain to be the year of Black Power, and the police were readying themselves. By the beginning of 1968 most American cities were preparing for war—building up their arsenals, sending under-cover agents into black neighborhoods like spies into enemy territory, recruiting citizenry as a standing reserve army. The city of Los Angeles, where thirty-four people had been killed in an August 1965 riot in the Watts section, was contemplating the purchase of bulletproof armored vehicles, each of which could be armed with a .30-caliber machine gun; a choice of smoke screen, tear gas, or fire-extinguishing launchers; and a siren so loud it was said to disable rioters. "When I look at this thing, I think, My God, I hope we'll never have to use it," said Los Angeles deputy police chief Daryl Gates, "but then I realize how valuable it would have been in Watts, where we had nothing to protect us from sniper fire when we tried to rescue our wounded officers." Such talk had become good politics since California governor Pat Brown had been defeated the year before by Ronald Reagan, largely because of the Watts riots. The problem was that the vehicles cost $35,000 each. The Los Angeles Sheriff's Office had a more cost-effective idea—a surplus army M-8 armored car for only $2,500.

In Detroit, where forty-three people died in race riots in 1967, the police already had five armored vehicles but were stockpiling tear gas and gas masks and were requesting antisniper rifles, carbines, shot-guns, and 150,000 rounds of ammunition. One Detroit suburb had purchased an army half-track—a quasi tank. The city of Chicago purchased helicopters for its police force and started training 11,500 policemen in using heavy weapons and crowd control techniques in preparation for the year 1968. From the outset of the year, the United States seemed to be run by fear.

On January 4, thirty-four-year-old playwright LeRoi Jones, an outspoken Black Power advocate, was sentenced to two and a half to three years in the New Jersey State Penitentiary and fined $1,000 for illegal possession of two revolvers during the Newark riots the previ-ous summer. In explaining why he had imposed the maximum sentence, Essex County judge Leon W. Kapp said that he suspected Jones was "a participant in formulating a plot" to burn Newark on the night he was arrested. Decades later, known as Amiri Baraka, Jones became the poet laureate of New Jersey.

In Vietnam, the war U.S. officials were forever telling correspondents was about to end still seemed far from over.

When the French had left in 1954, Vietnam was divided into a North Vietnam ruled by Ho Chi Minh, who had largely controlled the region anyway, and a South Vietnam left in the hands of anti-communist factions. By 1961 the Northern communists had gained control of half the territory of South Vietnam through the Viet Cong, which met with little resistance from the Southern population. That year the North began sending troops of their regular army south along what became known as the Ho Chi Minh Trail to complete the takeover. The U.S. responded with increased involvement though it had always been involved—in 1954 the U.S. had been financing an estimated four-fifths of the cost of the French war effort. In 1964 with North Vietnam's position steadily strengthening, Johnson had used an alleged naval attack in the Gulf of Tonkin as the pretext for open warfare. From that point on, the Americans expanded their military presence each year.

In 1967, 9,353 Americans were killed in Vietnam, more than doubling the total number of Americans previously killed, which now stood at 15,997, with another 99,742 Americans wounded. Newspapers ran weekly hometown casualty reports. And the war was also taking a toll on the economy, at a cost of an estimated $2 billion to $3 billion a month. During the summer, President Johnson had asked for a large tax increase to stanch the growing debt. The Great Society, the massive social spending program that Johnson had begun as a memorial to his fallen predecessor, was dying from lack of funds. A book published at the beginning of 1968 called *The Great Society Reader: The Failure of American Liberalism* contended that the Great Society and liberalism itself were dying.

New York City mayor John Lindsay, a liberal Republican with presidential aspirations, said on the last day of 1967 that if the country could not allocate more money to cities under current spending plans, then "the obligations that the United States feels it has in Vietnam and elsewhere ought to be reexamined."

The U.S. government, involved in an intense race with the Soviet Union to be first to the moon, had been forced to cut back on its space exploration budget. Even the Department of Defense was prioritizing, asking Congress at the first of the year for permission to delay or cancel orders for hundreds of millions of dollars' worth of low-priority military equipment and facilities so that more money would be available to meet the cost of the war in Vietnam.

On the first day of the year, President Johnson launched an appeal to the American public to curtail plans for foreign travel in order to help reduce a growing deficit in international payments, which he blamed in part on the fact that Americans had been going overseas in increasing numbers. Secretary of State Dean Rusk said that tourists must "share the burden." Johnson asked people to put off nonessential travel plans for at least two years. He also proposed a mandatory curtailment on business investments abroad and a tax on travel that Tennessee Democratic senator Albert Gore called "undemocratic."

Many in France, where there is an understandable tendency toward a Francocentric view of events, felt that Johnson had taken these measures as reprisal against the admittedly too haughty de Gaulle. The Paris daily *Le Monde* said Johnson's proposals were offering Americans an opportunity "to concentrate their resentment on France."

With the war increasingly expensive and unpopular, U.S. government officials were under intense pressure to make it look better in 1968. R. W. Apple of *The New York Times* reported:

> "I was in a briefing the other day," a middle-level civilian said, "and the man briefing us came out and said it: 'An election year is about to begin. And the people we work for are in the business of reelecting President Johnson in November.' "

The thrust of this new public relations campaign was to try to make South Vietnam look as though it were worth fighting for. With U.S. officials instructed to convince the American public that the South had an effective fighting force, they had to try to get the South Vietnamese army to accomplish something that could be cheered. Equally important, they had to try to clean up the embarrassing corruption in the South Vietnamese government and to somehow portray its head, Nguyen Van Thieu, contrary to all evidence, as an inspiring leader who motivated his people to sacrifice for the war effort. The already troubled relationship between the press and the U.S. government was certain to get worse in 1968.

A New Year's editorial in the official Hanoi newspaper, *Nhan Dan,* stated that "our communications lines remain open as ever" in the face of bombing and asserted that "the political and moral unity of our people has strengthened."

President Ho Chi Minh's New Year's message said the people of North and South Vietnam were "united as one man." The seventy-eight-year-old president, in an at least half-accurate forecast, predicted, "This year the United States aggressors will find themselves less able than ever to take the initiative and will be more confused than ever, while our armed forces, dashing forward with the impetus of new successes, will certainly win many more and still greater victories."

He extended best wishes to all friendly nations and to "the progressive people in the United States who have warmly supported the just struggle of our people."

Clearly the ranks of such "progressive people," to use Ho's term, were growing. Not only had pollsters noted a slippage in support for the war, but increasing numbers were willing to demonstrate against it. In 1965, when the Students for a Democratic Society, SDS, had called for an antiwar demonstration in Washington, many, including some in the old pacifist movement, complained that the SDS had failed to criticize the communists, and there were many disagreements on tactics and language. Still, they had assembled twenty thousand in their April march on Washington, which had been the largest antiwar march to date. But by 1967 the SDS and the antiwar movement had avoided the old arguments of the cold war and experienced a remarkably successful year. The National Mobilization Committee to End the War in Vietnam, the Mobe, a coalition of old-time pacifists, new and old leftists, civil rights workers, and youth, had mounted a peaceful demonstration of tens of thousands in San Francisco. In March, they rallied a few hundred thousand people to march behind Martin Luther King, Jr., in New York City from Central Park to the United Nations.

In the fall, for Stop the Draft Week, ten thousand mostly young antiwar demonstrators participated in what became a street fight with the Oakland, California, police. The antiwar movement was also breaking away from King's nonviolent tactics. These protesters did not allow themselves to be dragged into police wagons. They charged police lines and retreated behind makeshift barricades in the street. Students at the University of Wisconsin tried the old tactic of sitting in at a university building, several hundred strong, to protest the presence of Dow Chemical recruitment. The Madison police did not drag the protesters away but used Mace and clubs, which so outraged the public that soon the police were fighting several thousand.

Dow, evil-corporation poster child of the 1960s, produced the napalm used against soldiers, civilians, and landscape in Vietnam. First developed for the U.S. Army during World War II by scientists at Harvard, napalm was a clear example of the military using educational institutions to develop weaponry. Originally the name *napalm* was given to a thickener that could be mixed with gasoline and other incendiary material. In Vietnam the mixture itself was called napalm. The thickener turns the flame into a jellylike substance that can be shot a considerable distance under pressure. As it burns with intense heat, it sticks to the target, whether vegetal or human. According to the National Student Association, of the seventy-one demonstrations that were mounted on sixty-two college campuses in October and November 1967, twenty-seven of them were directed against Dow Chemical.

Only one of the seventy-one demonstrations was about the quality of education.

On a Saturday in late October 1967, the Mobe had organized an antiwar demonstration in Washington, with protesters gathering at the Lincoln Memorial and then crossing the Potomac to march on the Pentagon. An antiwar activist from Berkeley, Jerry Rubin, was there with a New York City friend from the civil rights movement, Abbie Hoffman. Hoffman managed to grab media attention during the Washington march by promising to levitate the Pentagon and exorcize it by spinning it around. He did not deliver on his promise. Norman Mailer was there and wrote about it in *Armies of the Night,* which was to become one of the most read and praised books of 1968. The poet Robert Lowell, linguist and philosopher Noam Chomsky, and editor Dwight MacDonald were among the marchers. These were more than just spoiled and privileged draft-dodging kids, which had been the popular way to characterize the antiwar movement or, as Mailer put it more sympathetically in his book, "the drug illumined and revolutionary young of the American middle class." This was clearly becoming a broad-based and diverse movement. "Join us!" demonstrators shouted at the soldiers guarding the besieged Pentagon, as though intoxicated by their sudden power to recruit more and more supporters.

In the first week of 1968, five men, including Dr. Benjamin Spock, the author and pediatrician, and the Reverend William Sloane Coffin, Jr., chaplain of Yale University, were indicted on charges of conspiring to counsel young men to violate the draft law. In New York City, Dr. Spock said that he hoped "one hundred thousand, two hundred thousand, or even five hundred thousand young Americans either refuse to be drafted or to obey orders if in the military." Spock's arrest in particular garnered attention because conservatives for some time had been blaming what they termed his permissive approach to child rearing for creating this spoiled and quarrelsome generation. But after the arrests, a *New York Times* editorial stated, "It is significant that the two best-known leaders of this challenge to the draft are a pediatrician and a college chaplain, men especially sensitive to young America's current moral dilemma."

On January 4, Bruce Brennan, a thirteen-year-old from Long Island with shoulder-length hair, was charged with truancy. His mother, who owned the Clean Machine, a shop where Bruce worked that sold psychedelic paraphernalia and peace symbols, and his father, the president of a management consulting firm, said that Bruce was being singled out because of his involvement in the peace movement. The youth said he had missed school eleven times because of illness and twice to march in peace demonstrations. The mother said her son had become involved in the movement when he was twelve.

Despite all of this opposition, Lyndon Johnson, after five years in office, seemed a solid favorite to win another term. A Gallup poll released on January 2 showed that just less than half the population, 45 percent, believed it was a mistake to have gotten involved in Vietnam. On that same day, an hour and twenty minutes before the end of the New Year's cease-fire, 2,500 Viet Cong attacked a U.S. infantry fire support base fifty miles northwest of Saigon in an area of rubber plantations, killing 26 Americans and wounding 111. These were the first Americans to die in Vietnam in 1968. The U.S. government reported 344 Viet Cong killed. The United States had a policy of reporting the number of enemy bodies left on the field—a Vietnam War propaganda innovation called "the body count"—as though if the tally rose high enough, America would be declared the winner.

A Republican state-by-state survey released at the beginning of the year indicated that their only hope to unseat Johnson was New York governor Nelson Rockefeller. Richard Nixon, the party predicted, would narrowly lose, as Nixon tended to do. Michigan governor George Romney had become the object of too many jokes when he reversed his support for the Vietnam War, claiming he had been "brainwashed." The dry-witted Democratic Minnesota senator Eugene McCarthy commented, "I would have thought a light rinse would have done it." California governor Ronald Reagan hoped he could step into the vacuum created by Romney. But he had been an elected official for less than a year. Besides, Reagan was considered too reactionary and would likely be completely routed, as would Romney. The Republican Party knew about routs. It was a sensitive topic. In the last election their candidate, Barry Goldwater, running against Johnson, had sustained the worst defeat in American history. He also had been too reactionary. A liberal like Rockefeller might have a chance.

In 1967 some Democrats had talked about replacing Johnson in 1968, but incumbents are hard to remove in American political parties, and "Dump Johnson" movements such as ACT, the Alternative Candidate Task Force, were not expected to have much impact. The only Democrat who was given any hope of unseating Johnson was the fallen President Kennedy's younger brother Robert. But Robert, the junior senator from New York, did not want to step in. On January 4 Kennedy once again reiterated his position that despite differences of opinion with the president over Vietnam, he expected to support him for reelection. Years later, Eugene McCarthy speculated that Kennedy did not think he could beat Johnson. So in November 1967, McCarthy decided that he would be the antiwar alternative to Johnson, announcing his candidacy at a Washington, D.C., press conference that was said to be the most low-key and unexciting campaign kickoff in the history of presidential politics. "I don't know if it will be political suicide," journalist Andrew Kopkind reported the senator saying at the conference. "It will probably be more like an execution."

Now, on the first day of the new year, McCarthy said that he was not at all disheartened by the lack of public response to his candidacy. He insisted that he would not "demagogue the issue" of the war to gain supporters and argued in his unheated prose that the Vietnam War was "draining off our material resources and our manpower resources, but I think [it is] also creating great anxiety in the minds of many Americans and really also weakening and debilitating our moral energy to deal with the problems at home and also some other potential problems around the world."

In November 1967 McCarthy had said that he hoped his candidacy would cause dissidents to turn to the political process rather than the "illegal" protest to which they had been driven by "discontent and frustration." But a month later, SDS leaders Tom Hayden and Rennie Davis and other antiwar figures had started planning for 1968. High on the agenda was a series of street demonstrations in Chicago during the Democratic convention the following summer.

The Yippie! movement—only later in the year was the exclamation turned to acronym by inventing the name Youth International Party— was founded that New Year's Eve, according to the official though not entirely factual story, at a Greenwich Village party, the product—so said its founders, Abbie Hoffman and Jerry Rubin—of an evening of marijuana. "There we were, all stoned, rolling around on the floor," Hoffman later explained to federal investigators. Even the name Yippie!—as in both the cheer and the counterculture label *hippie*— showed a kind of goofy brilliance much appreciated by young militants and very little appreciated by anyone else.

On the first day of the year, the United Nations announced that 1968 was to be the "International Year for Human Rights." The General Assembly inaugurated the yearlong observations with a worldwide appeal for peace. But even the pope, in his January 1 peace message, admitted that there were "new terrible obstacles to the achievement of peace in Vietnam."

The Vietnam War was not the only threat to peace. In West Africa the most promising of the newly independent African states, oil-rich

Nigeria, had for the past six months descended into civil war between the ruling ethnic groups and the Ibo, who represented eight million of the twelve million people in a small eastern region which they called Biafra. Biafra happened to be where the oil was that made Nigeria promising.

Major General Yakubu Gowon, the Nigerian head of state, announced in his Christmas message, "We shall soon turn the corner to a happier period." About the civil war he said, "Let's put our shoulders to the wheel and end it by March thirty-first." But he did little to promote national unity, never traveling outside of Lagos and rarely making himself visible there. Government officials from the east had begun a good news campaign similar to U.S. official information from Vietnam, reporting on mutinies in the Biafran army. At the beginning of the year, the government gave a news conference to present eighty-one policemen from the east who had defected to Lagos. But reporters noted that none of these defectors were members of the Ibo tribe. The government then showed small Biafran uniforms as evidence that the enemy was fighting with children.

The Biafrans were doing surprisingly well, continuing to hold most of their territory and inflicting large numbers of casualties on the numerically superior Nigerian army.

In 1960, when Nigeria had become an independent nation, it was often cited as an example of successful African democracy. But conflicts among regions and 250 ethnic groups with different languages became increasingly bitter, and in January 1966 Ibos overthrew the government and killed the elected leaders. In June Gowon came to power in a second coup and slaughtered thousands of Ibos who were resented for their ability to adapt to modern technology. The curtailing of democracy further exacerbated regional conflicts, and on May 30, 1967, the eastern region, dominated by Ibos, seceded from Nigeria and formed the Republic of Biafra.

After six months of fighting, the war had reached a stalemate. Lagos itself was only once under attack when a plane exploded while attempting a bombing mission over the city. But reporters were finding that the hospitals were filled with wounded soldiers, and that the military put up roadblocks to confiscate the heavier, better-built cars for use at the front. At the outset of the war international observers had thought that Gowon would be able to control his troops so that there would be relatively few civilian casualties. But by January 1968, it was reported that more than five thousand Ibo civilians had been slaughtered by angry mobs while Nigerian troops looked on. Nigerian troops took the Biafran port town of Calabar and shot at least one thousand

and according to some reports as many as two thousand Ibo civilians. As is often true of civil wars, if this war continued, it seemed certain to be a particularly vicious and bloody conflict.

In Spain, Generalissimo Francisco Franco was in his twenty-ninth "year of peace" since seizing control of the country during its civil war. Still a repressive dictatorship, Spain was credited with being less repressive than its neighbor Portugal, which was ruled by the autocratic António de Oliveira Salazar. In recent years resistance to the Franco regime had been crushed by bloody purges in which thousands of Spaniards were shot or imprisoned. The resistance having been destroyed, the repression eased. Some of the refugees from the civil war had even returned. But in 1967 a new generation—students—began demonstrating against the regime. They threw stones and shouted, "Liberty!" and "Death to Franco!" On December 4, Franco's seventy-fifth birthday, students put up a poster that said, "Franco, Murderer, Happy Birthday."

1968 did not begin peacefully in Spain. At the University of Madrid, the School of Technical Sciences was closed by police after students protested against the regime. This in turn led hundreds of medical students to demonstrate the following day, angrily throwing rocks at police. By mid-January, the government had closed the Schools of Philosophy and Letters, Economics, and Political Science because of anti-Franco demonstrations. Having won the right to student organizations in 1967, the 1968 students were demanding that the student leaders imprisoned after the 1967 demonstrations be released and that the government agree never again to allow police to invade the sanctity of university campuses, a historic principle recognized in most of Europe. But students were also becoming more politically involved in noncampus issues, especially issues of trade unions and worker rights.

On New Year's Eve, Israeli foreign minister Abba Eban urged the Arabs of the Middle East to "assert their will" and demand that their leaders negotiate a peace with Israel. In June 1967 Israel had gone to war with its Arab neighbors yet again. De Gaulle was furious because, as a close ally of Israel and a supplier of Israeli weapons, he had demanded that Israel not go to war unless attacked. But the state of Israel had already suffered attacks by the Arabs on several occasions since its creation, and once the Egyptians blocked the Gulf of Aqaba, the Israelis became convinced that another coordinated attack by the Arabs was about to be launched. So they attacked first. De Gaulle reversed French policy from pro-Israel to pro-Arab. Explaining this new policy at a November press conference, the General referred to Jews as "an elite people, self-assured and domineering." In 1968 de Gaulle was still trying to explain the statement and assure various Jewish leaders that it was not an anti-Semitic remark. He insisted that it was a compliment, and he may have thought it was, since the adjectives so perfectly described himself.

The Soviet Union, another former ally of Israel until 1956, also was upset. It had armed the Arabs and supplied their battle plans and was embarrassed to see Israel defeat Soviet-backed Egypt, Syria, and Jordan in only six days.

The Israelis had tried something different. In this war they confiscated land—the green Golan Heights from Syria, the rock-bound Sinai from Egypt, and the West Bank of the Jordan River, including the Arab-held sector of Jerusalem, from Jordan. Then they tried to negotiate with the Arabs, telling them that they would give back the land in exchange for peace. But to their complete frustration, the Arabs showed no interest in the offer. So on New Year's Eve, Abba Eban delivered a radio message in Arabic stating, "The policy adopted by your leaders for the last twenty years is bankrupt. It brought continuous catastrophe upon all the people of the region." 1968, he insisted, should be the time for a change in Arab policy.

In the meantime, the Israeli government appropriated 838 acres from the former Jordanian sector of Jerusalem to establish a Jewish settlement in the Old City. Fourteen hundred housing units were planned, including four hundred for Arabs who were removed from the Old City.

Like the words *black* and *Yippie!*, *Palestinian* first entered the popular vocabulary in 1968. Previously, there had not been a separate cultural identity for these people, who had not been thought of as a distinct nationality, and the usual phrase for Arabs living in Israel had been just that, "Arabs in Israel." It was less clear what an Arab in the West Bank of the Jordan River was since this area was thought of as Jordan, and hence Arabs there, culturally identical to those on the other bank of the Jordan, were thought of as Jordanians. When an American newspaper reported from the West Bank, the dateline read "Israeli-occupied Jordan."

At the beginning of 1968, the word *Palestinian* was generally used to refer to members of Arab guerrilla units, which were also frequently referred to in the Western press as terrorist organizations. These groups used the label *Palestinian,* as in the Palestine Liberation Front, the Palestinian Revolution, the Palestine Revolutionary Youth Movement, the Vanguard for Palestine Liberation, the Palestinian Revolutionaries

Front, and the Popular Front for the Liberation of Palestine. At least twenty-six such groups were operating before the 1967 war. In the leftist counterculture, these groups were termed "nationalist" and were gaining support, though they had little backing from the mainstream in Western countries. The support of such groups by SNCC was further isolating the once leading civil rights organization.

A week before the year 1968 began, Ahmed al-Shuqayri resigned as leader of one of the dominant Arab groups, the Palestinian Liberation Organization, PLO, founded in 1964. He was most famous for his unfulfilled threat to "drive the Jews into the sea." Accused by fellow Palestinians of failing to deliver on his promises, and of deceptiveness and sometimes outright lying, a rival organization, Al Fatah, rejected the leadership of the PLO under al-Shuqayri. Al Fatah, which means "Conquest," was led by Abu Amar, who had become legendary among Arabs as a guerrilla fighter since al Fatah's disastrous initial raid in 1964 when they tried to blow up a water pump but failed to detonate the explosives and were all arrested when they returned to Lebanon. Abu Amar was a nom de guerre for a thirty-eight-year-old Palestinian whose real name was Yasir Arafat.

At the outset of 1968, eight of these Palestinian organizations announced that they had established a joint command to direct guerrilla operations against Israel. They said that raids would be escalated but would not be directed toward Israeli civilians. Their spokesman, a Palestinian heart surgeon, Isam Sartawi, said that their organization sought "the liquidation of the Zionist state" and would reject any proposal for a peaceful solution to the Middle East. "We believe only in our guns, and through our guns we are going to establish an independent Palestine."

More bad news appeared on the cover of the January issue of the *Bulletin of the Atomic Scientists*. The hands of a clock on the cover showed seven minutes to midnight. The clock, which symbolically indicated how close the world was inching to nuclear devastation, had said twelve minutes to midnight ever since 1963. The *Bulletin*'s editor, Dr. Eugene Rabinowitch, said the clock had been reset to reflect the increase in violence and nationalism.

On the other hand, on the first day of the year, Eliot Fremont-Smith began his *New York Times* review of James Joyce's resurrected *Giacomo Joyce* by saying, "If beginnings mean anything, 1968 should be a brilliant literary year."

After considerable debate in 1967, the British announced on the first day of 1968 that they would replace John Masefield as poet laureate with Cecil Day-Lewis, a writer of mysteries and an Oxford poetry professor. The poet laureate is an official member of the queen's household with a ranking somewhat above caretaker but below deputy surveyor. When Masefield died in May after being poet laureate for thirty-seven years, many said that in the late 1960s the whole idea of an official poet was old-fashioned.

In the first week of 1968, Bob Dylan was back, having vanished for a year and a half after breaking his neck in a motorcycle accident. His new album, *John Wesley Harding,* was welcomed by both critics and fans because after his foray into "folk rock," the term used when he started to accompany his songs with electric guitar, he began 1968 true to his folk-singing roots, with acoustic guitar and harmonica, and with piano, bass, and drum backup. *Time* magazine said, "His new songs are simple and quietly sung, some about drifters and hoboes, with morals attached, some with religious overtones, including 'I Dreamed I Saw St. Augustine' and a parable about Judas Priest. The catchiest number is the last, a swinging proposal called 'I'll Be Your Baby Tonight.' " But it was Dan Sullivan for *The New York Times* who pointed out that the Texas outlaw John Wesley Hardin had no *g* in his last name and suggested that Dylan, after depriving so many words of their final *g,* "apparently felt he should return one."

Football was beginning to threaten baseball as the leading American sport. On January 1, 1968, 102,946 people, the largest crowd ever to attend a Rose Bowl, saw an extraordinary University of Southern California player named Orenthal James Simpson score two touchdowns for a total gain of 128 yards and defeat Indiana 14 to 3.

"The big cliffhanger for 1968," wrote Bernadine Morris in *The New York Times,* "is whether hemlines, officially poised above the knees for several seasons, are ready to take a plunge of a foot or so to calf level." A story circulating in January that the Federal Housing Administration had issued a wordy directive to employees stating that wearing miniskirts in cold weather would lead to a buildup of fat molecules on the legs turned out to be a hoax.

However, it was true that the British government was losing tax revenue on miniskirts. The 12.5 percent sales tax charged on skirts, in order to exempt children's clothing, specified that only skirts that measured twenty-four inches waist to hem were taxable. The fashionable women's skirt length in Britain in the winter of 1968 was between thirteen and twenty inches.

But the leading fashion concept for 1968 was that there were no limits or taboos. Conformity was out of fashion, and writers were predicting a continuing trend toward a liberating diversity in what people could wear.

It was an important year for women, not because of skirt lengths but because of events such as Muriel Siebert announcing on January 1 that she had become the first woman to own a seat on the New York Stock Exchange in its 175-year history. Seibert, a thirty-eight-year-old blond woman from Cleveland known to her friends as Mickey, had decided to ignore the advice of numerous men in the financial world that it would be wiser to let a man buy the seat. "It was last Thursday," she said. "The board of governors approved my membership. I went to the exchange and handed over a check covering the balance of the $445,000 seat purchase plus the $7,515 initiation fee. I walked outside and bought three bottles of French champagne for the people in my office. I still couldn't believe it was me. I was walking on cloud nine."

It seemed little would be without controversy this year. The good news might have been that Christiaan Barnard of the Groote Schuur Hospital in Cape Town, South Africa, had successfully transplanted the heart of a twenty-four-year-old into Philip Blaiberg, a fifty-eight-year-old dentist. This was the third heart transplant, the second by Barnard but the first that medical science regarded as successful. Barnard started 1968 and spent much of the year as an international celebrity, signing autographs, giving interviews with his easy smile and quotable statements, which from the outset in January was frowned upon by his profession. Barnard pointed out that despite his sudden fame he still earned only his $8,500 yearly salary. But there were also doubts about his feat. A German doctor called it a crime. A New York biologist, apparently confusing doctors with lawyers, said that he should be "disbarred for life." Three distinguished American cardiologists called for a moratorium on heart transplants, which Barnard immediately said he would ignore.

In theory, the operation involves two doomed patients. One gives up his heart and dies but would have died in any event; the other is saved. But some doctors and laymen wondered if doctors should be deciding who is doomed. Shouldn't everyone hope for a miracle? And how is it decided who receives a new heart? Were doctors now making godlike decisions? The controversy was not helped by Barnard, who said in an interview in *Paris Match,* "Obviously, if I had to choose between two patients in the same need and one was a congenital idiot and one a mathematics genius, I would pick the latter." Controversy was also fueled by the fact that Barnard came from South Africa, the increasingly stigmatized land of apartheid, and that he had saved a white man by removing a black man's heart and implanting it in him. Such an irony was not likely to be overlooked in a year like this.

Ever since Fidel Castro's 1959 New Year's victory, the beginning of every year has been marked in Havana on January 2 with an anniversary celebration in the broad, open space known as Plaza de la Revolución. In 1968, for the ninth anniversary of the revolution, something new was added—a sixty-foot-high mural of a beautiful young man in a beret. This young man was the thirty-eight-year-old Argentine Ernesto "Che" Guevara, who had been killed in Bolivia two months earlier while carrying out the new Cuban approach to revolution.

This new approach had been described in a book called *Revolution in the Revolution* by Régis Debray, a young Frenchman who had become enamored of the Cuban revolution. The book, translated into English in 1967, was a favorite of students all over the world, with its premise certain to appeal to the impatience of youth. Debray wrote of tossing out the old Marxist-Leninist theories about slowly fomenting revolution. Instead, according to Debray, revolutions began by taking the initiative with an army raised from rural people. That was Castro's strategy in the mountains of his native Oriente province. And it was what Che was doing in Bolivia. Only in Che's case, it had not worked out well, and in November a photograph circulated of a Bolivian air force colonel displaying Che's half-naked corpse. Debray, too, had been caught by the Bolivian army, but rather than killing him, the Bolivians kept him in a prison in a small town called Camiri. In the beginning of 1968 Debray was still there, though the Bolivians allowed his Venezuelan lover, Elizabeth Burgos, to come to the prison so the couple could be married.

So in 1968 Fidel Castro's close friend and co-revolutionary became a martyr, a canonized saint of the revolution—forever young, to borrow a phrase from Bob Dylan, bearded and bereted, with those smiling eyes, the pure revolutionary in deeds and clothing. At the José Martí International Airport in Havana, a poster of the martyr appeared with the message "Youth will intone the chants of mourning to the chatter of machine guns and cries of war. Until victory, forever."

All over Cuba the phrase was written, "Until Victory, Forever." Sixty thousand students in gray high school uniforms marched past Castro's reviewing stand, and as each group passed they declared, loudly and enthusiastically, "Our duty is to build men like Che." "*Como Che*"—to be like Che, to have more men like Che, to work like Che—the phrase filled the island. The cult of Che had begun.

Castro announced that this year the celebration would not include a display of Soviet weapons, explaining that such a parade was too expensive, in part because the tanks tore up the pavement on the Havana streets.

There were other troubling signs for Moscow, which began the year with a shaky economy and an unpopular trial of four intellectuals accused of spreading anti-Soviet propaganda after they campaigned in favor of Andrei Sinyavsky and Yuli Daniel, two writers in prison for the past two years because they had published their work in the West. The Six Day War in the Middle East had been a humiliation for the foreign policy of Leonid I. Brezhnev, chief of the Soviet Communist Party, at a time when collective farming was failing, attempts at economic reform had fizzled, youth and intelligentsia were growing restless, and nationalist movements such as that of the Tatars were becoming troublesome. The people of the Soviet bloc, especially young people, were increasingly rejecting the stances and language of the cold war. Yugoslavia's Josip Broz Tito had long annoyed Moscow with an air of independence, but now Romania's Nicolae Ceauşescu had begun to exhibit the same tendency. Even in Czechoslovakia, where the Soviets had their most loyal and pliable leader, Antonín Novotný, the population seemed restless. In April 1967 the *Bratislava Pravda,* the Slovak Party organ, had conducted a poll in Czechoslovakia and found a shocking general rejection of the Party line. Only half blamed the Western imperialists for international tension, and 28 percent said that both sides were responsible. Perhaps most shocking, only 41.5 percent blamed the United States for the Vietnam War, a stance with which even the populations of America's closest allies would not have been in agreement. By the fall, Czech writers were openly demanding more freedom of expression, and students from Prague's Charles University were demonstrating in the streets.

In the fall of 1967 a series of meetings of the Czechoslovakian Central Committee had gone very badly for Novotný. His slavish loyalty to Moscow had been rewarded by his appointment as first secretary of the Czechoslovakian Communist Party in 1953. In 1958 he had become president of Czechoslovakia. Now, an increasing number of Central Committee members, reacting in part to Novotný's relentless hatred of the 4.5 million Slovaks who constituted a third of the nation's population, felt he should give up one position or the other. The president barely managed to save himself in a December meeting of the ten-member presidium of the Communist Party by closing the session "because it was Christmas." The committee had agreed to reconvene the first week of January.

In the meantime, Novotný plotted. He tried to intimidate his opponents by spreading a rumor that the Soviet Union was poised to step in to preserve his position. But this backfired, turning key figures against him only further. He then plotted a military intervention that would affirm his positions and arrested his opponent, the Slovak Alexander Dubček, whom he despised. But a general informed Dubček of the plot and Novotný was outmaneuvered again.

So President Novotný began the new year with a broadcast to the nation that was intended to be conciliatory. He promised that Slovakia, always at the end of Prague's priorities, would suddenly be a leading concern in all economic planning. He also attempted to placate writers and students by promising that everything progressive, even if from the West, would be permitted. "I do not mean only in the economy, engineering, and science," he added, "but also in progressive culture and art."

The Central Committee met again on January 3 and removed Novotný as first secretary of the Party, replacing him with Dubček. There was not enough consensus to remove him as president, but Novotný had suffered a major and bitter defeat. The people of Czechoslovakia were not told that their world was about to change until Friday, January 5, when Radio Prague announced the "resignation" of Novotný as first secretary and the election of Dubček. Czechs had not realized Novotný was in trouble, and most of them had no idea who this Alexander Dubček was. In a closed society, the most successful politicians operate out of the public eye.

But while all this was happening, curiously little was heard from the ironfisted Soviet leader. Brezhnev had visited Prague in December, and it had been widely reported that he had made the trip to ensure the preservation of the beleaguered Czech leader. But in fact, when Novotný, whom Brezhnev never liked in spite of the Czech leader's vaunted loyalty, was removed, Brezhnev told Novotný, "*Eto vashe delo*"—That's your problem.

In Washington, Secretary of Defense Robert S. McNamara was preparing his annual report to Congress, in which he wrote, "In the 1960s the simple bipolar configuration which we knew in the earlier post–World War II period began to disintegrate. Solid friends and implacable foes are no longer so easy to label, and labels which did useful service in the past, such as 'free world' and 'iron curtain,' seem increasingly inadequate as descriptions of contending interests within and between blocs and of new bonds of common interest being slowly built across what were thought to be impenetrable lines of demarcation."

On Friday, at the end of the first week of 1968, the weekly summary of Vietnam casualties showed that 185 Americans, 227 South Vietnamese, and 37 other allied servicemen had been killed in action. America and its allies reported killing a total of 1,438 enemy soldiers. That was the first week, and so 1968 began.

CHAPTER 2

HE WHO ARGUES WITH A MOSQUITO NET

The people were dissatisfied with the party leadership. We couldn't change the people, so we changed the leaders.
—ALEXANDER DUBČEK, *1968*

O N JANUARY 5, 1968, the day Dubček took over as leader of the Czech Communist Party, while Czechs and Slovaks cheered, his wife and two sons could not help crying at the miserable fate that had befallen him.

At the center of one of the most dramatic moments in the history of Soviet-dominated Central Europe stood a gray, ambiguous man. Despite being six feet four inches tall, all his life Alexander Dubček was always described as unobtrusive. But he was not as dispassionate as he appeared. By the time he had deposed Novotný, whose nickname was Frozen Face, the animosity between the two men had a twenty-three-year history.

When Dubček took office at age forty-six, he did not seem youthful. Tall, enigmatic, often a dull speaker, but the inspiration for millions of energized youth, Dubček in some ways resembled Senator Eugene McCarthy. In fact, he had come very close to being born in the Midwest.

"I was conceived by a pair of Slovak socialist dreamers, who happened to immigrate to Chicago," Dubček wrote. In 1910, Stefan Dubček, an uneducated Slovak carpenter, weary of a Slovakia repressed by the Austro-Hungarian Empire and without opportunities, walked out of his mountain home along a curving bank of the Danube until he had reached Budapest, the domed and tree-lined capital of his oppressors. There he organized a socialist cell in a furniture factory and dreamed of overthrowing the monarchy. The factory management quickly realized what he was doing and fired him. Soon after, he immigrated to America, which he had been told was a land of democracy and social justice. He settled into a Slovak community on Chicago's North Side.

American capitalism seemed a harsh system, neither as free nor as just as he had been told, but at least he could speak his political beliefs without being arrested, and he would not get drafted into World War I to fight for the monarchy he hated. The entry of the United States into the war was a blow to American socialists, who were generally opposed to war—and had believed Wilson's promise that he would keep the United States out of war. Stefan, a pacifist—a belief that would reemerge in his son, Alexander, at a critical moment in history—went to Laredo, Texas, to meet up with Quakers and other pacifists who could help him get across the border to sit out the war in Mexico. But he was caught, arrested, fined, and imprisoned for a year and a half. When he was released, he returned to Chicago and met and married a young Slovak, Pavlina, who, unlike Stefan, was a devout communist. At Pavlina's urging, Stefan studied Marx. When his sister in Slovakia wrote that she was getting married, he sent her a lengthy political questionnaire with which to screen the prospective groom. Stefan became very excited about the revolution in Russia, and in a letter to Slovakia in 1919 he wrote, "In America you can have most things but you certainly can't have freedom. The only free country in the world is the Soviet Union."

After nearly a decade of struggle for socialism, Stefan was disappointed with the United States and Pavlina missed her country, so in 1921 they took their baby and, with Pavlina pregnant, moved back to Slovakia to a newly created Czechoslovakia, and that is how Alexander Dubček, born a few months later, came to be a Czechoslovakian. He had many relatives on both sides in America, though he had no contact with them until near the end of his life when they started writing him letters after the fall of communism.

The new country where Stefan vowed to build socialism at first seemed exciting. Czechoslovakia had been thought up by a Prague professor, Tomáš Garrigue Masaryk. At first the country seemed as though it would be an equal union among Bohemians, Moravians, and Slovaks. To Slovaks this was an enormous reversal of history, because since the tenth century they had always been the downtrodden and abused fiefdom of some powerful state. The Czech lands, Bohemia and Moravia, had had a late-nineteenth-century industrial revolution that had produced a literate middle class, including bureaucrats and technocrats with which to staff a new government. But after one thousand years of rule by the Magyars of Hungary, Slovakia was an impoverished agricultural region much like the neighboring part of Poland. Few Slovaks could read or write even in their native Slovak language. Most were peasants on very poor land. They had first expressed their nationalism in 1848, a year of rebellion not unlike 1968 except that the events were limited to Europe. In 1848 the Slovaks rose up against the Hungarians and demanded equal rights in a document known as Demands of the Slovak Nation. This became the model for Slovak nationalism, and its author, Ludovit Stur, became the Slovak national hero long before and after Masaryk. By a strange coincidence, when Stefan and Pavlina Dubček moved back to Slovakia, they settled into a cottage where Stur had been born in 1815, and it was there that Alexander Dubček was born.

The Slovaks' Hungarian masters and Czech neighbors had always regarded them with condescension. If Slovaks had listened closely to Masaryk, they would have realized that he harbored that same contempt. He tended to characterize Slovaks as backward, lacking political maturity, and being "priest-ridden"—all familiar, pejorative Czech stereotypes of Slovaks.

But Masaryk enjoyed great popularity among not only the Czechs but the Slovaks. At the end of World War I, he traveled to America and gained the support of Woodrow Wilson; then he moved to Paris, where in October 1918 he formed a united Czechoslovakian government, managed to get it recognized by the allies, and returned two months later to a newly created nation in which he was the national hero.

From the beginning there was the "Slovak problem." The Slovaks demanded that the new nation be called Czecho-Slovak and not Czechoslovakia, but the Czechs refused to grant that small hyphen of separation. This was the first of many arguments the Slovaks lost.

Little Alexander had almost no memory of childhood in Slovakia except a tame deer that lived behind the church and a St. Bernard dog that it grieved him to give up. He would be seventeen the next time he saw Slovakia. If Slovakia was backward, it was not nearly as underdeveloped as Kirghizia in the Soviet Union, where the Dubčeks moved voluntarily in 1925 to raise their children on an agricultural cooperative.

Soviet Kirghizia, now called Kyrgyzstan, was four thousand miles from Slovakia, near China. It was not enough in the Iron Age to have metal for plowshares, and nearly the entire population was illiterate, since Kirghiz was not a written language. The Dubčeks never reached their original destination. After traveling twenty-seven days, the rail line ended in a barren place called Pishpek and there they stayed, living in decrepit, abandoned military barracks. They helped build a farming cooperative, bringing in tractors. The local people, who had never seen one, ran after them, shouting, "Satan!" In the early years, there was so little food that Dubček remembered eating raw sparrow eggs in the shell. From there they went to the Russian industrial center of Gorkiy. Stefan did not bring Alexander back to Slovakia until 1938, when Stalin decreed that foreigners had to take Soviet citizenship or leave.

Alexander was now seventeen, and the exciting new Czechoslovakia was twenty years old and full of disorder and disillusionment. He had inherited his parents' ideology but for a long time, it seemed, not their rebellious natures. He was an orthodox, Soviet-educated communist. During World War II he was a partisan in a band of guerrilla fighters known as the Jan Ziska Brigade, named after a fifteenth-century fighter. They fought a rear guard action against the Germans. Years later his official Party biography made much of this wartime experience. He was wounded twice in the leg. His older brother was killed. In 1945 his father, Stefan, was deported by the Germans as a communist to Mauthausen concentration camp. There he found one Antonín Novotný, a prominent Czech communist who had also been deported. Novotný vociferously vowed that if he survived, he would never again have anything to do with politics.

In 1940, in a house where his father was being hidden, Alexander met Anna Ondrisova, about whom he said, "I think I was in love at first sight." In 1945 Dubček married her and remained in love with her until she died in 1991. Rare for such an orthodox communist, Dubček married her in a church. When in 1968 Dubček became leader of Czechoslovakia, he was the only chief of a European communist country who had been married in a church.

Czechoslovakia is the one country that became communist by a democratic vote. Unfortunately, as often happens in a democracy, the politicians were lying. In 1946 Czechoslovakia, newly liberated by the Soviet Red Army, voted for a communist government that promised there would be no collectives established and that small businesses would not be nationalized. By 1948 the communists had complete control of the country, and in 1949 the government began taking over the economy, nationalizing all enterprises, turning farms into state collectives.

Alexander Dubček was a hardworking, serious-minded Slovak Party official carefully sidestepping the issue of Slovak nationalism. He was Slovak enough to be acceptable at home, but not so much that it would be of concern to the Party leadership in Prague. In 1953 he became regional secretary for an area of central Slovakia. That year Stalin died and Khrushchev began dismantling the most rigid excesses of Stalinism—everywhere but in Czechoslovakia. That same year Frozen Face Novotný was appointed first secretary of the Communist Party. Novotný was poorly educated and his career had shown little promise until he displayed a flair for fabricating evidence in Stalinist purges such as the campaign against the number two government figure, Party secretary-general Rudolph Slansky. Slansky was a brutal member of the dictatorship, probably guilty of many crimes, but he was tried and executed for Zionism. It did not matter that Slansky, far from being a Zionist, had disagreed with the Soviet Union's early support of Israel. The word *Zionist* was being used not to designate supporters of Israel but to refer to people of Jewish origin, which Slansky was.

Before the Slansky trials, Novotný and his wife had once been invited to the home of Foreign Minister Vladimir Clementis, and Novotný's wife had admired the Clementises' porcelain tea service. After Clementis was executed in the Slansky purges, with the help of Novotný's doctored evidence, Novotný bought the porcelain for his wife.

Paper pulp for construction was made from millions of library books full of dangerous Western ideas. The people of Czechoslovakia were listened to and closely watched by a tight network of secret police agents and neighborhood snitches performing their patriotic duty for the revolution. The citizenry had almost no contact with the West and only limited connections with the rest of the Soviet bloc.

Dubček's job was developing the backward Slovak economy. He stood by patiently while the simplest of ideas were rejected. He and other leaders in his town of Banska Bystrica meekly approached Party leaders to suggest that a new cement factory be relocated to a spot that would not only avoid pollution in the town, but also had plentiful limestone deposits, since cement was made from limestone. The town had even offered to cover the expenses, which, he could demonstrate in his carefully detailed plans, would not be great. The proposal was rejected as the meddling of "narrow-minded bourgeoisie of Bystrica." Industrialization was too important to be left to a bunch of backward Slovaks. The cement factory was built by the original plan, showering the town, like so many Slovak towns under the industrialization program, with dust, while the entrance to town was marred with an overhead cable railroad to transport limestone.

Dubček said nothing. He seldom criticized the government or the Party, either, for incompetence or brutality. In 1955 he was rewarded with a place at the Higher Party School in Moscow. He seemed thrilled by the honor and the opportunity to improve on what he regarded as a poor education. He felt that he lacked "ideological training." But his three years of advanced ideology in Moscow turned out to be a vague discipline, because Khrushchev had denounced Stalin, leaving the school uncertain about what it should be teaching. Dubček returned from a reforming Soviet Union to a still-Stalinist Czechoslovakia in which Novotný had now become president. Since Novotný still headed the Party, the country was, for the first time, under one-man rule.

Students and young people were not afraid to show their displeasure. At cultural festivals in both Prague and Bratislava, they openly demanded more political parties, access to Western books and magazines, and an end to the annoying buzz, the jamming, that accompanied broadcasts of Radio Free Europe and the BBC World Service.

Dubček's new education was rewarded with the position of regional secretary of Bratislava. He was now one of the important Slovaks. He still believed in blind Party loyalty, but to whom? Coming from Moscow, he was very aware that Novotný and Khrushchev were not saying the same things. Dubček was careful not to express his animosity toward Novotný, though Novotný made no effort to hide his animosity toward Slovakia. According to Dubček, Novotný was "particularly ignorant about almost everything that concerned Slovakia and Czecho-Slovak relations, which was, of course, depressing for me." In 1959, changes in the constitution dismantled the few remaining vestiges of Slovak self-government. While the Slovak people were enraged, the Slovak leaders were anxious only to please Novotný and serve Prague.

Dubček had disdain for the special recreation area Novotný had built for Party officials to spend their weekends. "The place itself was very nice, located in a charming part of the Vltava River Basin," he recalled. "But I detested the whole idea of it—the isolated luxury enjoyed by the leadership under police protection." His enduring image of Novotný was his passion for a card game called "marriage." The bureaucrats looking for advancement were eager to be invited to play marriage with Novotný, who dealt out the deck inside a huge beer barrel he had built in front of his house for the purpose of hosting these card games. Dubček did not play and instead spent the periodic obligatory weekends at the retreat playing with children or going for long walks in the forest.

Occasionally he had open conflict with Novotný. "These confrontations," he later wrote, "arose when I dared to offer differing opinions first on investment priorities in Slovakia and later on the rehabilitation of victims of the 1950s repressions." But as a second-rung figure,

Dubček could do little to change government, and he said and did very little. He was a Communist Party careerist.

In the early 1960s, Dubček served on the Kolder Commission, which looked into redressing government abuse in the 1950s. This work made a lasting impression on him. "I was dumbfounded," he later wrote, "by the revelations of what had been going on in Czechoslovak Party circles in Prague in the early 1950s." It is still not certain if he really had not known of these abuses before. But he did seem deeply shaken by the revelations of the Kolder Commission, and so did many other officials. Novotný came under tremendous pressure to reorganize his government. In 1963, when because of the commission's findings the Slovak Central Committee was able to remove the first secretary they regarded as a Novotný quisling, it was the quiet Alexander Dubček they chose to replace him. This was done over the shouting of Novotný, who stormed out of the session and never again attended a meeting of the Slovak Central Committee.

In the mid-sixties, life became more difficult for Novotný. His friend Khrushchev was replaced in 1964 by his plotting protégé Brezhnev at the same time that the Czechoslovakian economy had taken disastrous turns. The economy had been catastrophic for years, but the Czech lands had started out at a level so far above those of everyone else in the Soviet bloc that it took years before the consequences of mismanagement became devastating. Slovakia, lacking the Czechs' starting advantage, had been suffering for a long time. But now even the Czechs were experiencing food shortages, and the government had ordered "meatless Thursday." With the combination of uncertain support in Moscow and unhappy people at home, Novotný eased up on the police state. Censorship became less severe, artists, writers, and filmmakers were allowed more freedom, and some travel to the West was allowed.

It was still a very repressive state. The literary magazine *Tvar* was shut down. There were limits to what could be written, spoken, or done. But Czechoslovakians flourished with the small margin of freedom they had been finally allowed. With the West no longer completely cut off, Czech youth immediately tapped into the vibrant Western youth culture wearing *Texasskis*—blue jeans—and going to clubs to hear the big beat, as rock and roll was called. Prague had more young people with long hair, beards, and sandals than anywhere else in central Europe. Yes, in the heart of Novotný's Czechoslovakia, there were the unshorn rebel youth of the sixties—hippies—or were they the rebel youth of the fifties, beatniks? On May 1, 1965, May Day, when the rest of the communist world was celebrating the revolution, the youth of Prague had crowned the longhaired, bearded beatnik, visiting poet Allen Ginsberg, *Kraj Majales,* King of May. "Ommm," chanted Ginsberg, the Jew turned Buddhist, who even while embracing Eastern religion was to many young Prague residents the embodiment of the exciting new world in the West. For his coronation speech he clanked tiny cymbals while chanting a Buddhist hymn. After a few days of following him through the dark, ornate back streets of the center city, the secret police had him deported. Or, as he wrote it in a poem,

And I was sent from Prague by plane by detectives in Czechoslovakian business suits

And I am the King of May, which is the power of sexual youth,

And I am the King of May, which is industry in eloquence and action in amour,

And I am the King of May, which is old Human poesy, and 100,000 people chose my name,

And I am the King of May, and in a few minutes I will land at London Airport. . . .

But as Stefan Dubček would have readily pointed out, one is not completely free in America, either. When Ginsberg returned to the United States, the FBI placed his name on a list of dangerous security risks.

For all its repression, despite the mustached men in Czechoslovakian business suits, Prague was becoming popular. In 1966 three and a half million tourists visited the country, a fifth of them from the West. Czech movies such as *Closely Watched Trains* and *The Shop on Main Street* were being seen around the world. Miloš Forman was one of several Czech directors sought internationally. Czech playwrights, including Václav Havel, were earning international reputations. Havel, perhaps not the most theatrical but the most politically stinging of the Prague playwrights, mounted plays of absurdist antitotalitarianism that would never have been seen in the Soviet Union. In *The Memorandum,* a bureaucracy prevents creative thinking by imposing a made-up language called Ptydepe. Havel often laughed at the language of communism. In another play, a character burlesques Khrushchev's habit of concocting meaningless folkisms. The Havel character asserts, "He who argues with a mosquito net will never dance with a goat near Podmokly."

In November 1967 a small group of Prague students decided to do what they were now hearing of students doing in the West. They held a demonstration. The issue was poor heat and lighting in the dormitories—neither the first nor the last student movement to start on a seemingly banal issue. They discovered, as many students in the West were also beginning to find, that it was fun to demonstrate. They marched in the dark of early evening, carrying candles to symbolize the dim light by which they said they were forced to study. It looked as merry as a Christmas procession when they headed up the narrow stone streets to Hradčany Castle, which housed the government. Suddenly they found their way blocked by police, who clubbed the few demonstrators to the cobblestone pavement and then dragged them off. About fifty needed hospitalization. The press reported simply on "hooligans" attacking the police. But by then people could decipher the code, and word spread quickly of the beatings, creating an even larger protest movement. By the end of 1967 students were handing out flyers and debating with anyone who would engage them on the street, and they looked very much like students in Berlin, Rome, or Berkeley. True, they were being watched by secret police, but so were American and Western European student demonstrators.

During the 1960s both Slovak nationalism and Novotný's animosity toward Slovaks grew. In 1967 the Slovaks defied the government and the Soviets by cheering Israel's victory in the Six Day War. By 1968 the Middle East had become a favorite political metaphor in the Soviet bloc. It was a sign of trouble in Poland that the Poles, instead of showing their loyalty to Soviet interests, thrilled to the spectacle of the Jews defeating Soviet-trained troops. In March 1968, when Romania wanted to assert its independence, it strengthened its ties to Israel.

After January 5, the removal of Novotný as Party chief filled Czechoslovakia with hope, excitement, and gossip. One of the favorite stories concerned why Brezhnev had not come to Novotný's defense. When Khrushchev was replaced by Brezhnev, Novotný had been so upset by the undoing of his Soviet friend—they had even spent vacations together—that he had actually called the Kremlin. Whatever Brezhnev's explanation, Novotný was not satisfied and he angrily threw down the phone, hanging up on the new Soviet leader. Brezhnev had a very long memory.

In 1968 both the Soviet Union and the people of Czechoslovakia put their hopes and trust in a tall, mournful-looking man with a faint smile, a man who had never shown great flair or imagination, which in any event were not qualities the Soviets encouraged. Dubček had no foreign experience. Except for the Soviet Union, he had been abroad only twice, both times in 1960, when he had spent two days in Helsinki and had gone to a Party conference in Hanoi.

But Dubček and many of his colleagues in the new government were of a unique generation, people who grew up with Nazi occupation, who saw a world of good and evil in which the Soviet Union was the force for good, the hope for the future. Zdeněk Mlynář, who became part of the Dubček government, wrote, "The Soviet Union was, in that sense, a land of hope for those who desired a radical departure from the past after the war and who also, of course, knew nothing of the real conditions in the Soviet Union."

The real question of the time was not why the Soviets accepted Dubček, but why the Czechoslovakians did. After twenty years of Stalinism, the nation was hungry for change, and they decided that Dubček might deliver it. As Mlynář pointed out, before 1968 the people of Czechoslovakia never learned very much about the character of their leaders, and so if this new one seemed difficult to read, they were accustomed to that. And by chance he was well suited for the youth of 1968. He was nonauthoritarian, a fact that seemed to be confirmed by his uneasiness in public and his dull speaking style. Young Czechoslovakians liked this awkwardness. In the end it would translate into a fatal tendency to make decisions too slowly, always the weak point of antiauthoritarianism. But in a small group he could be extremely persuasive. Most exciting of all, he was a leader with a habit of listening to others. Perhaps what had been true of Ludovit Stur, the officially outcast Slovak nationalist in whose house he was born, was also true of Dubček, as Dubček had said in an unorthodox speech three years earlier defending Stur: "He understood all the principal social and economic problems and the tendencies of his period, and he understood that everything must change."

Dubček's weeping family could see the spot he was in. He had to convince the energized people that he was a reformer, show the old-line figures in the Party and government, the Novotný men, that he could be trusted, and demonstrate to the satisfaction of Moscow that he was in control of this uncontrollable situation.

Dubček never mastered the situation. He simply tried to steer it, balancing the opposing forces, using the skills he had hewn as a Party man. He made no attempt to purge Novotný supporters. Years later he would speculate that this may have been his greatest mistake. There had been a 5 to 5 split in the presidium, what the Soviets had started calling a Politburo, that forced the vote to the Central Committee. And so these powerful bodies, normally packed with the chief's men, were full of old-time communists who had been loyal to Novotný and did not really like Dubček. Even his chauffeur and the secretarial staff in his office were Novotný people.

Being a Slovak further complicated his position because Slovaks expected him to now strike a blow for Slovak nationalism, whereas the Czechs muttered about "a Slovak dictatorship."

Meanwhile the country was full of factions with demands and expectations. The journalists wanted to know what to expect from censors under the new regime. Dubček offered no guidance on this or many other urgent issues. Later, historians spoke of the "January silence." Dubček seemed to have come to power completely unprepared, with only a few vague notions: He wanted to help the Slovaks, improve the economy, respond to the demand for more freedom. But he had no programs, and he had the Novotný loyalists and the Kremlin to watch at his back.

He did not seem comfortable in Prague, a large and grandiose capital for a man who had fit in in Bratislava, with its few streets along the Danube, an occasional dilapidated ornate building from the old empire, filled in with blocks of low-ceilinged Stalinist housing for the people and a lone castle on a weedy hill. What few relics there were in Bratislava were crumbling, as were the new buildings. But now at age forty-six, Dubček suddenly was working in palaces, being driven by Novotný's man through a town of European grandeur.

The silence of Dubček created a vacuum in which many things could grow. On January 27 a newsstand appeared in the historic center of the city selling newspapers from around the world from both socialist and capitalist countries. The shop provided a reading room where coffee was served. In the evening people would fill the little room and sit and read Russian, West German, French, and British newspapers. Without censorship, the national press flourished, with newspapers vastly increasing their press runs and still being sold out early in the morning. There had never been unfettered press like this anywhere in the Soviet bloc. The papers were filled with stories of government corruption. They also attacked, exposed, and ridiculed Soviet government. They would fight one another for circulation by running bigger and better exposés of Soviet purges or Czech venality. Novotný, never before scrutinized by the press, was exposed. He and his son, it was revealed, used a government import license to obtain Mercedeses, Alfa Romeos, Jaguars, and other Western cars with which to amuse women. When they got tired of a particular car, they could always sell it to friends at an enormous profit. Novotný could not survive the scandal, and without Dubček ever seeking it, on March 22 Novotný was forced to resign from the presidency.

The following day Dubček and his leaders were summoned to a Warsaw Pact meeting in the East German city of Dresden with its still burned and bombed out center. Significantly, Romania was not invited. In the winter of 1968 Moscow was far more troubled by Romania than by Czechoslovakia. While Dubček was trying to be the good disciplined communist, Romania's Nicolae Ceauşescu had been showing increasing independence since the aftermath of the Six Day War, when Romania became the only Soviet bloc country not to sever diplomatic ties with Israel. Czechoslovakia had been the first to follow the Soviets and cut ties, which in the eyes of many Czechs had made Novotný look too subservient. In late February the Romanians walked out of a Communist Party International Conference in Budapest. Even worse, two weeks later, at a meeting of the Warsaw Pact, the Soviet military alliance, in Sofia, Bulgaria, Romania refused to sign a communiqué endorsing Soviet and American nuclear weapon reduction. Romania said it was protesting the way the two superpowers dominated the dialogue without conferring with smaller countries.

So if the Soviets were upset with someone in the bloc, Dubček did not expect it to be him. Only weeks before he had written an article in Moscow's *Pravda* in which he said, "Friendship with the USSR is the foundation of our foreign policy."

Dubček had thought the Dresden meeting would be an economic conference. Suddenly he felt on trial. One by one the other leaders, the Poles, the East Germans, accused him of failing to be in control of the Czechoslovakian situation. Dubček looked to his one ally, János Kádár of Hungary. The Nationalists back in Bratislava could have laughed at the spectacle of a Slovak turning for help to their old oppressor. Even Kádár attacked him. What seemed to most trouble everyone, and especially Brezhnev, was that the press was running wild, writing about whatever they wanted, completely out of the control of government. What the Soviet Union demanded of its satellite country leaders was first and foremost that they be in control. The press had actually played a role in Novotný's dismissal from the presidency and was still demanding he be expelled from the Central Committee and even the Party.

They were right. Even after Dresden, when Dubček first realized the extent to which he was upsetting the Soviet bloc, he was unable to rein in the press. Freedom for their own press as well as access to Western media was to the Czechoslovakian people of primary importance. There was no subject on which there was less room for compromise.

But there was no turning back. Czechoslovakia could no longer live in isolation. Suddenly Prague was watched, talked about, even seen on television in many lands, and what the Czechs and the Slovaks were doing in the beginning of 1968 sent shock waves through the entire communist world and attracted the attention of young people throughout the West. Suddenly a Prague student who had never seen the rest of the world, bearded and in *Texasski* jeans too stiff and too blue, felt part of a liberating world youth movement.

CHAPTER 3

A DREAD UNFURLING OF THE BUSHY EYEBROW

Societies have always been shaped more by the nature of the media by which men communicate than by the content of the communication.

—MARSHALL McLUHAN AND QUENTIN FIORE,
The Medium Is the Massage, *1967*

L IKE AN UNNOTICED TREE falling in the forest, if there is a march or a sit-in and it is not covered by the press, did it happen? From Martin Luther King, Jr., and John Lewis to Stokely Carmichael and H. Rap Brown, there was wide disagreement on tactics within the civil rights movement, but they all agreed that an event needed to attract the news media. And it became obvious to the violent and nonviolent alike that violence and the rhetoric of violence were the most effective way to get coverage.

Mohandas K. Gandhi himself, the master of nonviolence who had inspired the movement, had understood this very well. He went to great trouble to try to get Indian, British, and American coverage of every event he organized, and he often spoke of the value of British violence in order to entice the media. It is the paradox of nonviolence. The protesters can be nonviolent, but they must evoke a violent reaction. If both sides are nonviolent, there is no story. Martin Luther King used to complain about this, but after he met a man named Laurie Pritchett, he understood that it was a reality.

Pritchett was the police chief in Albany, Georgia, in 1962 when Martin Luther King's Southern Christian Leadership Conference had singled out the town for a campaign of nonviolent resistance. The area in rural southwestern Georgia was infamous for segregation and had been the object of one of the first federal suits for voting rights under the 1957 Civil Rights Act. Little Albany, with seventy-five thousand people, about a third of whom were black, was the biggest population center in the area, and SNCC, with the encouragement of local blacks, decided to launch a voter registration drive there. The registration drive expanded to desegregation of public buildings, including the bus station, and Martin Luther King was brought in.

There were numerous encounters between the protesters and the law over several months, with mass arrests, including of King, but at no point did the polite, well-spoken sheriff use violence. Pritchett had been able to anticipate the protesters' every move because he had informants from the Albany black community. Because there was no violence, King and the other leaders were never able to get Robert Kennedy and the Justice Department to intervene as they had in other places. Federal intervention makes a bigger story. Worse, reporters liked Pritchett. He was folksy and pleasant. He told them that he had studied Martin Luther King's use of nonviolence and that he had adopted nonviolent law enforcement. King responded to criticism from civil rights activists who said he always remained safely removed from the action, by letting himself be arrested in Albany. But this forced him to cancel a valuable television appearance on *Meet the Press,* only to be personally released from jail by Pritchett himself, who said that "an unidentified Negro man" had paid bail and related fines. Many assumed that King's father, a distinguished Atlanta figure sometimes called Daddy King, had gotten his son out. King could go to jail because his daddy would get him out. In truth, the wily Pritchett had simply released him.

The entire Albany campaign was a disaster. After Albany, the civil rights leaders learned to avoid the Pritchetts and target towns that had hotheaded police chiefs and angry, volatile mayors. "The movement had a really gut sense of what it took to get in the news and stay in the news," said Gene Roberts, a North Carolina native who covered civil rights for *The New York Times.* During the 1965 march in Selma, Alabama, Martin Luther King noticed that a *Life* magazine photographer, Flip Schulke, had put down his cameras to help someone being beaten by police. Later King sought out the photographer and told him that they needed him not to help demonstrators, but to photograph them. He said, "Your role is to photograph what is happening to us."

In 1965 in Selma, a heavy, middle-aged woman named Annie Lee Cooper hit the sheriff full force with a punch. This got the attention of photographers, who started clicking off pictures as three sheriffs took hold of the woman. She then dared the sheriff to hit her, and he swung his billy club around and struck her so hard on the head that reporters noted the sound. They also got the picture—Sheriff Clark swinging his billy club at a helpless woman. It ran on the front page of newspapers throughout the country. SNCC's Mary King said, "The skillful use of the news media for public education is the modern equivalent of the 'pen,' and the pen is still mightier than the sword."

As the civil rights movement became more media conscious, Martin Luther King became its star. He was the first civil rights leader to become a media star and consequently was far more famous and had far more immediate impact than his predecessors or contemporaries. Ralph Abernathy said, "We knew that we had developed into symbols." King was often accused by people in the movement of stealing the spotlight, taking all the credit by taking all the bows. In truth, that was how the movement used him. He was seldom the innovator. But he was the eloquent speaker, the charismatic presence that made events work on television. He was a reluctant star, more at home in a church than at a demonstration or a press conference. He once said, "I am conscious of two Martin Luther Kings. I am a wonder to myself. . . . I am mystified by my own career. The Martin Luther King that the people talk about seems to me somebody foreign to me."

After Albany, television became an integral part of every campaign strategy. Within King's organization, the Southern Christian Leadership Conference, Andrew Young served as the chief adviser on media, or at least on white-controlled media. He understood that to get on television every day, they had to provide daily messages that were short and dramatic, what are now called sound bites, and that these had to be accompanied by what television called "a good visual." Young emphasized and King quickly grasped that the daily Martin Luther King statement should be no more than sixty seconds. Many SNCC activists thought King had gone too far, that he and his organization overused media. They believed that he was creating short-term news events, whereas they wanted to work more within southern society to create fundamental changes—a slow, off-camera process.

But the reality was that by 1968, the civil rights movement, the Black Power movement, the antiwar movement, even Congress and conventional politics had become deeply involved with the question of how to get a television cameraman, in the words of then CBS correspondent Daniel Schorr, "to push the button."

Two innovations in television technology completely changed broadcast news—videotape and direct satellite transmission. Both were developed in the 1960s, and though neither one came into full use until the 1970s, by 1968 they had already begun to change the way broadcast journalists thought. Videotape is inexpensive, can be reused, and does not have to be processed before broadcasting. In 1968 most television news was still shooting sixteen-millimeter black-and-white film, usually from cameras mounted on tripods, though there were also handheld cameras. Because the film was expensive and time-consuming to process, it could not be shot indiscriminately. The cameraman would set up and then wait for a signal from the correspondent. When the correspondent judged that the scene was becoming interesting— sometimes the cameraman would make the decision himself—he would give a signal, and the cameraman would push the button and start filming. "You could shoot ten minutes to get one minute," said Schorr, "but you couldn't shoot two hours."

What became apparent to Schorr was that it was "a matter of decibels. . . . As soon as somebody raised his voice and said, 'But how can you sit there and say so and so'—I would press the button, because television likes drama, television likes conflict, and anything that indicates conflict was a candidate for something that might get on the air— on the Cronkite show that evening, which was what we were all trying to do."

The presence of cameras started to have a noticeable impact on civility in debates. Schorr recalled in covering the Senate, "They frequently raised their voice for no reason at all, just because they knew that it would get our attention by doing that." But it was not only politicians in chambers that turned strident to get the button pushed. Abbie Hoffman understood how this worked, Stokely Carmichael understood it, and so did Martin Luther King. In 1968, after a decade of working with news media, King realized that he was losing the television competition. He complained to Schorr that television was encouraging black leaders to say the most violent and inflammatory things and had very little interest in his nonviolence. "When Negroes are incited to violence, will you think of your responsibility in helping to produce it?" King asked Schorr.

"Did I go on seeking menacing sound bites as my passport to the evening news?" Schorr asked himself in a moment of soul-searching. "I'm afraid I did."

The other invention that was changing television was live satellite transmission. The first transmission from a satellite was the tape-recorded voice of President Dwight Eisenhower giving Christmas greetings on December 18, 1958. Early satellites, such as the "Early Bird," were not *geostationary*—they did not maintain their position relative to the earth—and so could receive from any point on earth only at certain hours of the day. The satellite transmission of a major story required so many lucky coincidences that they rarely happened in the first few years. In those days, stories from Europe usually aired the next day in the States, after film could be flown in. The first story from Europe to be aired the same day on American television was not a satellite transmission. In 1961, when the Berlin Wall was first erected, the construction started so early in the day that with the time zone advantage, CBS was able to fly film to New York City in time for the evening news. President Kennedy complained that the half day it took to break the story on television had not allowed him enough time to formulate his response.

Fred Friendly, the head of CBS news, understood that satellites, with instant transmissions, would eventually become accessible from most places in the world at any time of day and that this awkward invention would one day change the nature not only of television news, but of news itself. In 1965, he wanted a live satellite broadcast from somewhere in the world on the Cronkite evening news, which came on at 7:00 P.M. New York City time. Looking for a place in the world that could send to Early Bird at seven New York City time, he found Berlin, which had been a major story for several years. Schorr was placed at the Berlin Wall, always a good visual, and it was—*live!* Schorr's entreaties that nothing was happening at the Wall in the middle of the night were useless. He was missing the point. The point was that it would be live.

"So indeed, I stood there," Schorr recounted. "This is the wall, behind here is where East Germany is, and all. And then, because we were there with lights on, you would hear dogs barking. Dogs started to bark and 'you would hear dogs barking sometimes chasing some poor East German who was trying to escape. I don't know that that is happening right now'—a lot of crap! But it was live."

CBS even talked a court in Germany that was trying an accused Nazi into holding a session after midnight so that it could be carried live rather than filming the normal day session and playing it that night. The age of live television news had begun.

According to U.S. military spokesmen, the second week of 1968, the week of the president's State of the Union address, marked a wartime record for the number of enemy soldiers killed in one week: 2,968. The previous record week had been the one ending March 25, 1967, in which only 2,783 enemy had been killed. The week also ended with Secretary of State Dean Rusk defending his foreign policy before a genial dinner audience of 1,500 in San Francisco as the police used clubs against 400 antiwar demonstrators outside. Three more American servicemen asked Sweden for political asylum on Friday, January 12. The previous Tuesday, 4 sailors had deserted the aircraft carrier *Intrepid* and were granted Swedish resident visas.

Race issues were also becoming more difficult. The shifting mood, already labeled "white backlash," was in part a reaction to rising crime and to the fact that young people and their counterculture stars openly used forbidden drugs, but it was mostly a reaction to black riots in northern cities. In one of his both bizarre and typical moments of self-discovery, Norman Mailer in his 1968 book *Miami and the Siege of Chicago*—one of three Mailer books published that year—described waiting for a Ralph Abernathy press conference for which the civil rights leader was forty minutes late. "The reporter became aware of a peculiar emotion in himself, for he had not ever felt it consciously before"—only slightly more modest than Charles de Gaulle, Mailer often referred to himself in third person singular—"It was a simple emotion and very unpleasant to him—he was getting tired of Negroes and their rights." But a more important revelation followed: "If he felt even a hint this way, then what immeasurable tides of rage must be loose in America?"

Originally, as most southerners sensed correctly, the civil rights movement fit comfortably into the prejudice most of the rest of the country felt toward the South. The movement seemed heroic when heading south and taking on drawling Neanderthals with names like Bull Connor. But in 1965, Martin Luther King began to champion the issue of "open housing" in northern cities. To most of white America, this was something different. They were not just trying to go to school and ride buses in Alabama, they were trying to move into our neighborhoods.

King and other leaders had also started devoting an increasing amount of time to opposing the war in Vietnam. By 1967, when King became an outspoken Vietnam War critic, he was the last major civil rights figure to do so. Most of the Congress of Racial Equality, CORE, and SNCC had turned antiwar in 1965 and 1966. Many of King's advisers in the Southern Christian Leadership Conference were reluctant to attack the government in time of war. In 1967 the Mobe and its leader David Dellinger, a World War II draft resister, made an all-out effort to bring King into the antiwar movement. Dellinger had also had advisers telling him that the antiwar movement was getting too involved with black leaders and it was alienating potential supporters of the antiwar cause. Many whites saw the involvement of black leaders as stepping outside the legitimate turf of a civil rights leader. Never mind the fact that only 11 percent of the population was black while

23 percent of the combat soldiers in Vietnam were. Blacks were now trying to dictate foreign policy. Heavyweight boxing champion Muhammad Ali, perhaps the one black figure who was even better than King at using the media, had refused the draft, saying, "I ain't got no quarrel with the Viet Cong." He was convicted of draft evasion, and a week after Johnson's State of the Union speech, Ali's appeal was rejected.

Ali had changed his name from Cassius Clay, which he said was a "slave name," when he became a Black Muslim, in 1963. The Black Muslims, Black Power, and especially the increasingly visible Black Panthers, who advocated violence, robberies, and shoot-outs with the police, were frightening to white people. The flames in black ghettos the summer before had for many been the final blow. King said that Black Power advocates such as Stokely Carmichael provided white people with the excuse they needed. "Stokely is not the problem," King said. "The problem is white people and their attitude."

For the ruling Democrats, the response to urban violence was a growing threat. An aide to Vice President Hubert Humphrey told *Time* magazine, "Another summer of riots could really sink us next fall." King opposed Johnson and had no loyalty to the Democrats, but he had more far-reaching fears of this so-called backlash. "We cannot stand two more summers like last summer without leading inevitably to a right-wing takeover and a fascist state," King said.

On January 12, President Johnson gave his State of the Union address. Never before in history had the annual address received so much television coverage. Not only did all three networks and the new National Educational Television station, the forerunner of PBS, carry the speech, but all four set aside time after the address to have guests come on and discuss what had just been heard. CBS canceled *Green Acres, He and She,* and *The Jonathan Winters Show* for its unprecedented two and one half hours of coverage. NBC sacrificed a *Kraft Music Hall* special starring Alan King and *Run for Your Life* to give two hours of coverage. ABC postponed its drama *Laura* developed by Truman Capote as a star vehicle for Jackie Kennedy's sister, Lee Bouvier Radziwell. For the analysis that preempted Eddie Albert and Eva Gabor, CBS had Senate minority leader Everett Dirksen. But the most extensive analysis was by NET, which had started the new trend by devoting more than three hours to the 1967 State of the Union address. For the 1968 speech, they put no time limit on their coverage, a concept unheard of in commercial television, and lined up such stars as Daniel Patrick Moynihan; Carl Stokes, the black mayor of Cleveland; and economist Milton Friedman.

If the speech was a barometer for the direction the country was turn-ing, the news was not good for liberalism. The Great Society, Johnson's catchphrase for the extensive list of social programs that were supposed to define his presidency, was mentioned only once. The audi-ence of Congress, cabinet members, and top-ranking military greeted the speech with the appropriate periodic applause that always seasons these events. According to *Time* magazine, the president was inter-rupted by applause fifty-three times, although it reported no genuine enthusiasm to most of these outbursts. The one prolonged standing ovation came when Johnson said, "The American people have had enough of rising crime and lawlessness in this country."

In place of new social programs, Johnson announced the Safe Streets Act, a new narcotics law with more severe penalties for the sale of what had become a campus favorite, LSD. He also called for gun control legislation to stop "mail order murder," which was the only statement in the fifty-minute speech that received applause from Senator Robert Kennedy.

Johnson responded to Hanoi's offer of talks—on condition that the United States cease bombing and other hostile acts—by saying, "The bombing would stop immediately if talks would take place promptly and with reasonable hopes that they would be productive." He then angrily recalled the enemy's violation of the New Year's truce, adding, "And the other side must not take advantage of our restraint as they have done in the past." This was an important point, since there were calls for another cease-fire for the upcoming Vietnamese New Year, Tet.

A Gallup poll released two days after the speech showed more people seeing Johnson as hawkish than saw either Nixon or Reagan that way. In a time when politicians were divided more commonly into doves and hawks, for peace or for war, than into Democrats and Repub-licans, this was significant. Both Nixon and Reagan had been regarded as unelectable, and one of the reasons had been their hawkishness.

In a *New York Times Magazine* article titled "Why the Gap Between LBJ and the Nation?" Max Frankel suggested that Johnson's problem was not so much that he handled the media badly, but that he was just not convincing:

But the measure of Mr. Johnson's trouble is not only Vietnam—perhaps not even Vietnam. It is his failure to persuade much of the country of his own deep belief that his war policy is right. Were he to succeed, his critics, even in the opposition, might at least respect the genuineness of his purpose. As it is, a great many of them seem to have concluded that he is beyond rational debate, merely afraid to concede a "mistake" or too timid to risk retreat. . . . He rehearses many of his public performances and studies some afterward. He has tried every combination of television lighting known to theatrical science and uttered every genre of political address.

Frankel quoted the president comparing himself to the Boston Red Sox's spectacular slugger Ted Williams. Despite all his records and considerable accomplishments, when Ted Williams stepped up to the plate fans often booed. "They'll say about me," Johnson explained, "I knock the ball over the fence—but they don't like the way he stands at the plate." The *Times* ran a follow-up letter to the editor signed by five members of the history department at Cornell:

On the other hand, there are similarities between the men that the President evidently chose to overlook: (1) Boston fans booed Williams not because of his stance but because he seldom delivered in the clutch; (2) Williams's problems were often caused by rudeness, immaturity and unsportsmanlike conduct with the public and the press; (3) Williams could never make a hit in left field either; (4) when faced with a new obstacle, like the Boudreau shift, Williams never chose to outsmart it but insisted on escalation to right field.

The day after the address, Martin Luther King, the most reluctant to denounce the war of all the civil rights leaders, called for a massive march on Washington in early February to protest "one of history's most cruel and senseless wars."

"We need to make clear in this political year, to congressmen on both sides of the aisle and to the president of the United States, that we will no longer tolerate, we will no longer vote for men who continue to see the killings of Vietnamese and Americans as the best way of advancing the goals of freedom and self-determination in Southeast Asia."

Traditionally the first day of Congress is a perfunctory one, but the start of the second session of the Ninetieth Congress in mid-January was marked by five thousand women, many dressed in black, marching and singing in protest over the war in Vietnam. They were led by eighty-seven-year-old Jeanette Rankin, the first woman member of Congress.

On January 21 a concert called "Broadway for Peace 1968," billed as "the greatest array of stars ever," was to have one performance at New York's Philharmonic Hall. Among those contributing their time to the event were Harry Belafonte, Leonard Bernstein, Paul Newman, Joanne Woodward, Eli Wallach, Carl Reiner, Robert Ryan, Barbra Streisand, and one of the biggest television stars of the year, Tommy Smothers. The proceeds went to the campaigns of antiwar senatorial and congressional candidates, many of whom were on hand to meet their supporters after the program.

Even Wall Street was turning against the war. The brokerage house Paine Webber, Jackson, and Curtis was running full-page newspaper ads explaining why peace was in the interest of investors and "the most bullish thing that could happen to the stock market."

Four days after the State of the Union address, Robert Kennedy attended the annual black-tie dinner of the Rochester, New York, Chamber of Commerce and asked for a show of hands for or against pursuing the war. About seven hundred were opposed. Only about thirty to forty hands indicated approval of war policy.

Yet Johnson was still considered the front-runner for the election in November. The January Gallup poll showed 48 percent approving of the way he handled his job, continuing an upward trend since a low of 38 percent the previous October. The day after his address, with only eight weeks to New Hampshire's opening primary election, pro- and anti-Johnson Democratic pundits agreed with those in the Republican Party that the president would probably beat Eugene McCarthy by a margin of 5 to 1.

The same day as Johnson's speech, as though ordered by Johnson himself, the North Vietnamese and Viet Cong, after ten days of the heaviest fighting of the war, stopped all ground combat. The U.S. military guessed that the enemy was gathering fresh troops and supplies. The Selective Service announced that a total of 302,000 men would be drafted into the army in 1968, an increase of 72,000 over 1967.

Since American democracy imposes no limits on a citizen's delusions of grandeur, there is always this question: If you were invited to the White House, would you give the president a piece of your mind, thereby publicly displaying bad manners, or would you be nice and waste the opportunity?

In January 1968, Eartha Kitt, a small and delicate-looking black cabaret singer, who had built her career in trendy Paris Left Bank clubs of the late 1950s, was confronted with such a decision when the president's wife, Lady Bird Johnson, invited her to a "ladies' lunch" at the White House. In conjunction with the president's newly outlined concerns, the topic was "What Citizens Can Do to Help Insure Safe Streets." Some fifty women were seated in the yellow-walled family dining room, ten to a table, with matching gold-rimmed plates and gold cutlery. The meal went from crab bisque to Lady Bird's favorite peppermint dessert. Woman after woman, mostly from privileged white backgrounds, spoke about their theories of the causes of street crime. But the fifty sat in stunned silence as Kitt leaned against the podium and said in her distinct porcelain voice, "You send the best of this country off to be shot and maimed. They rebel in the street. They will take pot and they will get high. They don't want to go to school because they're going to be snatched off from their mothers to be shot in Vietnam."

Different reporters were leaked slightly different versions of the encounter. In the *Time* magazine version she said, "No wonder the kids rebel and take pot—and in case you don't understand the lingo that's marijuana."

After a moment of silence, Mrs. Richard J. Hughes, wife of the Democratic governor of New Jersey, said, "I feel morally obligated. May I speak in defense of the war?" She said her first husband had been killed in World War II and that she had eight sons, one an air force veteran. "None wants to go to Vietnam, but all will go, they and their friends." She added that none of her sons smoked marijuana, and the guests, somewhat relieved, applauded while Kitt stared at her with arms folded.

Mrs. Johnson, noticeably pale, some said on the verge of tears, stood up and walked to the podium, somewhat in the way a good hostess would hurry to a trouble spot at a cocktail party to smooth it over, and politely suggested, "Because there is a war on—and I pray that there will be a just and honest peace—that still doesn't give us a free ticket not to try to work for better things such as against crime in the streets, better education, and better health for our people. Crime in the streets is one thing that we can solve. I am sorry I can't speak as well or as passionately on conditions of slums as you, because I have not lived there."

Kitt, the daughter of South Carolina sharecroppers, who as a teenager supported her family from a Harlem sweatshop, explained, "I have to say what is in my heart. I have lived in the gutters."

Mrs. Johnson, with candor and remarkable grace, replied, "I am sorry. I cannot understand the things that you do. I have not lived with the background you have."

And there it was, America in microcosm—the well-intentioned white liberals unable to comprehend black anger. Everyone wanted to comment on the widely reported incident, many applauding Kitt's courage, many appalled by her rudeness. Martin Luther King said that although the singer was the First Lady's guest, it was "a very proper gesture" because it "described the feelings of many persons" and that the "ears" of the Johnsons are "somewhat isolated from expressions of what people really feel."

Gene Roberts was removed from his beloved civil rights beat at *The New York Times* in the beginning of 1968 and reassigned to Saigon. Compared to civil rights, the Vietnam story seemed quiet. "I thought I had left the action." In Washington he got a round of briefings from the U.S. government. At the CIA briefing he asked if a recent battle had been a victory. The CIA official said, "There are six good reasons to consider this a victory." He went through the six reasons. Roberts then asked, "Is there any reason to consider it a defeat?"

"There are eight good reasons to consider it a defeat," the official replied, and he listed them.

At the White House, Roberts was briefed by a top-ranking member of the administration whose identity he promised not to expose. "Forget the war," he was told. "The war is over. Now we have to win the peace. The thing to keep your eye on is"—and he said this as though revealing a secret code—"IR8 rice."

"What?"

"IR8 rice!" The U.S. government had done large-scale experiments and found that IR8 rice had two high-yield crops a year. This, he assured Roberts, was the big story in Vietnam at the moment.

Roberts arrived in Saigon shortly after the Western New Year and started asking about IR8 rice. No one had heard of it. Finally, he learned that a rice festival was being held in the most secure province of South Vietnam. In fact, it was an IR8 rice festival. Crude bleachers were set up in the small rural village. In a corner, several farmers were squatting on their haunches, chewing on long blades of grass. All over the world farmers cluster and chew on grass. Roberts, who grew up in a farming area, recognized the scene and decided that a chat with these farmers would probably be worthwhile. He walked over with his translator and squatted by them.

"What do you think of this IR8 rice?"

The farmer exploded in an angry staccato burst of sound. The interpreter said, "He has some reservations about it." Roberts then insisted that the translator give a word-for-word first-person translation. He asked the question again. Again syllables spat out of the farmer's mouth as though from an automatic weapon.

"Basically," the interpreter explained, "he said, 'Fuck IR8 rice.'"
The other farmers were nodding in approval as the farmer continued

and the translator said, " 'My daddy planted Mekong Delta rice and so did his daddy and his daddy before that. If it was good enough for all those generations, why do we need something different?' "

The other farmers were still nodding enthusiastically.

"Well," Roberts wanted to know, "if you feel that way, why did you come to the IR8 rice festival?"

The farmer barked out more syllables. "Because *your president*"— he was referring to South Vietnamese president Nguyen Van Thieu as he pointed his finger at Roberts—"your president sent a bunch of men with rifles who ordered me onto the bus."

Somehow, Roberts reasoned, there was a story in this, but it was difficult. His government source had been promised anonymity. But there was the program—or its failure. While he was still laboring on the IR8 rice story, his turn came up for the daily breaking news story. Fighting had broken out in Da Nang on the northern coast of South Vietnam near the old provincial capital of Hue. This was near the north-south border, and there had been rumors of a big North Vietnamese push across the border. Roberts got on a plane for Da Nang. As the plane banked for the north, he looked out the window and saw Saigon below—in flames. He never did write the IR8 rice story.

Early that morning, January 30, the Vietnamese New Year, the air base at Da Nang was hit as part of an attack by sixty-seven thousand pro–North Vietnam troops on thirty-six provincial capitals and five major cities including Saigon.

In the middle of the preceding night, fifteen men led by Nguyen Van Sau, an illiterate farmer from the outskirts of Saigon, had gathered in a Saigon garage. Nguyen Van Sau had joined the cause four years earlier, assigned to a sabotage battalion in Saigon. He had recently been admitted to the People's Revolutionary Party as a reward for his good work. He and his group had been quietly moving ammunition and explosives hidden in baskets of tomatoes into the neighborhood around the garage. Far more than the many deeds done by the other sixty-seven thousand, the work of this group of slightly more than a dozen fighters would come to epitomize around the world what was called the Tet Offensive. What was special about Nguyen Van Sau's group was that their attack had the best press coverage.

His mission was to attack the U.S. embassy, which was a convenient location for coverage by the Saigon-based press corps, many of whom lived in the neighborhood. Up until then, most Vietnam War battles were reported on after they happened, or at best, if the battle was long enough, reporters would get in at midbattle. But from the U.S.

embassy, their lines of communication were uninterrupted, stories could be filed in the neighborhood, film could be quickly shipped. And they had the time difference on their side. The attack occurred on January 30, but it was still January 29 in the United States. By January 30 and 31, the United States and the rest of world had the story in pictures and on film. American GIs were seen taking cover in the U.S. embassy compound, American corpses were seen lying still, being dragged, carried away on the back of vehicles. Viet Cong bodies were piling up. For several days, Americans saw images of U.S. soldiers either dead or ducking behind walls.

Nguyen Van Sau and his group had packed into a taxi and a small Peugeot delivery truck and sped to the embassy, where they opened fire at the guards. The first report of the attack reached Associated Press's New York bureau about fifteen minutes later, while the assailants were blowing the first hole in the compound wall. They rushed in firing, killing the first two guards, who seemed to have also killed Nguyen Van Sau. The guerrillas further penetrated the compound with rockets. News reports were already describing the attackers as "a suicide squad." At 7:30 that morning, with the battle still in progress, it was 6:30 in the evening in New York and NBC Television's *Huntley-Brinkley Report* had the story, though without film. They reported twenty suicide attackers holding the building. The report had some confusion about who was firing from the building and who was in the compound. But Americans got the idea, more or less. Finally, military police were able to use a jeep to ram open the front gate, which had been locked shut by the guards at the first moment of attack. Behind the MPs came the press corps with cameras to document the bodies, bullet holes, fallen embassy seal. By 9:15 the embassy had been secured and one of the most famous battles of the Vietnam War was over. Eight Americans had been killed.

Everyone in Nguyen Van Sau's group was killed. It had been a suicide mission. They had been given no plan for escaping. The 67,000 Viet Cong guerrilla fighters of the Tet Offensive had taken on a South Vietnam with almost 1.2 million soldiers, of which 492,000 were American. General William C. Westmoreland, who often bolstered his arguments with body counts of enemy dead, immediately claimed that the attack had failed and cost the enemy many lives. But he had been saying that he had seen "the light at the end of the tunnel" in the war and he was not being very much believed anymore. In truth, after a week the Viet Cong had failed to hold a single city and had lost about half of its fighting force. With seven more years of fighting, the guerrilla fighters of the Viet Cong never again played a leading role because they had been so diminished in the Tet Offensive. The fight was carried on by the regular troops of the Vietnam People's Army, which Americans called the North Vietnamese army. It is now thought that Viet Cong four-star general Nguyen Chi Thanh had opposed the Tet plan, believing it was foolish to engage a superior force in conventional warfare, but he was killed in an American bombing before the issue was decided.

The attack had succeeded probably better than the North Vietnamese realized, because, though it was a military failure, it was a media success. At a loss to explain this kind of suicide warfare, U.S. intelligence officers at the time concluded that this lone successful aspect must have been its goal, that the North Vietnamese had launched the Tet Offensive to win a public relations victory. The results were dazzling. Today we are accustomed to war appearing instantly on TV, but this was new in 1968. War had never been brought to living rooms so quickly. Today the military has become much more experienced and adept at controlling media. But in the Tet Offensive, the images brought into living rooms were of U.S. Armed Forces in shambles, looking panicked, being killed.

By February 1968, Cronkite on CBS and Chet Huntley and David Brinkley on NBC were experiencing the highest ratings they had ever known. At a time when fifty-six million American homes had televisions, Cronkite was reaching more than eleven million homes and Huntley/Brinkley was reaching more than ten million homes. Expensive satellite transmissions instantly relaying footage from Japan to New York City were being used regularly by all three networks for the first time that month. The government could no longer control the public image of the war. *New York Times* television critic Jack Gould wrote, "For the huge TV audience the grim pictures unfolded in the last week cannot fail to leave the impression that the agony of Vietnam is acute and that the detached analyses of Secretary of State Dean Rusk and Secretary of Defense Robert S. McNamara, who appeared yesterday on 'Meet the Press,' could be incomplete."

The print media was also giving more attention to the war than they ever had before. *Harper's* magazine and the *Atlantic Monthly* put out special Vietnam War issues. *Harper's* entire March issue, on sale in February, was devoted to a Norman Mailer article about the antiwar movement that powerfully criticized U.S. policy. *Atlantic Monthly's* entire March issue was devoted to a piece by Dan Wakefield also about antiwar sentiment. Though both magazines were more than a century old and neither had ever done single-article issues, both said it was a coincidence that they were producing such issues at the same time on the same subject.

Photography was being used in this February explosion of media as it rarely had been before. The normally black-and-white *Time* magazine used color. The Tet Offensive happened to coincide with an internal debate at *The New York Times*. The photo department wanted the paper to use more than occasional small and usually cropped pictures, and after much arguing, the *Times* agreed that if they were supplied with pictures worthy of it, they would give a big picture spread.

Photographer Eddie Adams was roaming Saigon in morning light with an NBC crew when he came upon Vietnamese marines with a man in tow, his arms tied behind his back, badly beaten. Suddenly Adams saw the chief of South Vietnam National Police, General Nguyen Ngoc Loan, draw his sidearm. The prisoner turned a downcast eye as General Loan held his arm straight out and fired a bullet into the man's head. Adams had photographed it all. He developed the pictures and placed them on the drum of an electronic scanner that sent them to New York and around the world. The *Times* agreed that these were unusual pictures worthy of a different kind of spread. On February 2 a photo ran on the top of the front page of a small man, hands bound, face distorted by the impact of a bullet from the handgun in General Loan's outstretched arm. Below ran another picture of a South Vietnamese soldier, grief on his face as he carried his child, killed by the Viet Cong. On page twelve was more— three pictures marked "Prisoner," "Execution," and "Death," showing the Adams sequence of the killing. These photos won more than ten photojournalism awards and were and still are among the most remembered images of the war.

The world was learning what this war looked like in more detail than had ever happened in the history of warfare. Later in the year, John Wayne released a film on Vietnam, *The Green Berets,* starring and co-directed by himself. Renata Adler, reviewing for *The New York Times,* declared the film "stupid," "false," and "unspeakable." Richard Schickel in *Life* magazine agreed with all of these adjectives but further stated, "The war being fought here bears no resemblance whatever to the reality of Vietnam as we have all, hawks and doves alike, perceived it to be through the good offices of the mass media." Neither John Wayne nor any other American filmmaker had ever needed to contend with this before. Up until then, most war films did not look like the real thing, but now, even if the war was in a distant land, the public would know because it had seen the war.

1968 was the first year Hollywood filmmakers were permitted an unrestricted hand in the portrayal of violence. Censorship regulations were replaced by a ratings system so that Hollywood warfare could be portrayed looking as gruesome as network television war, though the first films to use the new violence, such as the 1968 police thriller *Bullitt* and the 1969 western *The Wild Bunch,* were not war movies.

Another problem with war films was that every day the public was picking up better war stories in the news media than they could find in the Hollywood war clichés. The fast talker from Brooklyn and the quiet "What are you going to do after the war?" scene did not stand up to real stories such as that of Marine Private Jonathan Spicer, a funny, offbeat son of a Methodist minister in Miami. Spicer refused to fight and so was assigned to be a medical corpsman. The scorn of his fellow marines was soon silenced because Spicer seemed to be fearless, dragging wounded marines out of the line of fire, protecting them with his own body. One March day in Khe Sanh, a shelling began as the corpsmen were trying to evacuate wounded, and Spicer was ordered into his bunker. When the marines were trapped in Khe Sanh, each time they tried to evacuate wounded, the Viet Cong would shell. Spicer saw the marines were having trouble getting the wounded loaded, so he ran over to help and was caught in a shell burst. At the field hospital only yards away, Spicer was pronounced dead. Such field units are not set up for major surgery and normally only patch up the patient and send him on to a full hospital. But this doctor thought he could save Spicer and opened his chest, massaged his stopped heart, plugging up a hole with his finger until he could stitch it closed, and brought the young man back to life. This was not a Hollywood story, though, and three days later Private Spicer, nineteen years old, shipped to a hospital in Japan, died of his wounds.

Now that people could watch the war, many did not like what they saw. Anti–Vietnam War demonstrations involving hundreds of thousands were becoming commonplace around the world. From February 11 to 15, students from Harvard, Radcliffe, and Boston University held a four-day hunger strike to protest the war. On February 14, ten thousand demonstrators, according to the French police, or one hundred thousand, according to the organizers, marched through Paris in the pouring rain, waving North Vietnamese flags and chanting, "Vietnam for the Vietnamese," "U.S. Go Home," and "Johnson Assassin." Four days later, West Berlin students did a better job of imitating American antiwar rallies when an estimated ten thousand West Germans and students from throughout Western Europe chanted: "Ho, Ho, Ho Chi Minh"—reminiscent of the American "Ho, Ho, Ho Chi Minh, the NLF is gonna win." Ho Chi Minh had called his movement the National Liberation Front. German student leader Rudi Dutschke said, "Tell the Americans the day and the hour will come when we will drive

American antiwar poster depicting a draft card being burned
(Imperial War Museum, London, poster negative number LDP 449)

you out unless you yourselves throw out imperialism." The demonstrators urged American soldiers to desert, which they were already doing, applying to Sweden, France, and Canada for asylum. In February, the Toronto Anti-Draft Program mailed to the United States five thousand copies of its 132-page paperback, *Manual for Draft Age Immigrants to Canada,* printed in the basement of an eight-room house by U.S. draft dodgers living in Canada. In addition to legal information it gave background information on the country, including a chapter titled "Yes, John, There Is a Canada." By March even the relatively moderate Mexico City student movement held a demonstration against the Vietnam War.

The Selective Service had been planning to call up 40,000 young men a month, but the number was ballooning upward to 48,000. The Johnson administration abolished the student deferment for graduate studies and announced that 150,000 graduate students would be drafted during the fiscal year that would begin in July. This was a severe blow not only for young men planning graduate studies, among them Bill Clinton, a senior at Georgetown's School of Government who had been appointed a Rhodes Scholar for graduate study at Oxford, but also for American graduate schools, which claimed they would be losing 200,000 incoming and first-year students. One university president, remarkably free of today's rules of political correctness, complained that graduate schools would now be limited to "the lame, the halt, the blind, and the female."

At Harvard Law School Alan Dershowitz began offering a course on the legal paths to war resistance. Five hundred law professors signed a petition urging the legal profession to actively oppose the war policy of the Johnson administration. With 5,000 marines in Khe Sanh surrounded by 20,000 enemy troops who could easily be replaced and resupplied from the northern border, the seven days ending February 18 broke a new record for weekly casualties, with 543 American soldiers killed. On February 17, Lieutenant Richard W. Pershing, grandson of the commander of American Expeditionary Forces in World War I, engaged to be married and serving in the 101st Airborne, was killed by enemy fire while searching for the remains of a comrade.

President Johnson was slipping so far in the polls that even Richard Nixon, the perennial loser of the Republican Party, had caught up to him. Nixon's most feared competitor in the Democratic Party, New York senator Robert Kennedy, who still insisted he was a loyal Johnson Democrat, gave a speech in Chicago on February 8 saying that the Vietnam War was unwinnable. "We must first of all rid ourselves of the illusion that the events of the past two weeks represent some sort of victory," Kennedy said. "That is not so. It is said the Viet Cong may not be able to hold the cities. This is probably true. But they have demonstrated, despite all our reports of progress, of government strength and enemy weakness, that half a million American soldiers with 700,000 Vietnamese allies, with total command of the air, total command of the sea, backed by huge resources and the most modern weapons, are unable to secure even a single city from the attacks of an enemy whose total strength is about 250,000."

As the Tet Offensive went on, the question was inescapable: Why had they been caught by surprise? Twenty-five days before Tet, the embassy had intercepted a message about attacks on southern cities including Saigon but did not act on it. A sneak attack during Tet was not even a new idea. In 1789, the year the French Revolution erupted and George

Washington took his oath of office, Vietnamese emperor Quang Trung took the Chinese by surprise by using the cover of Tet festivities to march on Hanoi. Not as undermanned as the Viet Cong, he attacked with one hundred thousand men and several hundred elephants and sent the Chinese into a temporary retreat. Wasn't Westmoreland familiar with this widely known story of Quang Trung's Tet Offensive? A small statue of the emperor, a gift from a Vietnamese friend, stood in General Westmoreland's office. Again in 1960, the Viet Cong had scored a surprise victory by attacking on the eve of Tet. Holiday attacks were almost a tradition in Vietnam. North Vietnamese general Vo Nguyen Giap had started his career catching the French by surprise on Christmas Eve 1944.

Now the same General Giap was on the cover of *Time* magazine. On the inside was a several-page color spread, an unusual display for *Time* magazine in the sixties, showing dead American soldiers.

"What the hell's going on?" said CBS's Walter Cronkite, reading reports from Saigon off camera. "I thought we were winning the war."

In a year with no middle ground, Walter Cronkite remained comfortably in the center. The son of a Kansas City dentist, Cronkite was middle class from the Middle West with a self-assured but never arrogant centrist point of view. It became a popular parlor game to guess at Walter Cronkite's politics. To most Americans Cronkite was not a know-it-all but someone who did happen to know. He was so determinedly neutral that viewers studied his facial movements in the hopes of detecting an opinion. Many Democrats, including John Kennedy, suspected he was a Republican, but the Republicans saw him as a Democrat. Pollsters did studies that showed that Cronkite was trusted by Americans more than any politician, journalist, or television personality. After seeing one such poll, John Bailey, chairman of the Democratic National Committee said, "What I'm afraid this means is that by a mere inflection of his deep baritone voice or by a lifting of his well-known bushy eyebrows, Cronkite might well change the vote of thousands of people around the country."

Cronkite was one of the last television journalists to reject the notion that he was the story. Cronkite wanted to be a conduit. He valued the trust he had and believed that it came from truthfulness. He always insisted that it was CBS, not just him, that had the trust of America. *The CBS Evening News with Walter Cronkite,* since it had begun in 1963, was the most popular television news show.

A difference in generations labeled "the generation gap" was not only dividing society, but was apparent in journalism as well. Author

David Halberstam, who had been a *New York Times* correspondent in Vietnam, recalled that the older reporters and editors who had come out of World War II tended to side with the military. "They thought we were unpatriotic and didn't believe that generals lied." Younger reporters such as Halberstam and Gene Roberts created a sensation, both in public opinion and in journalism, by reporting that the generals were lying. "Then came another generation," Halberstam said, "who smoked pot and knew all the music. We called them the heads." The heads never trusted a word from the generals.

Walter Cronkite was from that old World War II generation that believed generals and which Halberstam had found to be such an obstacle when he first started reporting on Vietnam. But, though his thirty minutes of evening news did not reflect this, Cronkite was growing increasingly suspicious that the U.S. government and the military were not telling the truth. He did not see "the light at the end of the tunnel" that General Westmoreland continually promised.

It seemed that in order to understand what was going on in Vietnam, he would have to go and see for himself. This decision worried the U.S. government. They could survive temporarily losing control of their own embassy, but the American people would never forgive their losing Walter Cronkite. The head of CBS News, Richard Salant, had similar fears. Journalists were sent into combat, but not corporate treasures.

"I said," Cronkite recalled, "well, I need to go because I thought we needed this documentary about Tet. We were getting daily reports, but we didn't know where it was going at that time; we may lose the war; if we're going to lose the war, I should be there, that was one thing. If the Tet Offensive was successful in the end, it meant that we were going to be fleeing, as we did eventually anyway, but I wanted to be there for the clash."

Walter Cronkite never saw himself as a piece of broadcast history or a national treasure, any of the things others saw in him. All his life he saw himself as a reporter, and he never wanted to miss the big story. Covering World War II for United Press International, he had been with the Allies when they landed in North Africa, when the first bombing missions flew over Germany, when they landed in Normandy, parachuted into the Netherlands, broke out of the Bulge. He always wanted to be there.

Salant's first response was predictable. As Cronkite remembered it, he said, "If you need to be there, if you are demanding to go, I'm not going to stop you, but I think it's foolish to risk your life in a situation like this, risk the life of our anchorman, and I've got to think about it."

His next thoughts were what surprised Cronkite. "But if you are going to go," he said, "I think you ought to do a documentary about going, about why you went, and maybe you are going to have to say something about where the war ought to go at that point."

The one thing Dick Salant had been known for among CBS journalists was forbidding any kind of editorializing of the news. Cronkite said of Salant, "If he were to detect any word in a reporter's report that seemed to have been editorializing at all, personal opinion, he was dead set against it—against doing it at all. Not just mine. I'm talking about any kind of editorializing of anybody."

So when Salant told Cronkite his idea for a Vietnam special, Cronkite answered, "That would be an editorial."

"Well," said Salant, "I'm thinking that maybe it's time for that. You have established a reputation, and thanks to you and through us we at CBS have established a reputation for honesty and factual reporting and being in the middle of the road. You yourself have talked about the fact that we get shot at from both sides, you yourself have said that we get about as many letters saying that we are damned conservatives as saying that we are damned liberals. We support the war. We're against the war. You yourself say that if we weigh the letters, they weigh about the same. We figure we are about middle of the road. So if we've got that reputation, maybe it would be helpful, if people trust us that much, trust you that much, for you to say what you think. Tell them what it looks like, from your being on the ground, what is your opinion."

"You're getting pretty heavy," Cronkite told Salant.

Cronkite suspected that all the trust he had earned was about to be diminished because he was crossing a line he had never before crossed. CBS also feared that their news show's top ratings might slip with Walter's transition from sphinx to pundit. But the more they thought about it, the more it seemed to Cronkite and Salant that in this moment of confusion, the public was hungering for a clear voice explaining what was happening and what should be happening.

When Cronkite arrived in Vietnam, he could not help looking happy, back in war correspondent's clothes, helmet on head, giving a thumbs-up sign that seemed completely meaningless in the situation. But from the start Cronkite and his team had difficulties. It was hard to find a friendly airport at which to land. When they finally got to Saigon on February 11, they found themselves in a combat zone. Westmoreland briefed Cronkite on how fortunate it was that the famous newsman had arrived at this moment of great victory, that Tet had been everything they had been hoping for. But in fact that same day marked the twelfth day since the Tet Offensive had begun, and though the United States was gaining back its territory, 973 Americans had already died fighting off the Viet Cong attack. Each week was breaking a new record for American casualties. In one day, February 9, 56 marines were killed in the area of Khe Sanh.

In Khe Sanh, where U.S. Marines were dug in near the north-south border, the battle was worsening, and Hanoi as well as the French press were starting to compare it to Dien Bien Phu, where the Vietnamese overran a trapped French army base in 1954. The French press took almost as much glee as the North Vietnamese in the comparison.

In Washington, speculation was so widespread on the idea that the United States might turn to nuclear weapons rather than lose Khe Sanh and five thousand marines that a reporter asked General Earle G. Wheeler, chairman of the Joint Chiefs of Staff, if nuclear weapons were being considered for Vietnam. The general reassured no one by saying, "I do not think that nuclear weapons will be required to defend Khe Sanh." The journalist had not mentioned Khe Sanh in his broad question.

There was a waiting list for correspondents to get a day in Khe Sanh, but Walter Cronkite was not to make the list. It was considered too dangerous. The U.S. military was not going to lose Cronkite. Instead he was taken to Hue, where artillery was smashing the ornate architecture of the onetime colonial capital into rubble. The Americans had once again secured Hue, Cronkite was told, but when he got there marines were still fighting for it. On February 16, U.S. Marines of the 5th Regiment's 1st Battalion took two hundred yards in the city at a cost of eleven dead marines and another forty-five wounded. It was in Hue that Americans first became familiar with the stubby, lightweight, Soviet-designed weapon, the AK-47, equally effective for a single-shot sniper or spraying ten rounds a second. The weapon was to become an image of warfare in the Middle East, Central America, and Africa.

What most disturbed veteran war correspondent Cronkite was that soldiers in the field and junior officers told him completely different versions of events from those given him by the commanders in Saigon. This was the experience of many who covered Vietnam. "There were so many patent untruths about the war," said Gene Roberts. "It was more than what is today called spin. We were told things that just weren't true. Saigon officers and soldiers in the field were saying the opposite. It produced a complete rift between reporters and the U.S. government."

Report from Vietnam by Walter Cronkite aired on February 27 at

10:00 P.M. eastern time. Cronkite fans, who seemed to include almost everyone, were thrilled to see Walter in Vietnam, out on the story, where in his heart Cronkite always believed he belonged. Then, after the last station break, he was back where CBS thought he belonged, behind a desk, dressed in a suit. He stared into the camera with a look so personal, so straightforward and devoid of artifice, that his nine million viewers could almost believe he was talking directly to each of them. The impression of sincerity was helped by his insistence on writing his own script:

> To say that we are closer to victory today is to believe, in the face of evidence, the optimists who have been wrong in the past. To suggest we are on the edge of defeat is to yield to unreasonable pessimism. To say that we are mired in stalemate seems the only realistic, though unsatisfactory, conclusion. On the off chance that military and political analysts are right, in the next months we must test the enemy's intentions in case this is indeed his last big gasp before negotiations. But it is increasingly clear to this reporter that the only rational way out then will be to negotiate, not as victors but as an honorable people who lived up to their pledge to defend democracy, and did the best they could.
> This is Walter Cronkite. Good night.

It was hardly a radical position. Few of its premises would have been acceptable to most leaders of the antiwar movement. But at a time of polarization, where every opinion was either for the war or against it, Walter Cronkite's statement was against the war. He was not of the sixties generation, he was of the World War II generation, his career had been built on war. Cronkite thought supporting democracy against communism was such a given that it never occurred to him his open backing of the cold war was a violation of his own neutrality. Now he was saying that we ought to get out. Of course, by this time he was not alone. Even the conservative *Wall Street Journal* editorial page said, "The whole Vietnam effort may be doomed."

Yet despite all his troubles, Johnson reacted to the Cronkite special as though now, for the first time, he had a real problem. There are two versions of Johnson's response. In one version he said, "If I've lost Cronkite, I've lost middle America." In the other the president was quoted saying, "If I've lost Cronkite, I've lost the war."

The show was said to have had a great effect on the president. Cronkite insisted that his role was greatly exaggerated. "I never asked Johnson about it, though we were pretty friendly. But there is no question that it was one more straw on the camel's back, perhaps no more

*Hue, the former Vietnamese capital, after being bombed
into rubble by the United States, February 1968
(Photo by Marc Riboud/Magnum Photos)*

important than that, but the camel, the back of the camel, was getting ready to collapse."

What is as important for broadcast history, Cronkite's ratings went up rather than down after giving his opinion, and few broadcasters would ever again wrestle with his and Salant's qualms about a little editorializing. In fact, starting in 1968 there was a noted increase in political opinion from entertainers, disc jockeys, and radio talk show hosts. Suddenly everyone on the air, regardless of his or her credentials, was being asked to state a position on issues from Vietnam to the plight of inner cities. The other new trend was for political figures to appear on television entertainment programs, most notably Johnny Carson's *Tonight* show but also such shows as *Rowan & Martin's Laugh-In* and *The Smothers Brothers Comedy Hour*. Some found this increased blending of news and entertainment disturbing. Jack Gould wrote in *The New York Times*, "It is only a matter of time before Chet Huntley and David Brinkley will be donning fetching leotards for their nightly pas de deux and Clive Barnes"—the *Times* theater critic at the time—"will be reviewing the New Hampshire primary."

Decades after the Tet Offensive special Cronkite said, "I did it because I thought it was the journalistically responsible thing to do at that moment. It was an egotistical thing for us to do . . . it was egotistical for me to do and for CBS to permit me to do." When again would a broadcast star submit himself to Cronkite's brand of self-criticism?

CHAPTER 4

TO BREATHE IN
A POLISH EAR

I want to rule as Thou dost—always, secretly.
—ADAM MICKIEWICZ,
Dziady, *or* Forefathers' Eve, *1832*

The communication of opposites, which characterizes the
commercial and political style, is one of the many ways in which
discourse and communication make themselves immune against
the expression of protest and refusal.
—HERBERT MARCUSE, One-Dimensional Man, *1964*

N O ONE was more surprised to discover a student movement
in "the happiest barracks in the Soviet camp" than the
students themselves. Happy barracks is perverse Polish humor. It was
not that the Poles were happy, but that they had managed to secure
from the Soviets certain rights, such as freedom to travel, that had been
denied in other Eastern European countries. They were certainly
happier than the citizens of Novotný's Czechoslovakia. The Polish
government would even sell $5 in hard currency to a Pole who wished
to go abroad.

By 1968, the belief that the Soviet bloc was crumbling had been
widespread in Western academic circles for a number of years. In the
summer of 1964, a group of economics and business experts offered a
series of seminars in Moscow, Poland, Czechoslovakia, and Yugoslavia
on the disintegrating bloc. Clark Kerr, president of the University of
California at Berkeley, participated, sensing trouble in the communist
world, but without the slightest notion that he would return to campus
in the fall to face the first important student uprising in the West.

Now many thought the hour had arrived for the Eastern bloc. When
Dubček came to power in Czechoslovakia and Brezhnev rushed to

Prague, experienced Soviet watchers were quick to recall October 1956, when Nikita Khrushchev rushed to Warsaw faced with the onetime disgraced Władysław Gomułka, now managing a political comeback and overwhelmingly popular. Despite Khrushchev's intervention, Gomułka came to power, and this Polish defiance had been all the encouragement needed for the Hungarians to rise up against Moscow. Was Brezhnev's unsuccessful rush to Prague a prelude to uprisings in the Soviet bloc?

This was Moscow's great fear. They had newly rebellious Romania to worry about, and Tito's Yugoslavia. Even Fidel Castro's Cuba had been causing them trouble. In the midst of Soviet difficulties with Romania, a February meeting of world Communist Parties in Budapest was boycotted by Cuba, which was in the midst of an anti-Soviet purge in its government. In January the Cuban Communist Party had "discovered" a pro-Soviet "microfaction" in its midst and prosecuted and convicted nine pro-Soviet Cuban officials for being "traitors to the Revolution." One Cuban official was sentenced to fifteen years in prison, eight were given twelve-year sentences, and twenty-six others received two-to-ten-year sentences.

But while Poles had a reputation in Eastern Europe for rebelliousness, Poland was not high on Moscow's lengthening list of worries for 1968. Gomułka, though at sixty-three he had outlasted Khrushchev, had lost some of his popular appeal. He understood that he had to balance Polish nationalism with Moscow relations and avoid the kind of debacle Hungary suffered in 1956. But the 1956 Soviet invasion of Hungary and the accompanying world condemnation had been difficult for the Soviets as well. Gomułka understood that the Kremlin had weaknesses and there were chances for concessions. The Soviet economy had been performing badly, and the Soviets could not afford the kind of hostility in the West that was produced by the crushing of Hungary in 1956. So with Moscow hesitant to act, it seemed a good time to test the limits. What those limits were was unknown, but all the bloc leaders, including Dubček, understood that there were at least two things the Kremlin would not accept: withdrawing from the Warsaw Pact military alliance and challenging Moscow's power monopoly.

Władysław Gomułka was the kind of enigma that CIA agents and KGB agents could earn their salaries trying to analyze. He was an antinationalist with a streak of Polish nationalism, a man with a history of rebellion against Moscow and yet a leader eager for good Soviet relations, an alleged anti-Semite married to a Jew. Being married to that woman would make anyone an anti-Semite, Polish Jews used to joke. Marian Turski, who covered the Gomułka years for the Polish weekly

Polityka, said, "In a way there was something in common between him and de Gaulle . . . a very selfish man with a very large, unlimited ego."

Gomułka was juggling at least three problems at once, all of which tugged in different directions: internal discontent partly but not entirely related to the failure of the economy, Moscow's paranoia, and an internal power struggle with an ambitious general who plotted for years to replace Gomułka. According to Jan Nowak, head of the Polish-language service of Radio Free Europe at the time, Interior Minister Mieczyslaw Moczar began plotting Gomułka's overthrow as early as 1959.

Moczar had not read Marx or Lenin or, for that matter, many other books. Uneducated and unrefined, he understood power and wanted to turn the "happy barracks" into a police state run by him. He was one of a group of extreme Polish nationalists known as the Partisans who had fought the Nazis together from inside Poland. The Partisans were bitter rivals of the so-called Muscovite faction that backed Gomułka, those who had fought the Germans by fleeing to Russia and joining up with the Soviets. The Jews, forced to flee Poland, became Muscovites and not Partisans. To help bring himself and the Partisans to power, Moczar did something that had often been done in Polish history: He played the Jewish card.

By the eighteenth century, Poland had the largest concentration of European Jewry since the 1492 expulsion from Spain. But the Poles became increasingly anti-Semitic, and during World War II many Poles, while they resisted German occupation, cooperated in the murder of all but 275,000 of the 3.3 million Jews living in Poland. After the war, Jewish survivors faced further massacres and pogroms by Poles. Socialism had not ended anti-Semitism, as it had promised, and wave after wave of Jews left Poland in response to periodic outbreaks of it. The Polish government encouraged Jews to immigrate to Israel, offering them passports and transportation to Vienna. How does a smart Jew talk to a dumb Jew? went a popular Jewish joke in Poland. The answer: On the telephone from Vienna.

By the mid-1960s only about thirty thousand Jews remained in Poland, and most of these identified more with the Communist Party than with Judaism. Despite recurring Polish bigotry, they were oddly comfortable, convinced that communism was the only hope for constructing a just society and ending anti-Semitism. In fact, communism would make both Judaism and anti-Semitism obsolete. Anti-Semitism, like Judaism, was a thing of the past in Poland.

In 1967, Moczar discovered that the Gomułka government had been infiltrated by Jews. Many of the Muscovites who supported Gomułka were Jewish, and many of them held high-ranking positions in his government.

The Polish anti-Semite accepted and needed no proof that Jews were foreigners, that they were not loyal to Poland, and that they were agents of foreign governments. In Poland, a Polish Jew is always called a Jew. A Pole by definition is Christian. Jews were often accused of siding with the Soviets against Poland or with the Israelis against the Soviets. Now Moczar was suggesting that they were guilty of both.

All of this came together in 1967 when the Arabs were defeated by the Israelis in the spectacular Six Day War. Poles congratulated Israel. Gomułka received transcripts of telephone calls of congratulations to the Israeli embassy by high Polish officials of Jewish background. Of course, the transcripts had been produced by the Moczar faction, and no such communication had taken place. But it was hard for Gomułka to ignore this accusation.

The Israeli embassy had been getting flowers and notes of congratulations from all over Poland, though not from officials of his government. The congratulations were not all coming from Jews, either. Poles asked, were not the Israeli fighters Poles—the very people who had left Poland through Vienna? Suddenly a Jew from Poland was a Pole. Was not the Israeli Defense Force, the Haganah, founded by Poles? Actually, it was founded by a Jew from Odessa, Vladimir Jabotinsky, but it was true that many Israeli soldiers were of Polish origin. Had not the *jojne,* an anti-Semitic stereotype of the cowardly Jew, gone to war? *Jojne poszedl na wojne*—the *jojne* went to war—it even rhymed in Polish. And the *jojne* even won, beating Soviet-trained troops in six days. It was a wonderful joke, and everyone—not the Jews, but the Poles—was laughing a little too loudly.

Gomułka was not a great lover of Russians, but he knew this was not a good time to be laughing at them. Since the fall of the Soviet Union it has been learned that at the time of the Six Day War, Brezhnev sent nuclear submarines into the Mediterranean. He then called Johnson on the hot line, and the two labored to keep Israel from marching to Damascus. While this was going on, Gomułka and other Eastern European leaders were meeting with Brezhnev. Notes by Gomułka's secretary indicate that news of the Arab defeat, step by step, was reaching Brezhnev while he was meeting with Gomułka and other leaders. The Russians had a sense of not only defeat but humiliation. Gomułka returned to Warsaw, deeply troubled, saying that the world was inching toward war, and then he received reports from Moczar, the minister of the interior, and the head of the secret police that Polish Jews were sympathizing with Israel. The report said nothing about the fact that non-Jewish Poles were doing the same thing.

On June 18, 1967, in a speech to the trade union congress, Gomułka spoke of "Fifth Columnist" activities, and that speech was interpreted as a signal that the purge of Jews or, as it was known, "the anti-Zionist campaign" could now begin. The terms *Fifth Columnist,* to indicate an underground traitor, and *Zionist* were now to be found in proximity. Zionists were to be rooted out and removed from high places. The worker's militias, always available in the service of the government, dutifully began demonstrating against the Zionists. But the word *syjoninci,* meaning "Zionist," was not well known, and some workers, told to demonstrate against the *syjoninci,* carried placards saying, "*Syjoninci do Syjamu*"—"Zionists Back to Siam."

While Gomułka had Moczar on one flank and Moscow on the other, a Polish dissident movement was growing among students. University students were an unlikely source of discontent, since they were the privileged children of good communist families. From the rubble of a society that became a nightmare, their parents had built through communism a society of greater social justice and, for those of Jewish origin, a society that did not tolerate racism.

Toward the end of World War II, with the Red Army rapidly driving the Germans west, the Polish Home Army rose up against the Germans in Warsaw, expecting the Soviet arrival. But the Soviets didn't come, and both the Home Army and the capital city were destroyed. The Soviets said they were held up by German resistance, the Poles say the Germans wanted a crushed and supplicant Poland. According to the Soviets, Warsaw was 80 percent destroyed. According to Polish historians, it was 95 percent rubble.

When the Red Army entered the capital, only a tenth of the population, 130,000 people, still lived in Warsaw, huddled on the far side of the river or camped in dangerously unstable ruins. For the Polish communists, almost the first order of business was to rebuild the historic center of Warsaw, the cultural showcase of the capital, with its fine old pastel buildings, the imposing Roman-style national theater with tall colonnades and bas relief ornament, and the university with its gardened and gated campus. There, behind the black iron gates on the leafy campus, in the restored historic center of a ruined city, the daughters and sons of the communists who built the new Poland studied peacefully.

It wasn't exactly a democracy. There wasn't exactly free speech. It was a little like German playwright Peter Weiss's 1964 play, *The Perse-cution and Assassination of Jean-Paul Marat as Performed by the Inmates of the Asylum of Charenton Under the Direction of the Marquis de Sade* or, as it became popularly known after Peter Brook's British production and 1966 film, *Marat/Sade*. Not only did this play start a vogue for long titles, but it was one of the most talked-about international works of theater in the mid-1960s. Expressing the senti-ments about freedom of young people in much of the world, *Marat/Sade* takes place on the eve of Bastille Day 1808. It is a little after the French Revolution, and the people are sort of not quite free. In the end, following a song titled "Fifteen Glorious Years," the inmates sing:

And if most have a little
and few have a lot
You can see how much nearer
our goal we have got.
We can say what we like
without favor or fear
and what we can't say
we will breathe in your ear.

Polish communist youth, not always in agreement with their parents, felt this "unfreedom," as another extremely popular German writer of the mid-sixties, philosopher Herbert Marcuse, called it. Poland and much of the Soviet bloc exemplified Marcuse's theory that the communication of opposites obstructed discourse. To criticize the government or "the system" in Poland required an aptitude for speak-ing opposites in reverse. *Polityka*, a weekly considered to be liberal and free thinking, reported on Dubček and Czechoslovakia, though mostly in the form of criticism. It often reported in reverse. If a student protested, *Polityka* would not report on it. But they might report that the student had recanted his protest letter and might even enumerate some of the lies he told, which he now retracted. From this, the Polish reader could learn of the protest letter and even a bit of its contents. When Mieczysław Rakowski, the editor of *Polityka* who decades later became the last first secretary of the ruling Polish Communist Party, wanted to criticize the government, he would write an article praising the government and then a week later run an article criticizing his arti-cle. He would breathe in your ear.

As Polish youth became more adept at being dissidents, they mastered another technique of spreading information. They would leak to the foreign press whatever they wanted the Polish people to know. *The New York Times* and *Le Monde* were favorite recipients. But any news media would work, as long as it was read the next morning by Jan Nowak and his staff in Vienna, where the Polish-language service of Radio Free Europe was based. The Polish service and the Czech service would work together, so that the Poles could be informed about events in Czechoslovakia and the Czechs were informed on events in Poland. By 1968 each knew the other had a student movement. They also knew that the United States had a student movement. They had no trouble, even through the Polish press, learning about Martin Luther King and sit-ins in the South and American student movements that used demonstrations to protest the Vietnam War. The leading official Polish newspaper, *Trybuna Ludu*, the *People's Tribune*, contained little news on Poland in 1968, though a great deal on the Vietnam War and the Middle East, which was mostly about how Israel had taken a lot of land and did not plan to give it back. They also reported extensively on the civil rights and antiwar movements in the United States. The sit-ins and marches that began to characterize American campuses were reported in the official communist press. But as 1968 began, few Polish students imagined using such methods in Poland.

Ironically, in the happy barracks foreign press was not suppressed. A Pole could go to a library and read *Le Monde* or the British *Guardian*. But these papers were accessible only to the few who could read French or English, including many students. Otherwise Poles had to wait for the broadcast on Radio Free Europe.

Students, tourists, even businessmen when traveling abroad would stop off at Radio Free Europe in Vienna and give information. But many refused to work with Radio Free Europe, for this cold war generation had grown up with the capitalists as the enemy, rehearsing for defense in the event of an American nuclear attack in scarce and overcrowded schools, a shortage blamed on the high cost of the fallout shelters each school had to contain.

Leading dissident Jacek Kuroń said, "I knew that Radio Free Europe was done by the CIA. I didn't know for sure, but I thought so. But it was the only means I had. I would have preferred to use a more neutral media but there was no other." But despite his negative feelings about them, the Radio Free Europe staff admired and trusted him. Nowak said of Kuroń, "He is one of the most noble human beings I have met in my life."

An alternative to Radio Free Europe was *Kultura*, a Polish-language newspaper written by a group of Poles who lived together in Paris. *Kultura* could get five thousand copies into circulation in Poland, which was often too few, too slowly.

Kuroń said, "My greatest concern was getting information to the Polish people. Who was beaten, who was arrested. I was a central information point and had to distribute the information." He gestured toward a white phone in his small, dark Warsaw apartment. "Through this phone I used to telephone Radio Free Europe several times a day to give them information because it was broadcast back to Poland immediately. One time I was telling them about seven people in prison, and two political police walked into the apartment and told me to come with them. 'Who is it you are arresting?' I asked.

" 'We are arresting you, Jacek Kuroń.' "

Kuroń was holding the phone with Radio Free Europe still on the line, and the arrest was recorded and broadcast instantly.

Radio Free Europe broadcasted in Poland from 5:00 A.M. to midnight, seven days a week. Broadcasts were by native-speaking Poles. There was music, sports, and news every hour on the hour. The station claimed strict objectivity without editorializing, though few believed this. Few cared. The station was listened to with the expectation that it was a Western point of view. But it was full of information on Poland that came from inside Poland.

The Polish government jammed the station, but this served as a guide. If a Pole turned on the station and heard that familiar engine roar in the background, it meant this was important programming. The words could still be deciphered. "Jamming was our ally," said Jan Nowak. "It made people curious about what they were hiding."

One day in 1964, an average-size, blond, fairly typical-looking young Pole stopped by Radio Free Europe in Vienna on his way back to Poland from Paris. He was only eighteen years old, a young disciple of two older, well-known dissidents: Kuroń and Karol Modzelewski. The young man talked with enthusiasm about a vision of a socialism that was both democratic and humane. Four years later, in 1968, Alexander Dubček would call this "communism with a human face."

Nowak recalled the young man, whose name was Adam Michnik: "He was boyish in appearance but had astounding intellectual maturity for his years." Michnik was born in 1946, a post-Holocaust Jew from Lwov, which is now in the Ukraine but at the time of his birth was still in Poland. Before the war, when such a world still existed, his father's family were impoverished, traditional shtetl Jews. His mother came from an assimilated Cracow family. Both parents were communists, and his father had been arrested for Party activities before the war. But Adam grew up in a communist world, with Rosa Luxemburg and Leon Trotsky, he says, by coincidence both Jews, for heroes.

"The only way I know I am Jewish is anti-Semites call me a Jew," said Michnik, which is to say that he never thought very much about being Jewish until 1968.

In 1965 he was a history student at the University of Warsaw, one of about fifty young students who gathered around Kuroń and Modzelewski, a twenty-seven-year old researcher in the History Department and a Communist Party member. They were all communists. Michnik said of Kuroń and Modzelewski, "They were the heroes, the leaders."

Jacek Kuroń, like Michnik, was from Lwov, but he had been born before the war. In 1965 he was already thirty-one. His mother had a law degree and was married when she became pregnant with Jacek. She often complained bitterly that "she was made for better things." Kuroń's father was a mechanical engineer and a leader in the Polish Socialist Party. But he disliked the Soviets, and his contact with them made him increasingly anticommunist. In 1949, when Jacek decided to join the Communist Party at the age of fifteen, his father vehemently opposed his decision.

Originally, Kuroń and Modzelewski's discussion groups were government sponsored. Communist youth had an opportunity to meet with Party officials and ask questions in small groups of close-knit friends. But by the 1960s the questioning was sometimes so harsh that the Party officials simply wouldn't answer. In response to a Modzelewski speech to younger students, the government closed down the Union of Socialist Youth—ZMS—his discussion group at the University of Warsaw. Banned from the university, the ZMS continued to meet in private apartments, with about fifty students attending.

After many long conversations, Kuroń and Modzelewski concluded that the system in power in Poland was not the one Marx had written about. It was not Marxism but used the name, used many labels to confuse and delude people. In 1965 they decided to write and distribute photocopies of an anonymous open letter calling the ruling system a fraud without justice and freedom. The two young men left their words unsigned because they did not want to experience Polish prison. But somehow the political police had been told of their activities and burst into the apartment where they were photocopying. The police simply confiscated the original and warned them that if they distributed any of the copies, they would face a prison sentence.

Had there been no further retribution, they might have heeded the warning. But Kuroń's wife lost her job as an assistant professor, and both Kuroń and Modzelewski experienced continual harassment. After several months, they decided that they had no choice but to bring their protest into the open, start an open debate, and go to prison for it.

Kuroń and Modzelewski signed their open letter and next to their signatures stated that they expected to receive three years in prison for this act. "We were exactly right," Kuroń recalled.

They distributed only twenty copies, but they also got a copy to Jerzy Giedroyc, who published *Kultura* in Paris and saw to it that more than five thousand copies were distributed in his publication. The letter was translated into Czech and then into most European languages. It was read in Spanish in Cuba and in Chinese in the People's Republic. Students in Paris and London and Berlin read it.

At age nineteen, Adam Michnik was sent to prison for the first time, with his reluctant heroes, Kuroń and Modzelewski.

By January 1968 the dissident movement had become a major force among students at the University of Warsaw. But it had little impact, was not even known beyond that lovely gated campus. Modzelewski had said that they were cordoned in and had to break out. He always warned that when they did, the government would attack.

That opportunity to break out came with a production of a play called *Dziady* by early-nineteenth-century poet Adam Mickiewicz, unquestionably the most revered writer in the Polish language. Not a prolific writer, Mickiewicz's unmatched reputation rests largely on an epic poem of rural Lithuanian life, *Pan Tadeusz*, and the play, *Dziady*. Among the first priorities of rebuilding the old center of Warsaw after the war had been the reconstruction of the gardened plaza built in 1898 to mark the centennial of Mickiewicz's birth. High in the center of a rose garden among the weeping willows stands the poet reproduced in bronze. To stage *Dziady* in Warsaw was no more controversial than a production of *Hamlet* in London or Molière in Paris.

Under communism, just as in previous regimes, studying this play was an essential part of a child's education. *Dziady*, sometimes translated into English as *Forefathers' Eve*, begins with the ritual summoning of the *dziady*, deceased ancestors. The hero, Gustav, dies in prison and returns to earth in the form of a revolutionary named Konrad. Throughout the play the rebellious antiauthoritarian message is unmistakable, as is the Polish nationalist message, since much of the play is about the struggle of Polish political prisoners at the hands of the Russian oppressor. But there were also demons, a priest, and angels. This is an extremely complicated piece of theater, difficult to stage and consequently the great challenge of Polish directors.

1968 was a great directorial moment for theater, a moment in which traditions were challenged, while the stage remained one of the important sources of social commentary. In New York, Julian Beck and his wife, Judith Malina, tried to break down the last barriers of traditional staging with their Living Theater. In their Upper West Side Manhattan living room they had begun directing works by difficult moderns, including García Lorca, Bertolt Brecht, Gertrude Stein, and the contemporary New York absurdist writer and social critic, Paul Goodman. They moved into theaters and lofts, where instead of selling tickets they collected contributions, and eventually traveled to Paris, Berlin, and Venice, living as a free-form commune with much fame and very little money. Julian built spectacularly original sets from scraps, and he directed occasionally, though it was more often Judith, the daughter of a German Hasidic rabbi and an aspiring actress who gave readings of German classic poetry, who was the director, especially of plays in verse. Increasingly political, the two boasted of having broken the barrier between politics and art. By 1968, their theater was a strong antiwar force and performances usually ended with not only applause but cries of "Stop the war!" and "Empty the jails!" and "Change the world!" The plays increasingly made contact with the audience. Sometimes actors served the audience food, and in one production an abstract painting was created in the course of the performance and then auctioned off to the audience. *Theater of Chance* determined lines by throws of the dice. Kenneth Brown's *The Brig*, about brutality in a Marine Corps prison, allowed actors to improvise their abuse of the prisoner.

Peter Brook's inventive direction of *Marat/Sade* was also influencing theater around the world. In New York Tom Stoppard's *Rosencrantz and Guildenstern Are Dead* opened in January, viewing Shakespeare's *Hamlet* from the perspective of its two least important characters. At the same time Joseph Papp mounted a production of *Hamlet* in a modern setting starring Martin Sheen. Clive Barnes wrote in *The New York Times*, "An aimless Hamlet for Philistines who wish to be confirmed in their opinion that the Bard is for the birds." Richard Watts, Jr., in the *New York Post* called it "lunatic burlesque, at times satirically amusing, at others seemingly pointless." All of which may have been true, but still, Papp was celebrated for his boldness at a time when boldness was admired above almost all else. In April his production of *Hair: The American Tribal Love-Rock Musical*, largely about the hippie life with very little story, was moved to Broadway directed by Tom O'Horgan, who sent actors panhandling and distributing flowers in the audience. Barnes, in a very positive and enthusiastic review, warned the public, "At one point—in what is later affectionately referred to as 'the nude scene'—a number of men and women (I should have counted) are seen totally nude and full, as it were, face." On the nudism in *Hair, Paris Match* pointed out that there were also those who objected to the naked back of Marat being visible from the bathtub in Brook's production.

In Dubček's Czechoslovakia, once-underground playwrights such as Václav Havel and Pavel Kohout were becoming international stars combining the Czech Kafkaesque tradition of absurdist wit and a dangerous, Beck-like fusion of art and politics. Communist bureaucracy was a favorite target. Papp's Public Theater presented a production of Havel's *The Memorandum* starring Olympia Dukakis, in which office workers struggle with a made-up language.

So it was not surprising, with avant-garde theater flowering everywhere, especially in neighboring Czechoslovakia, that the Polish National Theater's production of *the* Polish classic would try something different. The play, with its political side but also a religious side rooted in Slavic Christian mysticism, was often presented in precommunist Poland as a religious and mystical piece. Under communism it was generally seen as political. Instead of choosing between a political play and a religious one, director Kazimierz Dejmek used both to create a complex production steeped in early Christian ritual but at the same time very much about the struggle for Polish freedom. Gustav/Konrad was played by Gustaw Holoubek, one of Poland's most respected actors, who made the role one of inner struggle and uncertainty.

Like an old, well-known melodrama in which everyone knows the lines of the hero and villain, *Dziady* has always had its familiar moments certain to provoke applause. Most of these lines are nationalist in tone, such as, "We Poles have sold our souls for a couple of silver rubles," and the Russian officer's words, "It's no wonder they hate us so: For full one hundred years, they've seen from Moscow into Poland flow such a sewage-laden stream." These moments were part of the Polish experience of going to *Dziady*. The play was anticzar, which was perfectly acceptable Soviet thinking. It was not anticommunist. It said nothing about communists or Soviets, which it predates. In fact, the way it was taught and usually produced under communism was to emphasize the political messages. Far from an anti-Soviet symbol, the play had been originally mounted the previous fall as part of celebrations for the fiftieth anniversary of the October Revolution that brought the Communists to power in Russia.

It was the attention paid to Christian religious belief in this production that disturbed the government, since communism rejects religion. Still, no one regarded this as an important departure from orthodoxy. *Trybuna Ludu* gave the production a negative but not particularly impassioned critique, simply stating that it was a mistake to think that mysticism played as big a role in the drama as politics. For the play to work, the critic argued, Mickiewicz has to be seen as a predominantly political writer. But the production was a popular success, playing to packed and enthusiastic houses and extended for months. Adam Michnik went. "I thought it was a fantastic production. Really stirring," he said.

Then the government did a strangely unwise thing: It closed down the revered national play at the National Theater. Worse, it gave a closing date, January 30, and leaked it to the public two weeks in advance so that everyone knew that January 30 would be the last performance by order of the police. Poles were used to censorship, but it was never announced in advance. The government almost seemed to be inviting a demonstration. Was it looking for an excuse for repression? Was this General Moczar plotting again? Historians still argue about this. Amid all the plot and counterplot theories, the possibility is often raised that the government just acted stupidly. Michnik remembered, "The decision to close the play was proof that the government was stupid and did not understand Poles. Mickiewicz is our Whitman, our Victor Hugo. . . . It was an outburst of communist barbarism to attack Mickiewicz."

The night of January 30, after the final curtain, three hundred students from the University of Warsaw and the National Theater School demonstrated in front of the nearby National Theater, marching only a few hundred yards to the statue of Adam Mickiewicz. They did not see this as a particularly defiant act. They were just communist youth reminding their parents of the ideals of communism. Michnik said, "We decided to lay flowers on the poet's monument." Michnik himself, known to the authorities as "a troublemaker," did not march.

"We thought a Czech-style evolution was possible," said Michnik. The students did not fear a violent response. "Since 1949 there had never been a police act against students in Poland," Michnik reasoned with perhaps too much logic. There among the willows, in front of the rose garden with Mickiewicz frozen in bronze in midrecital, his right hand touching his chest, three hundred students were beaten with clubs by truckloads of "workers" who arrived at the protest ostensibly to talk to students but clubbed them instead. Thirty-five students were arrested.

Not surprisingly, there was no press coverage of the incident. Michnik and a fellow student dissident, Henryk Szlajfer, spoke with a *Le Monde* correspondent whom Michnik characterized as "an extremely dangerous man. Very reactionary and mostly interested in promoting himself." But the two young communists had few options if they wanted the Polish people to know what had happened. From *Le Monde* the story would be picked up by Radio Free Europe in Vienna and broadcast throughout Poland. But the two were seen talking to the correspondent by the secret police, and when the article ran in *Le Monde*, Michnik and Szlajfer were expelled from the university.

All of this connected expediently with the "anti-Zionist campaign." Michnik, Szlajfer, and numerous students who had demonstrated were Jewish. This is not surprising considering the university dissidents were from good communist families, who had taught their children they had an obligation to fight for a more just society.

But this was not the government's explanation for Jews in the student movement. The government, which had been removing Jews from their jobs throughout the bureaucracy, accusing them of Zionist plots, now said that the so-called student movement had been infiltrated by Zionists. The arrested students were interrogated. If they were not Jewish, they were asked, "You are a Pole. Why are you always with the Jews?" Non-Jews were asked to give them the names of Jewish leaders.

When interrogating a Jew, the police would begin, "You are Jew?"

Often the student would answer, "No, I am a Pole."

"No, you are a Jew."

It was a very old dialogue in Poland.

PART II

PRAGUE SPRING

The first thing for any revolutionary party to do would be to seize communications. Who owns communications now controls the country. Much more than it's ever been true in history.

—WILLIAM BURROUGHS, *interviewed in 1968*

CHAPTER 5

ON THE GEARS OF
AN ODIOUS MACHINE

Employees are going to love this generation. . . . They are going
to be easy to handle. There aren't going to be any riots.
—CLARK KERR, *president of the
University of California at Berkeley, 1963*

Our young people, in disturbing numbers, appear to reject all
forms of authority from whatever source derived and they have
taken refuge in the turbulent and inchoate nihilism whose sole
objectives are destructive. I know of no time in our history when
the gap between generations has been wider or more potentially
dangerous.
—GRAYSON KIRK, *president of
Columbia University, 1968*

B Y THE SPRING OF 1968, college demonstrations had
become such a commonplace event in the United States, with
some thirty schools a month erupting, that even high schools and
junior highs were joining in. In February, hundreds of eighth graders
jammed the halls, took over classrooms, and set off fire alarms at
Junior High School 258 in the Bedford-Stuyvesant section of Brooklyn.
They were demanding better food and more dances.

Protesters understood that with constant protest they had to do
more than just march carrying a sign in order to make the newspapers.
A building had to be seized, something had to be shut down. To protest
Columbia University's plans to build a new school gymnasium displac-
ing poor black residents of Harlem, a student hopped into the steel
scoop of an earthmover to obstruct construction. In mid-March, the
Columbia antiwar student movement called for a daylong boycott of
classes to protest the war. In all, 3,500 students and 1,000 faculty
members stayed out of classes. About 3,000 students looked on at the

University of Wisconsin in Madison as antiwar protesters planted 400 white crosses on the lawn of Bascom Hill near the administration building. A sign read "Bascom Memorial Cemetery, Class of 1968." Joseph Chandler, a former student, then working at the Madison-based Wisconsin Draft Resistance Union, said, "We thought the campus ought to look like a graveyard, because that's where most of the seniors are headed." The first week of spring, between 500 and 1,000 students took control of the administration building at Howard University, the leading black university, and refused to leave. They were protesting the lack of black history courses in the curriculum. Then black students seized a building at Cornell. Students blocked a building at Colgate.

And it was not only students. *The New York Times* reported on March 24 that hippies had taken over New York's Grand Central Station and "transformed a spring be-in to a militant antiwar demonstration," which in turn led to a lengthy article on the possibility that hippies, whom the establishment had defined as undermotivated types, were turning into political activists. But these particular hippies were in fact Yippies!, from Abbie Hoffman's Youth International Party, which had always been political.

In Italy, students protesting inadequate facilities carried a long red flag from building to building on the University of Rome campus as the university was reopened after being closed for twelve days in mid-March because of violence. On the first day alone, two hundred students were injured by police, and by the second, faculty members protesting police brutality had joined the demonstrators. Some were calling for the resignation of the rector for having called in the police in the first place. The students made clear that they intended to continue demonstrating. The Italian communists were attempting unsuccessfully to take control of the student movement.

By early spring 1968 a German student association had organizations in 108 German universities and represented three hundred thousand German students. They had organized around protesting the war in Vietnam but had started moving on to German issues such as the recognition of East Germany, the resignation of high officials with Nazi-tainted pasts, and the right of students to have more of a say in their own education.

Meanwhile, after being quiet for a generation, Spanish students were demonstrating against an openly fascist regime that in April sanctioned a mass for Adolf Hitler in Madrid. Spring began with the University of Madrid again closed because of student demonstrations. The university did not reopen for classes until thirty-eight days later in May.

In Brazil, armed violence that killed three protesters in the opening months of 1968 failed to keep students from protesting the four-year-old military dictatorship.

Japanese students were violently protesting the presence on their soil of the U.S. military machine engaged with Vietnam. This generation whose parents had brought ruin on their country with militarism—a country that had suffered through history's only nuclear attack— was vehemently antimilitary. The student organization Zengakuren was able to turn out thousands of protesters to block a U.S. aircraft carrier, in service in Vietnam, from docking in a Japanese port. The Zengakuren also protested, sometimes violently, such local issues as the confiscation of land from farmers to build an international airport at Narita, twenty-five miles east of Tokyo. The Japanese government was considering the passage of repressive security laws to control the Zengakuren.

The Zengakuren had been the student group that made Walter Cronkite realize how television was to be used in the sixties. Cronkite had been with a CBS television crew in Japan to report a 1960 visit there by President Eisenhower. But so many Zengakuren had turned out to protest the visit that Eisenhower decided not to land. The Zengakuren, however, content that a CBS television crew was there to record their protest, remained. Tens of thousands arrived throughout the day to protest, the television crew their only audience. With no U.S. president, Cronkite wanted to leave, but his route to the CBS vehicle was blocked by the huge crowd, which was at its most dense around the cameras. "It suddenly occurred to me," Cronkite recalled, "that the easiest way for me to get to the top of the hill was to join the Zengakuren. So I got the pictures, tucked the film in my pockets, and came down off the truck and grabbed ahold—they had all linked arms—I linked arms with one of these Japanese. He smiled at me, and he said, '*Banzai! Banzai, Banzai!*' as he flailed his arms angrily. And I started yelling, '*Banzai! Banzai! Banzai!*' and I went to the snake dancing up the hill shouting, '*Banzai Banzai Banzai!*' They were all having a wonderful time with me and I got up to the top of the hill and there was our car, so I said, 'Well, good-bye.' And they said, 'Good-bye.' And I got in the car and got to the airport."

In the United Kingdom students had started out by demonstrating against the U.S. war in Vietnam and had moved on to local issues such as the size of government grants for education and control over the universities. By spring there had already been major protests at Oxford, Cambridge, and numerous other British universities. Of greater concern to the British government than the antiwar movement was a tendency for protesters to attack anyone who seemed to represent the British government. In March, when British defense secretary Denis Healey gave a talk at Cambridge, students broke through police lines and attempted to overturn his car. Soon after that, Home Secretary James Callaghan was heckled by students at Oxford who attempted to throw him into a fish pond. Gordon Walker, the secretary of state for education and science, was prevented from delivering a speech at Manchester University. Unable to speak, he attempted to exit but had to step over the bodies of students sprawled across his path. American officials were not immune. When an American diplomat, a press officer from the U.S. embassy, made the mistake of appearing in front of Sussex University students, they attacked him with wet paint. British protesters also had a good sense of media. In April they turned the water in the fountain in Trafalgar Square red.

Violence requires few ideas, but nonviolent resistance requires imagination. That is one of the reasons so few rebels are willing to embrace it. The American civil rights movement learned as it went along, making many mistakes. But by the mid-1960s the movement, especially SNCC, had thrilled the world with its imagination and the daring of its ideas, inspiring students as far away as Poland to stage sit-ins. By 1968, all over the world, people with causes wanted to copy the civil rights movement. Its anthem, Pete Seeger's "We Shall Overcome"—a folk song turned labor song that Seeger had turned into a civil rights song when sit-ins began in 1960—was sung in English from Japan to South Africa to Mexico.

The civil rights movement began to grab the world's attention on February 1, 1960, when four black freshmen from the Agricultural and Technical College of North Carolina in Greensboro went into a Woolworth's, bought a few items, and then sat at the "whites only" lunch counter, and one of them, Ezell Blair, Jr., asked for a cup of coffee. Refused service, they just sat there until the store closed. The technique had been tried out a number of times before by civil rights workers to test the reaction. But these four, without the backing of any organization, went much further. The next day they returned with twenty students at 10:30 in the morning and sat all day. A waitress, refusing service, explained to the press, "It's a store regulation—a custom." The students vowed to sit every day at the counter until they were served. Every day they jammed the Woolworth's lunch counter with more and more students. Soon they were sitting in at other counters in Greensboro and then in other towns. Within two weeks of the first sit-in, national and international press were reporting on its broad significance. "The demonstrations were generally dismissed at first as another college fad of the 'panty-raid' variety," reported *The New York Times*. "This opinion lost adherents, however, as the movement spread from North Carolina to Virginia, Florida, South Carolina and Tennessee and involved fifteen cities."

"Sit-ins took the existing civil rights organizations completely by surprise," said Mary King, a white volunteer for SNCC. They amazed Martin Luther King's newly established Southern Christian Leadership Conference and shocked the older organizations such as CORE. But the press was drawn to them and the public was impressed by them. SNCC was largely born out of the desire to invent stunning new approaches like this.

In 1959 there were twenty thousand students on the sprawling leafy campus of the University of Michigan at Ann Arbor. There was little sign of the civil rights movement or any radical politics. But in February 1960, inspired by the sit-ins in Greensboro, Robert Alan Haber, a University of Michigan undergraduate, announced the formation of a new group called Students for a Democratic Society, SDS. To start up the new organization he recruited two people with roots in the traditional Left: Sharon Jeffrey, a sophomore whose mother was an important figure in the United Auto Workers union, and Bob Ross from the South Bronx, whose grandparents' circle had been Russian revolutionaries and who loved jazz and beat poetry. They had also approached the studious, hardworking editor of the *Michigan Daily*, Tom Hayden. Hayden, who came from a small town not far from Ann Arbor, was consumed with his newspaper, a professional operation considered one of the best college papers in the country. He was more interested in another organization that began at the University of Michigan, a group that lobbied for the founding of a Peace Corps.

SDS wanted to recruit a network of student leaders across the country. Their timing was perfect. The February sit-ins in Greensboro had inspired American youth, made them long to be doing something, too. Hayden later wrote, "As thousands of Southern students were arrested and many beaten, my respect and identification with their courage and conviction deepened." Haber, Jeffrey, and Ross began by joining picket lines in Ann Arbor in solidarity with the sit-ins in Greensboro. Hayden covered them for the *Daily* and wrote sympathetic editorials. In the spring, SDS invited black civil rights workers from the South to come to Ann Arbor and meet northern white students. Hayden covered the event, although he was by now the editor in chief of the paper, an ambition he had worked hard to fulfill.

Hayden, age twenty, had a transforming summer in California. He

1968 poster
(Schomburg Center for Research in Black Culture)

went to Berkeley, was handed a leaflet, asked for a place to stay, and found himself living with student activists. The Berkeley campus was well organized, and he wrote a series of long articles for the *Daily* about "the new student movement." He went to the Livermore laboratories, where America's nuclear arsenal had been developed. He interviewed nuclear scientist Edward Teller, who madly explained how nuclear war could be survived and how one was "better dead than Red." At the 1960 Democratic convention in Los Angeles, he met Robert Kennedy, who at thirty-nine seemed to Hayden very young for a politician. Hayden watched Kennedy's older brother get nominated and was deeply moved by John Kennedy's speech, even though his new radical friends had already dismissed Kennedy as a "phony liberal." Hayden had not yet learned that liberals were not to be trusted. He also interviewed Martin Luther King, who told him, "Ultimately, you have to take a stand with your life."

He sent articles to the *Daily* about the emerging new Left. Back in Michigan, the university administration accused him of inventing the news rather than reporting on it. He knew that there was a new Left, but he realized that the faculty and most people in America were still completely unaware of it.

Hayden spent his senior year dreaming of going south and participating. He took food to blacks in Tennessee driven out of their homes for registering to vote. But he wanted to do more. "I was chafing to graduate; the South was beckoning," he later wrote. He did graduate and went south as an SDS liaison with SNCC. But he quickly learned that SNCC was well staffed and didn't need him. Hayden felt alone in his very arduous and at times dangerous task in the South. "I didn't want to go from beating to beating, jail to jail," Hayden wrote. In December 1961, from a jail cell in Albany, Georgia, he wrote to his fellow SDS organizers in Michigan proposing a meeting to try to make SDS a larger, more important organization like SNCC. SDS had eight hundred members around the United States paying $1 in dues a year. It needed to define itself in order to grow.

In June 1962, the small circle of young people who called themselves SDS activists, some sixty people, met in Port Huron, Michigan, where as a boy Tom Hayden used to fish with his father. Hayden, playing Jefferson to Haber's Adams, was asked to draft a document that would be "an agenda for a generation." Looking back, Hayden was amazed at the grandiose terms of the project. "I still don't know," he wrote decades later, "where this messianic sense, this belief in being right, this confidence that we could speak for a generation, came from." But the resulting document, known as the Port Huron Statement, to a remarkable extent did capture the thoughts, sensibilities, and perspective of their generation. By 1968, when it had become clear to older people that a younger generation thought very differently, the Port Huron Statement was seized on as an insight into how they thought. College students of 1968 had been in junior high school when it was written but were now required to read it in sociology and political science courses.

It was not a manifesto for the entire generation. It was clearly addressed to upper-middle-class whites—privileged people who knew they were privileged and were angry about this injustice. The statement began:

> We are people of this generation, bred in at least modest comfort, housed in the universities, looking uncomfortably to the world we inherit.

Remarking that neither southern blacks nor college students were allowed to vote, the statement called for participatory democracy. "The goal of society and man should be human independence." The statement rebuked the United States for its use of military power, which it said had done more to stop democracy than stop communism. The document steered a careful course between communism and anticommunism, denying any support to either. What became known as the "New Left" had been defined, a Left that had little use for liberals, who could not be trusted, or communists, who were authoritarian, or capitalists, who robbed people of freedom, or anticommunists, who were bullies. And if the New Left was American, it sounded very much like the 1968 students of Poland, France, and Mexico. Allen Ginsberg, who always said things a little more forcefully than others around him, wrote:

> And the Communists have nothing to offer but fat cheeks and
> eyeglasses and lying policemen
> and the Capitalists proffer Napalm and money in green suitcases
> to the Naked . . .

The civil rights movement continued to dazzle with creative new approaches. In 1961 SNCC invented "Freedom Rides"—a good name always being important in the marketing of an idea. Freedom Riders rode on buses, blacks in white sections, whites in black sections, using the wrong rest rooms at each stop, provoking white racism all over the South. Freedom Riders became legendary. James Farmer, one of the creators of the tactic, said, "We felt that we could count on the racists of the South to create a crisis, so that the federal government would be compelled to enforce federal law." White southerners responded with violence, and that attracted the kind of media coverage that made civil rights workers heroes around the world. A Montgomery, Alabama, newspaper reported on one of the first Freedom Rides:

> Two adamant "Freedom Riders"—battered and bruised from beatings administered by a white mob—vowed Saturday afternoon to sacrifice their lives if necessary to break down racial barriers in the South. They were beaten into insensibility by the mob who attacked 22 integrationists after they debarked from a bus here Saturday morning.

Angry mobs reacted so violently to these integrated busloads that the Kennedy administration asked for "a cooling-off period" and CORE dropped Freedom Riding as too dangerous. This only made SNCC increase its riders, many of whom ended up spending forty-nine days in an antiquated dungeon fortress in Mississippi called Parchman Penitentiary.

In 1963, an estimated 930 civil rights demonstrations were carried out in eleven southern states with twenty thousand people arrested. A young generation around the world grew up watching and thrilling to these David-against-Goliath tactics. To them the civil rights movement was a mesmerizing spectacle, nourishing idealism and schooling activism. There was also an appeal to machismo, because the civil rights worker always faced significant danger. The more the racists resisted, the more heroic the rights worker appeared. What could be more admirable than standing up to racist bullies who were filmed attacking peaceful young people?

Then in 1964 came the most influential strategy of all. It was called Mississippi Freedom Summer. Those old enough to participate, to act at last, would be—sometimes unwittingly—trained to lead their generation.

1964 began with the nation still in mourning for the murder of a young president in whom so much optimism had been invested. But as the year went on, there was an excitement in the air captured in a recording by Martha Reeves and the Vandellas, "Dancing in the Street." 1964 was a year of new beginnings. It was the year Americans got their first glimpse of the Beatles, with their salad bowl haircuts and strange collarless suits, so sexless that the fashion was doomed not to last. It was the year liberalism overran conservatism in the Johnson-Goldwater election. It was the year the Civil Rights Act of 1964 was emphatically passed, despite the solid opposition of the entire congressional delegations of Alabama, Arkansas, Georgia, Louisiana, Mississippi, North Carolina, South Carolina, and Virginia—not by chance, the only section of the country where Goldwater had done well against Johnson. But the most exciting event of the year was the Mississippi Freedom Summer.

Freedom Summer was the idea of Harlem-born, Harvard-educated SNCC leader and philosopher Bob Moses and activist and later U.S. congressman Allard Lowenstein. At a time when the civil rights movement was focused on the important but not visually dramatic work of registering black voters in the South, they realized that the work would get much more media attention if they put out a call for white northerners to come to Mississippi for the summer to register black voters.

If any of the almost one thousand volunteers had any doubt of the dangers of their work, early in the summer three SNCC workers, James Chaney, Andrew Goodman, and Michael Schwerner, disappeared in a remote swampy section of Mississippi. Schwerner was an experienced civil rights worker, but Goodman was a fresh volunteer from the North and Chaney was a local black volunteer. The drama unfolded through-out the summer as SNCC struggled to get FBI cooperation, and each clue, such as the discovery of their car, painted an ever darker picture. Finally, on August 4, forty-four days after the three were reported miss-ing, a tip by an FBI informer led to the discovery of their bodies twenty feet under an earthen dam south of the town of Philadelphia, Missis-sippi. All three had been shot to death. Chaney, the black man, had been brutally beaten first.

Yet not one volunteer backed down, although one underage volun-teer was forced to leave by his parents. In fact, Moses had to ask that volunteers stop coming because SNCC workers could not train all the new recruits they were getting.

Among those who went south that summer was the son of an Italian machinist in Queens, New York, who was studying philosophy at Berkeley. Born in 1942, Mario Savio was six feet two inches tall, thin, and gentle in demeanor. He stammered so badly that he had struggled to deliver his high school valedictorian address. He was a Roman Catholic who like many Catholics embraced Catholic morality while being at odds with the Church itself. At a younger age he had dreamed of becoming a priest.

In 1964, twenty-one-year-old Savio was walking across the Berkeley campus, and at Telegraph and Bancroft, a narrow strip of land that had been designated the area for political activity, someone handed him a leaflet about a demonstration by the local civil rights movement against unfair hiring practices in San Francisco. Savio later remembered, "I said, 'Oh, demonstration, okay.' These demonstrations had the moral cachet of the campus. Absolutely, they had won out over football games, no doubt about it."

So with little internal debate, Savio went to the demonstration. An elderly woman shouted at him, "Why don't you go to Russia!" and he tried to explain to her that his family was from Italy.

For the first time in his life, Mario Savio was arrested. In the lockup a man named John King casually asked him, "Are you going to Missis-sippi?" When Savio learned of the Mississippi Freedom Summer, he knew he "had to be there." Most of the volunteers felt that way, they had to be there. Savio went. In Mississippi he would knock on the screen door of a poor black sharecropper. Politely, the head of the household, looking a little scared, would say that he just didn't want to vote. Savio would ask him if his father had ever voted.

"No, sir."

"Did your grandfather ever vote?"

"No, sir."

"Do you want your children to vote?"

Then he had them, and they would come with him into town, averting the glares of hatred of half the citizens, and risk their lives to register to vote. "I don't know where I got the nerve to say such a thing," Savio said years later. But he always remembered those people he had persuaded to risk their lives.

The experience shaped Savio and a generation of white northerners. They arrived in Mississippi looking clean and young. They were greeted by local workers, and they crossed arms and held hands to form a tight chain, singing "We Shall Overcome," swaying sightly as they sang of "white and black together," which for that moment they were. They spent the summer being young and brave, risking their lives, getting beaten and jailed. Like Albert Camus's doctor in *The Plague,* which everyone was reading, they were doing something, fighting society's pestilence. They left in September, experienced activists. Freedom Summer probably did more to develop radical campus leadership than all the efforts of SDS. The volunteers returned north in the fall energized, moved, committed to political change, and trained in one of the finest schools of civil disobedience in American history.

Savio returned to Berkeley, the incoming president of the local Friends of SNCC, in a fever of political commitment, only to find that the university had rescinded the right to political advocacy on campus even from that small strip of land at Telegraph and Bancroft where he had first learned of a demonstration. How could he say nothing in defense of his own rights when he had convinced those Mississippians to risk everything for theirs? He remembered them in their silence and dignity, demanding softly in rural Mississippi accents to "reddish," to register.

"Am I a Judas?" Savio asked himself, still steeped in the imagery of the Church. "I am going to betray the people that I endangered now that I am back home? Forget all about that. Was that reality? Or is it just a fantasy? A little childish game? I did my little childish game in Mississippi, and now I am back to the serious stuff of becoming whatever I was going to become (I had no idea what that was anyway)?"

Drawing from the lessons of Mississippi, where even knocking on doors was done in pairs, the Berkeley free speech advocates did nothing alone, always en masse. On October 1, 1964, a civil rights worker named Jack Weinberg, who had also gone to Mississippi for Freedom Summer, was arrested on the Berkeley campus. He had defied the prohibition of political advocacy on campus by sitting at a table filled with civil rights literature. He was placed in a police car, which was surrounded by protesters. With no real plan, students trained in the civil rights movement sat down. More and more students came, immobilizing the car for thirty-two hours.

When Mario Savio leaped on top of the police car to make a speech, he first removed his shoes so as not to damage the car. Later, he did not even recall when he had decided to jump on the car. He just did it. He stammered no longer, and his eloquence instantly anointed him the spokesperson of what came to be known as the Berkeley Free Speech Movement.

A graduate philosophy student, Suzanne Goldberg, who later married Savio, said that "his charisma came from sincerity." She remembered, "I would see him around Berkeley carrying signs, but when I heard him speak I was amazed at the sincerity. Mario had the ability to make things ordinary and understandable without using rhetoric. He believed that if people knew all the facts, they couldn't help but do the right thing—which most of us know is not true. He had a naïve faith in people. He would talk to people at great length, certain that he could convince them."

Though Mario Savio did not have the eloquence of Martin Luther King, or the lawyerly precision of Tom Hayden, he loved language and used it to simplify. At Berkeley his stammer appeared only occasionally, the Queens accent remained. His speeches, devoid of rhetorical flourish, always seemed to say "It's all so clear." Only in his eyes could a real fire be seen. The sweep of his arms and his persistent hand gestures reflected his Sicilian origins. The tall, lanky, bowed stance revealed his humility, recalling Gandhi's teaching that a political activist should be so mild that the adversary, once defeated, does not feel humiliated. A favorite Savio phrase was "I ask you to consider." According to legend, Savio, during one of his stays in prison, approached a large, burly inmate and, apropos of nothing, bet him that if he poured a glass of water on the man's head, the inmate would do nothing to retaliate against his skinny attacker. The man took the bet, and Savio filled two glasses of water. He simultaneously poured one glass on the other inmate's head and one on his own. He won the bet.

Two months after the sit-in at the police car, Savio led a takeover of Sproul Hall, a university building, which resulted in the largest mass arrest of students in U.S. history. Before the seizure of the building, Savio made what may be the only student speech of the sixties that is remembered. He said:

There's a time when the operation of the machine becomes so odious, makes you so sick at heart, that you can't take part, you can't even tacitly take part, and you've got to put your bodies upon the gears and upon the wheels, upon the levers, upon all the apparatus, and you've got to make it stop. And you've got to indicate to the people who run it, to the people who own it, that unless you are free, the machine will be prevented from working at all.

Most of the leaders of the Free Speech Movement had participated in the Freedom Summer. They took Bob Dylan's stirring civil rights song, "The Times They Are A-Changin'" and made it their own. Joan Baez sang it for them at one of their pivotal demonstrations, and overnight Dylan's song for the civil rights movement became the anthem of 1960s student movements.

But the Free Speech Movement, like most sixties movements, claimed to be too democratic to have leaders. Savio always denied being the singular leader. It was because of him, though, more than any other single figure, that students entering college in the mid-1960s thought of demonstrating as a natural act. Savio made the connection from the civil rights movement to the student movement. From Warsaw to Berlin, to Paris, to New York, to Chicago, to Mexico City, students were stirred by the tactics and oratory of Mario Savio and the Free Speech Movement. The names, the sit-ins, the arrests, the headlines, the fact that they won their demands for on-campus activism— all this became legend to students entering a university in the mid-1960s. Unfortunately, what was forgotten was the grace and civility of a rebel who walked in his socks on a police car in order not to scratch it.

Mario Savio and Tom Hayden were not particularly interested in the fashion of the times. In 1968, when Tom Hayden organized demonstrations at the Chicago convention, he still dressed very much like the journalist from the *Michigan Daily*. But if Hayden gave 1968 its statement of principles and Savio its spirit—its style was best expressed by an over-thirty man from Worcester, Massachusetts. In his entire lifetime, perhaps in all of history, there was no year that was better suited for Abbie Hoffman than 1968. It must have seemed extraordinary to him that year that the world had come around to his way of doing things. He used to say that he had been born with the decade, in 1960, and that was probably how it felt to him.

Abbie Hoffman was one of the first Americans to fully appreciate the possibilities and the importance of living in what was becoming a media age. He was the New Left's clown, not because he was clownish, but because in a very calculated way he understood that the New Left was in need of a clown, that a clown could publicize their issues, that a clown was not ignored. Above all, Abbie Hoffman did not want to be ignored. And like all good clowns, he was very funny. He was a master of the put-on, and those who understood put-ons laughed while the others joined the television cameras waiting when he promised to spin and levitate the Pentagon, not understanding why he was not in the least bit embarrassed, or the slightest bit disappointed, when he failed to do so.

In 1960, the year he said he was "born," he was twenty-four years old, having actually been born in 1936. He was the same age as Black Panther Bobby Seale, a junior at Brandeis when Tom Hayden first traveled fifty miles to the University of Michigan, six years older than Mario Savio, and a decade or more older than undergraduate college students in 1968. Hoffman had a sense that he was running late. He had never gone to a political demonstration until 1960, when as a graduate student at Berkeley he participated in a huge outcry against capital punishment led by Marlon Brando and other celebrities after Caryl Chessman, who had kidnapped two women and forced them to perform oral sex, was sentenced to death for his crime. But on May 2, after Hoffman's first taste of political activism failed, the state of California killed Chessman.

That same year, Hoffman married and had two children and spent the next few years trying unsuccessfully to master fatherhood and a conventional life. In 1964, to his great frustration, he watched Freedom Summer on television. The following summer, the last time that large numbers of white volunteers went south, Hoffman was among them. He returned to the South the next two years, when few others went, working for SNCC. Hoffman had not only missed Freedom Summer, he had missed another 1964 watershed in the civil rights movement, the Democratic convention in Atlantic City. The convention belonged to Johnson, heir to the Kennedy administration. Johnson's running mate, Hubert Humphrey, his protégé Walter Mondale, and other leaders of the liberal establishment, fearing they would lose the South to Goldwater, refused to seat the delegates of the Mississippi Freedom Party. This split the movement in two, largely on generational lines. The older civil rights leaders such as Martin Luther King were used to the idea that the Democratic Party was not a dependable friend and required work. But SNCC lost faith in working with anyone from the white establishment. Bob Moses was angry. Young leaders such as Stokely Carmichael had no more patience. They began talking about Black Power, about black people going their separate way.

Only a few weeks before the Democratic convention, it was alleged that North Vietnamese gun boats had fired on U.S. destroyers in the Gulf of Tonkin. Johnson retaliated by attacking North Vietnam and got Congress to pass the Tonkin Gulf Resolution, which empowered the president to take "any means necessary" to protect South Vietnam. There has been much evidence, including a cable from one of the destroyers, that the attack may never have taken place. In 1968 the Senate held hearings on the subject but never resolved it conclusively. The suspicion has endured that the Tonkin incident, whether it occurred or not, was seized by Johnson as a pretext to pursue the war. Tom Hayden said, "When the Democratic Party was agreeing to the Tonkin Gulf Resolution at the same time they were refusing to seat the Mississippi Freedom Party, that was a turning point for me."

The following year Stokely Carmichael went to Mississippi intending to form a local black political party in one of the counties there. He chose Lowndes County because it was 80 percent black. The all-white Mississippi State Democratic Party had a white rooster for a symbol. Searching for a predator that would devour a rooster, Carmichael called his party the Black Panthers. More than a year later two Californians, Huey Newton and Bobby Seale, talked to Carmichael about starting their own California party for which they borrowed the name Black Panther. Not seating the Mississippi Freedom Party at the 1964 convention had radicalized the civil rights movement and profoundly changed the history of the 1960s in America.

One year after the Freedom Summer, the southern civil rights struggle was no longer center stage. Black Power was shifting attention to northern cities. Stokely Carmichael, Bob Moses, and all the diverse elements of the civil rights movement could agree on the importance of stopping the war and on little else.

Hoffman appeared not to have noticed this shift. In the spring of 1965, he opened the Snick Shop in his native Worcester, selling crafts made by poor blacks in the South while his fellow SNCC workers, H. Rap Brown, Stokely Carmichel, Julius Lester, and others were selling books and pamphlets on Black Power. Stokely Carmichael admired him for his physical courage. It was somewhat more than physical courage—an irresistible pull toward the vortex. When demonstrators were attacked, he stepped to the front and did everything he could to be the most visible. But when SDS organized its first antiwar rally in Washington, Hoffman did not even go. His most publicized comment about opposing the war at the time was that everyone should protest by going to Jones Beach on Long Island on a summer day wearing only bathing suits.

In 1968 Julius Lester published his seminal work, *Look Out, Whitey! Black Power's Gon' Get Your Mama!* Lester wrote about how it had been fine for SNCC to have "white and black together" in the words of the Pete Seeger anthem, when they were fighting southern racism, but once they went north it became clear that white people, not southerners, were the problem. "The mask," he said, "began to slip from the North's face." He noted the media value of Black Power—it was provocative.

> The cry for black power has done more to generate black consciousness than anything else. The term is not new, having been used by black people like Richard Wright and James Boggs, as well as whites like Charles Silberman. It achieved world wide notice, though, on the highways of Mississippi during the Meredith March, when SNCC organizer Willie Ricks condensed what everybody had been saying, "Power for black people!" and said, "Black Power!" (Ricks is not one to mince words.)
> What had been a dull march turned into a major news event. Everybody wanted to know what this Black Power was. If SNCC had said Negro Power or Colored Power, white folks would have continued sleeping easy every night. But BLACK POWER! Black. That word. BLACK! And the visions came of alligator infested swamps arched by primordial trees and moss dripping from the limbs and out of the depths of the swamp, the mire oozing from his skin, came the black monster and fathers told their daughters to be in by nine instead of nine-thirty. . . . BLACK POWER! My God, the niggers were gon' start paying white folk back, . . . The nation was hysterical. Hubert Humphrey screamed, ". . . there is no room in America for racism of any color." He must have been lying because black people know of 48 states at least that have so much room for racism there's hardly room for anything else.

SNCC had never been more than 20 percent white, but in December 1966, seven months after Carmichael became head of SNCC, the organization narrowly passed—19 to 18, with 24 abstentions—a measure barring white people. It was Bob Moses, the man who had brought a thousand volunteers south two summers before, who ordered the expulsion. Hoffman was furious and struck back in an article in that month's *Village Voice,* where he originated his hip first-person colloquial style—a style that New York publications have been imitating ever since. He attacked SNCC's Achilles' heel: the fact that, as in many of the sixties movements, SNCC organizers had been doing a great deal of sleeping with one another. These were young people working closely together, often in great danger. As SNCC worker Casey Hayden said, "If you were lucky enough to have a bed, you might feel bad if you didn't share it." SNCC had tried to keep this information within the organization, because people were not only having sex, they were having *interracial* sex, black men with white women, and there was absolutely nothing that so provoked white racists as this. Abbie Hoffman wrote that white women had been lured into the organization and seduced and were now being thrown out: "I feel for the other whites in SNCC, especially the white females. I identify with all those Bronx chippies that are getting conned out of their bodies and bread by some dark skinned sharpie."

In July 1967, when riots erupted in American cities, Johnson appointed an eleven-member presidential commission headed by Illinois governor Otto Kerner to study and recommend solutions to "civil disorders." In March 1968, the Kerner Commission released its controversial but much praised study in which racism was said to be the key problem. It accused the news media of exaggerating violence and underreporting on the poverty of inner cities and said, "A new mood has sprung up among Negroes, particularly among the young, in which self esteem and enhanced racial pride are replacing apathy and submission to 'the system.' "

The report, which sold so widely that by April 1968 it was number two on *The New York Times* nonfiction bestseller list, called for drastic increases in federal spending. "The vital needs of the nation must be met; hard choices must be made, and, if necessary, new taxes enacted." Unfortunately, that same day Arkansas Democrat Wilbur Mills, who as chairman of the House Ways and Means Committee was the leading figure on taxes, announced that the cost of expanding the war in Vietnam could force a tax increase. That was what the commission meant by hard choices. New York City mayor John Lindsay, a member of the Kerner Commission, was one of an increasing number, including Robert Kennedy, who were complaining that the cost of the war was keeping the country from its social responsibilities.

But the most quoted and remembered line of the report was "Our nation is moving toward two societies, one black, one white—separate and unequal." And that was exactly what was happening in the militant movements of the Left as well. Mirroring society, black and white activists were increasingly separated.

By 1967 Abbie Hoffman had become a militant for the privileged whites. He protested capitalism and commercialism by burning money and urging others to do the same. Burning money was not an idea that would resonate with rural southern blacks or urban northern ones. But what was significant to Hoffman was that setting fire to money attracted television cameras, because it was visual. In 1967, when he finally turned his attention to the antiwar movement, his concern was how to get it onto television. In May of that year he formed the Flower Brigade, made up of young antiwar activists with what had become the hippie uniform—long hair, flowered clothing, bell-bottomed blue jeans, headbands, beads—a uniform that seemed to draw cameras. Hoffman, waving an American flag, wore a cape that said "Freedom."

Hoffman had learned from the civil rights movement that even creative nonviolence can go unnoticed unless the participants are attacked. The Flower Brigade was designed to get attacked. He trained the members in the defensive crouch that he had been taught in the civil rights movement. And they were attacked, young women beaten, American flags torn out of their hands. It made for powerful photographs, and the Flower Brigade was momentarily the talk of the peace movement. Hoffman told the press that they were poorly equipped from "uptown florists" but had plans to "grow our own." He boasted that "dandelion chains are being wrapped around induction centers," where draftees were processed into the military.

Now established as one of the leading "hippies" of New York's East Village, Hoffman joined a group called the Diggers, founded by a group of actors from San Francisco, the San Francisco Mime Troupe. He explained the difference between a Digger and a hippie in an essay titled "Diggery Is Niggery" for a publication called *Win*. Diggers, he said, were hippies who had learned to manipulate the media instead of being manipulated by them. "Both are in one sense a huge put-on," he wrote.

The Diggers were named after a seventeenth-century English free land movement that preached the end of money and property and inspired the idea of destroying money and giving everything away for free as revolutionary acts. Hoffman staged a "sweep-in" on Third Street in the East Village, usually one of Manhattan's dirtiest streets. The police did not know how to respond when Hoffman and the Diggers took to the block with brooms and mops. One even walked up to a New York City cop and started polishing his badge. The policeman laughed. Everyone laughed, and the *Village Voice* reported that the "sweep-in" was "a goof." Later that year Hoffman staged a "smoke-in" in which people went to Tompkins Square Park and smoked marijuana, which was pretty much what everyone had been doing anyway.

"A modern revolutionary group," Hoffman explained, "headed for the television station, not for the factory."

Hoffman's partner and competitor was Jerry Rubin, born in 1938 to a blue-collar Cincinnati family. The story in January 1968 of Rubin and Hoffman rolling on the floor in drug-induced stupors while founding the Yippie! movement is exactly the opposite of what it appears to be. Instead of being the embarrassing reality leaked to the press by some disloyal insider, it was in fact a planted story. In reality, Rubin and Hoffman had given a great deal of sober thought to the creation of the movement. Hoffman, in his "free" period, wanted to call the group the Freemen. In fact, his first book, *Revolution for the Hell of It*, was published in 1968 under the nom de plume Free. But after long discussion, the Freemen lost out to Yippie! It wasn't until later in the year that it occurred to them to say it stood for Youth International Party.

No one was certain how seriously to take Abbie Hoffman, and that was his great strength. One story tells much about the elusive clown of the sixties. In 1967, Hoffman got married for a second time. The June 8 "wed-in" was also publicized in the *Village Voice*, which said, "Bring flowers, friends, food, fun, costumes, painted faces." The couple was to be joined "in holy mind blow"—dressed in white with garlands in their hair. The I Ching, the Chinese Book of Change that was used to interpret the future three thousand years ago and in 1968 reemerged as popular mysticism, was read at the ceremony. The groom was visibly under the influence of marijuana and giggled uncontrollably. *Time* magazine covered the wed-in for its July 1967 issue on hippies but did not mention the "beflowered couple" by name. Abbie Hoffman was not a widely known name until 1968. But after the wed-in, without any publicity, the bridal couple went off to the decidedly bourgeois Temple Emanu-El on Manhattan's affluent Upper East Side, where Rabbi Nathan A. Perilman quietly performed a traditional Reform Jewish wedding.

Jews in disproportionate numbers were active in student movements in 1968 not only in Poland, but in the United States and France. At Columbia and the University of Michigan, two of SDS's most active campuses, SDS was more than half Jewish. When Tom Hayden first went to the University of Michigan, he noted that the only political activists were Jewish students from leftist families. Two-thirds of the white Freedom Riders were Jewish. Most of the leaders of the Free Speech Movement at Berkeley were Jewish. Mario Savio, the notable exception, said:

I'm not Jewish, but I saw those pictures. And those pictures were astonishing. Heaps of bodies. Mounds of bodies. Nothing affected my consciousness more than those pictures. And those pictures had on me the following impact, which other people maybe came to in a different way. They meant to me that everything needed to be questioned. Reality itself. Because this was like opening up your father's drawer and finding pictures of child pornography, with adults molesting children. It's like a dark, grotesque secret that people had that at some time in the recent past people were being incinerated and piled up in piles. . . . Those pictures had an impact on people's lives. I know they had an impact on mine, something not as strong but akin to a "never again" feeling which Jews certainly have had. But non-Jews had that feeling, too.

People born during and directly after World War II grew up in a world transformed by horror, and this made them see the world in a completely different way. The great lesson of Nazi genocide for the postwar generation was that everyone has an obligation to speak up in the face of wrong and that any excuse for silence will, in the merciless hindsight of history, appear as pathetic and culpable as the Germans in the war crimes trials, pleading that they were obeying orders. This was a generation that as children learned of Auschwitz and Bergen-Belsen, of Hiroshima and Nagasaki. Children who were told constantly throughout their childhood that at any moment the adults might decide to have a war that would end life on earth.

While an older generation justified the nuclear bombing of Japan because it had shortened the war, the new generation once again, as children, had seen the pictures and they viewed it very differently. They had also seen the mushroom clouds of nuclear explosions on television because the United States still did aboveground testing. Americans and Europeans, both Eastern and Western, grew up with the knowledge that the United States, which was continuing to build bigger and better bombs, was the only country that had ever actually used one. And it talked about doing it again, all the time—in Korea, in Cuba, in Vietnam. The children born in the 1940s in both superpower blocs grew up practicing covering themselves up in the face of nuclear attack. Savio recalled being ordered under his desk at school: "I ultimately took degrees in physics so even then I asked myself questions like 'Will this actually do the job?' "

Growing up during the cold war had the same effect on most of the children of the world. It made them fearful of both blocs. This was one of the reasons European, Latin American, African, and Asian youth were so quick and so resolute in their condemnation of U.S. military action in Vietnam. By and large, theirs was not a support of communists, but a distaste for either bloc imposing its power. To American youth, the execution of the Rosenbergs, the lives ruined by Senator Joseph McCarthy's hearings, taught them to distrust the U.S. government.

Youth around the globe saw the world being squeezed by two equal and unsavory forces. American youth had learned that it was important to stand up to both the communists and the anticommunists. The Port Huron Statement recognized that communism should be opposed: "The Soviet Union, as a system, rests on the total repression of organized opposition, as well as a vision of the future in the name of which much human life had been sacrificed, and numerous small and large denials of human dignity rationalized." But according to the Port Huron Statement, anticommunist forces in America were more harmful than helpful. The statement cautions that "an unreasoning anti-Communism has become a major social problem."

This first started to be expressed in the 1950s with the film characters portrayed by James Dean, Marlon Brando, and Elvis Presley, and the beat generation writings of Ginsberg and Jack Kerouac. But the feeling grew in the 1960s. The young invested hope in John Kennedy, largely because he too was relatively young—the second youngest president in history replacing Eisenhower, who at the time was the oldest. The inauguration of Kennedy in 1961 was the largest change of age ever at the White House, with almost thirty years' difference between the exiting and entering presidents. But even under Kennedy, young Americans experienced the Cuban missile crisis as a terrifying experience and one that taught that people in power play with human life even if they are young and have a good sense of humor.

Most of the people who arrived at college campuses in the mid-1960s had a deep resentment and distrust of any kind of authority. People in positions of authority anywhere on the political spectrum were not to be trusted. That is why there were no absolute leaders. The moment a Savio or Hayden declared himself leader, he would have lost all credibility.

There was something else that was different about this generation. They were the first to grow up with television, and they did not have to learn how to use it, it came naturally, the same way children who grew up with computers in the 1990s had an instinct for it that older people could not match with education. In 1960, on the day of Eisenhower's last news conference, Robert Spivack, a columnist, asked the president if he felt the press had been fair to him during his eight years in the White House. Eisenhower answered, "Well, when you come down to it, I don't see much what a reporter could do to a president, do you?" Such a sentiment would never again be heard in the White House. Kennedy, born in 1917, was said to have understood television, but it was really his brother Robert, eight years younger, who was the architect of the Kennedy television presidency.

By 1968 Walter Cronkite had reached what for him was a disturbing conclusion, that television was playing an important part not only in the reporting of events, but in the shaping of them. Increasingly around the world, public demonstrations were being staged, and it seemed clear to him that they were being staged for television. Street demonstrations are good television. They do not even need to be large, they need only enough people to fill the frame of a television camera.

"You can't put that as the only reason they were in the streets; demonstrations took place before television, but this was an added incitement to demonstrate," Cronkite reflected decades later. "Particularly as television communications in the world showed them that this was successful in different communities, they obviously felt, well, that's the way you do it. And so it was epidemic around the world."

This generation, with its distrust of authority and its understanding of television, and raised in the finest school of political activism, the American civil rights movement, was uniquely suited to disrupt the world. And then they were offered a war they did not want to fight and did not think should be fought. The young people of the generation, the ones who were in college in 1968, were the draftees. The Haydens and Savios, and Abbie Hoffmans, too young for Korea and too old for Vietnam, had not faced a draft. These younger members of the sixties generation, the people of 1968, had a fury in them that had not been seen before.

CHAPTER 6

HEROES

Let us decide not to imitate Europe; let us combine our muscles and our brains in a new direction. Let us try to create the whole man, whom Europe has been incapable of bringing to triumphant birth.
— FRANTZ FANON, The Wretched of the Earth, *1961*

1968 WAS SUPPOSED TO BE Johnson's year. As winter thawed toward spring, every one of the numerous men who were dreaming of the White House was calculating his chances of beating the incumbent president. And in every one of those hypothetical contests, Johnson was favored to win. But even those not running for president were running against Johnson. Martin Luther King and his Southern Christian Leadership Conference announced a plan to have hundreds of thousands of poor people, white and black, march on Washington in the spring. Poverty, instead of being hidden, would be displayed openly and put on television. The Reverend Ralph Abernathy, the number two leader in the movement, said, "We're going up there to talk to LBJ, and if LBJ doesn't do something about what we tell him, we're going to put him down and get us another one who will."

But by March 12, 1968 was no longer necessarily Johnson's year. That day Johnson won his first primary, an easy contest in New Hampshire in which the incumbent was opposed only by the improbable senator Eugene McCarthy, the candidate *Life* magazine one month earlier had labeled "a conundrum." The shock was that the president on that snowy New Hampshire day had defeated the conundrum by a mere 230 votes. Around the world, the news was reported as though the unknown senator had just been elected president, or at the very least had defeated Johnson. While Warsaw students were fighting

Martin Luther King, Jr.'s, last campaign, 1968
(Schomburg Center for Research in Black Culture)

police in the streets and Czechs were drifting ever further from Soviet control, the Soviet Party newspaper, *Pravda,* said that the primary results showed that the Vietnam War "has become the main and decisive question of the 1968 presidential election." In Spain, where the University of Madrid was closed, the Catholic newspaper *Ya* predicted that the November elections would "turn upside down for Johnson." In Rome, where students had shut down the university, the left-wing press was declaring a victory for the antiwar movement.

Nelson Rockefeller, governor of New York, who was not on the Republican ballot in New Hampshire, conducted a disappointing write-in campaign in which he garnered only 10 percent of the vote. After the primary, he announced his decision not to run, leaving the Republican field open to what to many was the unthinkable: another Nixon nomination. Nixon had little time to gloat, because Robert Kennedy announced that he too was a candidate, raising the terrifying specter in Nixon's mind of a rerun of the campaign that had almost ended his career—another Nixon-Kennedy showdown. But first Kennedy would have to unseat the incumbent. On March 31 came the bombshell: President Johnson went on television and announced, "I shall not seek and I will not accept the nomination of my party as your president."

Suddenly the front-running Democratic incumbent was out of the race, and no one was sure what would happen next. "It was America that was on a trip; we were just standing still," said Abbie Hoffman. "How could we pull our pants down? America was already naked. What could we disrupt? America was falling apart at the seams."

Historians have debated Johnson's reasons ever since. McCarthy supporters and antiwar activists claimed victory—that they had convinced the president he could not win. In subsequent years, it has been revealed that Johnson's hawkish cabinet had advised him that escalation of the war was politically impossible and the war was militarily unwinnable. Johnson did, along with his resignation, announce a limited halt to bombing and the intention to seek peace negotiations with the North Vietnamese. But the president was not acting like the well-known LBJ. There had been good reasons to believe he might have won reelection. It could have been that the snowstorm had kept over-confident Johnson supporters home the day of the primary and the narrowness of his victory was only a fluke. Even if New Hampshire did mean real trouble ahead, Johnson did not usually avoid tough political contests. After the New Hampshire primary, *The Times* of London predicted the result would "anger" Johnson and "should activate the politician within him." Some have said that his wife urged him not to run. *The New York Times* speculated that the primary inducement was that the war was going badly.

From March 8 to 14, the world experienced yet another international debacle caused by the U.S. involvement in Vietnam. The war was costing the United States about $30 billion annually. And the $3.6 billion balance of payments deficit was considered so enormous that such measures as travel curbs were viewed as pointless Band-Aids. The United States was financing the war with gold reserves, which were now at only half of their post–World War II high of $24.6 billion. The value of the dollar was fixed to gold, and speculators looking at these figures concluded that the United States would not be able to maintain the fixed price of gold at $35 an ounce. The United States, according to the theory, would not have sufficient reserves to sell at $35 to all buyers, which would force up the price of gold. Those who held gold would make enormous profits. The same thing had happened to sterling in November 1967 when the British devalued the pound. Gold speculators went on a buying spree that set off a panic that the press called "the biggest gold rush in history." More than two hundred tons of gold worth $220 million changed hands on the London gold market,

setting a new single-day record. So much gold was going into Switzerland that one bank had to reinforce its vaults for the added weight.
Economists around the world were predicting disaster. "We're in the
first act of a world depression," said British economist John Vaizey.

While the world angrily watched America's Vietnam spending desta-
bilize the global economy, the war itself ground on uglier than ever. On
March 14 the U.S. command reported that 509 American servicemen
were killed and 2,766 had been wounded in the past week, bringing
total casualties since January 1, 1961, to 139,801, of whom 19,670
had been killed. This did not approach the 33,000 dead in three years
of fighting in Korea. But for the first time the total casualties, including
wounded, was higher in Vietnam than in Korea.

On March 16 the 23rd Infantry Division, the so-called Americal
Division, was fighting in central Vietnam along the murky brown
South China Sea in the village of Son My, where they slaughtered close
to five hundred unarmed civilians that day. Much of the killing was in
one hamlet called My Lai, but the action took place throughout the
area. Elderly people, women, young boys and girls, and babies were
systematically shot while some of the troops refused to participate.
One soldier missed a baby on the ground in front of him two times
with a .45-caliber pistol before he finally hit his target, while his
comrades laughed at what a bad shot he was. Women were beaten with
rifle butts, some raped, some sodomized. The Americans killed the live-
stock and threw it in the wells to poison the water. They threw explosives into the bomb shelters under the houses where villagers had tried
to escape. Those who ran out to avoid the explosives were shot. The
houses were all burned. Tom Glen, a soldier in the 11th Brigade, wrote
a letter to division headquarters reporting the crimes and waited for a
response.

Whatever the reason for Johnson's withdrawal from the presidential
race, it created a strange political reality. The Democrats had Minnesota's Eugene McCarthy, the peace candidate who had barely bothered
to articulate any program beyond the single issue, and New York senator Robert Kennedy, who, according to the February issue of *Fortune*
magazine, was more disliked by business leaders than any other candidate since the 1930s. The youth of 1968, famously alienated and
removed from conventional politics, suddenly had two candidates they
admired vying for the nomination of the ruling party. The fact that
these two politicians, both from the traditional political establishment,
had managed to earn the faith and respect of young people who scoffed
at the labels "Democrat" and "liberal" was remarkable. No one

believed they would have the field to themselves for long. The political establishment would run its own candidate, no doubt Vice President Hubert Humphrey, but for the moment it was exhilarating. A McCarthy ad showing the senator surrounded by youth carried the headline OUR CHILDREN HAVE COME HOME.

Suddenly there's hope among our voting people.

Suddenly they've come back into the mainstream of American life. And it's a different country.

Suddenly the kids have thrown themselves into politics, with all their fabulous intelligence and energy. And it's a new election.

When the following year Henry Kissinger became Nixon's security adviser, he gave an interview to *Look* magazine in which he demonstrated his extraordinary ability to speak with authority while being completely wrong.

I can understand the anguish of the younger generation. They lack models and they have no heroes, they see no great purpose in the world. But conscientious objection is destructive of a society. The imperatives of the individual are always in conflict with the organization of society. Conscientious objection must be reserved for only the greatest moral issue, and Vietnam is not of this magnitude.

It was clear that Kissinger was incapable of understanding "the anguish of the younger generation." To begin with, this was a generation with a long list of heroes, though neither Kissinger nor those he admired were to be found on this list. For the most part, the list did not include politicians, generals, or leaders of state. Young people all over the world had these heroes in common, and there was an excitement about the discovery that like-minded people could be found all over the world. For Americans, this was an unusually international perspective. It could be argued that because of the birth of satellite communications and television, this was the first global generation. But subsequent generations have not been this cosmopolitan.

What was also unusual for Americans was that so many of the revered figures were writers and intellectuals. This is perhaps because to a very large extent theirs was a movement from the universities. Perhaps the single most influential writer for young people in the sixties was Algerian-born French Nobel Prize laureate Albert Camus, who died in 1960 in an automobile crash at age forty-seven, just as what should have been his best decade was beginning. Because of his 1942 essay, "The Myth of Sisyphus," in which he argued that the human condition was fundamentally absurd, he was often associated with the existential movement. But he refused to consider himself part of that group. He was not a joiner, which is one of the reasons he was more revered than the existentialist and communist Jean-Paul Sartre, even though Sartre lived through and even participated in the sixties student movements. Camus, who worked with the Resistance against the Nazi occupiers of France editing an underground newspaper, *Le Combat,* often wrote from the perspective of a moral imperative to act. His 1948 novel, *The Plague,* is about a doctor who risks his life and family to rid his community of a sickness he discovers. In the 1960s, students all over the world read *The Plague* and interpreted it as a call to activism. Mario Savio's famous 1964 speech, "There's a time when the operation of the machine becomes so odious . . . you've got to put your bodies upon the gears . . . and you've got to make it stop," sounds like a line from *The Plague.* "There are times when the only feeling I have is one of mad revolt," Camus wrote. American civil rights workers read Camus. His books were passed from one volunteer to the next in SNCC. Tom Hayden wrote that he considered Camus to be one of the great influences in his decision to leave journalism and become a student activist. Abbie Hoffman used Camus to explain in part the Yippie! movement, referring to Camus's words in *Notebooks:* "The revolution as myth is the definitive revolution."

By 1968 there was another intellectual it seemed everybody wanted to quote: Marxist-Hegelian revisionist revolutionary Herbert Marcuse. His most appealing idea was what he called "the great refusal," the time to say "No, this is not acceptable"—another idea that was expressed in Savio's "odious machine" speech. Marcuse, a naturalized American citizen who had fled the Nazis, was on the faculty of Brandeis when Abbie Hoffman had been a student there, and Hoffman was enormously influenced by him, especially by his book *Eros and Civilization,* which talked about guilt-free physical pleasure and warned about "false fathers, teachers, and heroes." The most talked-about Marcuse book of the late sixties, *One-Dimensional Man,* was published in 1964. It denounced technological society as shallow and conformist and put into the carefully orchestrated discipline of German philosophy all of the sentiments of the 1950s James Dean–style rebels and the 1960s student revolutionaries. *The New York Times* called Marcuse "the most important philosopher alive."

In 1968, at the age of seventy, Marcuse taught at San Diego State, where he could be seen fussing over his rust-colored cat and enjoying the hippos at the zoo, an avuncular white-haired figure whose impact was felt across the globe. The students who forced the University of Rome to close in March of that year carried a banner with three Ms that stood for Marx, Mao, and Marcuse.

While more conventional thinkers insisted that technology would create more leisure time, Marcuse warned that it would instead imprison people in unoriginal lives devoid of creative thinking. He warned that though technology appeared to help the dissenter, it would actually be used to muffle protest. People were being anesthetized into a complacency that was mistaken for happiness. Goods and services were rendering mankind useless and incapable of real thought. There was an increase in media, but it espoused less and less variety of ideas. People in today's world who "surf" through eighty or more television stations, only to find less there than when they had only four choices, might be beginning to grasp Marcuse's vision for a technological age in which people think they have more choices but the choices lack significant differences. In an age of abundance, when technology has made individuals extraordinarily efficient, why do people spend even more time working, and why is so much work mindless instead of stimulating? One of the first Marxists to lose faith in the Soviet system, Marcuse saw the West as also in a state of "unfreedom" and often suggested that revolution may be the only path to true freedom.

Marcuse, the aging professor, seemed to warm to the role of guru to the student radicals. He frequently discussed their movements. He warned Abbie Hoffman on "flower power" that "flowers have no power" other than the force of the people who cultivate them—one of the few occasions on which Hoffman had no reply. But as Marcuse freely admitted, many of the young rebels who talked about his ideas had never read him. His work is written in the German dialectic tradition. Marcuse achieved popularity without ever developing an accessible writing style. Luis Gonzalez de Alba, one of the student leaders in Mexico, described finally settling down to read some Marcuse simply because President Gustavo Díaz Ordaz had accused the movement of being influenced by the philosopher.

> I opened *One-Dimensional Man* and got as far as page five. *Eros and Civilization* had been a terrible bore. And now I had to read another of Marcuse's books, all because Díaz Ordaz had happened to mention "the philosophers of destruction."

A Martinique-born psychiatrist named Frantz Fanon became an international figure after he wrote a book in 1961 called *Les damnés de la terre*. Translated into twenty-five languages, the book was read by U.S. college students under the title *The Wretched of the Earth*. Fanon had finished his French medical studies in Algeria in 1953, where he joined the Algerian National Front and became a leader in the fight for Algerian independence. This alone was credentials enough in the French youth movement that began in the late fifties by opposing French policy in Algeria. Independent Algeria, like Cuba, came to be regarded as a symbol of resistance to the established order of the world. Not a predictable anticolonialist tirade, *Wretched of the Earth* examines the psychology not only of colonialism, but of overthrowing colonialism and the kind of new man that is required to build a postcolonial society.

By explaining the complexity of the inner struggle to break with colonialism, *Wretched of the Earth* wielded an important influence in the United States on the American civil rights movement, where it helped make the connection between oppressed American blacks trying to rise up from white rule and oppressed African Muslims trying to free themselves from Europeans. This was the theme of the Black Muslim movement, especially under Malcolm X, who like Fanon was born in 1925, but in 1965 had been murdered, it appeared, by fellow Black Muslims, though this was never proven. Black Muslim boxer Muhammad Ali, as he defied the white establishment, was often seen as a standard-bearer for emerging poor nations. Eldridge Cleaver called Ali "the black Fidel Castro of boxing."

Even Martin Luther King, Jr., identified the civil rights movement with the struggle of underdeveloped nations. In 1955 he said of the Montgomery boycott, "It is part of a world-wide movement. Look at just about any place in the world and the exploited people are rising against their exploiters. This seems to be the outstanding characteristic of our generation."

Eldridge Cleaver became a sixties icon largely through his literary ability. Cleaver first went to prison at the age of eighteen for smoking marijuana. He later went back for rape. Released from prison in 1966, he joined the staff of the counterculture magazine *Ramparts*—famous for being charged with a crime for its 1968 cover of burning draft cards. The magazine staff encouraged him to publish the essays he had written while in prison, essays that expressed harsh self-criticism along with harsh criticism of the world that created him. Cleaver was virtually unknown until 1968, when his book of essays, *Soul on Ice,* was published and he was credited by critics, including in *The New York Times Book Review,* with a brash but articulate voice. His timing was perfect: In 1968, what was wrong with American society was a leading question in America. A June Gallup poll showed that white people by a ratio of three to two did not believe America was "sick," but black people by a ratio of eight to seven did. *Soul on Ice* was published at almost the exact same moment as the Kerner Report on racial violence and, as *The New York Times* review pointed out, confirmed its findings. "Look into a mirror," wrote Cleaver. "The cause is you, Mr. and Mrs. Yesterday, you, with your forked tongues."

Shortly before the publication of his book, Cleaver had brokered an important black-white alliance in California. The New Left there had formed a political party, the Peace and Freedom Party, which had gathered one hundred thousand signatures to put its candidates on the California ballot. Through Cleaver, the party was able to establish a coalition with the Black Panthers, by agreeing to the Panther platform of exempting blacks from the military, freeing all blacks from prison, and demanding that all future trials of blacks be held with an all-black jury. Cleaver was to be nominated as the party's presidential candidate, with Jerry Rubin as his running mate. Cleaver's new wife, Kathleen, a SNCC worker, was to be a state assembly candidate, as was Black Panther Bobby Seale. It was during Cleaver's campaign that he called for "pussy power" at an event he labeled "Pre-erection Day" and an alliance with "Machine Gun Kellys"—that is, anyone with firearms who was willing to use them. In October he received loud applause from a packed theater with an overflowing crowd at Stanford University, when he said of the governor of California, "Ronald Reagan is a punk, a sissy, and a coward, and I challenge him to a duel to the death or until he says Uncle Eldridge. I give him a choice of weapons—a gun, a knife, a baseball bat, or marshmallows."

1968 was the best year Eldridge Cleaver had. The following year, accused of involvement in a Black Panther shoot-out in Oakland, he fled to Cuba and then to Algeria. By the time he finally returned to the United States in 1975, he had no following left.

If the truth be told, which it rarely was except in private, most of the white Left found the Black Panthers a little bit scary. While most of the New Left whites were from the comfortable middle class, and most of the civil rights blacks such as Bob Moses and Martin Luther King were well educated, the Black Panthers were mostly street people from tough neighborhoods, often with prison records. Dressing in black with black berets and posing for photos with weapons, they intended to be scary. They preached violence and urged blacks to arm themselves for a coming violent revolution. They might have gotten little sympathy and few admirers except for two things. By 1968 it was becoming clear that the political establishment, especially in certain fiefdoms such as Mayor Richard Daley's Chicago and Governor Ronald Reagan's California, was prepared to use armed warfare against unarmed demonstrators. In April Daley announced that he had given his police force orders to "shoot to kill" any arsonist or anyone with a Molotov cocktail and "shoot to maim" any looters, a license to open fire on any civil disturbance. Once Reagan became governor in 1967, along with cutting the state budget for medical care and education, he initiated a policy of brutalizing demonstrators. Following an October 16, 1967, attack on antiwar demonstrators in Oakland that was so barbarous it was dubbed "bloody Tuesday," he commended the Oakland Police Department for "their exceptional ability and great professional skill." Young, privileged white people were starting to be treated by police the way black people had been for a long time.

In January 1968, after an attack on seven hundred antiwar activists picketing Secretary of State Dean Rusk's speech in San Francisco, one of the jailed victims, a Berkeley student, said of the attacking police, "They wanted to kill and would have if they could have gotten away with it. I know now that they were out to put Huey away, except Huey had the good sense to defend himself."

The reference was to Huey Newton, who founded the Black Panthers in California in 1966 and became the Peace and Freedom Party candidate for the U.S. House of Representatives from the Berkeley-Oakland district in 1968 while in prison awaiting trial in connection with the death of one and wounding of another Oakland policeman in a 1966 shoot-out. The first trial, in the summer of 1968, ended in a mistrial, as did two subsequent ones. Almost all of the major trials of Black Panthers ended in mistrials, acquittals, or convictions overturned on appeal, further fueling the suspicion that they were being persecuted by the police. In the course of the trials, plausible evidence of police brutality turned up, including in one case, allegedly murdering two suspects in their beds. The Black Panthers were increasingly being seen as victims of violence, martyrs who courageously stood up to the police.

It was a time of great strife within the black community, as former Negroes struggled to define the new black. By 1968 many of the greats of black culture were being regularly attacked by blacks. In *Soul on Ice,* Eldridge Cleaver savagely turned on James Baldwin, arguably the most respected black writer of the first half of the 1960s. After admitting how he thrilled to find a black writer of Baldwin's skill, Cleaver concludes that Baldwin had "the most grueling, agonizing, total hatred of the blacks, particularly of himself, and the most shameful, fanatical, fawning, sycophantic love of the whites that one can find in the writing of any black American writer of note in our time." Cleaver, who accused other blacks of hating blacks, managed in his one small book to denounce not only Baldwin, but Floyd Patterson, Louis Armstrong, Joe Louis, Harry Belafonte, Lena Horne, and Martin Luther King. Jazz star Louis Armstrong was an "Uncle Tom," according to Cleaver, a black man who pandered to the white racist population with his big eyes and big teeth.

Basically, Cleaver saw blacks who succeeded as sellouts. Malcolm X, who had been murdered, Muhammad Ali, stripped of his boxing title, Paul Robeson, forced into exile—these were all authentic black heroes, whereas Martin Luther King was to be scorned for his Nobel Prize. Cleaver wrote, "The award of a Nobel Prize to Martin Luther King, and the inflation of his image to that of an international hero, bear witness to the historical fact that the only Negro Americans allowed to attain national or international fame have been the puppets and the lackeys of the power structure." Once that is concluded, it is an easy step to the litmus test: If a black person achieves recognition, is he or she not thus proven to be a lackey?

Lincoln Theodore Monroe Andrew Perry, more popularly known as Stepin Fetchit, age seventy-six, struck back angrily in 1968 when a CBS television special entitled *Black History—Lost, Stolen, or Strayed*, narrated by black comedian Bill Cosby, presented Stepin Fetchit as an early racist stereotype. Stepin Fetchit, a friend of boxer Muhammad Ali, said, "It was not Martin Luther King that emancipated the modern Negro. It was Stepin Fetchit." He contended that it was his imitators but not he who did the eye-rolling, foot-shuffling kind of performance. "I was the first Negro to stay in a hotel in the South," he said angrily. "I was the first Negro to fly coast to coast on an airliner. I wiped away the image of rape from the Negro, made household work, somebody it was all right to associate with." Then he attacked some of the new movies, such as *Guess Who's Coming to Dinner*, in which Spencer Tracy and Katharine Hepburn's daughter brings home to dinner her fiancé, played by Sidney Poitier, who is a handsome, wonderfully artic- ulate, brilliant young doctor. The white dad, Tracy, struggles with the idea without ever expressing a racist thought and in the end gives in, apparently proving that intermarriage is okay if the black man is one of the leading citizens in America. Stepin Fetchit said that the film "did more to stop intermarriage than to help it," asserting that at no point in the film did Poitier actually touch the woman playing his fiancée. The comedian said Poitier and other contemporary black stars "are tools. Like in a bank. You put one Negro up front, but you won't find any other in the place."

New black heroes were made and old ones dropped every day. By 1968 Muhammad Ali was one of the few black heroes who were unassailable from the Left. Youth and blacks had admired him when in 1967 he was stripped of his boxing license for refusing the draft. The play *The Great White Hope* starred James Earl Jones as the newly discovered black hero, the first black heavyweight champion, Jack Johnson. Johnson had been unapologetic, or in 1968 terms a black champ, not a Negro, and the way he was driven from boxing seemed to parallel Muhammad Ali's own story.

In these hard times for black heroes, not surprisingly, Martin Luther King was frequently criticized. Many civil rights activists, especially those in SNCC, used to jokingly refer to him as "de Lawd." Beginning in 1966, King would occasionally be booed by SNCC activists while speaking or shouted down with cries of "Black Power!" King once responded, "Whenever Pharaoh wanted to keep the slaves in slavery, he kept them fighting among themselves."

He had often been accused of stealing more media attention than he deserved. This might have been true. He was a media natural; that was how he had become a leader. He sometimes reflected on what a good life he could have had if he had not gotten involved in civil rights. He was the privileged son of a distinguished Atlanta clergyman. He had not been born into the poverty and discrimination he was trying to end. He wasn't even aware that racism existed until the sixth grade, when his white friend stopped playing with him because they had gone off to different schools.

As a doctoral student at Boston University, he impressed young women with his care and clothes, unusually well outfitted for a graduate student. Coretta Scott, his future wife, recalled, "He had quite a line." She termed it "intellectual jive." He was a small, unimpressive-looking man until he began to speak. From the beginning he was picked for leadership roles because of his speaking abilities and because he seemed to the press to be much older and more mature than he was. He was only twenty-six years old and a newcomer to Alabama when he became leader of the Montgomery bus boycott.

He often spoke of his own life as something he had no choice in. "As I became involved and as people began to derive inspiration from their involvement, I realized that the choice leaves your own hands. The people expect you to give them leadership."

Although born in 1929, a decade before the older sixties leaders such as Tom Hayden, King thought like a sixties activist—dreaming of something bigger than just the South and an issue larger than segregation. He felt part of an international movement toward freedom.

The FBI under J. Edgar Hoover, whom Eldridge Cleaver called "America's flattest foot," pursued King relentlessly. It spied on him, photographed him, planted informants around him, recorded his conversations. Ostensibly, Hoover was searching for a communist link and convinced Attorney General Robert Kennedy, who committed most of his worst decisions in the service of the cold war, that there was enough cause for concern for Kennedy to okay the wiretaps. King, who clearly saw the failings of capitalism and on rare occasions expressed admiration for Marx, was careful to avoid too much of this type of rhetoric. As far as formal communist ties, all that could be shown is that he knew one or two people who may have at an earlier date had communist connections.

What the FBI turned up was merely very solid evidence that the Reverend Martin Luther King, Jr., had constant sexual relations with a long list of women. Close associates occasionally warned him that the movement might be hurt if stories got out. King once said, "Fucking's a form of anxiety reduction." And few people in the movement could criticize him, since most of them were indulging on occasion as well. "Everybody was out getting laid," said political activist Michael Harrington. But King did it more often—not by chasing women: They pursued him everywhere he went.

The FBI presented photographs and other evidence to select journalists. But no one wanted to report this story. In the 1960s such a story was considered beneath the dignity and ethics of journalists. In 1965 the FBI went so far as to send taped proof of sexual affairs to King and his wife along with a note suggesting that the only solution was for him to take his own life.

But these attacks were not nearly as disturbing to King as the sense that his day was over, that no one really believed in nonviolence anymore. In 1967 he said, "I'll still preach nonviolence with all my might, but I'm afraid it will fall on deaf ears." By 1968 he was clearly depressed, talking constantly about death, and growing fat from compulsive eating. A Nobel Peace Prize did little to cheer him. He told Ralph Abernathy, "Maybe we just have to admit that the day of violence is here, and maybe we have to just give up and let violence take its course. The nation won't listen to our voice. Maybe it will heed the voice of violence."

He said that he was living in a "sick nation." His speeches became morbidly focused on death. He compared himself to Moses, who led his people out of slavery but died on a mountaintop in Jordan in view of the promised land.

In the spring he was periodically spending time in Memphis to support a garbage workers' strike. These segregated jobs for blacks paid only slightly above minimum wage, with no vacation or pensions—an example of how black people were kept from the prosperity of America. An attempted demonstration on March 28 was a disaster for King, with marchers turning to violence, battling police, and demolishing storefronts. On April 3 King returned to Memphis to try again and was greeted by a sarcastic and ridiculing press corps. On the evening of April 4 he was resting in his hotel, preparing his next week's sermon at his church in Atlanta where his father had preached before him, a sermon titled "America May Go to Hell," when he was shot in the right side of the face. He died minutes later.

The day of violence was indeed at hand, as King had predicted. As news spread that King had been killed by an escaped white convict named James Earl Ray, violence spread in the black sections of 120 American cities, with rioting reported in 40. The National Guard moved into many cities that were being burned and looted. That was

April 7, 1968, in Washington, D.C., after the riots
following Martin Luther King, Jr.'s, assassination
(Photo by Burt Glinn/Magnum Photos)

when Chicago's mayor Richard Daley gave his infamous "shoot to kill" order. Millions of dollars of property was destroyed in black neighborhoods, and black people were killed—twelve in Washington, D.C., alone. King, no longer a suspected Uncle Tom with a Nobel Prize, was dead, not yet forty, killed by a white man, at last an authentic black martyr. Stokely Carmichael said, "Now that they've taken Dr. King off, it's time to end this nonviolence bullshit."

CHAPTER 7

A POLISH CATEGORICAL IMPERATIVE

Gross: Good God! Don't you make yourself sick?
Ballas: Do we make ourselves sick, Mr. P?
(Pillar shakes his head.)
Of course we don't. When the good of Man is at stake nothing
will make us sick.

—VÁCLAV HAVEL, The Memorandum,
first performed in the United States in 1968

O N MARCH 8, several hundred University of Warsaw students, a demonstration so small it could have fit in one of the lecture halls, marched to the rector's office, demanded to see him, and shouted, "No studies without freedom!" Then they marched through the gated campus. This would have seemed a minor incident on an American campus in 1968, where thousands were marching, seizing buildings, forcing schools to close, but nothing like this had happened in Poland before. Workers' militia, trained to fend off any attempt at "counterrevolution," about five hundred of them, arrived by truck in civilian clothes but wearing the red and white of the Polish flag on armbands. They said they wanted to talk to the students, but after a short time talking they took out clubs and in the presence of two hundred police officers chased the students through the campus, beating them while the police arrested those who attempted to flee.

The students were shocked by the brutality and by the unprovoked invasion of the campus in violation of all tradition. After years in which periodic dissident acts led by Jacek Kuroń and Karol Modzelewski had been able to attract only a handful of other dissidents, the government's ruthlessness had created a real movement. The following day twenty thousand students marched through the center of Warsaw. Once again they were clubbed by plainclothesmen. Among those arrested were Kuroń, Modzelewski, and their young protégé, Adam Michnik.

Young Polish communists, the children of the country's elite, made up this new and unprecedented movement. Three of them were children of government ministers. Many had parents who were important Party members. Up until then, an idealistic young Pole, not entirely in agreement with his or her parents, still joined the Communist Party in order to change it, to force it to evolve. Now they were seeing that it was a brutal system prepared to use violence to oppose any change.

The pre–World War II generation of Polish communists had a cynicism that the postwar generation, raised in safety and security, did not learn until 1968. Konstanty Gebert, who was only fifteen years old, joined the protest movement in 1968. His father, who had been a communist organizer in the United States before the war and had returned to Poland after the war to build the new communist state and was serving as a diplomat, was a tough, old-time communist who knew about demonstrations and being arrested. Young Konstanty imagined that his father would be proud of his son, out demonstrating in the streets like a good communist. But that wasn't how his father saw it.

"My father disapproved that I was a hysterical kid engaging in politics, which was terribly disappointing for me. . . . I was brought up in a communist mentality. So here comes a demonstration that shouts socialism, freedom, independence. I thought it was great. I joined it. We fight the police, whatever. I come back home three hours late. 'Dad, we fought the police! For independence!' I was expecting he'd crack open a bottle of vodka and we'd have a great time. They locked me up at home for three days. Exactly what I would do if it happened to my kid. Fifteen years is not the right age for fighting on the streets. But what heartbreak. I thought I'd become one of the boys. Just like Dad."

Young Poles very quickly did learn that it was dangerous and violent to protest in the streets. But far from intimidating them, this brought them out. The next day, students met to protest the arrests and the invasion of their campus and the closing of *Dziady*. Students from the Polytechnical School went out into the streets, cheering Czechoslovakia, denouncing Minister of Interior Moczar and his "Gestapo," and throwing rocks at the police, who responded with tear gas. Traffic police cordoned off the area and plainclothesmen were brought in by truck. They leaped out of the vehicles and once again began clubbing. Other students, demonstrating in a small group by the University of Warsaw campus in front of a church where the heart of composer Frédéric Chopin is buried, were also beaten by plainclothesmen.

On March 11, thousands of students marched into the center of

Warsaw to the gray, totalitarian, art deco facade of the Polish Communist Party headquarters. There, with Party officials looking down from a sixth-floor terrace, the police again emerged, pounding young skulls with thick clubs, knocking young people to the ground, beating them bloody, and dragging them away. Some fought back, throwing debris at police. The battle lasted two hours. The few thousand demonstrators were a small number compared to those who had gathered in Berlin, Rome, and other Western cities to protest the Vietnam War, but for a Soviet bloc country it was a startling occurrence, reported as a front-page story around the world.

Outside the university campus, trucks full of plainclothesmen who arrived were greeted by demonstrators shouting, "Gestapo!" In 1968 there was hardly a demonstration from Warsaw to Berlin to Paris to Chicago to Mexico City that did not compare police to the Nazi storm troopers. In Warsaw, these plainclothes shock troops who arrived by truck, the ones the students called Gestapo, were often workers' militia, who were told that the student protesters were privileged kids who lived in the best apartments and took trips to Paris, all of which was by and large true. Although there were plentiful reports of workers refusing to get in trucks and declining participation in counterdemonstrations, pitting the workers against the students was a successful government strategy. On March 11, before the day had ended, students and militia had battled for almost eight hours on the streets of Warsaw. The government closed factories early for workers to stage counterdemonstrations denouncing the students as "Fifth Columnists."

That same day, March 11, students simultaneously demonstrated in Gdansk, Cracow, Poznan, Wroclaw, and Lodz, all attacked by police with clubs and sometimes with water cannons and tear gas. Students borrowed some of the techniques they had read about from the American civil rights movement. They staged boycotts and sit-ins. At first many students did not understand that they had to actually sit down in a sit-in.

The government reasoned that Warsaw and bourgeois Cracow had demonstrations because of their large elite student populations. But the strong working-class communist roots of the populations in Lodz and Gdansk made it more difficult to explain demonstrations in those cities. In Gdansk the student demonstrators asked the workers to join them. It was well known that in the United States, antiwar demonstrators were calling out to people to "join us!" The students in Gdansk had no more luck with the workers than did the students in Washington with the National Guard. In Poznan students shouted, "Long live the workers of Poznan," but the workers did not join the movement there, either.

Jacek Kuroń recalled, "Before the play, we students wanted to approach the workers. But in very shy and timid ways. No one expected such an outburst. And when it came, the government explained that the students were spoiled privileged Jews, children of the elite."

"In 1968, students had a motto, 'There is no bread without freedom,' " recalled Eugeniusz Smolar, a student activist son of an influential Party member. "Workers thought this a ridiculous slogan—there is no freedom without bread. Bread always comes first. Most of us had never gone without bread. We didn't understand each other." For years to come the government was able to contain protest because either the workers did not support the students and intelligentsia or the students would not support the workers.

Demonstrators carried signs and shouted slogans denouncing the Polish state-controlled press, which wrote of the student movement as hooliganism but refused to actually cover the demonstrations or write about the issues. "Lying press" became one of the leading student grievances. A February writers conference that first attempted peacefully to raise the issue of censorship and the closing of *Dziady* was first mentioned in *Trybuna Ludu* a month later, at the end of March, after weeks of open protests, sit-ins, and street battles. But the violence was being widely reported around the world. In Vienna, Jan Nowak had only to sift through the daily accounts of *Le Monde* and *The New York Times* and other papers in order to broadcast the events in Polish throughout Poland.

In Lodz, Joanna Szczesna was a seventeen-year-old freshman in the university. From a lower-class background, she was a bookworm who had learned of the evils of capitalism from nineteenth-century French novels. She was grateful to be living in a socialist country. "I didn't think that I wasn't free. I could say whatever I wanted at the university. In March, a student at the University of Warsaw who was from Lodz came home and said that Warsaw students had demonstrated against censorship, against the closing of a play, and that the police had beaten them up.

"Maybe I lived in the world of my books, but I was shocked," said Szczesna. "I didn't read the newspaper except the movie section, but now I looked and it was so different. The newspaper talked of hooligans, adventurers, children of the rich, Zionists. This was unacceptable. It was clear that I should participate. There was something in the air—a kind of excitement."

She signed a petition and joined a march protesting the arrests of students and demanding the press write the truth. Her mother,

Jadwiga, a clerk who had always dreamed of being a social worker, feared that there might be violence and insisted on coming along to protect her. For their defense she carried an umbrella. About one thousand people had joined the march when they were suddenly confronted with workers, some of whom knew Jadwiga.

"What are you doing here!" one of the workers demanded of her.

Jadwiga, umbrella at the ready, answered, "What are you doing here!"

A three-day sit-in was declared. The government cut the campus phone lines so that one part of the university did not know what another part was doing. There was a rumor in Joanna's part that the rest of the university had given up. But her mother, Jadwiga, arriving with sandwiches for her daughter, had just come from another part of the university, where she had brought sandwiches to her daughter's boyfriend, and she told her daughter's group that the other areas were still striking. After twenty-four hours, when students started talking of abandoning the sit-in, it was Joanna Szczesna who made the first speech of her life, insisting that they carry through on what they said they would do and proposing following the sit-in with a hunger strike.

"I was an adult, but I was also a child," Joanna said. "I wanted to make our parents join us. I knew that if I went on a hunger strike, my mother would attack the Communist Party headquarters." Someone in the underground heard the speech and asked her to join, and that was how Joanna Szczesna, age seventeen, became a political dissident who would later work with Kuroń, Modzelewski, and Michnik.

The Party said the demonstrators were being manipulated by old Stalinists. The government would not admit that the demonstrations were spontaneous. According to the *Trybuna Ludu*, "The events of March 8 did not emerge deus ex machina. They were preceded by long preparation, many campaigns of smaller size and range but in all preparing both leaders and participants for drastic measures." The leaders they named were Modzelewski and Michnik. But while they and other leaders were in prison, demonstrations around Poland had become a daily occurrence. In fact, they were not being coordinated by anyone. "When I heard I was completely surprised," said Jacek Kuroń, who was also in prison at the time. "We had had a little contact with Wroclaw, but this was all the universities." A series of leaders had been elected for the March 8 demonstration, but they had all been arrested. Most subsequent attempts to pick leaders also resulted in their arrests.

Two weeks of demonstrations around Poland followed. Many demonstrators carried signs saying, "Warsaw Students Are Not

Alone," and burned copies of the official newspapers that were not reporting on the movement.

The government may have been caught off guard, but no one was more astonished than the students themselves. Eugeniusz Smolar said that after years of small discussion groups, "it was a surprise to find out these issues were popular. It was a big surprise that so many at Warsaw University rose up, and a bigger surprise that every major university in the country responded."

It seemed that without discussion many young Poles were questioning their society. Smolar said, "There was something in the air that communism just wasn't offering the freedom they wanted." The communist regime had inadvertently revealed itself to its communist youth. Smolar's wife, Nina, a graduate student at the time, said, "Anti-Semitism was a complete surprise and the violence was another surprise."

Faced with spreading nationwide protest, the 1967 anti-Zionist campaign raged on in 1968. To many Polish communists, especially Jews such as the Smolars, this seemed to completely contradict their idea of what the Communist Party was. All the communist states had banned the expression of anti-Semitism. Adam Michnik said, "When I saw anti-Semitic articles I had never seen such a thing. It was fascism. It wasn't allowed. Until then anti-Semitism was an abstract term. I thought in Poland after the Holocaust, anti-Semitism was impossible." Kuroń said, "Before the war I had seen anti-Semitic communists, but never before as state policy." But to a government desperate to explain the nationwide protest movement, a theory of Zionist conspiracy suited its needs perfectly.

On Michnik's arrest on March 9, interrogators demanded, "Mr. Michnik, after you are released, will you immigrate to Israel?"

"Only if you immigrate to Russia," was his defiant response. But he was pressured, told he would be released if he agreed to go to Israel. Poland wanted finally to be rid of its Jews. Gomułka announced that, as had been done the previous year during the Six Day War, emigration passports were being made available for any Jews wishing to go to Israel.

On March 15, an article appeared in the *Trybuna Ludu* explaining what Zionism was.

It is a fact commonly known that money collection among the Americans of Jewish descent brought hundreds of millions of dollars to Israel. These funds enable Israel to develop its economic potential and its army, to wage aggressive wars against the Arab states [the latest was the third war with the Arabs] and also serve to cover expenses connected with the occupation of the Arab lands. . . . The Zionist leaders are calling for aid to finance the Israeli expansionist policy supported by the imperialist powers, specifically the USA and West Germany. With the help of Israel, Imperialism desires to abolish progressive Arab governments, strengthen its control over Arab petroleum and transform the Middle East into a springboard against the Soviet Union and other socialist states. In justification of the aggressive policy of Israeli ruling circles and pandering to Imperialism, the Zionist propaganda attempts to make world public opinion believe that Israel struggles for its existence and that it is threatened by the Arabs who wish to "drive Israel to the sea". . . .

But increasingly the word *Zionist* was becoming code for "student organizer." The problem, the government insisted, was caused by a Zionist plot, a Stalinist conspiracy. It was overindulgent parents and Stalinist professors, all of whom happened to be Jewish, who had coddled a few devious people such as Kuroń, Modzelewski, and Michnik. On March 26 the *Trybuna Ludu* attacked professors, singling out the colleges of philosophy, economics, and law—the ideological departments. "These scholars systematically defended revisionist factions, while using their authority and privileged scientific and university position, whenever these factions came into conflict with the state law or university regulation." Misguided by having received a Stalinist education, these professors coddled dangerous and persistent subversives:

> Threatened by sanctions, each time they turned to their science professors for protection. During various sessions and meetings they defended the students with the excuse that "young people must have their fling" and in fact though they spoke ambiguously, the professors were encouraging the students' political activity. Some professors even defended them in court. W. Brus, appearing as a witness for the defense in the trial against K. Modzelewski, characterized him as . . . "an honest, idealistic man committed to the cause of building socialism and awakening the political interests of the young." It is difficult to imagine a more clear-cut encouragement to the remaining members of the group.

W. Brus, Wlodzimierz Brus, was one of many university professors of Jewish background who was removed from his position early in

March. Now the government began removing more professors and instructors from the faculty, most of them of Jewish origin. Beginning March 12, the government began singling out Jewish students as leaders of the movement. Three highly placed government officials of Jewish backgrounds were removed from their positions and informed that their children were student leaders. Purges, mostly of Jews, followed. Poets, philosophers, and professors of Jewish origin throughout the Polish university system were accused of complicity in the conspiracy, and many were fired. On March 18, Roman Zambrowski, a former member of the Politburo, was found to be one of the plotters of the student movement and was removed from the Party. Zambrowski had no particular tie to the student movement, but he was a Jew and a political adversary of Moczar. His son, Antoni, a student accused of being a leader, had no connection to the movement. It became clear to the students as more and more Jews lost their jobs and more and more students were beaten and arrested that the government had chosen its line on the uprising and the students' grievances were not going to be addressed.

The other factor that spurred on the spontaneous student uprisings was the events in Czechoslovakia. Polish students carried signs saying, "*Polska Czeka na Dubčzeka!*"—"Poland Awaits Its Dubček!" Some historians say Dubček was doomed the minute those signs went up in Warsaw. Moscow's nightmare from the moment Dubček had come to power in January was that Czechoslovakian reform would spark a movement that would sweep across central Europe.

Poles cherish a heroic image of themselves, unshared by and little known in the outside world. One of their self-glorifying images is that of the defiant Pole. According to the Polish version of history, the Czechs allowed German occupation and the Poles resisted. The Czechs accepted communism in 1948 and the Poles resisted. The Poles rebelled in 1956 and supported the uprising in Budapest, while the Czechs said nothing and remained loyal to Moscow. Poles recall the fact that they sent a food shipment to support the Hungarian rebels, but the trucks had to pass through Czechoslovakia, where they were stopped. In the complicated pecking order of central Europe's national images, Poles say that in 1956 "the Hungarians acted like Poles, the Poles like Czechs, and the Czechs acted like pigs."

Now the Czechs, whom the Poles had sneered at under Novotný's Stalinist anachronism, were becoming the vanguard communist nation, the one to be followed. "It was surprising to see the Czechs ahead of us.

They were supposed to be the opportunists and cowards," said Eugeniusz Smolar.

Neither the government nor the students could fully understand this
unorganized movement. The activists, cut off from their leaders, didn't
know what to do with it. "We were just not prepared for either the
brutal response of the government or the popular response of the
people," said Eugeniusz Smolar. "We just were not prepared."

On March 22, with the Western press full of stories of student sit-ins
in Cracow, Warsaw, and other Polish cities, and with the Polish press
writing only of Zionists, hooligans, Stalinists, and troublemakers, the
Soviet public read of Polish unrest for the first time. That same day
Tass, the Soviet news agency, reported on the removal of Novotný from
his second post as president of Czechoslovakia while *Pravda,* the Soviet
Communist Party newspaper, and *Izvestia,* the government newspaper,
reported at length on the "anti-Soviet agitators" in Poland.

Also on March 22, the Yippies—Abbie Hoffman, Jerry Rubin, and
Paul Krassner—attended a meeting in Lake Villa, Illinois—a gathering
of what had come to be known as the New Left, the youth movements
of 1968. The meeting was called by the Mobe, the National Mobilization Committee to End the War in Vietnam. Tom Hayden and Rennie
Davis of the SDS were also there. The topic was how to protest during
the Democratic Party convention that would take place in Chicago the
following August. Blocking the city traffic with a funeral march as
Johnson was nominated was one suggestion. An attack on the convention was another. Abbie Hoffman—rebel, clown, and media genius—
was, as always, outrageous. He sat through the meeting smoking
marijuana and throwing out ideas. One was calling for an end to paid
toilets. Another was a gesture on the part of the Mobe in support of
Polish student protesters. Neither suggestion was adopted.

On March 24, while sit-ins were spreading to every university in
Poland and more and more "Zionist conspirators" were being
removed from office, a letter was released from the bishops of the
Polish Catholic Church saying that the student movement was "striv-
ing for truth and freedom, which is the natural right of each human
being. . . ." The bishops went on to say that the "brutal use of force
disgraces human dignity." This letter was the beginning of a new
alliance in Poland. Never before had the Catholic Church and the leftist intelligentsia fought on the same side. According to Michnik, this
letter caused a radical change in thinking. "Traditionally the Left in
Poland is anticleric," said Michnik. "I was too until 1968. When the
Church issued a letter supporting the students, for the first time I

thought maybe the Church is not an enemy. Maybe it could be a partner in dialogue."

On March 28 three thousand students in Warsaw demonstrated,
demanding an end to censorship, free trade unions, and a youth movement independent of the Communist Party. It was to be the last demonstration. Eight university departments were closed and one thousand of
the University of Warsaw's seven thousand students were left without a
curriculum and told they would have to reapply for entry. Another
thirty-four were expelled. "All of us have had enough of mass meetings. There will be and can be no tolerance of trouble-mongers and
people of ill will," the *Trybuna Ludu* announced.

With almost a thousand students in prison, the student movement
was shut down. The government continued to find Zionist ringleaders
to be removed from their posts.

The universities were irreparably damaged as many of the best
faculty members fled to escape anti-Semitism and were replaced by
party hacks. A Pole had only to express desire to move to Israel and
show proof of Jewish origin to leave. One man was stopped because he
could not show that he was Jewish. His only proof was a paper from
the government denouncing him as a Zionist. All but about one thousand Jews left the country, essentially ending Judaism in Poland.

But Eugeniusz and Nina Smolar stayed. "March 1968 was the last
time anyone believed the system could evolve," said Eugeniusz.
"People used to join the Communist Party to change it. To do
anything, to be a player, you had to be in the Party. After March 1968
people who joined were much more cynical, using the Party as a vehicle for personal advancement."

Michnik was another Jew who stayed. But he stayed in prison. He
was later asked if when sitting in prison, with the university destroyed
and its intellectual life silenced, he had thought he'd made a huge
mistake. Without hesitation, this small, energetic man jutted out his
jaw and said, "I never thought that. Part of my education was the
silence of my parents during the trials of 1935. You must always
protest against dictatorship. It is what Immanuel Kant called a cate-
gorical imperative."

Smolar said, "The 1968 generation was born of fire. They learned
from experience and were active in all the movements that followed."
They did learn to join with both the church and the workers, or, as a
writer put it in *Trybuna Ludu* in unwittingly prophetic language, "The
events at the University pointed out that apart from the prevailing
naïveté and credulity some students had great potential, were ideolog-

ically committed and willing to change the country for the better. We now wait for this capital to bear fruit."

Joanna Szcesna was only nineteen the first time she went to prison. She amused the other prisoners by reciting *Gone With the Wind* and the Galsworthy novels. In 1981, when the movement had grown, joined by workers and clergy, to such size that the government declared martial law in an attempt to contain it, Joanna's mother, Jadwiga, was the oldest woman interned. Joanna said, "I think I was a bad influence on her."

CHAPTER 8

POETRY, POLITICS, AND A TOUGH SECOND ACT

I have left Act I for involution
and Act II. There mired in complexity
I cannot write Act III
　　　　　　—EUGENE MCCARTHY, *"Lament of
　　　　　　　an Aging Politician,"* 1968

1968 WAS ONE OF THOSE rare times in America when poetry seemed to matter. Telephone service in New York City in 1968 offered a "dial-a-poem." A government pilot program that year sent poets around the country to public high schools to give readings and discussions. The response was wildly enthusiastic. In Detroit, poet Donald Hall was trapped in a hallway at Amelia Earhart Junior High School by excited students shouting, "Say us a poem!" Obligingly he shouted one, but then the crowd had doubled with new arrivals and he had to read it again.

Robert Lowell, born to a patrician Boston family in 1917, the year of John Kennedy's birth, seemed a poet for the sixties. Like the Mobe's David Dellinger, who was from a similar background, Lowell was a pacifist who had served a prison term rather than fight in World War II. In the sixties, he was a frequent fixture at antiwar rallies. By 1968 he was the most visible American poet, because he campaigned with Eugene McCarthy.

Allen Ginsberg, born in 1926, was closer in age to Lowell than he was to the students of 1968. But Ginsberg, even in his forties, balding and a bit paunchy, with his thick beard and wreath of wild dark hair, had both the personal spirit and literary style that characterized the sixties. He was really a fifties figure, a central figure of the beat generation. But by 1968 many of the beats had faded. Jack Kerouac was dissipated from alcohol and did not approve of the antiwar movement. He accused his old friend Ginsberg of being unpatriotic. Neal Cassady died in Mexico in early 1968 while undertaking a fifteen-mile hike following a railroad line. He said he would pass the time counting railroad ties. But along the way he managed to get himself invited to a wedding party, where he spent hours drinking and taking Seconal. He was found the next day along the railroad tracks where he had spent the rainy night. Suffering from overexposure, he soon died, exiting in that free and offbeat style that had made his group famous. According to legend, his last words were, "Sixty-four thousand nine hundred and twenty-eight."

Despite losing many friends to alcohol and drugs, Ginsberg was a passionate believer in certain drugs, especially marijuana, psilocybin, and LSD. In fact, although he was a determined adversary of the Vietnam War and the American military and industrial war machine, there were three other topics that he seemed to bring up on most occasions. One was fair treatment for homosexuals. Always extremely candid in his poetry, some said graphic, about his own sexual preference, he was a gay rights activist before the term was invented. And he always championed his theories on the beneficial uses of narcotics as well as the unfair persecution of users. He was also a persistent believer in the value of Buddhist chants. By 1968, when Eastern religion had become a trend, it was easy to forget that Ginsberg had been very serious about his Buddhism for a number of years. Hinduism was also in vogue, especially having a guru, a new enough word in 1968 for the press to usually offer the pronunciation (goo-roo).

Mahesh Yogi, who gave himself the title Maharishi—"great sage"— had found a formula for instant meditation, which he promised would deliver *samadhi,* a holy state of expanded consciousness, without going to all the trouble of fasting and endless prayer. He converted Europeans by the thousands to "Transcendental Meditation" before arriving in the United States in 1968, bringing with him a fad for Indian clothes and Indian music. Many celebrities, including the Beatles and the Beach Boys, followed the Maharishi Mahesh Yogi. But when the Beatles went to India to spend three months studying under the Maharishi, Ringo Starr, always said to be the least reflective of the quartet, returned with his wife, Maureen, to his suburban London mansion after ten days, unhappy with the great sage's accommodations. "Maureen and I are a bit funny about our food, and we don't like spicy things," Ringo explained.

The Maharishi was of limited appeal to poet and seasoned chanter Ginsberg because he opposed LSD and urged young people to accept the draft. Ginsberg continued to chant, oppose the war, and champion the rights of homosexuals and the use of hallucinogenic drugs.

By the 1960s Ginsberg had become one of the most venerated living poets and was invited to speak around the world, though in many of these countries, including the United States, the Soviet Union, Cuba, Czechoslovakia, and Italy, he found himself in legal difficulties for the things he said.

Known for his kindness, he is still remembered in his East Village, New York, neighborhood as a soft-spoken gentleman. His free-form passionate verse was from its first publication both controversial and widely recognized as brilliant. He sometimes gave readings with his father, Louis, who was also a poet. Louis, a New Jersey schoolteacher, could not resist the more than occasional pun in his comments and wrote well-constructed, lyric poetry, often in rhymed couplets. The relationship was one of love and mutual respect, though Louis thought his son should be a little less free-form. He also thought his son should not use scatological words that embarrassed people and wished he would be a little less forthcoming about his homosexuality. But that was the way Allen was. He talked publicly about whom he loved, whom he lusted after, and how. Once he went too far and referred to an extramarital dalliance of his father's, and Louis got him to remove the lines. Their readings together, in the age of "the generation gap," were considered a great show—Louis in his tweeds and Allen in his beads.

In 1966 they had appeared together in the Ginsberg hometown of Paterson, New Jersey. Louis read to his many local fans, and the more famous son read political poems but also his poem about Paterson. They talked about how father and son had visited Passaic Falls the day before, Louis calling it an intimate moment shared. Then Allen, who always volunteered the unrequested detail, said that while at the falls he had smoked marijuana, which had added greatly to the experience. The next day Paterson mayor Frank X. Graves, contending that he had received numerous calls about the drug confession, got a bench warrant for the younger Ginsberg's arrest, whereupon the police found and detained a man with a beard and glasses, mistaking him for the wanted poet, who was by then safely back in the East Village.

By 1968, when they appeared together at the Brooklyn Academy of Music, a bearded, pot-smoking hippie was more commonplace, though it was still curious to see the two together. Louis began by punning and Allen began by chanting a mantra that *The New York Times* reviewer said was longer than any of his poems. They ended the evening with a family squabble about LeRoi Jones's recent illegal firearms possession conviction. To the son it was clear the black playwright had been framed—to the father it wasn't. The audience was also divided, and each Ginsberg had his cheerers.

LeRoi Jones was also one of the popular poets of the 1968 generation. His most famous line was fast becoming "Up against the wall motherfucker this is a stick-up." A 1967 East Village "affinity group" named themselves "the Motherfuckers" after the Jones poem. An affinity group used intense intellectual debates as an underpinning for carrying out the kind of media-grabbing street theater that Abbie Hoffman could do so well. During the New York City garbage strike, the Motherfuckers hauled garbage by subway from the redolent mountains of it left on the sidewalks to the newly opened Lincoln Center.

The bestselling poet of 1968 was Rod McKuen, who penned rhythmic little bon mots that he read in a raspy voice suggestive either of emotion or bronchitis. A Hollywood songwriter, clean-shaven with V-neck sweaters, McKuen was a long way from the beats. But by early 1968 he had already sold 250,000 volumes of his unabashedly sentimental verse. His two books, *Stanyan Street and Other Sorrows* and *Listen to the Warm,* were selling more than any book on *The New York Times* fiction bestseller list, although they were not listed, because poetry was not included on bestseller lists. With characteristic self-effacing candor, he said in a 1968 interview, "I'm not a poet; I'm a stringer of words." When he came down with hepatitis, fans by the hundreds sent him stuffed animals. To many, he and his fans seemed unbearable.

If a songwriter is a poet, stronger candidates were available in 1968 than McKuen. Bob Dylan had made his position clear by choosing the stage name Dylan. There was a distant relation between his richly worded lyricism and that of the Welsh poet Dylan Thomas. The Doors named their group from a line of William Blake's poetry: "the doors of perception." In *Life* magazine, Jim Morrison, lead singer of the Doors, was called "a very good actor and a very good poet," in fact "an amplified poet in black leather pants." It did not matter that the words at times would not have conveyed the point without the embellishment of Morrison's shrill screams. Paul Simon and Art Garfunkel, whose ballads featured lyrics full of metaphor and imagery, were to many fans poets. But the songwriter of the pair, Paul Simon, dismissed the idea. "I've tried poetry, but it has nothing to do with my songs. . . . But the lyrics of pop songs are so banal that if you show a spark of intelligence, they call you a poet. And if you say you're not a poet, then people think you're putting yourself down. But the people who call you a poet are people who never read poetry. Like poetry was something defined by Bob Dylan. They never read, say, Wallace Stevens. That's poetry."

On the other hand, few doubted that Ginsberg was a poet and no one that Ezra Pound was one, the octogenarian artifact of the birth of twentieth-century poetry, now sitting out his days in Italy. Despite Pound's fascism and anti-Semitism, he and his politically conservative protégé T. S. Eliot remained on the cultural list of the 1968 generation. Even without studying poetry, the lineage was clear. If there had been no Pound, there would have been no Eliot and there would have been no Dylan Thomas, no Lawrence Ferlinghetti, no Allen Ginsberg. Or they would have written very differently.

Ginsberg acknowledged his debt to Pound, so the Jewish poet or, as he liked to say, Jewish Buddhist poet wanted to visit Pound. When he did in 1967 in Venice, he did not recite his own poetry. Instead, after dinner he rolled marijuana in cigarette paper and, without comment, smoked it. Then he played records for the elderly poet—the Beatles' "Yellow Submarine" and "Eleanor Rigby," Bob Dylan's "Sad-Eyed Lady of the Lowlands," "Absolutely Sweet Marie," and "Gates of Eden," and Donovan's "Sunshine Superman." Pound smiled as he listened, seemed particularly to enjoy certain lines, tapped his ivory-handled cane to the music, but never said a word. Ginsberg was later assured by the elderly poet's longtime partner, Olga Rudge, that if he had not appreciated the offering, he would have walked out of the room.

Just who was and wasn't a poet was becoming an issue.

Politics had much to do with tastes in poetry. Russian poets, especially if they were politically outspoken, were garnering huge followings among college students in the West. Yevgeny Yevtushenko was having a big year in 1968, both in political controversy at home and in artistic recognition abroad. Born in 1933, he belonged to a new school of Russian lyric poetry. Critics frequently suggested that others from the new school, such as Boris Pasternak's protégé Andrey Voznesensky, also born in 1933, were better poets. But in the 1960s Yevtushenko was the most famous working Russian poet in the world. In 1962 he published four poems highly critical of the Soviet Union, including "Babi Yar," about a massacre of Jews unsuccessfully covered up by the Soviets.

In 1965, when Ginsberg was in Russia, in between being thrown out of Cuba and being thrown out of Czechoslovakia, he met with his famous Russian colleague. Yevtushenko told Ginsberg that he had heard many scandalous things about him but did not believe them. Ginsberg assured him that they were probably true. He explained that since he was a homosexual and that was the reality he lived in, the scandals came from his willingness to speak openly about his experiences.

The Russian grew visibly uncomfortable as he said, "I know nothing of such matters." Ginsberg quickly changed the subject to another favorite, drug use. Yevtushenko said, "These two subjects—homosexuality and narcotics—are not known to me, and I feel they are juvenile preoccupations. They have no importance here in Russia to us."

In 1962, when British composer Benjamin Britten wrote *War Requiem*, he was not thinking about Vietnam. He was commemorating the reopening of Coventry Cathedral, bombed during World War II. The text came from Wilfred Owen's poems about World War I. But by 1968 *War Requiem* was considered to be "antiwar," and anything that was antiwar had a following. Wilfred Owen's nearly forgotten poems were being read again, not only because they expressed a hatred of war, but because of his sad life story. Owen had been a company commander in World War I who discovered his poetic talent while venting about his war experiences. He almost went on to a brilliant literary career, but a week before the war ended he was killed in combat at the age of twenty-five and most of his work was published posthumously. In 1968 not only was the poetry of Owen becoming popular again, but also that of Rupert Brooke, another young poet who died in World War I. The poet-victim of war seemed to be an irresistible setting for literature in 1968. Even Guillaume Apollinaire, the French writer who died the day before World War I ended from a shrapnel wound to the head months earlier, was attaining cult status in 1968. Better known in the art world as the critic who promoted Picasso, Braque, Derain, his own mistress, Marie Laurencin, and many others—the inventor of the word *surreal*—he was also a poet. In 1968, when a new English translation of *The Poet Assassinated* was published, Richard Freedman, reviewing it for *Life,* said, "A half-century after his death Apollinaire is more than ever a big man on campus."

It seemed the literary capital of writers who had opposed wars, any wars, was on the rise. Hermann Hesse, the German pacifist who moved to Switzerland to evade military service in World War I, was enjoying a popularity among youth greater than he had known during most of his life. Although he died in 1962, his novels, with an almost Marcusian sense of the alienating quality of modern society and a fascination with Asian mysticism, were perfectly suited to the youth of the late sixties. He might have been amazed to discover that in October 1967 a hard-driving electric rock band would name itself after his novel *Steppenwolf*.

According to the twenty-four-year-old Canadian lead singer, guitar and harmonica player, John Kay, the group, best known in 1968 for "Born to Be Wild," had a philosophy similar to that of the hero of the Hesse novel. "He rejects middle-class standards," Kay explained, "and yet he wants to find happiness within or alongside them. So do we."

In 1968, it seemed everyone aspired to be a poet. Eugene McCarthy, senator and presidential candidate, published his first two poems in the April 12 issue of *Life* magazine. He said that he had started writing poetry about a year before. Since no one in the working press believes that a politician does anything just by chance in an election year, *Life* magazine columnist Shana Alexander pointed out, "Lately McCarthy has discovered, with some surprise, that people who like his politics also tend to like poetry. Crowds surge forward eagerly when they learn Robert Lowell is traveling with the candidate."

This turn toward verse showed in McCarthy an understanding of his supporters that was surprising in a candidate who was seldom caught doing anything to curry favor. Most of the time, conventional political professionals and the journalists who covered them did not understand him at all. McCarthy would skip speeches and events without warning. When television host David Frost asked him what he wanted his obituary to say, McCarthy answered without the least suggestion of irony, "He died, I suppose." His tremendous popularity on college campuses and among the youth who did not like conventional politics initially arose because, until Kennedy entered the race, he was the only candidate committed to an immediate end to the Vietnam War. Early in his campaign, the antiwar leftists such as Allard Lowenstein, who had constructed his candidacy, were so frustrated by the senator's ambiguous style and lack of passion that they started to fear they had picked the wrong man. Some thought they should appeal to Bobby Kennedy, Lowenstein's first choice, one last time. But McCarthy's style appealed to young people who disliked leaders and appreciated a candidate who didn't act like one. They talked about him as though he were a poet who later became a senator, although the less romantic truth that he was able to reinvent himself as a poet in midcampaign may be a more impressive stunt.

It was *Life*'s Shana Alexander who had labeled him a "conundrum," explaining, "One's first response to him is surprise. Admiration, if it comes, comes later." Perhaps part of his appeal to college students was that he looked and sounded more like a professor than a candidate. Asked about the riots in the black Los Angeles neighborhood of Watts, he mystified everyone by comparing them to a peasant uprising in 1381.

"McCarthy for President" campaign poster, 1968
(Chicago Historical Society)

Norman Mailer, in describing the candidate's faults at the campaign's final hours in Chicago, may have hit on exactly the source of his appeal to young antiwar activists of 1968:

He spoke in his cool, offhand style, now famous for its lack of emphasis, lack of power, lack of dramatic concentration, as if the first desire of all men must not be the Presidency, but the necessity to avoid any forcing of one's own person (as if the first desire of the Devil might be to make you the instrument of your own will). He had insisted after all these months of campaigning that he must remain himself, and never rise to meet the occasion, never put force into his presentation because external events seemed to demand that a show of force of oratorical power would here be most useful. No, McCarthy was proceeding on the logic of the saint, which is not to say that he necessarily saw himself as one (although there must have been moments!) but that his psychology was kin: God would judge the importance of the event, not man, and God would give the tongue to speak, if tongue was the organ to be manifested.

Given how unusual a year this was, it may have made sense for McCarthy to publish his poetry in midcampaign, but the contents of the poem seem ill chosen. Why would someone running for the office of president of the United States volunteer that he felt mired in Act II and could not write Act III? Asked to explain his poem, why he could not write the third act, he said, "I don't really want to write it," which for many supporters, reporters, and political professionals confirmed the suspicion that he did not really want to be president. But the senator mused on, "You know the old rules: Act I states the problem, Act II deals with the complications, and Act III resolves them. I am an Act II man. That's where I live. Involution and complexity."

McCarthy mused further about everyone from Napoleon to FDR and finally came to his rival Robert Kennedy. "Bobby is an Act I man. He says here's a problem. Here's another problem. Here's another one. He never really deals with Act II, but I think maybe he's beginning to write Act III. Bobby's tragedy is that to beat me, he's going to have to destroy his brother. Today I occupy most of Jack's positions on the board. That's kind of Greek, isn't it?"

Whatever similarities existed between Gene McCarthy and the late John Kennedy, they were seen by few other than the Minnesota senator himself. On the other hand, Bobby Kennedy, many hoped, might be like his brother. But others appreciated that he was not in any way like his older brother Jack except for the Cape Cod Yankee accent and a trace of family resemblance around the eyes. Robert was born in 1925, eight years after Jack. He was not entirely a part of the World War II generation because he had been too young to serve, though his adolescence was steeped in the thinking and experiences of that time, including having his brother, ten years older, killed in combat. By 1950 he was already twenty-five, too old to experience childhood or adolescence in the 1950s. So he was born on a cusp, not quite one generation or the other, tied to the older generation by his family. In the 1950s he participated in the cold war, even serving as a lawyer for the infamous anticommunist senator Joseph McCarthy. The relationship did not last long, and Kennedy would later describe it as a mistake. He said that though misguided, he had been genuinely concerned about communist infiltration. But perhaps a better explanation lay in the fact that his father had gotten him the job.

Robert Kennedy struggled to live up to his father and his big brothers. Having missed World War II, he always admired warriors, men at war. In 1960 at a Georgetown party he was asked what he would like to be if he could do it all over again, and he said, "A paratrooper." He lacked his big brothers' ease and charm. But he was the one who understood how to use television for the charming president, arranging for John Kennedy to be the first television president by hiring the first media adviser ever employed by a White House. John, understanding little of television, was a natural because he was easy, relaxed, and witty, and he smiled handsomely. Little brother Bobby, who understood television perfectly well, was terrible at it, looking awkward and intense because he was awkward and intense. John used to laugh at Bobby's serious nature, calling him "Black Robert." Seeing how it turned out, it is now easy to think that, with his sober intensity, he always looked like a man slated for a cruel destiny. "Doom was woven in your nerves," Robert Lowell wrote of him.

He was slight, lacking the robust appearance of his brothers, and unlike his brothers, he was genuinely religious, a devout Roman Catholic, and a faithful and devoted husband. He loved children. Where other politicians would smile with babies or strike an instructive pose with children, Bobby always looked as though he wanted to run off and play with them. Children could sense this and were happy and uninhibited around him.

How did this man who worshiped warfare, wished he had been a paratrooper, was a cold warrior, even authorizing wiretaps on Martin Luther King because he feared he had communist ties—how did he become a hero of the sixties generation and the New Left? There was a moment when Tom Hayden had considered calling off the plans for Chicago demonstrations if Bobby was to be nominated.

In 1968 Robert Kennedy was forty-two years old and seemed much younger. Eight years earlier, when Tom Hayden had walked up to him at the Democratic convention in Los Angeles and brashly introduced himself, the chief impression Hayden walked away with was that he seemed so young. Perhaps that was why the boyhood nickname Bobby always stuck. There was Bobby, at the end of a tough day of campaigning, looking as if he were twelve years old as he settled into his evening ritual of a big bowl of ice cream.

Kennedy was obsessed with self-improvement and probably at the same time with finding himself. He carried books with him to study. For a time it was Edith Hamilton's *The Greek Way*, which led him to read the Greeks, especially Aeschylus. For a while he carried around Emerson. And Camus had his turn. His press secretary, Frank Mankiewicz, complained that he had little time for local politicians but hours to chat with literary figures such as Robert Lowell, whom he knew well.

Although busy with his campaign, he was eager to meet poet Allen Ginsberg. He listened respectfully as the shaggy poet explained his beliefs about drug enforcement being persecution. The poet asked the senator if he had ever smoked marijuana, and he said that he had not. They talked politics about possible alliances between flower power and Black Power—between hippies and black militants. As the lean senator was walking the stocky, bearded poet to the door of his Senate office, Ginsberg took out a harmonium and chanted a mantra for several minutes. Kennedy waited until Ginsberg fell silent. Then he said, "Now what's supposed to happen?"

Ginsberg explained that he had just finished a chant to Vishnu, the god of preservation in the Hindu religion, and had thus been offering a chant for the preservation of the planet.

"You ought to sing it to the guy up the street," said Kennedy, pointing toward the White House.

While he had little chemistry with Martin Luther King and the two always seemed to struggle to speak to each other, he struck up an immediate and natural friendship with the California farmworker leader César Chávez. With the slogan "*Viva la Huelga!*"—"Long Live the Strike!"—Chávez had launched successful national campaigns for what he called *la Causa,* boycotting California grapes and other products to force better conditions for farmworkers. Most self-respecting college students in 1968 would not touch a grape for fear it was a brand being boycotted by Chávez. He had organized seventeen thousand farmworkers and forced their pay to be raised $1.10 an hour to a minimum $1.75. Chávez was a hero of the younger generation, and Kennedy and Chávez, the wealthy patrician and the immigrant spokesman, seemed oddly natural together even if Bobby was famous for ending a rally with "*Viva la Huelga! Viva la Causa!*" and then, his Spanish seemingly failing to match his enthusiasm, "*Viva all of you.*"

Bobby even developed a rapport and sense of humor with the press. His standard campaign speech ended with a quote from George Bernard Shaw, and after a time he noticed the press took this as their cue to go to the press bus. One day he ended a speech, "As George Bernard Shaw once said—Run for the bus."

He had clearly evolved in profound ways since the death of his brother. He seemed to have discovered his own worth, found the things he cared about rather than the family's issues, and was willing to champion them even if it meant going against his old allies from those heady and revered days of his still-mourned brother's administration. To turn

against the war had been a deep personal struggle. He had named one
of his sons, born in 1965, after General Maxwell Taylor and another in
1967 after Averell Harriman and Douglas Dillon—three of the key
figures in pursuing the war.

Even if he was not a great speaker, he said extraordinary things.
Unlike politicians today, he told people not what they wanted to hear,
but what he thought they should hear. He always emphasized personal
responsibility in much the same terms, with a similar religious fervor,
as did Martin Luther King, Jr. Championing the right causes was an
obligation. While adopting a strong antiwar position, he criticized
student draft dodgers, going onto campuses where he was met by
cheering crowds and lecturing them on passing on their responsibilities
to less privileged people by refusing the draft. But he also said that
those who did not agree with what their government was doing in Vietnam were obligated to speak out because in a democracy the war was
being carried on "in your name."

McCarthy did some of this as well, telling his young supporters that
they had to work hard and look better for the campaign. Supporters
cut their hair, lowered hemlines, and shaved their faces to get "clean for
Gene."

But Kennedy went to extraordinary lengths to define what was
wrong and what needed to be done. He attacked the national obsession
with economic growth, a statement Hayden cited for its similarity to
the Port Huron Statement:

> We will find neither national purpose nor personal satisfaction in
> a mere continuation of economic progress, in an endless amassing
> of worldly goods. We cannot measure national spirit by the Dow
> Jones Average, nor national achievement by the Gross National
> Product. For the Gross National Product includes air pollution,
> and ambulances to clear our highways from carnage. It counts
> special locks for our doors and jails for the people who break
> them. The Gross National Product includes the destruction of the
> redwoods and the death of Lake Superior. It grows with the
> production of napalm and missiles and nuclear warheads. . . . It
> includes . . . the broadcasting of television programs which
> glorify violence to sell goods to our children.
>
> And if the Gross National Product includes all this, there is
> much that it does not comprehend. It does not allow for the
> health of our families, the quality of their education, or the joy of
> their play. It is indifferent to the decency of our factories and the

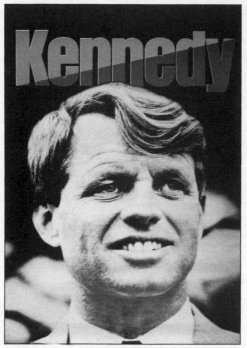

*"Robert Kennedy for President" campaign poster, 1968
(John F. Kennedy Library and Museum)*

safety of our streets alike. It does not include the beauty of our
poetry, or the strength of our marriages, the intelligence of our
public debate or the integrity of our public officials . . . the Gross
National Product measures neither our wit nor our courage,
neither our wisdom nor our learning, neither our compassion nor
our devotion to our country. It measures everything, in short,
except that which makes life worthwhile, and it can tell us everything about America—except whether we are proud to be Americans.

Could a man who said such revolutionary things actually get to the
White House? Yes, it was possible, because this, after all, was a
Kennedy. Most McCarthy supporters, at their most optimistic, thought
the campaign might stop the war but quietly believed their man was
unelectable. But Robert Kennedy had a real chance of becoming president, and though historians since have debated on what kind of presi-

dent he might have been, he was a man the younger generation could relate to and even believe in, a hero even in a year poisoned by King's murder.

Kennedy had endless energy for campaigning, and he might catch up to and pass McCarthy, he might even beat Hubert Humphrey, the vice president who would certainly pick up Johnson's mantle and step into the race. Even with that Nixon nightmare—another contest with a Kennedy—pollsters said Bobby could win. If he could catch up to McCarthy in the spring, he might be unstoppable. But then what weighed on Kennedy and most of his supporters and detractors was the thought that he might be unstoppable—unless someone stopped him with a bullet.

CHAPTER 9

SONS AND DAUGHTERS
OF THE NEW FATHERLAND

> How will it be to belong to a nation, to work in the spiritual
> tradition of a nation that never knew how to become a nation,
> under whose desperate, megalomaniac efforts to become a
> nation the world has had to suffer so much! To be a German
> author—what will that be? Back of every sentence that we
> construct in our language stands a broken, a spiritually burnt-
> out people . . . a people that can never show its face again.
> —THOMAS MANN, "*The Tragedy of Germany*," 1946

IT WILL NEVER BE completely comprehensible to other peoples
what it was like to be German and born in the late 1940s, the
concentration camps closed, the guilty scattered, the dead vanished.
The twenty-first-century public drama of Gerhard Schröder, born in
1944, elected chancellor of Germany in 1998, is a story of his generation. He never knew his father, who died in the war before he was born.
How his father died or who he was remained a mystery. While in office
as chancellor, Schröder found a faded photograph of his father as a
German soldier but could learn little else about him. The possibilities
were frightening.

After World War II, when there were not two but four Germanies—
the American, British, French, and Russian sectors—the policy in all
four sectors was what the Americans called "de-Nazification," a purge
of high and low Nazi officials from all responsible positions and war
crime trials for all ranking Nazis.

In 1947 the United States launched its Marshall Plan to rebuild
European economies. The Russians declined to participate and soon
there were two Germanies and two Europes and the cold war had
begun. In 1949 the United States established its own Germany, West
Germany, with a capital in Bonn, a city as far as possible from the East.

The Soviets responded with an East Germany whose capital was in the divided old capital of Berlin. By July 1950, when the cold war had become a shooting war in Korea, de-Nazification was quietly dropped in West Germany. Nazis, after all, had always been reliable anticommunists. But in East Germany, the purge continued.

There had always been a north and south Germany, Protestants in the north and Catholics in the south, with different foods and different accents. But there had never been an East and West Germany. The new 858-mile border had neither cultural nor historic logic. Those in the west were told they were free, whereas the easterners were oppressed by communism. Those in the east were told that they were part of a new experimental country that was to break with the nightmarish past and build a completely new Germany. They were told that the west was a Nazi state that made no effort to purge its disgraceful past.

Indeed, in 1950 West Germany, with U.S. and Allied approval, declared an amnesty for low-level Nazis. In East Germany, 85 percent of judges, prosecutors, and lawyers were disbarred for Nazi pasts, and most of these resumed their legal profession in West Germany by qualifying for the amnesty. In East Germany, schools, railroads, and post offices had been purged of Nazis. These Germans also were able to continue their careers in West Germany.

To many in both the east and west it was the Globke affair that crystallized how things were to be in the new West German Republic. In 1953 Chancellor Konrad Adenauer chose for state secretary of the Chancellory a man named Hans Globke. Globke was not an obscure Nazi. He had written the legal argument supporting the Nuremberg laws that stripped German Jews of their rights. He had suggested forcing all Jews to carry either the name Sarah or Israel for easy identification. The East Germans protested Globke's presence in the West German government. But Adenauer insisted that Globke had done nothing wrong, and he remained in German government until he retired to Switzerland in 1963.

In 1968 Nazis were still being discovered.

Edda Göring was in court trying to keep possession of the sixteenth-century painting by Lucas Cranach, *Madonna and Child*. It was of sentimental value since it had been given to her at her christening by her now deceased father, Hermann Göring. Göring, who had stolen the painting from the city of Cologne, had been founder and head of the Gestapo and the leading defendant at the showcase of de-Nazification, the Nuremburg trials. He killed himself hours before the scheduled time of his execution. The city had been trying to get the painting back ever since. Though Edda Göring had lost in court yet again in January 1968, her lawyers predicted at least two more rounds of appeals.

At the same time, evidence surfaced, actually resurfaced, that Heinrich Lübke, the seventy-three-year-old president of West Germany, had helped to build concentration camps. The East Germans had made the accusations two years earlier, but their documents had been dismissed as false. Now *Stern,* the West German magazine, had hired an American handwriting expert who said that the Lübke signatures by the head of state and the Lübke signatures on concentration camp plans were made by the same hand.

By 1968 questioning a high official on wartime activities was not new, except that now it was on television. The French magazine *Paris Match* wrote, "When you are 72 years old, and at the summit of your political career, the highest ranking person of state, and you are shown on television in front of 20 million viewers in the role of the accused, that is the worst."

In February two students were expelled from the university in Bonn for breaking into the rector's office and writing on the honor roll next to Lübke's name "Concentration Camp Builder." Following their expulsions, a petition signed by twenty of the two hundred Bonn professors demanded that Lübke address the issue publicly. The German president met with the chancellor, the head of government and the more powerful position in the German system. Chancellor Kurt Georg Kiesinger reviewed different options with the president, ruling out retirement or resignation. A few days later the president went on television denying the charges but saying, "Naturally, after nearly a quarter of a century has gone by, I cannot remember every paper I signed." It took more than ten months before he was finally forced to resign.

Chancellor Kiesinger, who had worked for the government of the Third Reich, had his own problems in 1968. He was called as a witness to the war crimes trial of Fritz Gebhard Von Hahn, accused of complicity in the murder of thirty thousand Greek and Bulgarian Jews in 1942 and 1943. From almost the moment the chancellor took the stand, it appeared that he himself was on trial. The defense had called him to explain that while he was serving in the Foreign Ministry, news on the deportation and killing of Jews was not passed on by his radio-monitoring department. But first he had to explain why he had a position in the Foreign Ministry. He said it was "a coincidence," but he did admit having been a Nazi Party member. He explained that he had joined the party in 1933, "but not out of conviction or opportunism."

For most of the war, he said, he had thought Jews were being deported to "munitions factories or places like that." Then did the radio department pass on news about the fate of deported Jews? "What information?" was Kiesinger's response. He denied knowing anything about killing Jews.

The Kiesinger government had come to power two years earlier in a reasonably successful attempt at a compromise coalition that offered political stability. But it was then that the student movement became most visible. A new generation had been angered and worried by the end of de-Nazification and the decision to remilitarize West Germany. The universities had become crowded owing to a policy, first established by the Allies, of offering military deferments to college students. Yet by 1967, despite growing university enrollment, only about 8 percent of the population attended university, still a small elite. Students wanted to be less elite and demanded that the government open up opportunities for enrollment. In March 1968 the West German Chamber of Commerce and Industry complained that German society risked producing more graduates than the number that could reasonably expect appropriate career opportunities.

On March 2, the day of the announcement, a prosecutor released Robert Mulke from prison on the grounds that the seventy-one-year-old was not in good enough health for prison. Mulke had been convicted three years earlier of three thousand murders while serving as assistant commandant of Auschwitz concentration camp.

In 1968 German student leaders estimated that they had six thousand militant students behind them. But they had the ability to mobilize many thousands more over a variety of issues. The Vietnam War, the illegal military dictatorship in Greece, and oppression by the shah of Iran were the three most popular foreign issues, but German issues occasionally rallied even more protesters. Fritz Teufel's Commune I organization and a Marxist student study group by coincidence also called SDS, Sozialistische Deutsche Studentenbund, were experienced and well organized.

One of the central themes of the student movement was that Germany was a repressive society. The implied word was "still," Germany was still repressive—meaning it had failed to emerge from the Third Reich and become truly democratic. The presence of Nazis in government was only an underlying part of this. The suspicion on the part of many students that their parents may have either done or countenanced horrendous deeds had created a generation gap far wider and deeper than anything Grayson Kirk was seeing at Columbia.

The fear of the past, or in many cases lack of a past, was recognized by many psychiatrists and therapists as a special problem of Germans of the postwar generation. Sammy Speier, an Israeli-born psychoanalyst in private practice in Frankfurt, wrote, "Since Auschwitz there is no longer any narrative tradition, and hardly any parents and grandparents are left who will take children on their lap and tell them about their lives in the old days. Children need fairy tales, but it is just as essential that they have parents who tell them about their own lives, so that they can establish a relationship to the past."

One of the surface issues was academic freedom and control of the university. The fact that this often stated issue was not at the root of the conflict is shown by the place where the student movement was first articulated, developed most rapidly, and exploded most violently. Berlin's Free University was, as the name claimed, the most free university in Germany. It was created after the war, in 1948, and so was not mired in the often stultifying ways of the old Germany. By charter a democratically elected student body voted with parliamentary procedure on the faculty's decisions. A large part of the original student body were politically militant East Germans who had left the East German university system because they refused to submit to the dictates of the Communist Party. They remained at the core of the Free University so that thirteen years after its founding, when the East Germans began erecting a wall in 1961, students from the Free University in the West attempted to storm the wall. After the wall was built, students from East Germany were unable to attend the Free University and it became largely a school for politicized West German students. With far greater intensity than American students, the students of West Berlin, the definitive products of the cold war, were rejecting capitalism and communism at the same time.

Berlin, partly because it was located at the heart of the cold war, became the center of all protest. East Germans were slipping into West Berlin, West Germans were slipping into the east. This second traffic was less talked about, and West Germany kept no statistics on it. In 1968, East Germany said that twenty thousand West Germans were crossing to East Germany every year. They were said not to be political, but this myth was disturbed in March 1968 when Wolfgang Kieling moved east. Kieling was a well-known German actor, famous in the United States for his portrayal of the East German villain in the 1966 Alfred Hitchcock movie *Torn Curtain* starring Paul Newman. Kieling, who had fought for the Third Reich on the Russian front, was in Los Angeles at the time of the Watts race riots for the shooting of *Torn Curtain* and said he had been appalled by the United States. He said that he was leaving West

Germany because of its backing of the United States, which, he said, was "the most dangerous enemy of humanity in the world today," citing "crimes against the Negro and the people of Vietnam."

In December 1966, Free University students fought in the streets with police for the first time. By then the American war in Vietnam had become one of the major issues around which the student movement organized. Using American demonstration techniques to protest against American policy, they quickly became the most noticeable student movement in Europe. But the students were also revolting against the materialism of West Germany and searching for a better way to achieve what East Germany had promised, a complete break with the Germany of the past. And while they were at it, they began demonstrating about tram fares and student living conditions.

On June 2, 1967, students gathered to protest Mayor Willy Brandt entertaining the shah of Iran. Once the guests were safely installed in the Opera House for a production of Mozart's *The Magic Flute,* the police attacked the Free University students outside with violent fury. Students fled in panic, but twelve were so severely beaten that they had to be hospitalized, and one fleeing student, Benno Ohnesorg, was shot and killed. Ohnesorg had not been a militant, and this had been one of his first demonstrations. The policeman who shot him was quickly acquitted, whereas Fritz Teufel, leader of the protest group Commune I, faced a possible five-year sentence in a lengthy trial on the charge of "sedition." The national student movement was built on anger over this killing, which was protested not only in Berlin but throughout Germany, demanding the creation of a new parliamentary group to oppose the German legislature.

On January 23, 1968, a right-wing Hamburg pastor, Helmuth Thielicke, found his church filled with students wanting to denounce his sermon. He called in West German troops to clear his church of the students, who were distributing pamphlets with a revised Lord's Prayer:

Our capital, which art in the West, amortized be Thy investments,
Thy profits come, Thy interest rates increase,
In Wall Street as they do in Europe.
Give us this day, our daily turnover.
And extend to us our credits, as we extend them to our creditors,
Lead us not into bankruptcy, but deliver us from the trade unions,
For thine is half the world, the power and the riches,
For the last two hundred years.
Mammon.

By 1968 theology students were also demonstrating, insisting that it was no longer acceptable to listen to church sermons without questions and dialogue in the service addressing the immorality of the West German state as well as moral outrage at the U.S. war against Vietnam. In effect the church was to become a discussion group for the purpose of heightening political and moral awareness. The most prominent of these theology student rebels was one of the student refugees from East Berlin, Rudi Dutschke, sometimes called Rudi the Red.

German SDS was well organized in the universities. On February 17, combining a good sense of timing with an impressive display of organization, the group hosted student activists from around the world to an international meeting against the American war in Vietnam. The International Vietnam Congress was the first large-scale international meeting of 1968 student movements and was being held at the height of the Tet Offensive when the Vietnam War was a mainstay of television programming around the world. In most countries, opposition to the war was not only one of the most popular causes—in many cases antiwar groups were the best-organized movements—but it was also the one issue they all had in common. Although an Iranian "revolutionary" attended, as did U.S. and Canadian militants, including two black Vietnam veterans who gave the clenched-fist salute and chanted arm in arm, "Hell, no, I ain't gonna go!"—too late, as they had already been—it was largely a European meeting of German, French, Italian, Greek, and Scandinavian students. They met for a twelve-hour session of speeches and discussions in an enormous hall of the Free University with an overflow of thousands sent to two other large halls. The main hall was decorated with a huge flag of the North Vietnamese National Liberation Front along with a banner emblazoned with Che Guevara's hard-to-refute statement: "The duty of a revolutionary is to make a revolution." Speakers ranged from Dutschke, to leaders of other national movements, to the playwright Peter Weiss, whose *Marat/Sade* was being quoted by students all over the world.

Many of the foreign activists were dazzled by the Germans. One of the speakers, Alain Krivine, twenty-seven, a French Trotskyite who would later become one of the leaders in the spring Paris uprising, said, "Many of the 1968 student tactics were learned earlier in the year in Berlin and Brussels anti–Vietnam War demonstrations. The anti–Vietnam War movement was well organized throughout Europe. Dutschke and the Germans were the pioneers in the hard demonstration tactics. We went there and they had their banners and signs ready

Anti–Vietnam War poster on a street
in Germany in 1968
(Photo by Leonard Freed/Magnum Photos)

and their security forces and everything with militaristic tactics. It was new to me and the other French."

Daniel Cohn-Bendit, the French-German student leader, was impressed with the way the German SDS had incorporated student issues into the larger protest. The French students invited Karl D. "Kaday" Wolf, the German SDS national chairman for 1968, to speak to students in France.

Born in 1940, Rudi Dutschke was the oldest of the German student leaders. Tariq Ali, leader of a British group called Vietnam Solidarity Campaign, VSC, and cofounder of a short-lived 1968 underground London review, *Black Dwarf,* described him as "of medium height with an angular face and a gentle smile. He always smiles with his eyes." With his long dark hair shaking and swaying and a stubble of beard that seemed to neither grow nor be shaved off, he was said to be an electrifying orator, but this skill was always met by German youth with an awkward embarrassment. Germans, it seemed, had learned to be wary of electrifying oration and would offer him only polite applause. Other student leaders had advised Dutschke to moderate his speaking style.

His speech at the Congress drew parallels between the struggle of the Vietnamese people and that of Europeans to overthrow the classist system. Then, as he often did, he compared their fight to change European society one institution at a time to Mao's famous Long March of 1934–1935, in which he gave his besieged movement a national presence by leading ninety thousand Chinese communists on a remarkably arduous trek across China, picking up small enclaves of support as they went. Of course, Dutschke didn't point out that half of Mao's original followers died along the way.

The talks had gone on for hours. Eric Fried was speaking. A recognized poet, he was what had become a rarity, a German Jew. Born in Austria in 1921, he had escaped the Nazis after his father was beaten to death. Though of a different generation, Fried was personally very close to a number of German student leaders, especially Dutschke. He was particularly valued by the German New Left because he was outspokenly anti-Zionist and pro-Palestinian. The German New Left, like many of their counterparts in Europe and the United States, saw the emerging Palestinian terrorist organization under the young Yasir Arafat as another romantic nationalist movement. But it was uncomfortable for these young Germans to back an organization so clearly bent on killing Jews, including Jews in Europe, so it was a considerable boost to have an actual Jewish survivor in their ranks. The switch away from supporting Israel had begun with the Six Day War and the rise of Arafat, but it also coincided with a growing lack of interest in nonviolence. That these Palestinians were interested only in violence simply meant that they could be seen as guerrilla fighters—like Che.

The expressions *peace movement* and *antiwar movement* were largely American and even in the United States were fast becoming old-fashioned in some leftist circles. European radicals were not as interested in an end to the war as in a North Vietnamese victory. They tended to see the Tet Offensive not as a tragic loss of life, but as a triumph for an oppressed people. The British radical Tariq Ali, using language that was also heard in Berlin, Rome, and Paris, said of Tet, "A wave of joy and energy rebounds around the world and millions more are suddenly, exhilaratingly, ceasing to believe in the strength of their oppressor."

We all carry our own history on our backs. The American activists wanted a stop to the aggression. The Europeans wanted a defeat of colonialism—they wanted the United States to be crushed just as the European colonial powers had been. This was particularly apparent in the French insistence that the marines in Khe Sanh might suffer the same humiliating defeat as had the French in Dien Bien Phu. The constant articles in the French press asking, "Is Khe Sanh another Dien Bien Phu?" had a barely concealed wishfulness to them. There was a touch of self-loathing to the European Left, especially the Germans, and all sins were compared to those of their own countries. To the French and British Left, the Americans were colonialists, to the Germans they were Nazis. Peter Weiss's 1968 *Vietnam Discourse* argued that the Americans in Vietnam were a Nazi-like evil.

The following morning an estimated eight thousand to twenty thousand people appeared on Kurfurstendamm, a wide boulevard lined with fashionable shops—used to launch expensive new fashion trends since West Berlin's isolation simplified market research. Amazingly, the students' ranks were swollen with hundreds of West Germans who had crossed East Germany, spending the night before in homes of Berlin comrades. *The New York Times,* which estimated "more than 10,000," called it "the biggest anti-American rally ever staged in the city." Through the cold, humid, gray streets of West Berlin, they carried with them a curious blend of cultures—portraits of Che Guevara, Ho Chi Minh, and Rosa Luxemburg, the Jewish leftist from Poland killed in Germany in 1919. They shouted the chant always heard at American antiwar marches—"Ho, Ho, Ho Chi Minh! NLF is gonna win!" They marched to the Opera House, where Benno Ohnesorg had been shot, and then to the Berlin Wall for more speeches. Dutschke said to a cheering crowd, "Tell the Americans the day and the hour will come when we will drive you out unless you yourselves throw out imperialism." But for all his apparent anti-Americanism, Red Rudi, said to be the most important student revolutionary in Europe, was married to an American theology student from Chicago.

The police, many on horseback, had been posted mostly to protect American military and diplomatic installations. But the demonstrators made no attempt to approach these areas. Demonstrators climbed two thirty-story construction cranes and attached huge Viet Cong and red flags. The demonstrators then booed as construction workers took the flags down and burned them. The city of West Berlin, working with the trade unions, was able to assemble an equally large counterdemonstration that chanted, "Berlin supports America" and "Throw Dutschke out of West Berlin."

The students from other countries returned from Berlin's February Vietnam demonstration exhilarated. The British mounted their own

demonstration on March 17, the second demonstration organized by
Tariq Ali and the VSC. The first, like most previous London demonstrations, had been smaller and without violence. But on this occasion,
thousands filled Oxford Street, a solid river of red flags and voices
chanting, "NLF is gonna win!" A German SDS contingent had urged
the VSC to try to take the U.S. embassy, but Tariq Ali did not believe
this was possible. When the crowd reached Grosvenor Square, to the
complete surprise of the VSC organizers, they broke through the police
line and started running for the embassy. Armed with clubs, mounted
British police charged with a brutality rarely seen in London. Mick
Jagger of the Rolling Stones was there and wrote about it in "Street
Fighting Man."

Aside from the imported issue of Vietnam and a worsening climate
in Northern Ireland, the biggest issue in Britain that year was racism.
Led by Enoch Powell, a member of Parliament, the country was seeing

Anti–Vietnam War demonstration in Grosvenor Square,
London, July 7, 1968
(Photo by David Hurn/Magnum Photos)

a virulent strain of what the American civil rights movement called white backlash set off by the Labour government's proposed Commonwealth Immigration Bill. As the British decolonized their empire, workers were being told that black and brown people from the former empire would be coming and taking away their jobs. "Keep Britain White," was Powell's slogan, and a number of workers groups demonstrated with this slogan. There was some amusement when a Kenyan diplomat was harassed entering the House of Commons by "Keep Britain White" hecklers who shouted, "Go back to Jamaica!" at the East African.

It was Germany that seemed a volatile place waiting for a larger explosion. On April 3 the violent left wing that would gain more prominence in the 1970s for such actions burned two Frankfurt department stores. On April 11, Rudi Dutschke was in front of a West Berlin drugstore about to buy medicine for his baby boy, Hosea Che—named for a prophet and a revolutionary—when Joseph Bachmann, a twenty-three-year-old out-of-work Munich housepainter, walked up to him and fired three bullets from a handgun. One hit Dutschke in the chest, a second in the face, and a third lodged precariously in his brain. This was the first attempt at a political assassination in Germany since the fall of the Third Reich. Arrested after a gun battle with the police, Bachmann explained, "I heard of the death of Martin Luther King and since I hate communists I felt I must kill Dutschke." Bachmann, who kept a picture of Hitler in his apartment and identified with him as a fellow Munich housepainter, was a devoted reader of a hate-mongering, right-wing paper called *Bild Zeitung, Picture Times*. The tabloid was owned by Axel Springer, Germany's most powerful press baron, whose papers slavishly supported all U.S. policies and viciously attacked leftist movements, both cheering and encouraging attacks against them. DON'T LEAVE ALL THE DIRTY WORK TO THE COPS! read one headline.

Bild Zeitung, launched in 1952, became the centerpiece of an empire of right-wing press that became the largest in Europe with *Bild*'s circulation of four million, the largest of any daily on the European continent. Fourteen Springer publications, including five daily newspapers, had a total circulation of fifty million. The papers were not only anticommunist but also racist, and many felt that they were appealing to the very beast the new Germany was trying to lay to rest. Springer always claimed that he spoke for the way the average German thought, which was exactly what many feared. Springer did not deny that the paper sometimes got carried away. "You should see me falling out of bed in the morning with surprise at what I read in my own papers," he once said.

It was not only students who were angered. Even before the shooting, two hundred writers had asked their publishers to boycott his papers. But while Bachmann's claim that the newspaper had inspired him resonated with many, Axel Springer himself was more complicated. He was known as an excellent employer who treated workers so well that despite his right-wing politics, organized labor supported him. And despite the Nazi-like tone of his papers, Springer was a strong supporter of Jewish causes, to which he contributed generously from his own fortune. He campaigned tirelessly for German reparation payments to Israel, and his papers were strongly pro-Israel. But in 1968, what Germany's New Left was most aware of was that the Springer press had declared war on them, demanding repressive laws to curtail demonstrations and to deal harshly with demonstrators, whom he called "terrorists." He urged vigilante violence against the students.

The response was immediate: The anger over the shooting instantly transferred to anger toward Springer, because of his campaign for years against the Left, but also from a long-simmering rejection of the notion that Europe could be run by powerful press barons. A forerunner of Murdoch and Berlusconi, with an empire that seems quaint today in its lack of broadcast holdings, the question remained—how was it that this man, scooped up by the British from Germany's rubble to run a radio broadcast, had become the most powerful opinion maker in Europe?

Only hours after the attack on Dutschke, a crowd of angry young people gathered in front of the nineteen-story steel-and-glass office block in the bohemian Kreuzberg section of Berlin. Springer had chosen the spot to build because it was defiantly right up against the Wall. He put a neon sign on the building that said, *"Berlin bleibt frei"*—"Berlin remains free." Police used water cannons to disperse the crowd of students who threw rocks and flaming torches. The following day, columns of students, arms linked, marched in waves toward the West Berlin Springer building. By the time they reached it, it was already fortified with barbed wire and riot police. The crowd chanted Dutschke's name and "Springer, murderer!" and "Springer, Nazi!" The police turned on their water cannons and began arresting demonstrators. At the City Hall demonstrators chanted, "Fascists!" and "Nazis!" The students also marched to the American radio station, where windows were broken. Munich demonstrators did better, actually managing to get inside the Springer building there before being driven off by police. Failing to take over buildings, students burned delivery trucks. Thousands of students also clashed with police in Hamburg, Esslingen, Hanover, and Essen. Mostly it was student clubs pitted against police water cannons, and the high-pressure water won the day. But the demonstrators stopped or delayed delivery of Springer papers. In Frankfurt they also stopped the leading West German business paper, *Frankfurter Allgemeine Zeitung,* because it was printed at a Springer plant. Demonstrators also appeared in front of Springer buildings in New York, London, and Paris. In London Tariq Ali led a group that broke away from a Martin Luther King memorial in Trafalgar Square and attempted to take over Springer offices. In Paris Alain Krivine recalled, "When Rudi was shot was the first spontaneous violent demonstration in Paris. The police were not even in riot gear, no helmets or shields, when suddenly the students in the Latin Quarter began to hurl tables and chairs at police."

In Germany, the event fell on an Easter holiday, and five days of street battles followed the shooting. In these riots two were killed—an Associated Press photographer and a student, both from objects thrown by students—and several hundred were wounded. Many hundreds were arrested. It was the worst German street rioting since before Hitler came to power. Remembering the consequences of German political instability, most West Germans did not approve of the street violence. In June 1968 the German magazine *Der Spiegel* conducted a poll in which 92 percent of Berlin citizens were opposed to "the use of violence by protesting students." The students were failing to appeal to the working class: 78 percent of Berliners under thirty from working-class homes said they opposed the student violence. Even some students were outspokenly opposed to the violence.

Dutschke survived his wounds and even wrote a letter to his would-be assassin, explaining his ideas of socialism. But Bachmann hanged himself in his prison cell.

Among the 230 students arrested in Berlin was Peter Brandt, the son of Willy Brandt, former Berlin mayor, minister of foreign affairs, and vice chancellor of Germany. Willy Brandt had always been the good German, the socialist who had opposed fascism and had nothing to hide in his past. But Peter said he was disappointed in his father, that since he had gotten into government he had lost his socialist fervor. He was a social democrat, the German equivalent of a liberal. "I never said that my father should leave office. That's not true," Peter stated. "But I think that he has changed and I regret it. He is no longer the same man. He is no longer the socialist who went to fight in Spain during the Civil War. We don't agree anymore." When his father suggested that he was spending too much time on politics and not enough on his studies, he said, "If I find that something needs to change, I find that it is my duty to do something to make that change happen."

One of Peter's professors warned his father, the vice chancellor, "In another six months your son Peter will become a communist."

Brandt shrugged. "Anyone who has not been a communist at the age of twenty will never make a good social democrat."

CHAPTER 10

WAGNERIAN OVERTONES OF A HIP AND BEARDED REVOLUTION

I had been raised on Errol Flynn's *Robin Hood* and the endless
hero actor fighting against injustice and leading the people to
victory over tyranny. The Cuban thing seemed a case of classic
Hollywood proportions.

—LeRoi Jones, The Autobiography of
LeRoi Jones/Amiri Baraka, *1984*

IN FEBRUARY 1968 a group of twenty young Americans
arrived in Havana from Mexico City. The trip had been organized by the American SDS. In the group was a twenty-year-old
Columbia University junior from New Jersey named Mark Rudd, who
had raised money for his Cuban trip by selling hashish at the West End
Bar, a student hangout in upper Manhattan.

The group met with the Vietnamese diplomatic delegation and were
surprised by their extreme courtesy. The Vietnamese ambassador said
that he understood there were important differences between the
American government and the American people. Though the students
accepted the ambassador's gracious remark with relief, Rudd seized the
occasion to point out that while he wished the ambassador's comments
had been correct, in reality, most Americans did support the war.

The Vietnamese diplomat smiled at the earnest young blond student.
"This will be a very long war," he said. "It has already lasted for us
more than twenty years. We can hold out much longer. Eventually the
American people will tire of the war, and will turn against it. Then the
war will end."

Rudd realized the ambassador was right. One of the diplomats said
he had fought in South Vietnam for seven years, living in tunnels and
emerging at night to attack the Americans. Everywhere in Cuba that
winter, there was news from Vietnam. A large neon sign over a main

Havana street, La Rampa, gave the current total of planes shot down. When the students went to the countryside, they found Cubans standing around transistor radios getting news of the Tet Offensive. Someone gave Rudd a ring that was said to have been made from the metal of a shot-down American plane.

The students met many Cubans who were their age, including Sylvio Rodriguez, who sang ballads in the style of Joan Baez. They spent time in the leafy tropical park with the famous ice-cream shop Coppelia. Rudd later remembered: "We hung out at Coppelia eating tomato ice cream and went to great parties with Afro-Cuban music, which I had never heard before and didn't quite understand. I saw in Cuba what I wanted to see: factories, farms, and institutions that were owned by the state, socialized. I wanted to see a different way to organize society. But I didn't see the obvious, that you can't have a one-party state, that you have to have elections."

Fidel Castro, bearded and in army fatigues, the surprising and slightly offbeat sensation of 1959, had become the New Left hero of 1968.

He had been neither bearded nor revolutionary in 1955 when he visited the United States looking for financing to overthrow the dictatorship of Fulgencio Batista, who had seized power three years earlier and had banned all political parties. Batista was corrupt and disliked, and Castro, Dr. Fidel Castro as he was known in the United States in deference to his law degree, was reasonable, earnest, clean-cut, and reassuringly middle class.

In December 1956 Castro landed a yacht in Oriente province with a fighting force of eighty-two. The Cuban government reported that almost all the rebels, including Castro, were killed. This was only a slight exaggeration; the casualties included all but a dozen survivors who made it into the Sierra Maestra mountains with Dr. Castro among them. This was not known for certain until a retired *New York Times* correspondent, Herbert L. Matthews, accomplished one of the most famous and controversial newspaper scoops of the twentieth century by finding Dr. Castro alive, bearded and talkative in his mountain hideaway along with eighteen colorful bearded rebels, including one who had been a pro baseball player in the United States.

The *Times* ran Matthews's interview as a three-part series on February 24, 25, and 26, 1957. It has often been attacked by anti-Castro elements for presenting Fidel as a sympathetic freedom fighter similar to a World War II partisan. Of course, Americans conveniently forget that many World War II partisans had also been communists. The most remembered attack on the Matthews series was a 1960 cartoon in the conservative *National Review* showing an avaricious-looking Castro hunkering down on an island labeled "The Cuban Police State." The caption read, "I got my job through the *New York Times.*"

But the *Times* was far from the only media outlet that ran favorable coverage of Dr. Castro at the time. A rabid anticommunist Hungarian exile named Andrew St. George wrote favorably of the Cuban rebels in *Look*; Jules Dubois gave sympathetic coverage in the Red-baiting, right-wing *Chicago Tribune*; photojournalist Dickey Chapelle spent three weeks with Castro for the extremely conservative *Reader's Digest. Time,* another right-leaning publication, ran thirty-two articles on the Cuban rebels in the two years leading up to their victory, most of them favorable. In December 1956 *Time* called Fidel "Lawyer Castro" and said that he was a "well born, well-to-do daredevil of 29."

American reporters always emphasized Castro's middle-class character, origins, and education and invariably mentioned his pure Spanish blood. It was never said, but it was reassuring to know, that the Cuban rebellion was no dangerous "Negro uprising." To the American press he was a good story, a colorful and uplifting tale of a struggle for freedom. But what was starting to become more important was that he made for great television. He looked dashing in fatigues, and his uncertainty in English showed a touchingly vulnerable, less assured side that in reality he never had. He was simply uncomfortable in English. Three months after Matthews's scoop, a CBS News team traveled to the green, thickly overgrown tropical mountains of Cuba's Oriente province and shot a prime-time news special that aired in May called *Rebels of the Sierra Maestra: The Story of Cuba's Jungle Fighters.*

Television had come along too late for the Mexican revolution. It had missed the romance of the beautiful Emiliano Zapata, famous for his exquisite horsemanship, and the wild, mounted northern bandits of Pancho Villa, although they were captured in the fifties by Hollywood with romantic rebel stars including Marlon Brando as Zapata. But now television had a live revolution, with the large and rugged-looking Dr. Fidel Castro and his heartthrob Argentine sidekick Che. The Barbudos, the bearded band of rebels, cigars clenched in their teeth, dressed in green, toted huge guns more impressive for portraits than military tactics—but the weapons were reminiscent of the Mexican revolution, which was the very image of a fabled Latin revolution. In between climbing down green slopes to attack the evil dictatorship and its underpaid and undermotivated henchmen, Fidel could squat in the jungle just south of Miami with CBS correspondent Robert Taber and speak into a microphone. Not nearly as graphic as the live warfare from Vietnam of 1968, this coverage felt immediate but was appealing in its bloodlessness.

Students tried to go to Cuba and fight for Fidel, but the rebels did not encourage them. Frenchman Régis Debray managed to fight with Che only later, in Latin America. Bernard Kouchner, age twenty the year of Fidel's triumph, was discouraged when he attempted to join up with Fidel and returned to France, where he went to medical school and formed Médecins Sans Frontières, Doctors Without Borders, a medical response to the ideals of third worldism. *The New York Times* reported that twenty-five Americans were fighting with Fidel and there may have been more, though only in a few cases do we know their names. Three sons of American sailors serving in Guantánamo joined up with the guerrilla forces, and unexplained gringos were occasionally referred to in rebel communications. In March 1957 a Berkeley undergraduate student, Hank di Suvero, wrote Herbert Matthews about the possibility of taking a group of friends with two jeeps to Oriente province after the spring semester to help Fidel. Mathews was kind enough not to dwell on the notion of Castro holding up the revolution until the spring semester was over, but he was discouraging, so instead di Suvero stayed at Berkeley that year and became one of the founders of the student political party SLATE, which was the beginning of activism on that campus.

It seemed everyone loved Fidel. Even Eisenhower negotiated secretly with Batista in 1958, trying to persuade him to step down and be replaced by a coalition that would include Castro. America and much of the world thrilled to the film footage of the bearded revolutionaries led by Fidel and Che, as photogenic as anyone Hollywood might have cast, triumphantly taking Havana on New Year's Day 1959. Everyone wanted Fidel on television. Both Ed Sullivan and Jack Parr flew down to do Fidel shows. But this euphoric state where television, journalists, the student Left, and the political establishment were all in love with Castro would not last for long.

Once in power, Fidel began executing hundreds of Batista supporters. Suddenly the political establishment, the same people who would defend capital punishment in the Chessman case the following year, were appalled by state executions. And the Left, the Abbie Hoffmans and Marlon Brandos, the activists and celebrities who would stand vigil by the California prison, protesting the Chessman execution, had not a word to say for Fidel's victims. But even within Cuba, revolutionary justice was being called into question. In March 1959 forty-four Batista airmen were tried for war crimes. Evidence that they had refused to bomb populations and had dumped their ordnance on fields led to their acquittal, whereupon the judge was replaced by a more loyal revolutionary and the forty-four were retried and all sentenced to prison terms. The minister of health, Elena Mederos, asked to resign, saying, "I am a different generation to you and your friends. We are quite opposed to each other in spirit. I must resign." But Castro was able to charm her into staying.

Executions and revolutionary justice were talked about and criticized in the United States, too, but the fundamental issue was revolution. Down from the mountains and secure in the capital, Dr. Castro and his middle-class white rebels were not shaving off their beards! This was the sixties, when extra hair was synonymous with rebellion. In 1961 Matthews came out with a book that put it succinctly: This was "a real revolution, not a changing of the guard, not a shuffling of leaders, not just the outs getting in but a social revolution on the direct line of the French Revolution of 1789."

As this reality became understood, in other countries the people of the establishment, with their fear and distrust of revolution, became vehemently anti-Castro. Many people could not decide. But a radical minority around the world, people who longed for revolution, believing it was the only hope for social change, the only way to move toward a more just society, were prepared to salute Fidel, whatever his faults, because he had not just taken power, he was really doing it— was really making a revolution. Fidel was in their pantheon, along with Ho Chi Minh and Mao. But Ho was a curious and stoic character, not hip like Fidel, and though Mao's revolution fascinated, they would never completely understand his vast and complex China. For many radical students, middle-class people who dreamed of revolution, Dr. Castro, the middle-class lawyer-turned-revolutionary, and his partner, Dr. Che Guevara, the middle-class doctor-turned-revolutionary, were their ideal radicals.

In November 1960 C. Wright Mills published *Listen, Yankee,* the first of a number of leftist essays to reach the bestseller list in the 1960s. Most of the others, such as Eldridge Cleaver's *Soul on Ice,* did not come until 1968. C. Wright Mills, a sociologist well respected in academic circles who died at the height of his popularity in the early 1960s, had been widely read since his 1950s book, *The Power Elite,* which told of the military-industrial complex before Eisenhower had coined the phrase in his 1960 farewell address. Mills had articulated a view of society's power structure that was felt by many of the New Left youth. According to Mills, the ruling class was made up of a new clique of politicians, corporate executives, and military commanders who maintained their hold on power by perpetuating the cold war. In *Listen, Yankee,* Mills broke all the rules of academic writing and as a result sold four hundred thousand copies. The book is written in the first-person voice of a fictitious Cuban revolutionary who speaks rapidly, his commentary richly woven with asides—a fair approximation of what Castro sounded like in Spanish. The Cuban talks not only of his own revolution, but of the need for revolution in America. In 1960, unlike 1968, talk of revolution in America was rarely heard.

While Cuba was thrilling the Left, it was alienating most of its U.S. admirers. In early 1959, Camilo Cienfuegos, the head of the rebel army, visited the United States to garner support, and the trip was disastrous. These Barbudos were no longer picturesque guerrilla fighters, they were unshaven and uncouth radicals. But two months later, in April, Fidel himself came to America, and for a brief moment the country succumbed to his seemingly irresistible charm. A toy manufacturer produced one hundred thousand olive drab caps that said "El Libertador" and had the 26th of July logo of Fidel's movement. Each cap came with a chin strap to which a black beard was attached. Fidel was particularly well received in New York at a huge Central Park rally. New York mayor Robert F. Wagner, Jr., gave him keys to the city. But in what proved to be an omen for the future, his most successful stops were at Columbia and other universities. By springtime, polls in the United States showed an almost even split between those opposed to Castro and those who either supported him or hadn't made up their minds. With a third to a fifth of the population solidly behind him, he had lost a great deal of support in the first six months of 1959.

The American press, once accused of coddling the bearded heroes, had turned so vehemently against the revolution, once they understood that it *was* a revolution, that Robert Taber, the CBS correspondent who had met with Castro in the mountains, decided to form an organization called Fair Play for Cuba Committee. Unfortunately, the short-lived organization is most remembered by the odd and unexplained evidence that Lee Harvey Oswald, John Kennedy's assassin, participated in it. But there was something more interesting about the group. Taber, by most accounts, was fairly apolitical and simply believed that the Cuban revolution was initiating interesting social and economic changes that were being ignored by the press. Among those he attracted to the organization were Jean-Paul Sartre and Simone de Beauvoir, Norman Mailer, James Baldwin, theater critic Kenneth Tynan, and Truman Capote. The group placed high-profile ads explaining the Cuban revolution. With very little political affiliation except for the French couple who were connected to the French Communist Party, they were still able to attract thousands of people to write-in campaigns and demonstrations. It was one of the first indications that the United States had a large body of left-leaning people who were not part of any leftist establishment—the people who came to be known as the New Left.

During the first two years of Castro's rule, the rift between Washington and Havana widened steadily. In early 1959 there were already hints of a U.S. invasion, and Castro made his famous remark about "two hundred thousand dead gringos" if they tried. On June 3, 1959, Cuba's Agrarian Reform Law limited the size of holdings and required owners to be Cuban. Sugar company stocks on Wall Street immediately crashed, while the U.S. government angrily and futilely protested. In October, Major Huber Matos and a group of his officers were arrested for their anticommunist political stances, stances that had matched Castro's own a year earlier, and tried for "uncertain, anti-patriotic, and anti-revolutionary conduct." By November 1959 the Eisenhower government had decided on the forcible removal of Castro and began working with Florida exiles toward that goal. Two months later the Fair Play for Cuba Committee began its activities. In February 1960 Cuba signed a five-year accord with the Soviet Union to trade Cuban sugar for Soviet industrial goods. Only a few weeks later a French ship, *Le Coubre,* carrying rifles and grenades, blew up in Havana harbor owing to causes still unknown today, killing seventy-five and injuring two hundred Cuban dockworkers. Castro declared a day of mourning, accusing the United States of sabotage, though he admitted that he had no proof, and in one of his more famous speeches said, "You will reduce us neither by war nor famine." Sartre, visiting Cuba, wrote that in the speech he found "the hidden face of all revolutions, their shaded face: the foreign menace felt in anguish."

The United States called back its ambassador, and Congress gave Eisenhower the power to cut the Cuban sugar quota, which Eisenhower insisted he would do not to punish the Cubans, but only if necessary for regulating U.S. sugar supplies.

On May 7 Cuba and the Soviet Union established diplomatic ties, and during the summer U.S.-owned refineries that refused to take Soviet oil were nationalized. When the Soviet Union pledged to defend Cuba from foreign aggression, Eisenhower dramatically cut the Cuban sugar quota. It appears that Cuba's drift toward the Soviet Union was fueling U.S. hostility, but in fact it is now known that back in mid-March, before the ties with Moscow were established, Eisenhower had already approved a plan for an exile invasion of the island. Throughout the 1960 summer election campaign, John Kennedy repeatedly accused the Republicans of "being soft" on Cuba.

On October 13, 1960, Cuba nationalized all large companies, and the following week, while Kennedy accused Nixon and the Eisenhower administration of "losing" Cuba, Eisenhower responded with a trade embargo, which Castro answered by nationalizing the last 166 American-owned enterprises on the island. By the time Kennedy was inaugurated in January, the U.S.-Cuban relationship appeared to have already reached the point of no return. Kennedy cut diplomatic relations with Cuba, banned travel to the island, and demanded that the Fair Play for Cuba Committee register as a foreign agent, which it refused to do. But Kennedy boasted, "We can be proud that the United States is not using its muscle against a very small country." Kennedy was different, a liberal with "a new frontier."

Then he did exactly what he had been proud of not doing, authorizing the invasion of Cuba by Cuban exiles. The so-called Brigade 2506, on April 17, was an extraordinary disaster. The exiles had convinced the United States that the Cubans would rise up against Castro and join them. But they didn't. Instead they rose up with impressive determination to defend their island against a foreign invader. The Cuban exiles also thought that if they got into trouble, the U.S. military would step in, which Kennedy was not willing to do. In three days, what came to be known as the Bay of Pigs invasion was over. Fidel had saved Cuba. As Dean Acheson so succinctly put it, "It was not necessary to call on Price Waterhouse to know that 1,500 Cubans wasn't as good as 250,000 Cubans."

The Bay of Pigs was an enormously significant moment in postwar history. It was America's first defeat in the third world. But it also marked a shift that had been taking place since the end of World War II. The United States had been founded on anticolonialism and had been lecturing Europe on its colonialist policies even as recently as Franklin Roosevelt. All the while, it had been developing an imperialism of its own—ruthlessly manipulating the Caribbean, Latin America, and even parts of Asia for its own benefit with indifference to the plight of the local inhabitants—while the Europeans, against their will, had been losing their colonies. America was becoming the leading imperialist.

At the time of the Bay of Pigs, France had lost a colonial war with Vietnam and was mired in one with Algeria. The year before, the British had given up fighting the Mau Mau and were now planning for Kenyan independence. The Belgian Congo was in a bloody civil war over its independence. The Dutch were fighting an independence movement in Indonesia and New Guinea. These were European problems, and a New Left in Europe was organizing over the issue of anticolonialism and the struggles of newly emerging nations. The Bay of Pigs brought the United States solidly into this debate, making writers such as Frantz Fanon, not to mention Ho Chi Minh, relevant to Americans and shaping the way the young Left in the United States and around the world would see Vietnam. To them the Bay of Pigs made Cuba a symbol of anticolonialism. The issue was no longer the quality of the Cuban revolution, but just the fact of it and that it had stood up to a huge imperialist nation and survived.

The Bay of Pigs invasion also drove a wedge between the liberals and the Left, who had united for a moment in the promise of a Kennedy presidency. Norman Mailer, a prominent Kennedy supporter and chronicler, wrote in an open letter, "Wasn't there anyone around to give you the lecture on Cuba? Don't you sense the enormity of your mistake—you invade a country without understanding its music." But it is significant that in the numerous protests against the invasion that took place around the country, a great many of the protesters were college students who had not been particularly political up until then. By his fourth month in office, it had become clear that the Kennedy administration was not just about the New Frontier, the Peace Corps, and the race to the moon. Exactly like his predecessor, this president wanted to use military power to back up cold war obsessions and would have no tolerance for small, impoverished countries that did not step into line. Young Kennedy enthusiasts such as Tom Hayden would soon start reappraising their support of him. Even the Peace Corps looked different. Was it really an organization by which people with ideals could help the newly emerging nations? Or was it a wing of U.S. government policy, which was colonialist and not, as it had always claimed, anticolonial?

The Bay of Pigs was one of the defining moments in a new generation's cynicism about liberals. By 1968 "liberal" had become almost synonymous with "sellout," and singer Phil Ochs amused young people at demonstrations with his song "Love Me, I'm a Liberal." The song's message was that liberals said the right things but could not be trusted to do them.

Fidel Castro is a seducer. He has always had an enormous ability to charm, convince, and enlist. He was so completely confident and self-assured that he was almost an irresistible force. He could just walk into a room or even a wide-open space and everyone present could feel,

Cuban government poster, 1968
(Schomburg Center for Research in Black Culture)

even in spite of themselves, a sense of excitement—a sense that something interesting was about to happen. He understood very well how to use this talent, made more important because he, and everyone else, had started to view the revolution as an extension of himself. Cuba too had a long history of seducing visitors, with its beauty and the richness of its culture, the grandeur of its capital like no other Caribbean city. And Fidel, who had been cheered on American college campuses, knew that Cuba still had a wealth of young supporters in the United States.

For all these reasons it became Cuban policy to bring over as many sympathetic Americans as possible to show them the revolution firsthand. Travel restrictions and economic embargoes could be circumvented by Cuban government–sponsored trips. Most of the visitors understood that the Cubans were out to seduce them. Some resisted and others didn't care to go. In either case, the result was usually the same. Most left deeply impressed with the Cuban revolution: the elimination of illiteracy, the construction of new schools across the island, the development of an extensive and effective health care system. The Cubans even experimented with feminism—increased roles for women, an antimachismo campaign, marriage vows in which the man pledged to help clean the house. These social experiments to build "a new man" were striking. And while it was a young revolution, it had a contagious excitement.

Most saw things that were wrong—too many police, too many arrests, no free press. But they also saw so much that was extraordinarily bold and experimental and inspiring. They were well aware that Cuba's enemies, chiefly the U.S. government and Cuban exiles, were opposed to the revolution not for the things that were wrong, but for the things that were right, and this made them focus on these important transformations.

Susan Sontag spent three months in Cuba in 1960 and found the country "astonishingly free of repression." While noting a lack of press freedom, she applauded the revolution for not turning against its own, as did so many revolutions. This would have been inspiring news to Huber Matos, serving his twenty-five-year term, or the fifteen thousand "counterrevolutionaries," many of them former revolutionaries, who were in Cuban prisons in the mid-1960s. But because leftists believed Cuba was being treated so unfairly by the same U.S. government that was brutalizing Vietnam, and because they were both infuriated by the United States and impressed by the genuine accomplishment of Castro, they had a tendency to overstate the case for Cuba. Some felt that they were only compensating for the obvious lies and misstatements of Cuba's enemies.

Cuba transformed LeRoi Jones. Born in 1934, he spent the fifties as a beat poet, focused on neither race nor revolution. In fact, he was less political than his colleague Allen Ginsberg, with whom he founded a poetry magazine in 1958. In 1960 he went on one of the Cuban-sponsored trips, this one for black writers. Like many other writers on such Fidel-sponsored junkets, he worried about being "taken" the way it was always said Herbert Matthews had been. "I felt immediately sure that the make was on," he wrote. It was hard not to feel that way as a guest of the government, shuttled from one accomplishment to the next by the Casa de las Americas, a government organization of earnest, well-educated young people who could talk about Latin American art and literature. The Casa was run by Haydée Santamaria, who had been a member of Castro's inner group since the beginning. Santamaria, later infamous for the persecution of insufficiently revolutionary Cuban writers, believed that it was impossible to be an apolitical writer, since being apolitical was in itself a political stance. Jones had been initially disappointed by the caliber of black writers on the trip.

He was the most distinguished. But he was struck by his contact with Latin American writers, some of whom attacked him for his lack of political commitment. The final step appeared to be on July 26, the anniversary of Castro's 1953 quixotically unsuccessful attack on an army fortress that had kicked off the revolution. After touring the Sierra Maestras with a group of Cubans celebrating the anniversary, he returned and described the scene in an essay, "Cuba Libre."

> At one point in the speech the crowd interrupted for about twenty minutes, crying, "Venceremos, venceremos, venceremos, venceremos, venceremos, venceremos, venceremos, venceremos." The entire crowd, 60 or 70,000 people, all chanting in unison. Fidel stepped away from the lectern, grinning, talking to his aides. He quieted the crowd with a wave of his arms and began again. At first softly, with the syllables drawn out and enunciated, then tightening his voice and going into almost a musical rearrangement of his speech. He condemned Eisenhower, Nixon, the South, the Platt Amendment, and Fulgencio Batista in one long, unbelievable sentence. The crowd interrupted again, "Fidel, Fidel, Fidel, Fidel, Fidel, Fidel, Fidel, Fidel, Fidel, Fidel, Fidel." He leaned away from the lectern, grinning at the Chief of the Army. The speech lasted almost two and a half hours, being interrupted time and again by the exultant crowd and once by five minutes of rain. When it began to rain, Almeida draped a rain jacket around Fidel's shoulders, and he relit his cigar. When the speech ended, the crowd went out of its head, roaring for almost forty-five minutes.

"Cuba Libre" is an essay that attacked Jones himself and the beat-bohemian lifestyle and held up the Cuban revolution as a model. Jones wrote, "The rebels among us have become merely people like myself who grow beards and will not participate in politics." The new black American, the black man as revolutionary, in part had his intellectual beginnings with "Cuba Libre."

The trip to Cuba became a kind of hajj, an obligatory journey that all leftists had to make at least once in their life. Writers went to discuss culture, activists to see the revolution, youth to cut cane and "do their share."

One of the less successful visits was by Allen Ginsberg, though even he was favorably impressed with what he found. He wrote of his arrival in early 1965, "Marxist Historical Revolutionary/futility with Wagnerian overtones/lifted my heart." He was put up, as all the Amer-

ican guests were in those days, at the Havana Riviera, which had a
state-of-the-architecture fifties facade. A little footbridge crossed a
pond to enter the not very high high-rise hotel with vistas of Havana
harbor over the curved shoreline drive, the Malecón, where wild waves
broke away and splashed over the wall onto the pavement. From his
luxury room he thought, as many had before, that "being treated as a
guest is a subtle form of brainwashing." His first night there, he met
three young gay poets who told him of police persecution of homosexuals, beats, and bearded longhairs—unless, of course, they were
bearded Fidelistas. They asked Ginsberg to complain to the government, which he did, only to be reassured by officials that it was an incident from the past. Ginsberg, having been persecuted by numerous
secret police, including the FBI, remained skeptical.

He quickly developed a following among young poets, who would
show up at his readings and be prevented from entering until Ginsberg
insisted. Interviewed by a Cuban reporter, he was asked what he would
say to Castro if they could meet. Ginsberg had three points: He
would ask him about the police persecution of homosexuals, then
he would ask him why marijuana was not legal in Cuba, and last he
would propose that opponents of the regime, rather than being
executed, be fed hallucinogenic mushrooms and then be given jobs
operating the elevators at the Havana Riviera.

"I just shot my mouth off," the poet later said. "I just continued
talking there as I would here in terms of being anti-authoritarian. But
my basic feeling there was sympathetic to the revolution."

The revolution quickly tired of his mouth. Haydée Santamaría told
him that he could discuss drugs and homosexuality with high officials,
but they could not have him spreading these ideas to the general population. "We have work to do and cannot afford these extra luxuries
that impede the senses," she said of his ideas about free drugs. Like
other visitors, Ginsberg remained impressed with the Cuban experiment in building a new society. But the Cubans were not impressed
with Ginsberg. The knock on the door finally came at 8:00 A.M. on a
morning after he had been out at parties most of the night. A government official with three uniformed guards told him to pack and put
him on the next outbound plane, which happened to be going to
Czechoslovakia, another country from which he would soon be
expelled.

The early months of 1968 were a revolutionary high point for Cuba.
The trials of pro-Soviet officials at the beginning of the year appeared
to represent a distancing from the Soviet Union, though it was not to

last long. Castro seemed more interested in China than in Russia, which, from the point of view of the New Left, was the correct choice. In 1968 China was in the middle of a wrenching process known officially as the Great Proletarian Cultural Revolution. It had been launched by Communist Party chairman Mao Zedong in 1966 to force out elements that he felt were undermining both his authority and the ideology of the revolution. It quickly turned into a power struggle between the Party chairman and the more moderate leaders in government. China too had its 1968 generation, the first Chinese born and raised in the revolution, and as in the rest of the world, they leaned to the Left. In the Cultural Revolution they were Mao's defenders, released from their schools to be vanguard "Red Guards," as they were labeled in May 1966 by student radicals at Qinghua University. Mao's stated purpose was to combat the creeping bourgeoisie mentality. In August he released his sixteen points "to struggle against and overthrow those persons in authority who are taking the capitalist road" and to bring education, art, and literature into line with socialist doctrine. For leftist ideologues around the world, the Cultural Revolution was a fascinating effort to purge, recommit, and purify their revolution. The Chinese appeared determined not to let their revolution descend into the venality and hypocrisy of the Soviets.

But in practice, the Cultural Revolution was both brutal and disastrous. Teenagers walked up to adults and ordered them to replace their shoes because they had been made in Hong Kong. Girls forcibly cut the long hair off women. The army protected libraries and museums from the Red Guard, who wanted to destroy everything that wasn't ideologically pure. Scholars were assaulted and publicly humiliated for knowledge of foreign languages. Given the extreme reverence for elders in the Chinese population, this behavior was even more shocking than it would have been in a Western country. Gradually society was becoming paralyzed by an almost universal fear. Even the Red Guard itself was split between students whose families were workers, peasants, soldiers, cadres, or martyrs of the revolution—"the five kinds of Red" singled out for special treatment—and the students from bourgeois backgrounds.

Many of the world's governments were less interested in the issue of Chinese revolutionary purity than that of Chinese political and economic stability. By 1968, for the first time in years there were signs of food shortages, caused by the Cultural Revolution. Western governments were even more interested in the impact the Cultural Revolution was having on the Chinese nuclear weapons program. China had become a nuclear power in 1964 and in 1966, the same year as the

象英雄四排和李文忠同志那样破私立公
把毛主席的最新指示落实到行动上。
为人民立新功

1968 poster from China of the Cultural Revolution showing a Red Guard with a book of Mao's teachings in hand. The caption says, "Establish a new standard of merit for the people: Just as the heroic 4th Platoon and Comrade Li Wen'chung worked to defeat selfishness and promote the common good, we should convert Chairman Mao's most recent directive into action."
(Library of Congress)

launching of the Cultural Revolution, had demonstrated the ability to deliver a warhead by missile to a target five hundred miles away. The program had not shown much progress since. This may have been one of the reasons that the Pentagon was not particularly alarmed by it, but others feared the Pentagon was too optimistic. Even with the instability of the Cultural Revolution, physicist Ralph E. Lapp warned in 1968 that by 1973 the Chinese would be capable of hitting Los Angeles and Seattle and they seemed on the verge of a hydrogen bomb, which in fact they did explode by the end of 1968.

Cuba's leaders were intrigued by the Chinese effort to purify their revolution. Revolutionary purity had been a favorite topic of the martyred Che, who had vehemently opposed all financial incentives because he feared they would corrupt the revolution. Castro was more pragmatic, and this disagreement, along with the fact that the actual revolution was over, led to Che's decision to resign from government and move on to another revolution.

Castro had declared 1968 to be "the year of the heroic *guerrillero*." It was to be a yearlong tribute to Che. As though obeying its own propaganda—the ubiquitous signs urging everyone to be like Che—the government itself actually became more like Che. Che, like the New Left, was scornful and distrustful of the Soviet Union, which he felt had compromised away all revolutionary principles. Castro began the year in an anti-Soviet spirit. He said that he expected to expand exports to the point where in two years he would no longer be dependent on the Soviets. Then, on March 14, he announced "the revolutionary offensive." The new offensive ended the remaining traces of privately owned business, closing without compensation fifty-five thousand small businesses, including fruit stands, laundries, garages, clubs, and restaurants. Many of Havana's famous restaurants were closed. In his four-and-a-half-hour speech—not exceptionally long for Fidel—he announced that in Havana alone, 950 bars were to be closed. He said that it was unfair for such people to earn $50 a day in a shop while others earned far less cutting cane. Like Che, he stated his opposition to financial incentives for work.

Cuba was trying to create people who worked for the good of society. Private entrepreneurs, he explained, were in opposition to the sort of "new man" they were trying to create. "Are we going to construct socialism, or are we going to construct vending stands?" Fidel demanded, and the crowd laughed and cheered. "We did not make a revolution here to establish the right to trade! Such a revolution took place in 1789—that was the age of the bourgeois revolution, the revolution of merchants, of the bourgeois. When will they finally understand that this is a revolution of socialists, that this is a revolution of Communists . . . that nobody shed his blood here fighting against the tyranny, against the mercenaries, against bandits, in order to establish the right for someone to make 200 pesos selling rum, or fifty pesos selling fried eggs or omelettes. . . . Clearly and definitely we must say that we propose to eliminate all manifestation of private trade!" The crowd shouted and applauded its approval.

In a March 16 speech announcing the closing of the national lottery, Castro said that such institutions only perpetuated "the mystique of money" that he was trying to end. He was seeking a more pure communism and said that he hoped eventually to completely abolish money. 1968 was the year of the "new man" concept. Che had sought to build the new man, the socialist who worked for the common good, was dedicated to the revolution, and was without selfishness and greed. Now the new man was sometimes referred to as "a man like Che." Castro first spoke of the new man in a speech in May 1967, but 1968, with the "revolutionary offensive" under way, was the year of the new man.

In the middle of his speech about the new offensive, Castro referred to another new phenomenon. "There almost exists an air route for those who take over planes." The week of Fidel's speech, National Airlines flight 28 took off from Tampa bound for Miami. After five minutes in the air, two Cuban exiles took out pistols, forced the flight attendant to open the cockpit, and shouted, "Havana! Havana!" It was the seventh recent hijacking to Cuba, the third that month. This one was by Cubans who had slipped out by boat but found they were homesick for their island home. Most of the hijackers, though, were Americans being pursued by U.S. law enforcement. Increasingly, hijacking became the exit for hunted black militants. Soon Cuba would be arranging entire houses for black American hijackers who remained as political refugees. Some are still there.

In 1968 the Cuban government treated the sudden influx of unwilling visitors with the hospitality the revolution showed to most visitors. The Cubans photographed all the passengers and then escorted them through the airport shops, where, like all visitors, they were encouraged to buy excellent Cuban rum and incomparable cigars. Then they were given a meal that usually included luxury items that were becoming scarce to Cubans, such as roast beef. The plane was refueled and the airline charged for fuel and landing rights—a weighty $1,000 bill for National flight 28. Then, many hours later, the flight returned to the United States, where customs, enforcing the embargo, would usually confiscate the rum and cigars. These reasonably comfortable encounters led to a long-lasting policy among pilots, crews, and passengers of remaining passive when confronted by hijackers. This was even the Federal Aviation Administration's recommendation.

Castro warned in his March speech that he might not continue his hospitality, pointing out that while he allowed the planes to return, planes and vessels stolen to flee to the United States were never returned to Cuba.

The regime's enemies in the United States had grown further entrenched. Alabama governor George Wallace, in his 1968 independent run for president, once again vilified Herbert Matthews for his interview with Fidel. Although the defeat at the Bay of Pigs appeared to demonstrate in irrefutable fashion that popular support in Cuba was on the side of the revolution and not with them, this did not silence the more extreme factions of the anti-Castro exiles, Cubans from the old dictatorship who were not particularly interested in the majority point of view. In the years since the failed invasion, they had become even more violent. In the spring of 1968, a group of Cuban exiles began attacking nations that maintained relations with Cuba, which in fact included the majority of nations in the world. The French tourism office in Manhattan, the Mexican consulate in Newark, travel agencies in Los Angeles, a Polish ship in Miami, and a British ship in New Orleans were among the targets of simple homemade bombs. An officer in a New York City bomb squad said, "It's lucky there aren't more of this particular kind of nut around because there is nothing tougher than trying to stop them." But in fact, many were caught through obvious slipups, such as leaving fingerprints. In December, U.S. district judge William O. Mehrtensin, sentencing nine Cubans—including a ten-year term for Orlando Bosch, a pediatrician and father of five—said, "These acts of terrorism are stupid. I cannot reasonably see any way to fight communism in this manner."

Fidel's admirers loved him as much as his enemies hated him. To the youth of the New Left in 1968—Americans, Western Europeans, Latin Americans—Cuba was the most exciting country in the world. Castro seemed to share their reservations about the Soviets. While the Soviet Union and Eastern Europe confronted their economic crisis by experimenting with free enterprise, Cuba, in the purist tradition of Mao, was going in the opposite direction. Todd Gitlin of the American SDS wrote, "Here apparently was the model of a revolution led by students, not by a Communist Party—indeed, in many ways against it." The world's youth wanted to see Cuba, and the Cubans wanted to show them their showcase of socialism. Such a bold experiment, so close to the United States, for all its faults, even with its milk shortage and executions, was impressive. Ginsberg, too, even after being deported, was impressed. The fierce opposition from the United States always gave the little sugarcane island a heroic aspect.

American SDS's official position on Cuba and other third world revolutions was called "critical support." When Todd Gitlin joined an SDS trip to Cuba in the beginning of 1968, like LeRoi Jones and Allen Ginsberg before him, he was determined not to be seduced by the excitement. He wrote, "I knew all about the terrible and laughable history of Westerners (Lincoln Steffens, George Bernard Shaw, H. G. Wells, Sidney and Beatrice Webb) making their pilgrimages to the East and trapping themselves in apologies; it wasn't going to happen to me." And so he steeled himself against the revolution's many charms with a list of questions about civil liberties, democracy, and the right of dissent.

Che images at the Cultural Congress in Havana in January 1968.
(Photo by Fred Mayer/Magnum Photos)

The trip began, as many of them did, traveling by way of Mexico City to circumvent U.S. travel restrictions. The Mexican government openly differed with the United States on Cuba and refused to cut off relations with its historically close Spanish Caribbean neighbor. But unbeknownst to the young Americans who traveled through Mexico City, the Mexican president, Gustavo Díaz Ordaz, had a paranoid fear of the Cuban revolution and carefully noted passenger lists on Havana-bound flights to record the Mexicans on board. When there were Americans, he would pass the list on to U.S. intelligence.

The SDS trip was timed to coincide with a weeklong international cultural congress. British historian Eric Hobsbawm reported on the week for the *Times Literary Supplement*: "Cuba was, of course, an ideal setting for such a Congress. It is not only an embattled and heroic country, though as Castro himself observed, a long way second to Vietnam, but a remarkably attractive one, if only because it is visibly one of the rare states in the world whose population actually likes and trusts its government." Among the luminaries at the conference were novelist Julio Cortázar and muralist David Siqueiros. A rumor circulated that

Siqueiros had been recognized as one of the plotters in the Trotsky assassination by an angry Trotskyist who kicked him in the shin.

The SDS group was put up in the Havana Libre, the former Havana Hilton, completed just before the revolution. This sterile, modern hotel was one of the first and last true high-rises built in Havana. The young radicals were comfortable there, eating crab and shrimp cocktails with Cuba libres. They visited factories, which admittedly they rarely did in the United States, and training programs, and a farm where field hands actually sang on their way to work. Gitlin tried to stay skeptical but said, "Mostly I saw energy, amazing commitment. Ordinary people seemed both mobilized and relaxed." It was an extraordinary combination to see a people energized by a young revolution, inspired by a charismatic leader, and yet with the calm, the music, the sensuality, the good humor, and the accessibility of Caribbean culture. Gitlin, Tom Hayden, other SDS leaders, and David Dellinger were there analyzing the revolution in between conversations about what to do in Chicago during the Democratic convention coming up in the summer.

Gitlin returned to the United States still full of reservations but impressed enough with his experience that he began to arrange other Cuban trips for SDS members. SDS was growing rapidly on college campuses and by 1968 had nearly one hundred thousand members.

Mark Rudd was in the first group to go on one of Gitlin's SDS-organized trips to Cuba. They were put up at the Riviera, the not quite high-rise over the footbridge by the bay. But they objected to the luxury and arranged to be moved to student housing in the abandoned mansions of the neighborhood. Everywhere they went in this year of the heroic *guerrillero,* they saw Che's portrait—on walls, in stores, in homes. Traveling by bus in the countryside, they looked down into a valley and saw Che's portrait, several acres large, fashioned in white rock and red earth. Rudd knew the teachings of Che: "The duty of every revolutionary is to make a revolution." He longed to be a revolutionary, to be "a man like Che." Soon he would be back on his Ivy League campus. He was eager to get back.

CHAPTER 11

APRIL MOTHERFUCKERS

NEVER EXPLAIN WHAT YOU ARE DOING. This wastes a good deal of time and rarely gets through. Show them through your action, if they don't understand it, fuck 'em, maybe you'll hook them with the next action.
— ABBIE HOFFMAN, Revolution for the Hell of It, *1968*

I SENSED IN MARK an embryo of fanaticism that made me feel slightly irrelevant in his presence." That is what Tom Hayden wrote about meeting Mark Rudd when he was twenty-nine years old and Rudd a twenty-year-old Columbia student.

In 1968 there was an expression, "Don't trust anyone over thirty." It was a cliché ironically offered as advice by Charlton Heston to young, rebellious chimpanzees in the 1968 Hollywood hit *Planet of the Apes.* In another 1968 movie, *Wild in the Streets,* a dictatorship by young people rounds up everyone over thirty-five and imprisons them in concentration camps, where they are kept helplessly high on LSD. The film was made by the over-thirty crowd, the same ones who insisted that youth trust no one over thirty. Twenty-year-olds never expressed such a ridiculous sentiment. In 1968, Abbie Hoffman turned thirty-two, as did Black Panther Bobby Seale. Hoffman's colleague Jerry Rubin turned thirty that year, and Eldridge Cleaver turned thirty-three.

But the college students of the late sixties were different from those of earlier in the decade. They were even more rebellious and perhaps less skilled at expressing that rebellion. Tom Hayden described Rudd as "a nice, somewhat inarticulate, suburban New Jersey kid with blue eyes, sandy hair, and an easy-going manner, non-descript in appearance, apparently having no time for changing clothes or engaging in sterile debate."

Rudd's style and manner were certainly different from those of Tom Hayden or Mario Savio, who were conservative dressers, notably articulate, and frequently engaged in long hours of debate with their movements. Hayden, who expressed himself with a brilliant clarity, may have found Rudd inarticulate by contrast, but the true difference was that Rudd, a tough, avid, and thoughtful reader, did not attach the importance that Hayden did to words. The younger rebels did not believe in civility. While Savio, perhaps the best student speaker of the sixties, was famous for the genteel removal of his shoes to avoid marking up a police car, one of Rudd's famous moments was sitting in the Columbia University vice president's apartment and pulling off his shoes.

Being a student in the late sixties was a different experience from being one in the early sixties. For one thing, there was the draft. Neither Abbie Hoffman nor Tom Hayden nor Mario Savio had been subjected to a draft—a draft that threatened to pull students into a war in which Americans were killing and dying by the thousands. Perhaps more important, the war itself, with its cruel and pointless violence, was seen on television every night, and no matter how much they reviled it, these students were powerless to stop it. They could not even vote if they were under twenty-one, though they could be drafted at eighteen.

Despite all these differences, one thing, unfortunately, had not changed—the university itself. If the American university has in recent years been thought of as a sanctuary for leftist thought and activism, that is a legacy of the late sixties graduates. In 1968, universities were still very conservative institutions. Academia had enthusiastically supported World War II, moved seamlessly to firm support of the cold war, and, though starting to squirm a bit, tended to support the war in Vietnam. This was why the universities imagined their campuses to be suitable and desirable places for such activities as recruitment of executives by Dow Chemical, not to mention recruitment of officers by the military. And while universities were famous for their intellectuals like Herbert Marcuse or C. Wright Mills, a more typical product was Harvard's Henry Kissinger. The Ivy League in particular was known as a bastion of conservative northeast elitism. Columbia University had Dwight Eisenhower as an emeritus member of its board of directors. Active members included CBS founder William S. Paley; Arthur H. Sulzberger, the septuagenarian publisher of *The New York Times*; his son Arthur O. Sulzberger, who would take over after his father's death later in the year; Manhattan district attorney Frank S. Hogan; William A. M. Burden, director of Lockheed, a major Vietnam War weapons contractor; Walter Thayer of the Whitney Corporation, a Republican fund-raiser who worked for Nixon in 1968; and Lawrence A. Wein, film producer, adviser to Lyndon Johnson, and trustee of Consolidated Edison. Later in the year students would produce a paper alleging connections between Columbia trustees and the CIA. Columbia and other Ivy League schools produced leaders in industry, publishing, finance—the people behind politics, the people behind war, the very people C. Wright Mills had identified in his book as "the power elite."

At Columbia the dean offered "sherry hours," in which students dressed in blazers and gray wool pants sipped pale sherry from cut-glass goblets while discussing campus issues. It was this vanishing world that the administration was struggling to preserve in 1968.

The disappointments felt by the new crop of students were not so different from those felt by the earlier group. Tom Hayden too had been disappointed in the University of Michigan, which he found to be in league with a corporate world. The new students may have just felt the same thing more intensely. Mark Rudd said of Columbia, "I entered the university expecting the Ivy Tower on the Hill—a place where committed scholars would search for truth in a world that desperately needed help. Instead, I found a huge corporation that made money from real estate, government research contracts, and student fees; teachers who cared only for advancement in their narrow areas of study; worst of all, an institution hopelessly mired in the society's racism and militarism." The prestigious schools, the ones that attempted to use their status to skim off the brightest, most promising of the generation, were the worst.

New York, albeit many blocks downtown in the East Village, had become the center of a hip counterculture. Abbie Hoffman and Allen Ginsberg and Ed Sanders—who had a group called the Fugs that was named after a word used by Norman Mailer in his novel *The Naked and the Dead* because he could not use his F-word of choice—were all in the East Village. Hoffman frequently appeared at East Village events with his special honey laced with a distillate of hashish. The East Village, a dilapidated section of the Lower East Side, had only recently acquired its name because the once beat Greenwich Village, now the West Village, had become too expensive. The enormously successful Bob Dylan still lived in the West Village. The same thing had happened in San Francisco, where Ferlinghetti remained in the North Beach section that the beats had made too fashionable, while the hippies moved out to the poorer, less central Fillmore and Haight-Ashbury sections.

The East Village became so famous for its "hippie" lifestyle that tour buses would stop by the busy shops of St. Mark's Place—or St. Marx Place, as Abbie Hoffman liked to call it—for tourists to view the hippies. In September 1968, East Village denizens rebelled, organizing their own bus tour to a staid section of Queens, where they questioned people mowing lawns and took photos of people taking photos of them.

San Francisco and New York were the bipolar epicenters of America's 1968 hip. This was reflected in rock concert producer Bill Graham's two halls, the Fillmore West in the Fillmore section of San Francisco and the Fillmore East, which he opened in 1968 on Second Avenue and Sixth Street in the East Village. The new rock concerts began in the neighborhood at what had been the Anderson Yiddish Theater. John Morris, who managed the Fillmore East, had been there years before to see the Anderson's closing show, *The Bride Got Farblundjet,* starring Menasha Skulnik and Molly Picon. Reopened by Morris, the theater featured such groups as the Fugs and Country Joe and the Fish, who were stars from their grizzly anti–Vietnam War satire, "I-Feel-Like-I'm-Fixin'-to-Die Rag." They then persuaded Graham to open an East Village Fillmore across the street.

Graham was not only a dominant force in 1968 rock music, he frequently gave benefit concerts for political causes, including one for the Columbia students when they went on strike in April. Rock music and college campuses had become closely connected. "The college market today accounts for more than 70 percent of the professional concert activities in the United States," said Fanny Taylor, executive secretary of the Association of College and University Concert Managers in 1968.

College students also represented a large share of record sales. In 1967, record sales in America had reached an all-time high of $1 billion, having doubled in ten years, and for the first time in history, record albums were outselling singles. These trends continued in 1968.

The late sixties are often remembered for heavily amplified music full of electronic vibrato, slow fades, and other gimmicks pleasing to drug users, much of it pioneered by the Beatles. Feedback and twelve-track tapes produced a complex and often loud sound from only a few musicians. Researchers at the University of Tennessee exposed guinea pigs to rock music over a period of three months at intervals designed to resemble what "the average discotheque goer" heard and found evidence of cell destruction in the cochlea, the part of the ear that transmits sound waves into nerve impulses. But college students, the important part of the market, were not blowing their ears out in 1968. They could barely forgive Bob Dylan for turning to rock in 1966 and cheered when, starting with "John Wesley Harding," Dylan returned to acoustic guitar and folk ballad—though never again to the pure folk sound of 1963.

In 1968 *Life* called the new rock music "the first music born in the age of instant communication." In June 1967 the Beatles had performed the first live international concert broadcast by satellite.

Life called the rock music of 1968 "an eclectic cornucopia." The year 1968 was a time of ballads with carefully crafted lyrics and a clear melody line. Peace activist and performer Joan Baez, at twenty-seven, was still playing to huge crowds, singing ballad versions of Dylan, the Rolling Stones, the Beatles, the poetic Leonard Cohen, and fellow folk protester Phil Ochs. The Cubans imitated her ballad style, and from there the soft and lyrical protest ballad spread through the entire Spanish-speaking world. Even the Basques began singing Baez-type ballads in their outlawed ancient language. Simon & Garfunkel, who had struggled in the early sixties because their style had more to do with Renaissance madrigals than rock and roll, reached new heights of popularity with their April 1968 album, *Bookends*. With songs such as "America" about the search for the country's soul, the album is considered by some fans to be their best. Crosby, Stills, & Nash and Neil Young sang ballads with a country sound, as did Creedence Clearwater Revival, though their instrumentals were highly amplified with electric instruments. Joni Mitchell, a twenty-four-year-old Canadian with long blond hair and a crystalline voice, became a star in the United States in 1968 with her ballads. Jerry Jeff Walker sang the sad story of Bojangles, a street performer. Pete Townshend, guitarist and songwriter for the Who, complained that music was getting too serious. Since popular music was being targeted more than ever before to youth, it might have been expected to be more playful. "There's no bloody youth in music today," said Townshend.

There was a surprising mobility among music genres. After sixteen years with a jazz quartet, Dave Brubeck broke up his group and began composing classical music. Three British musicians—Eric Clapton, Jack Bruce, and Ginger Baker—strayed from blues and jazz into rock music, calling themselves Cream. The group was greatly admired by the New York Philharmonic's conductor Leonard Bernstein, who at age fifty gave up full-time conducting at the end of the 1968 season. He was particularly taken with Ginger Baker, saying, "I mean, they've got a drummer who can really keep time."

The new record albums came with increasingly elaborate covers, many double flapped, their curiously costumed and staged photos set in swirling, throbbing graphics. The album covers were in fact designed for young people smoking marijuana or "dropping acid" to seemingly spend hours examining. Under the influence of drugs, everything appeared to be a double entendre with deep hidden meanings. A fairly straightforward film such as 1967's *The Graduate,* about a young man uncertain of his future in a world of shallow values, seemed laden with far deeper messages. Beatles songs were examined like Tennyson's poems. Who was Eleanor Rigby? *The Man with the Balloons,* Marco Ferreri's Italian film starring Marcello Mastroianni, tells the story of a disillusioned man with a bunch of balloons. He decides to find the breaking point of the balloons and discovers that each balloon is different. End of movie. Do you get it? The meaning of it all? It was this insistence that everything had a hidden deeper meaning that led to the unexpected success of the low-budget 1968 thriller, *Night of the Living Dead,* which was seen not as a zombie horror film, a type of cheap thriller that had been done repeatedly since the 1930s, but as a cogent satire on American society.

Singer Janis Joplin, who in 1968 was screeching out her voice with a California group called Big Brother and the Holding Company, said that she was not a hippie, because hippies believed in trying to make the world better. Instead she said she was a beatnik: "Beatniks believe things aren't going to get better and say, 'The hell with it,' stay stoned, and have a good time."

But while trying to make the world better, the hippie spent a great deal of time stoned and having a good time. Smoking marijuana was probably more commonplace among American college students in 1968 than smoking tobacco is today. It was commonly believed, and still is by many, that the government's drug enforcement apparatus was an instrument of repression and that a truly democratic society would legalize drugs.

It seemed America was divided into two kinds of people: those who lived the new way and those who were desperate to understand it. The secret of the surprise theatrical success *Hair,* "the American tribal love-rock musical," was that although virtually nothing happens in the course of it, it claimed to offer the audience a glimpse of hippie life, furthering the stereotype that hippies do absolutely nothing and do it with an inexplicable—surely drug-induced—enthusiasm. Newspapers and magazines often ran exposés on campus life. Why was Abbie Hoffman's wed-in covered in *Time* magazine? Because the news media and the rest of society's establishment were trying to understand "the younger generation." It was one of the "big stories of the year," along with the war they were refusing to fight. Magazines and newspapers regularly ran articles on "the new generation." Most of these articles had an undertone of frustration because the reporters could not understand whose side these people were on. To the establishment, they seemed to be against everything. An April 27, 1968, editorial in *Paris Match* said, "They condemn Soviet society just like bourgeois society: industrial organization, social discipline, the aspiration for material wealth, bathrooms, and, in the extreme, work. In other words, they reject Western society."

In 1968, a book was published in the United States called *The Gap*, by an uncle and his longhaired, pot-smoking nephew trying to understand each other. The nephew introduces the uncle to marijuana, which the uncle queerly refers to as "a stick of tea." But after he smoked it he said, "It expanded my consciousness. No kidding! Now I know what Richie means. I listened to music and heard it as never before."

Ronald Reagan defined a hippie as someone who "dresses like Tarzan, has hair like Jane, and smells like Cheetah." The lack of intellectual depth in Ronald Reagan's analysis surprised no one, but most of these analyses had little more to them. Society had not progressed beyond the 1950s, when the entire so-called beat generation, a phrase invented by novelist Jack Kerouac, was reduced on television to a character named Maynard G. Krebs, who seldom washed and would croak, "Work!?" in a horrified tone any time gainful employment was suggested. Norman Podhoretz had written an article in the *Partisan Review* on the beat generation titled "The Know-Nothing Bohemians." A rejection of materialism and a distaste for corporate culture were dismissed as not wanting to work. A persistent claim of a lack of hygiene was used to dismiss a different way of dressing, whereas neither beatniks nor hippies were particularly dirty. True, the occasional Mark Rudd was known for slovenliness, but many others were neat, even fastidious—obsessed with hair products for their new flowing locks and preening in embroidered bell-bottoms.

The public had a fixation on the subject of hair length, which gave the 1968 Broadway show its title. In 1968 there was actually a poster placed on two thousand billboards across the country that had a picture of a bushy-headed eighteen-year-old and said, "Beautify America, Get a Haircut." Joe Namath, the New York Jets quarterback, with medium-length hair and sometimes a mustache—whose courage and toughness did much to elevate football to a leading national sport in the late 1960s—was frequently greeted in stadiums by fans with signs

"Son, why don't you bring some of the New Left home for Cokes and cookies?"

saying, "Joe, Get a Haircut!" In March 1968, when Robert Kennedy was wrestling with a decision about running for president, he received letters saying that if he wanted to be president, he should get a haircut. There was an oddly hostile tone to these letters. "Nobody wants a hippie for President," one said. And, in fact, when he declared his candidacy, he did get a haircut.

By 1968, a wide range of commercial interests realized that "the generation gap" was a concept that could be marketed for profit. ABC Television launched a new series called *The Mod Squad,* seemingly unaware that "mod" was an already dated British word. The series was about three young cops—one looking like a young version of Mary from the folk-singing group Peter, Paul, & Mary, another like a cleaned-up young Bob Dylan, and the third like a sweet-faced Black Panther—all the provocative, violent, and churning counterculture suddenly rendered absolutely harmless. ABC's advertisements said, as though people actually talked like this, "The police don't understand the now generation—and the now generation doesn't dig the fuzz. The solution—find some swinging young people who live the beat, get them to work for the cops." The ABC ad went on to explain, "Today in television the name of the game is think young. . . . And with a whole breed of young adult viewers, ABC wins hands down."

In 1968 everyone held opinions on the generation gap, Columbia president Grayson Kirk's phrase from an April 12 speech at the University of Virginia that instantly became banal. André Malraux, who in his youth was known as a fiery rebel but in 1968 was part of de Gaulle's right-wing government, denied that there was a gap between generations and insisted the problem was the normal struggle of youth to grow up. "It would be foolish to believe in such a conflict," he said. "The basic problem is that our civilization, which is a civilization of machines, can teach a man everything except how to be a man." Supreme Court chief justice Earl Warren said in 1968 that "one of the most urgent necessities of our time" was to resolve the tensions between what he called "the daring of youth" and "the mellow practicality" of the more mature.

Then there were those who explained that the youth of the day were simply in transition to a postindustrial society. Added to the widely held belief that the new youth, the hippies, were unwilling to work was the belief that they would not have to. One study by the Southern California Research Council claimed that by the year 1985 most Americans would have to work only half the year to maintain their current standard of living and warned that recreational facilities were woefully underdeveloped for all the leisure time facing the new generation. These conclusions were based on the rising individual share of the gross national product. If the total value of goods and services was divided by the total population, including nonearners, the resulting figure was projected to double between 1968 and 1985. It was a widespread belief in the 1960s that American technology would create more leisure time, Herbert Marcuse being one of the few to argue that technology was failing to create leisure time.

John Kifner, a young *New York Times* reporter respected by student radicals at Columbia, wrote a January 1968 article from Amherst on marijuana and students, which contained the shocking news that the town was selling a great deal of Zig-Zag cigarette paper and no pouches of tobacco. The article introduced readers to the concept of recreational drugs. These students were doing drugs not to forget their troubles, but to have fun. "Interviews with students indicated that, while many drug takers appeared to be troubled, many did not." The article suggested that the drug lifestyle had been encouraged by media coverage. A high school principal in affluent suburban Westchester was quoted as saying, "There's no doubt this thing has increased since the summer. There were articles on the East Village in *Esquire, Look,* and *Life* and this provides the image for the kids."

Such articles described "college marijuana parties," although a more typical get-together would be students lying around smoking joints and reading such an article while uncontrollable giggling led to gasping, wheezing laughter. A popular way to pass a rainy day in the East Village was to get stoned and go to the St. Marks Cinema, where sometimes included in the triple feature for a dollar would be the old documentary on the dangers of marijuana, *Reefer Madness.*

Marijuana was a twentieth-century drug in the United States. It had never even been banned by law until 1937. LSD, lysergic acid diethylamide, or acid, was invented by accident in a Swiss laboratory in the 1930s by a doctor, Albert Hofmann, when a small amount of the compound on his fingertips resulted in "an altered state of awareness of the world." After the war, Hofmann's laboratory sold small amounts in the United States, where saxophonist John Coltrane, celebrated for his introspective brilliance, jazz trumpeter Dizzy Gillespie, and pianist Thelonious Monk experimented with the new drug, though not nearly as much as did the CIA. The substance was hard to detect because it had neither odor, taste, nor color. An enemy surreptitiously exposed to LSD might reveal secrets or become confused and surrender. This was the origin of the idea of slipping acid into the water cooler. Plans under consideration included slipping acid to Egypt's Gamal Abdel Nasser and Cuba's Fidel Castro so that they would babble foolishly and lose their followings. But Castro's popularity among the young would probably have been enormously magnified once Allen Ginsberg and others learned that Fidel, too, was an acid head.

Agents experimented on themselves, causing one to run outside to discover that cars were "bloodthirsty monsters." They also, in conjunction with the army, experimented on unknowing victims, including prisoners and prostitutes. The tests resulted in a number of suicides and psychotic patients and left the CIA convinced that it was almost impossible to usefully interrogate someone while under the influence of LSD. Acid experiments were encouraged by Richard Helms, who later, between 1967 and 1973, served as CIA director.

Timothy Leary and Richard Alpert, Harvard junior professors, studied LSD by taking it or giving it to others. Their work in the early sixties was well respected—until parents started complaining that their promising young Harvard student was boasting of having "found God and discovered the secret of the Universe." The pair left Harvard in 1963 but continued experiments in Milbrook, New York. In 1966 LSD became an illegal substance by an act of Congress and Leary's fame spread through arrests. Alpert became a Hindu and changed his name to Baba Ram Dass. In 1967, Allen Ginsberg urged everyone over the age of fourteen to try LSD at least once. Tom Wolfe's bestselling book that extolled and popularized LSD, *The Electric Kool-Aid Acid Test,* was published in 1968.

It was an unpredictable drug. Some people had a pleasant experience and others nightmarish cycles of mania and depression or paranoia known as "a bad trip." Students who took pride in being responsible drug abusers insisted that tripping be done under the supervision of a friend who did not take the drug but had experienced it before. To many, including Abbie Hoffman, there was a kind of unspoken fraternity of those who had taken acid, and those who had not were on the outside.

Disturbing stories began to appear in the press. In January 1968 several newspapers reported that six young college men suffered total and permanent blindness as a result of staring at the sun while under the influence of LSD. Norman M. Yoder, commissioner of the Office of the Blind in the Pennsylvania State Welfare Department, said the retinal area of the youths' eyes had been destroyed. This was the first case of total blindness, but in a case the previous May at the University of California at Santa Barbara, four students reportedly lost reading vision by staring at the sun after taking LSD. But many stories of LSD damage proved bogus. Army Chemical Corps testing failed to support the ubiquitous stories of LSD causing chromosome damage.

Acid was having a profound effect on popular music. The Beatles' 1967 *Sergeant Pepper's Lonely Hearts Club Band* album reflected in music, lyrics, and cover design the drug experiments of the group. Some of the songs were descriptive of fantasies experienced while under the influence of LSD. This was also true of the earlier song "Yellow Submarine," which was the basis of a 1968 movie. John Lennon's first imaginary voyage in a submarine was reported to be the result of an acid-doused sugar cube. To the audience, Sergeant Pepper was about drugs, one of the first of the acid albums—the coming of age of psychedelic music and psychedelic album design. Perhaps because of the drug use that went with listening to this music, *Sergeant Pepper* was said to have profound implications. Years later Abbie Hoffman said the album expressed "our view of the world." He called it

"Beethoven coming to the supermarket." But at the time, the ultra-conservative John Birch Society claimed that the album showed a fluency in the techniques of brainwashing that proved the Beatles' involvement in an international communist conspiracy. The BBC barred the airing of "A Day in the Life" because of the words "I'd love to turn you on" and Maryland governor Spiro Agnew campaigned to ban "With a Little Help from My Friends" because the fab four sang that that was how they "get high."

The Beatles did not invent acid rock, the fusion of LSD and rock music, but because of their status, they opened the floodgates. San Francisco groups had been producing acid rock for several years but by 1968 a few of these groups such as the Jefferson Airplane and the Grateful Dead became famous internationally while many others such as Daily Flash and Celestial Hysteria remained San Francisco acts.

The newly campus-focused music was not only about politics and drugs, it was also about sex. Rock concerts, like political demonstrations, were often the foreplay of a sexual encounter. Some singers were more open than others about this. Jim Morrison, the velvet-voiced rocker of the Doors, in tight leather pants, called himself "an erotic politician." In a 1969 Miami concert, he urged the audience to take off their clothes and then announced, "You want to see my cock, don't you? That's what you came for, isn't it." Janis Joplin, the scratchy-voiced balladeer, said, "My music isn't supposed to make you riot, it's supposed to make you fuck."

Most articles about the new lifestyle alluded with varying degrees of candor to the impression that these young people were having a lot of sex. Sex was now called "free love," because, with the pill, sex seemed free of consequences. It was not entirely free, as Mark Rudd learned his sophomore year at Columbia when he went on penicillin for the case of gonorrhea passed to him by a Barnard student who had gotten it from a married philosophy instructor. In fact, penicillin, discovered in the 1940s, had been the first pill to sexual freedom. The second, the oral contraceptive, was developed in 1957 and licensed by the Food and Drug Administration in 1960. As college physicians found, it rapidly overtook all other birth control methods and by 1968 had became commonplace on college campuses.

The popular slogan "Make Love Not War" made it clear that the two were interconnected—students could demonstrate against making war, and then, in the exhilaration of having stood with the thousands, survived the clubs and the tear gas, they would not uncommonly go off and make love. It was not only SNCC that was having fun. It was the

SDS and other student organizations that had constant meetings about the next thing to do and then, when the next thing came and they didn't know what to do, just acted spontaneously. But in between all these meetings there was a fair amount of sex. As a Detroit student told *Life* magazine, "We are not just eating and sleeping together, we're protesting the war together!"

Ed Sanders, whose Fugs sang much about fugging, called the mid-sixties "the Golden Age of fucking," which was as close as his plotless 1970 "novel of the Yippies," *Shards of God,* set in 1968, came to a theme. Many couples were made and unmade in the course of the movement. Tom Hayden's marriage to Casey Hayden, Mario Savio's to fellow Free Speech Movement activist Suzanne Goldberg, and Mary King's marriage to a fellow SNCC worker are just a few of the many marriages formed in the movements that did not last.

The attitude toward sex created an even deeper gap between generations. It was as though two completely different societies were cohabiting the same era. While Sanders was having his golden age in the East Village and Rudd was up at Columbia being saved by penicillin, City Councilman John J. Santucci, a Democrat, successfully pressured the Metropolitan Transportation Authority in 1968 to remove from subway cars posters for the film *The Graduate,* because they showed Anne Bancroft and Dustin Hoffman in bed together.

The change in sexual mores was not just American. Young women in the Mexican student movement of 1968 shocked Mexican society by carrying signs saying "Virginity Causes Cancer." The 1968 demonstrations in Paris began with a demand for coeducational dormitories. According to French myth, when President de Gaulle was told that the students at Nanterre wanted coeducational housing, the General, looking confused, turned to his aide and asked, "Why don't they just meet in the cafés?"

In the United States, only a few progressive schools such as Oberlin had mixed dormitories. Many universities allowed more freedom for men than women. The Ivy League had separate universities for women with completely different rules. Columbia men certainly had far more privileges than Barnard women, who were not allowed to live anywhere other than the women's dormitories for their first two years. It is strange to think of a nationwide controversy over an unknown coed's living arrangements, but that is what unfolded for several weeks in 1968 when a *New York Times* journalist decided to report on the life of college women—just one of hundreds of articles on "the new lifestyle." One sophomore bragged to the reporter, on condition that she not be identified by name, of how she had lied to the Barnard administration in order to be able to live off campus with her boyfriend.

Though the reporter respected her anonymity, Barnard, determined to weed out this public disgrace, followed the details and was able to identify the offender as a student named Linda LeClair and called for her expulsion. Students protested this treatment, many protesting that this could be happening only to a woman. But, strangely, the struggle of Linda LeClair—to cohabit or not cohabit—was not only covered on the front page of *The New York Times* for weeks, but it was also covered by *Time, Newsweek, Life,* and other national publications. Day after day the drama unfolded in the *Times*—how the Barnard School Council granted her a hearing, how hundreds went, how she argued for the rights of individuals, and finally how she was "wearing a bright orange shift and beaming brightly as she read the final verdict: no expulsion but banned from the school cafeteria."

In the *Times* coverage, it was also mentioned that many of the students questioned "shook their heads in amusement." To the outside press, this seemed an important story about a radically changing society. To the 1968 student, as to most of us today, it seemed hard to believe that such a petty affair would even make the newspapers.

Two days later, the *Times* was back with an article on LeClair's parents headlined FATHER DESPAIRS OF BARNARD DAUGHTER. In Hudson, New Hampshire, Paul LeClair said, "We just don't see eye to eye and just don't know what can be done about it . . . what an individual does is one thing, but when she starts influencing hundreds of people, it's wrong."

The president of Barnard, Martha Peterson, was not content with the minor rebuke of the council and moved to expel LeClair despite the decision. Students staged a sit-in, blocking Peterson's office. A petition, signed by 850 of Barnard's 1,800 students, protested the expulsion. The office was awash in letters supporting or attacking the college sophomore, declaring that she had become the symbol of everything from civil liberties to the decline of the American family.

Martha Peterson said, "We learned also to our regret that public interest in sex on the college campus is insatiable." But it was more than simply prying. The press was reflecting the common view that the "new generation" had a "new morality" and that for better or worse, the things youth were doing represented nothing less than a complete alteration in the values and mores of society with the far-reaching ramifications. Ed Sanders confidently wrote, "Forty years from now the Yippies and those who took part in the Peace-swarm of 1967–68 will be recognized for what they are, the most important cultural political force in the last 150 years of American civilization." It was believed, at times with panic, at times with joy, that the fundamental nature of human society was changing. *Life* magazine wrote, "A sexual anthropologist of some future century analyzing the pill, the drive-in, the works of Harold Robbins, the Tween-Bra and all the other artifacts of the American Sexual Revolution, may consider the case of Linda LeClair and her boyfriend, Peter Behr, as a moment in which the morality of an era changed." So with Hue under siege, marines dug in at Khe Sanh, the Biafran war growing harsher, the Middle East more volatile, the Senate investigating if the Gulf of Tonkin incident that was the pretext in August 1964 for the Vietnam War was a fraud, Rudi Dutschke and the German SDS on the streets of Berlin, Czechs and Poles defying Moscow—a Barnard student's decision to live across the street in her boyfriend's dorm room was front-page news.

Linda LeClair's boyfriend, Peter Behr, seems to have almost never been consulted in the controversy. She dropped out of school and the two joined a commune. Behr, who did get his Columbia degree, went on to be a massage therapist. Barnard relaxed the rules, saying only parental permission was needed to live off campus. But in the fall of 1968, Barnard women rebelled against even this.

There was one thing Mark Rudd, growing up in an affluent New Jersey suburb on the edge of impoverished Newark, always wished his parents could make him understand. Why had they not done more to stop the Nazis when they first came to power? Surely there must have been something they could have tried to do. Despite this nagging notion, he had not been a politically active high school student. He lived in well-to-do Maplewood, where his parents had moved late in life when his father started to succeed in the real estate market. His father was a lieutenant colonel in the army reserves who had anglicized his Jewish-sounding last name to avoid anti-Semitism in the military.

Like many of his age, Mark Rudd had as his introduction to radical politics *Sing Out!* magazine, a journal of folk singing and protest songs that led him to the music of Ledbelly, Woody Guthrie, and Pete Seeger. He loved to study, and many of the books he read came from his politically savvy girlfriend, the school intellectual. She even knew Herbert Marcuse's stepson, Michael Neumann, who later became Rudd's college roommate. Neumann's older brother, Tommy, was a member of the affinity group the East Village Motherfuckers.

Rudd never played sports. Years later he liked to say that sex was his exercise—reading and sex with his girlfriend, who then went away to Sarah Lawrence. Rudd wanted to go to the University of Chicago, a school that had distinguished itself by canceling its sports program. In the end he chose Columbia so that he could be close to his girlfriend. But as often happens, once in college, both formed other attachments.

Aside from its Ivy League conservatism, Columbia was a reasonable choice for Rudd. In this institution that had originated the phrase *generation gap,* Rudd was not a good match with the administration, but he was with the students. Like Rudd, most Columbia students were not athletes. Rudd was told that Columbia had managed to run up a record twenty-year streak without winning a football game. The half-time band performed distinctive numbers, including one titled "Ode to the Diaphragm." Fraternities barely existed. In the summer of 1968, Rudd and his friends rented a fraternity house on 114th Street for the summer, renaming it Sigma Delta Sigma—SDS.

In 1965, when Rudd first went to college, SDS was beginning to give up on its unsuccessful efforts to organize in the inner cities and recognize that college campuses offered the most fertile ground for recruitment. One night early in Rudd's freshman year, a man named David Gilbert knocked on Rudd's door and said, "We are having a meeting discussing things. Maybe you would like to come."

That was all it took. "It was a social thing," Rudd recalled. "People hang out. And the subculture is fun. There were drugs and girls. It was what was happening. Nobody thought about going to Wall Street in those days."

Rudd's life at Columbia was reshaped. He became an SDS campus radical, going to meetings and discussions, knocking on doors himself, and planning protests. There were many hours of meetings for every protest. "I liked talking about revolution—changing the world—make it a better place. Meetings were discussing important things, and it led to action. I must have gone to one thousand meetings in this five-year period. It was vastly different from my classes. The SDS people knew a lot. They knew a lot about Vietnam, about anticolonial revolutions, and nationalist movements."

But what was always important to Rudd was that the talk translated into action. "I've always valued people who could read, think, discuss, and act. That is my idea of an intellectual," Rudd recently said. He became known among radicals for his impatient taste for action—"the action faction," was what the SDS started calling the Rudd contingent at Columbia. Rudd had returned from Cuba with a quote from José Martí that had been used by Che: "Now is the time of the furnaces, and only light should be seen."

He came back from Cuba in March, in his own words, "fired up with revolutionary fervor." Square inch by square inch, his walls became covered with posters and pictures of Che—Che smoking, Che smiling, Che smoking and smiling, Che reflecting. In early spring Rudd had to go to a dentist, and confronted with the prospect of pain, he asked himself, What would Che do?

The business of the action faction at Columbia was deadly serious, though at times their pranks seemed more Yippie! than SDS. Or perhaps the activists, like most twenty-year-olds, were part adult and part teenager. Against the wishes of Rudd, the SDS voted in a meeting to confront the head of the Selective Service for New York City, an officer with the improbable name of Colonel Akst, who was to deliver a speech on campus. Rudd hated the idea of dignifying the Selective Service with probing questions. "What wimps," he complained, resolving to find another course of action.

At that time the SDS had recently acquired a new chapter that fit well with Rudd's action faction. The East Village Motherfuckers had joined the fast-growing SDS organization. The other necessary component for Rudd's plan was someone who could approach the colonel without being recognized, since by early spring 1968 Rudd and his comrades had already become too well known. By blind luck, a self-proclaimed Berkeley radical fell into Rudd's lap. He remembered hearing a friend complain of an irritating houseguest who talked a great deal about the revolution and violence and the importance of Berkeley as the revolutionary center of all that was happening. Rudd enlisted his help.

The colonel was to deliver his speech in Earl Hall, the religious center of the Columbia campus. "Red face shining beneath his proud cap," was Rudd's description of the colonel. Suddenly, from the back of the hall, the snare drums and fifes of "Yankee Doodle" were heard. While the audience turned to see the East Village Motherfuckers dressed as a hairy fife and drum corps, having given themselves the name "the Knickerboppers," the unknown Berkeley revolutionary ran to the stage and perfectly planted a coconut cream pie on Colonel Akst's red face. Rudd escaped down Broadway with the pie thrower, who, to Rudd's dismay, had gotten carried away with the theatricality of the moment and pulled a bandanna over his face as a disguise. Rudd, for lack of a better idea, hid him in the closet of his girlfriend's apartment.

Grayson Kirk, born in 1903, the president of Columbia, lived in a stately Ivy League home in Morningside Heights, the high ground in the north of Manhattan on which the campus is perched. He was a patrician who saw himself as the guardian of a tradition. Rudd termed him "a ruling-class liberal, a man who wanted to be progressive but whose instincts always held him to the power elite. He denounced the Vietnam War, not as immoral or wrongheaded, but simply as unwinnable." Kirk's only discernible fear, as he sat in his Morningside Heights mansion in the first week of April, was of seething and simmering Harlem below. He did want to placate "the Negroes," as he and many others still called them.

Looking out his window, Kirk could see chaos and the glow of fires. Martin Luther King had been killed, and Harlem was burning. As head of a university on the hill over Harlem, this was exactly what he dreaded.

Mark Rudd could see the same flames but had a very different reaction. Now the nonviolence movement—or, as Stokely Carmichael had put it, "this nonviolence bullshit"—was over, and Rudd, as he stood on Morningside Drive smelling smoke, was looking forward to a new age of Black Power. He was with his friend JJ, who believed in a world revolution in which the impoverished nations would overthrow the empires in a great global movement that would include the unseating of white power in America. Come the revolution and its overthrow of the power centers, everyone, black and white, would taste a new freedom never known before. JJ and Rudd, each with his thick mop of long, blondish hair, spent the night wandering through Harlem, watching burning and looting, police attacks, and barricades quickly constructed to block fire trucks. There is a strange ghostlike way an observer can walk unseen through the middle of a race riot simply by not being involved. "I saw the rage black people carry inside them," Rudd said later. He and JJ were convinced they were witnessing the beginning of the revolution.

Five days after the King assassination, Columbia was to hold a memorial service. Spied on, abused, smeared, and belittled in his short life, in death Dr. King had become a saint to be eulogized by many of the same people who had obstructed his cause. Here was Columbia University, thoughtlessly expanding into Harlem, taking over parks and low-cost housing to build more facilities for its wealthy campus. In 1968 a study of Harlem showed that in the past seven years Columbia University had forced 7,500 Harlem residents out of their homes and was planning on pushing out another 10,000. The university's connection to city government was demonstrated in 1959 when over the objections of a few Harlem leaders, a lease was negotiated for more than two acres of Morningside Park on which to build a gymnasium. Leasing public land to a private concern was unprecedented in city policy, and the rent charged was only $3,000 per year. After ground

was broken in February 1968, six students and six residents of Harlem
staged a sit-in to block the first bulldozers. A new gym to be built by
tearing down housing—a gym to which the people of Harlem were to
be denied access—was particularly controversial. Student protest eventually succeeded in creating a small door down on the Harlem side for
local use. But that was a student issue. The people of Harlem didn't
want the gym at all. They wanted housing. The university was also
trying to prevent a union from organizing their black and Puerto Rican
workers. Now Martin Luther King, killed in Memphis, where he had
gone to support the very kind of union Columbia was trying to keep
out, was to be eulogized there.

SDS students called a meeting. Something had to be done with this
Kafkaesque moment. Some argued that this was the turning point—the
time to break in and announce the death of nonviolence and the age of
Black Power, the beginning of the real revolution. But others argued
that to do this would be to cede the figure of Martin Luther King to the
white establishment. "Don't do that," some students argued. "He was
one of us."

What did happen, as Tom Hayden described it, was that "Mark
Rudd, a young SDS leader, simply walked on stage, took the microphone, and denounced the university elders for the hypocrisy of honoring King while disrespecting Harlem." Rudd does not remember
himself as the nonchalant figure Hayden and others described. In truth,
his legs were shaking in his boots as he managed to step in front of Vice
President David Truman. He said into the microphone, "Dr. Truman
and President Kirk are committing a moral outrage against the memory
of Dr. King." The microphone went dead. But Rudd continued, lecturing on how the university "steals land from the people of Harlem,"
praises King's nonviolent civil disobedience, but crushes such demonstration on its own campus.

It was the beginning of Columbia University's most memorable
spring.

It is remarkable how many of the movements of 1968 took on importance only because governments or university administrations adopted
repressive measures to stop them. Had they instead ignored them—had
the Polish government not closed the play and had they not attacked
the protesters, had the Germans ignored the demonstrators who were
largely protesting U.S., not German, policy—many would have been
forgotten today. As in the civil rights movement, by 1968 it was easy to
find a bad sheriff to keep a protest alive.

The SDS could count on Grayson Kirk and the Columbia administration. In April the university for unclear reasons banned indoor demonstrations, which was Rudd's cue to lead 150 students into the Low Library with a petition against IDA, the Institute for Defense Analyses. The students had demanded to know if Columbia was part of this organization that researched military strategy. The university had refused to confirm or deny participation, and the SDS now claimed that not only did the university belong, but Grayson Kirk and another Columbia trustee were on the board of the organization. The university fell into step, singling out six students, including Rudd, for disciplinary action. Instead of focusing just on the gym, the April 23 demonstration was now also about what had come to be called "the IDA Six." Then, as though to fuel the protesters even more, the day before the demonstration the university placed the six on probation. Now it was a demonstration not only against the gym and the IDA, but to "free the IDA Six."

That also happened to be the day Rudd issued his open letter in response to Kirk's speech about the "nihilism" of "growing numbers" of youth and the generation gap, in which he had called the Vietnam War "a well-meant but essentially fruitless effort." This was particularly offensive to an antiwar movement that saw the U.S. effort as an immoral attempt to bully a poor nation into submission.

Rudd's reply, in keeping with the tone of the rest of the letter, was titled "Reply to Uncle Grayson." It began "Dear Grayson." In it, he redefined what Kirk had called the generation gap. "I see it as a real conflict between those who run things now—you, Grayson Kirk—and those who feel oppressed by and disgusted with the society you rule— we the young people. . . . We can point, in short, to our meaningless studies, our identity crisis, and our repulsion with being cogs in your corporate machines as a product of and reaction to a basically sick society. . . .

"We will take control of your world, your corporation, your university, and attempt to mold a world in which we and other people can live as human beings."

He promised to fight Kirk over his support of the war, over the IDA, over his treatment of Harlem. But it was the ending for which Rudd's letter was most remembered:

> There is only one thing left to say. It may sound nihilistic to you, since it is the opening shot in a war of liberation. I'll use the words of LeRoi Jones, whom I'm sure you don't like a whole lot: "Up against the wall, motherfucker, this is a stick-up."

> Yours for freedom,
> Mark

The SDS's Todd Gitlin remarked, "It is interesting to note the civility preserved in Rudd's polemic, however: the correct grammatical 'whom.' " But to Rudd, a normally pleasant and not particularly rude person, who in an earlier speech had referred to Kirk as "that asshole," this manner of speech was a deliberate attack on the polite decorum of the Ivy League social order. He was acutely aware that this was not the way things were done at Columbia, and that was why he did them this way.

On April 23, a cool and gray day, the protesters were to meet at a sundial in the center of the gated Columbia campus. Rudd had been up the entire night before, preparing a speech by studying Mario Savio's "odious machine" speech. Looking on at the demonstrators from the nearby Low Library were about 150 right-wing students, the short-haired students the rest of Columbia referred to as "the jocks." One sign said, "Send Rudd Back to Cuba." Another, more disturbing one, said, "Order Is Peace." Only about three hundred protesters turned out at the sundial. But as speeches were made by various student leaders, the crowd grew. By the time it was Rudd's turn to speak, an event that was to be a prelude to marching on the library—thereby again violating the rule on indoor demonstrating—two things had happened. Vice President Truman had proposed a meeting, and the Low Library had been locked.

Suddenly the Savio-like speech seemed irrelevant. This was not the moment for grand oratory, Rudd reasoned. It was a moment in which to act. But SDS leaders never acted. Their job was to organize the debate out of which came a decision. So Rudd asked the demonstrators what to do. He told them about Truman's offer and that Low had been locked. Suddenly a demonstrator stood on the sundial and shouted, "Did we come here to talk or did we come here to go to Low?"

"To Low! To Low!" the crowd chanted as they began marching. Rudd, because he was a leader, desperately ran to catch up and take his place at the head of the march, linking arms with other leaders as the pulsating crowd pushed them toward the library.

"Here I was," said Rudd, "at the head of a demonstration about to burst into a locked building or else run headlong into a mob of right-wingers, and I had only the vaguest idea about what we were doing." The one idea he did have was that disruption would provoke the police and school administration into actions that in turn would build their own support. He had noted that this approach worked well at the University of Chicago and the University of Wisconsin. But what specifically they were going to do in a few minutes when they climbed to the top of the library steps, he did not know. When they got there, the doors were indeed locked.

Rudd looked around for something on which to stand and found a trash can. He climbed on top, from which commanding heights he would present the options for what to do next. But by the time he had mounted, the crowd was running away. A demonstrator had yelled, "Let's go to the gym site!" Rudd was standing on a trash can watching the entire demonstration deserting him in a dash toward Morningside Park, which was two blocks off campus. He shouted after them in an effort to remain relevant, "Tear down the fucking fence!" and then he jumped down and ran to regain the head of the group.

By the time Rudd reached the fence, the demonstrators had already tried to tear it down, to no avail. One SDSer was in handcuffs, and police were moving in. For lack of a better idea and because more and more police were arriving at the park, the demonstrators retreated to the campus. A group from the campus met them. It seemed to Rudd that everyone was tugging on him and offering opinions on what to do. He had surely failed as a leader. "Mark, you should act more aggressively," he was told, but also, "Mark, you should stop the anger in the crowd." He saw himself drowning in a deluge of competing advice. He stood on the sundial and weighed the options, along with a black student leader who did the same. Clearly neither of them was sure what to do, although at the moment, in Rudd's estimate, they had about five hundred students ready to do anything.

But what?

Other students made speeches about revolution. Back to Rudd. He talked about IDA. He talked about the gym. But what to do? Finally he said, "We'll start by holding a hostage!"

And they were off. Rudd's idea of a hostage was not a person. He wanted to hold a building—a sit-in. Sit-ins were, as he later put it, "a time-honored tactic of the labor and civil rights movement." He heard a voice scream, "Seize Hamilton Hall!" Yes, he thought. That's the idea. He shouted, "Hamilton Hall is right over there. Let's go!" And a mob chanting, "IDA must go!" moved toward the hall.

In Hamilton Hall, the dean, Henry Coleman, with his crew cut, approached Rudd, who was now starting to think about a real hostage. Rudd called out to the protesters that they should hold the building and not let the dean leave until their demands were met. They could decide later what the demands were. At last they had a course of action. "Hell, no, we won't go!"—which usually referred to refusing the draft—was being chanted by the crowd. They were holding a building and a dean.

From that moment on, events rode the leaders. Up went posters of Che, Stokely Carmichael, Malcolm X, and, somewhat anachronistically, Lenin, in the occupied building. Increasing numbers of blacks from Harlem, some rumored to be armed with guns, moved into the building. Later, Rudd admitted feeling scared as they all stretched out to sleep that night on the floors. "We were still really middle-class kids, and suddenly we were in a different league from the student protest we had begun that morning."

Immediately a racial divide was felt. White students wanted to keep Hamilton Hall open for classes because they did not want to alienate their base, the student body. But the black students, who felt their base was the Harlem community, wanted to seal up the building. After arguing points of view, they met separately. The whites had an SDS-style meeting, which included discussions of class struggle and imperialism in Vietnam and the fine points of the Bolshevik revolution. In the meantime, the blacks met among themselves and decided to close down the building and ask the whites to leave. "It would be better if you left and took your own building."

Sleepily and sadly, the white students gathered up blankets and pillows that had been brought by late-arriving sympathizers and headed out the front door of Hamilton Hall. Rudd said he had tears in his eyes as he looked back at his black comrades closing off the building with crudely constructed barricades. It was the SNCC experience again. 1968 was not a year for "black and white together."

Someone broke into the locked library, and like sleepy children the protesters silently climbed in. They wandered the building, drifting in and out of Grayson Kirk's office with its Ming dynasty vases and Rembrandt. A few took cigars; others looked through files for secret documents and later claimed to have come across information on real estate deals and Defense Department agreements. In the early morning Rudd found a telephone and called his parents in New Jersey.

"We took a building," Rudd said to his father, who had been learning of his activities on radio and television.

"Well, give it back," his father answered.

The front-page article in *The New York Times* the next morning, raising the student movement to at least the level of the Linda LeClair case, accurately reported the wild events of the day, differing from Rudd's own version only in that it credited him with knowing what he was doing. It read as though Mark Rudd, identified as the Columbia SDS president, had planned to lead the march from the sundial, to the park, and back to the sundial and then, at just the right moment, to call for the taking of a hostage. The reading public did not know that the SDS trained its "leaders" to discuss, not to make decisions. It also appeared to the *Times* that by bringing in some activists from Harlem, Rudd had involved CORE and SNCC and so Columbia was now part of a national protest campaign.

Tom Hayden came in from Newark. The Newark inner-city operation was being closed down, and he was about to move to Chicago, where SDS national headquarters was being established. After trying to live on a dollar a day with rice and beans and failing to recruit the support he had hoped for, he was astounded by what had occurred at Columbia.

> I had never seen anything quite like this. Students, at last, had taken power in their own hands, but they were still very much students. Polite, neatly attired, holding their notebooks and texts, gathering in intense knots of discussion, here and there doubting their morality; then recommitting themselves to remain, wondering if their academic and personal careers might be ruined, ashamed of the thought of holding an administrator in his office but wanting a productive dialogue with him, they expressed in every way the torment of their campus generation.

He felt that "he couldn't walk away." He offered his support, but in the SDS way made it clear that he was to have no leading role. The protesters seemed pleased to have him, even in a silent capacity. He speculated, "What could be more fitting, perhaps they thought, than to involve Tom Hayden, the (twenty-nine-year-old) old man of the student movement, in this turning point of history?"

The longer they held the buildings, the more students joined them. As they ran out of space, they moved to other buildings. By this point Rudd had resigned from the SDS because the group refused to join the students and occupy more buildings. By the end of the week, Friday, April 27, students held five buildings. *The New York Times* continued to give front-page space to the student strike and to describe it as an SDS plan.

Hayden was in a building. Abbie Hoffman had arrived. But no one was leading. Everyone was discussing. Each building arranged "strike committees." The blacks in Hamilton Hall, who had released their hostages shortly after the whites left, insisted on their autonomy from the other four buildings. Each building was having its own debates. Students were literally cranking out press materials around the clock on old-fashioned mimeograph machines. Banners went up on occupied buildings declaring them "liberated zones." Some borrowed the slogan from César Chávez's United Farm Workers, "*Viva la Huelga*" and others the old labor sit-in slogan "We Shall Not Be Moved."

The campus was divided. Some wore red armbands, for revolution. Others wore green armbands, meaning they supported the uprising but insisted on nonviolence. The jocks, the short-haired male students who wore Columbia blazers and ties, seemed to the student radicals to be comic and irrelevant leftovers from the past. Even when the jocks attempted to blockade supplies to the occupied buildings, the radicals laughed and taunted, "Columbia lines never hold"—a reference to the fact that they always lost at football.

By Friday, April 26, when Columbia announced the suspension of work on the gym and closed the university, it was not the only university that had been closed. Throughout the United States and the world, students cut Friday classes to protest the war in Vietnam. There was a noticeably large participation by American high school students who, starting in April, became increasingly organized, establishing by the end of the year their own chapters of the SDS and a network of almost five hundred underground high school newspapers. The Universities of Paris, Prague, and Tokyo were among those that participated. The Italian university system was barely functioning. That day alone there had been sit-ins, boycotts, or clashes in universities in Venice, Turin, Bologna, Rome, and Bari. The absolute power of senior professors remained the central issue, and the students continued, to the great frustration of the political establishment, to refuse an alliance with communists or other political parties. In Paris three hundred students stormed an American dormitory at Cité University in the southern part of the city over the issue of banning mixed-sex dormitories. It was noted with concern that this represented a successful attempt by student radicals from the suburban University of Nanterre to spread into other Paris universities. On the other hand, the University of Madrid announced that it would reopen for classes on May 6, thirty-eight days after being closed by student demonstrations.

In New York, it was an especially violent day. One girl was hospitalized from riots between pro- and antiwar students at the Bronx High School of Science, an elite public school. Three were hospitalized from Hunter College. But the campus that had captured world attention because of extensive press coverage was Columbia, where the police were now guarding the campus gates and occupying all buildings other than those occupied by students. Just off campus on 116th Street, the police troops waited in long green vans. Even though Kifner now wrote in the *Times* that the movement was leaderless, that Rudd was only an occasional spokesman, and that each building debated its next step with its own steering committee, the occupation was still widely reported as organized by the SDS and led by Rudd.

The Columbia Board of Trustees denounced what they called "a minority" that had caused the Columbia campus to close. Since there were estimated to be about 1,000 striking students and Columbia had 4,400 full-time undergraduate students in 1968, the claim that it was a minority was mathematically correct, though it was a very large minority. *The New York Times,* with its two seats on the Columbia board perhaps evident, wrote an editorial that said, "The riot, the sit in, and the demonstration are the avant-garde fashion in the world's campuses this year. To prove one's alienation from society is to be 'in' at universities as far apart as Tokyo, Rome, Cairo and Rio de Janeiro." This kind of thing is fine for Poland and Spain, where there is a "lack of avenues for peaceful, democratic change," the *Times* declared, "but in the United States, Britain and other democratic countries there is no such justification."

Even the *Times* credited WKCR, the Columbia University radio station, with being the hot media outlet of the week. With almost nonstop live coverage, WKCR was in the best position to clearly follow the chaotic events. On Friday morning the university ordered the station to discontinue broadcasting but relented in the face of a huge outburst of student protest. Rudd and other leaders, though they spoke with such reporters as the *Times*'s Kifner, kept in closest contact with the university paper, the *Daily Spectator,* and WKCR. Rudd often forewarned the campus radio station's anchor Robert Siegel of events. He had told him to cover the speech of Colonel Akst.

About ninety thousand antiwar demonstrators filled the Sheep Meadow in Central Park on Saturday. Coretta Scott King, Martin Luther King's young widow, spoke in the place that had been scheduled for him, reading King's "Ten Commandments on Vietnam," which denounced the White House version of the war. To the last commandment, "Thou shalt not kill," she received a thunderous round of applause. The police arrested 160 demonstrators, including 35 who attempted to march from the park to Columbia to show support for the students.

A rival demonstration led by the archbishop of New York, Terence Cooke, who had been installed only three weeks earlier in the presence of President Johnson, promised to rally sixty thousand in support of the war but managed to attract only three thousand war-supporting demonstrators.

In Chicago organizers said that twelve thousand antiwar protesters marched peacefully from downtown Grant Park, but the Chicago police, who attacked with Mace and clubs, said there were only about three thousand marchers. In San Francisco about ten thousand demonstrators marched against the war, including, according to organizers, several dozen servicemen in civilian clothing and several hundred veterans wearing paper hats that said "Veterans for Peace." In Syracuse, New York, an outstanding high school student, Ronald W. Brazee, age sixteen, who on March 19 had ignited his gasoline-soaked clothing near a cathedral as protest against the war, died. He had left a note that said, "If giving my life will shorten the war by even one day, it will not have been in vain."

In the meantime, the United States began a massive assault by Airmobile Division helicopters into South Vietnam's Ashau valley. Ten aircraft were lost in a single day of fighting. At almost the same time as the assault began, the siege of Khe Sanh ended. Six thousand U.S. Marines who had been dug in and cut off on a plateau since January were relieved by a thirty-thousand-man force of U.S. and South Vietnamese troops led by the helicopters of the 1st Air Cavalry in what was called Operation Pegasus. Correspondents with the relief force described the hills around Khe Sanh as "a moonscape." The earth had been churned into craters by the most intensive aerial bombing in the history of warfare—110,000 tons of U.S. bombs. It was not known if the two North Vietnamese divisions holding the marines in Khe Sanh had been driven off by the bombing or if the North Vietnamese army had never intended a costly final assault. In either case they were thought to have retreated to the Ashau valley, where they could strike Da Nang or Hue. In addition to the assault on the Ashau valley, an attempt to clear enemy troops from the Saigon area was mounted with the optimistic label Operation Complete Victory. Khe Sanh, where two hundred U.S. Marines died during an eleven-week siege and another seventy-one Americans were killed during the relief operation, was to be abandoned by the end of April.

That brief moment of optimism at the beginning of April when Johnson announced he would not run had already vanished by the end of the month. What had happened to the peace talks and the bombing halt? North Vietnam quickly announced that it would appoint representatives to begin talks. The United States then announced that W. Averell Harriman, seventy-six, a onetime Roosevelt liberal and cold war diplomatic veteran, would head up a U.S. team in Geneva or Paris. The United States also let it be known that New Delhi, Rangoon, or Vientiane would be agreeable sites for negotiating. The United States did not want the talks taking place in a communist capital, where the

South Vietnamese and South Koreans had no diplomatic mission. On April 8 North Vietnam proposed the Cambodian capital of Phnom Penh. On April 10 the United States rejected this even for preliminary talks, because there was no U.S. embassy there. Then, on April 11, North Vietnam proposed to have the talks in Warsaw and the United States promptly turned down the offer. By chance this was the same day that Johnson finally signed the Civil Rights Act in the hopes of calming black America; it was also the day 24,500 reserves were called up, bringing U.S. troop strength in Vietnam to a record 549,500—a day in which the United States claimed to kill 120 enemy and lose 14 American soldiers in fighting near Saigon. The next week the United States proposed ten sites, including Geneva, Ceylon, Afghanistan, Pakistan, Nepal, Malaysia, and India. But Hanoi rejected the ten and once again proposed Warsaw.

Diplomacy was not working any better up at Morningside Heights. On Monday, April 29, almost a week after the protest began, Columbia remained closed and the buildings remained occupied. There was, in fact, little diplomatic activity, since both the trustees and a majority of the faculty had come out against the insurrection. The school did try to negotiate with protesters in Hamilton Hall, since it was being held by black students with ties to Harlem and Columbia did not want to enrage Harlem. But the black students, holding to their promise to Rudd and the white students, refused to negotiate separately from the other students. Vice President David Truman invited Mark Rudd and several other student leaders to his comfortable professorial apartment on elegant Riverside Drive. The student rebels were seated at a polished mahogany table and served tea from a silver service set, all in the best Columbia tradition. Unfortunately, it was at this moment that Rudd decided to take off his boots. His only explanation was that his feet hurt. But the affront was reported in the *Times,* where Truman also described Rudd as a "capable, ruthless, cold-blooded . . . combination of a revolutionary and an adolescent having a temper tantrum."

The talks never found any common ground. Rudd told Truman that the students had taken over the university and demanded access to the bursar's office and the school's financing. Each "liberated" building evolved into its own commune. Young people living together on the floor, living the revolution, waiting for the siege, made for an emotional, romantic existence. One couple decided that they wanted to be married then and there in their occupied building. WKCR broadcast that a chaplain was needed at Fayerweather Hall, and William Starr, a university Protestant chaplain, answered the call. It was the kind of wedding *Life* magazine would have loved. The couple borrowed their wedding clothes. The groom, Richard Eagan, wore a Nehru jacket with love beads around his neck. The bride, Andrea Boroff, wore a turtleneck and carried daisies. More than five hundred people occupied Fayerweather, including Tom Hayden. A candlelight procession led the couple through a circle of hundreds of strikers to William Starr, who pronounced them "children of a new age." Even Hayden, who had already discovered the calamities of matrimony, found his eyes tearing. The couple called themselves Mr. and Mrs. Fayerweather.

Columbia, it seemed to these students, had become a revolutionary center. Students and student leaders from other universities and even high schools came to show their support. More and more people from Harlem, both organized groups and individuals, arrived on campus and staged large demonstrations. Stokely Carmichael and H. Rap Brown went to Hamilton Hall, which was now renamed Malcolm X University. Young people from Harlem had come onto campus chanting, "Black Power!" It was Grayson Kirk's nightmare.

In the dark early hours of Tuesday, April 30, hundreds of police began gathering around the university. At 1:30 A.M., WKCR advised students that an attack was imminent and they should stay in their dormitories. The police said that they had originally planned the assault for 1:30 but put it off several times for what they termed "tactical delays." It later was clarified that these delays were caused by a desire not to move until Harlem was asleep. At 2:30, armed with helmets, flashlights, clubs, blackjacks, and, according to witnesses, brass knuckles, they moved onto the campus in a militarylike operation in which the force of one thousand police officers broke off into seven target sectors. "Up against the wall, motherfucker," Rudd later recalled. "Some Columbia students were surprised to learn that cops really say that."

The police beat those who resisted; they beat those who didn't. Some officers arrested students according to procedure and led them to wagons. Others appeared to go berserk with clubs or blackjacks. Dragged into paddy wagons that completely blocked off two blocks of Amsterdam Avenue, 720 students were arrested. Students who occupied buildings were beaten as they tried to hold up the two-finger V sign. Students who tried to keep peace outside, clearly marked by their green armbands, were also beaten, as were some faculty members. In their report the police complained that they had not been told how many faculty supported the students or how many students were involved. Right-wing students, the jocks, who were cheering on the police, were also beaten. One hundred and forty-eight injuries were reported. It was one of those rare moments in American history when class warfare became open. The police, working-class people, resented these privileged youth who would not support the war that working-class children were fighting. The conflict was increasingly becoming a division of classes. College students were using "hard hat" as a term of derision, and the police attacked them with raw hatred. Marvin Harris, a Columbia anthropology professor who witnessed the raid, wrote:

> Many students were dragged down stairways. Girls were pulled out by the hair; their arms were twisted; they were punched in the face. Faculty members were kicked in the groin, tossed through hedges, punched in the eye. A diabetic student fell into a coma. One faculty member suffered a nervous collapse. Many students bled profusely from head wounds opened by handcuffs, wielded as weapons. Dozens of moaning people lay about the grass unattended.

The 120 charges of police brutality brought against the department were the most from any single incident in the history of the New York police.

The public was shocked. Initially the administration had the public relations advantage, due chiefly to *New York Times* coverage. A photograph had caught students in Kirk's office. Student David Shapiro, today a poet, was photographed at the president's desk in sunglasses with a purloined cigar. The *Times* abandoned all objectivity when deputy managing editor A. M. Rosenthal wrote an editorial disguised as a front-page news story centered on a quote from Kirk: "My God, how could human beings do such a thing." Vintage Kirk, the "such a thing" was not the brutal beating of hundreds of unarmed people, but acts of vandalism, which Rosenthal attributed to the students, but most witnesses—the *Times* didn't mention—including faculty members who signed affidavits, attributed to the police. Despite the claims of the New Left that such coverage was adopted by the rest of the media, both the press and the public were appalled by what happened and did not entirely blame the students. *Time* magazine wrote, "Much of the blame falls on President Grayson Kirk, whose aloof, often bumbling administration has proved unresponsive to grievances that have long festered on campus." The Columbia faculty formed a board that set up a commission of inquiry headed by Harvard professor Archibald Cox, who came to a similar conclusion.

Strangely, the entire cast—the students, the administration, the police—did it all over again. There were ongoing discussions about changes at the university. But the administration, which had provoked the original incident by singling out Rudd and five others, decided in late May to suspend Rudd and four others from Columbia. Such suspensions had particularly serious implications in 1968 because they meant the end of a student draft deferment and often a sentence to the Vietnam War. How did the students respond? By demonstrating. What did Rudd and the other four do with the demonstration? They took over Hamilton Hall. So then another one thousand police attacked, in a battle in which sixty-eight people, including seventeen policemen, were injured.

Rudd returned to campus, suspended from school and out on $2,500 bail and vowing to keep Columbia protests going through the spring and summer. *Time* magazine asked his parents in suburban Maplewood, New Jersey, where they had been receiving a flood of anti-Semitic letters with such phrases as "fucking Jew," what they thought of all that had happened with their son. His father pointed out that he had spent his own youth struggling just for enough money. "We're glad Mark has time to spend on activities like politics." Or, as his mother *kvell*ed, "My son, the revolutionary."

In August, when Kirk, to the relief of almost everyone, offered to retire at the age of sixty-four, the trustees debated for four hours whether or not accepting the offer would appear to be giving in to student rebels. In the end they accepted the resignation even though it was clear that the president had been forced out by the students.

"The issue is not the issue," Rudd had said. The point was not the treatment of Harlem or the fostering of the Vietnam War machine. The point was that the nature of American universities needed to be changed. Even the Cox Commission had denounced the authoritative nature of the Columbia administration, with some rules dating from the eighteenth century. Once students had a say, they could address the goal of breaking the tie between corporations and universities, getting the academy out of the business of weaponry, and getting America out of the business of war. Tom Hayden wrote in *Ramparts*, "The goal written on the university walls was 'Create two, three, many Columbias'; it meant expand the strike so that the U.S. must either change or send its troops to occupy American campuses." The goal seemed realistic.

CHAPTER 12

MONSIEUR, WE THINK YOU ARE ROTTEN

A man is not either stupid or intelligent, he is either free or not free.
— *Written on a wall of the Faculté de Médecine,*
Paris, May 1968

To be free in 1968 is to take part.
— *On a stairwell in the school of Science Politique,*
Paris, May 1968

Certain French students, having found out that students in other countries have shaken up and smashed everything, want to do the same.
— ALAIN PEYREFITTE, *French minister of education,*
explaining events, May 4, 1968

A
S SPRING CAME to rainy Paris, France's leader, the seventy-eight-year-old general, a man of the nineteenth century, with his near absolute power, ruling under the constitution he had written himself ten years earlier, promised stability, and delivered it.

The not quite octogenarian, not quite king, entertained fantasies of monarchy, in fact invited the pretender to the French throne, Henri Comte de Paris, to his palace for talks from time to time—the bethroned president with no crown playing host to the king with no throne. While de Gaulle had little tolerance for opposition, he acted as though he had moved beyond politics and its constant search for supporters to a kind of inevitable permanence. In 1966, ensconced in his palace's regal Salles des Fêtes, he was asked about his health and answered, "It is quite good—but don't worry, I shall die sometime."

On March 15, 1968, while Germany, Italy, Spain, the United States, and much of the world was exploding, *Le Monde* journalist Pierre

Viansson-Ponté wrote a now famous editorial in which he said, "France is bored." Around this same time, de Gaulle was smugly declaring, "France is in a satisfactory situation, whereas the Germans are having their political difficulties, the Belgians their language problems, and the British their financial and economic crisis." He continually emphasized that the French should be pleased with this dull peace that he had given them.

While de Gaulle infuriated the rest of the world, a poll released in early March by the conservative French newspaper *Le Figaro* showed that 61 percent of the French approved of his foreign policy, whereas only 13 percent disapproved. Of course, disapproving of de Gaulle could be complicated in France, as François Fontievielle-Alquier, a respected journalist, found out when he was brought to court in March 1968 on an eighty-seven-year-old law against criticizing the president. Prosecutors cited twelve passages in his new book, *Re-Learn Disrespect,* that fell under "attacks on the honor" of the head of state. The law passed on July 29, 1881, provided for prison sentences up to three years or fines from 100 to 300,000 francs ($20 to $60,000 at 1968 exchange rates) for "offenses" in the form of "speeches, shouts, threats uttered in public places, writings, articles in the press."

This was the three-hundredth time the law had been invoked since de Gaulle became president. In one case a man was fined 500 francs for shouting, "Retire!" as de Gaulle's car passed.

If the French said they were pleased with de Gaulle's foreign policy, almost no one else was. His peculiar brand of nationalism seemed to threaten most international organizations. The year 1967 had been particularly difficult, or at least a year in which *he* had been particularly difficult. He withdrew French forces from NATO, a formerly French-based organization, and threatened the survival of the European Common Market when for the second time he blocked British entry to the group. His famous statement after the Six Day War about Jews being a "domineering" people alienated French and American Jews and Gentiles. He even alienated Canadians by endorsing Québécois separatism from the town hall balcony in Montreal while on a state visit to Canada.

"It is clear to everyone that in de Gaulle the United States is dealing with an ungrateful four-flusher whose hand should have been called years ago," Gordon McLendon of Dallas said on his eight radio stations. Throughout the United States there were calls for boycotting French products. When a Gallup poll asked Americans to rate which countries they liked, France was near the bottom of the list, beating only Egypt, Russia, North Vietnam, Cuba, and the People's Republic of China. In a poll in which the British were asked to pick the most villainous man of the twentieth century, Hitler came in first but was followed by Charles de Gaulle, who beat out Stalin. In fourth place was British prime minister Harold Wilson. The usually good-humored West German foreign minister, Willy Brandt, said in early February that de Gaulle was "obsessed with power," though he was quickly forced to apologize for the remark.

Nor did all criticism come from outside of France, despite de Gaulle's tendency to prosecute. French of the next generation, the generation of John Kennedy, who should have been taking over, were anxious for their turn. This included fifty-two-year-old socialist François Mitterrand, who was still in line behind sixty-one-year-old Pierre Mendès-France, the leftist former head of government who had earned the contempt of the Right when he withdrew the French military from France's Vietnam war. But there were also new faces. While America's New Left was reading translations of Camus, Fanon, and Debray, France also produced a book for the establishment. A 1967 bestseller in France, *Le Défi Américain* by Jean-Jacques Servan-Schreiber, the publisher of the slightly left-of-center weekly news-magazine *L'Express*, was translated into English and in 1968 became an American bestseller known as *The American Challenge*. Servan-Schreiber looked to a post–de Gaulle era and his ambitions for himself in that world. His one run for elected office in 1962, a campaign for a National Assembly seat, was disastrous. But if political careers are launched with books, this one had a rare success. In France in its first three months it broke all postwar sales records. Servan-Schreiber's thesis was that in the next thirty years the United States would become so dominant that Europe would be little more than a colony. The European Common Market, despite the fact that on July 1, 1968, customs between member countries would cease, was failing to move forward fast enough and would disintegrate from lack of momentum.

The message of this book, often quoted in 1968 by European diplomats and entrepreneurs, was that Europe would have to become like America or would be eaten up by it. American companies, with $14 billion invested in Europe, were taking over. He warned that in the next thirty years they would all be living in what was called "the post-industrial society." He added, "We should remember this term, for it defines our future." Among the other prescient predictions: "Time and space will no longer be a problem in communications" and "The gap between high and low salaries in the post-industrial society will be considerably stronger than today." But he also endorsed the wide-spread belief in 1968 that by the end of the century Americans would be awash in leisure time. In thirty years, Servan-Schreiber predicted, "America will be a post-industrial society with a per capita income of $7,500. There will be only four work days a week of seven hours per day. The year will be comprised of 39 work weeks and 13 weeks of vacation."

He quotes a White House expert predicting, "Well before 1980, computers will be small, powerful, and inexpensive. Computing power will be available to anyone who needs it, or wants it, or can use it. In many cases the user will have a small personal console connected to a large, central computing facility where enormous electronic memories will store all aspects of knowledge."

The book was a warning: "America today still resembles Europe—with a fifteen-year head start. She belongs to the same industrial society. But in 1980 the United States will have entered another world, and if we fail to catch up, the Americans will have a monopoly on know-how, science, and power."

Servan-Schreiber foresaw, though his timetable was a little fast, the dangers of America as a singular superpower. "If Europe, like the Soviet Union, is forced out of the running, the United States will stand alone in its futuristic world. This would be unacceptable for Europe, dangerous for America and disastrous for the world. . . . A nation holding a monopoly of power would look on imperialism as a kind of duty, and would take its own success as proof that the rest of the world should follow its example."

To Servan-Schreiber there was little time and one major obstacle in the path of France's and Europe's modernization: a septuagenarian nineteenth-century general. "De Gaulle is from another time, another generation," said the forty-four-year-old editor who had flown a fighter for Free France during World War II. "He is irrational in a time that cries for rationality." Even the General's favorite pose, of the World War II hero, was wearing thin. Servan-Schreiber said, "I disapprove of heroes. Children who worship Batman grow up to vote for heroes. I hope that after de Gaulle the Europeans will be sick of heroes."

Servan-Schreiber represented a middle generation of Frenchmen, tired of the elderly de Gaulle but distrustful of the new youth culture. "I want my sons to grow up to be citizens of something that is impor-tant. I don't want them to be second class. A twenty-five-year-old with nothing to be proud of does stupid things like becoming a hippie or going to Bolivia to fight with the guerrillas or putting up a Che Guevara poster on his wall." Bored and suffocating France had two generation gaps: one between the World War II generation and their children, and the other between General de Gaulle and most of France.

De Gaulle's ten-year-old Fifth Republic and the protest movement that was about to consume the society where nothing was happening, both had their roots in Algerian independence. The French colony of Algeria, home to de Gaulle's Free French government-in-exile for a time during the war, began demanding its independence as soon as the war ended. It was the struggle of Algeria that inspired the writing of Frantz Fanon and greatly shaped the anti-imperialist movement of the 1960s. Mendès-France, who decolonized Indochina and Tunisia, could not get the political muscle to let go of Algeria. Although almost constant local resistance continued from the moment France took over in 1848, a million Frenchmen lived there, many for generations, and the French considered Algeria to be theirs. The French army, humiliated by the Germans and then humiliated by the Vietnamese, felt Algeria to be their final and non-negotiable stand.

At this point France was supposed to have been through with de Gaulle. After World War II he had considered it his mission to "save" France from the Left. In order to do this, he fostered the myth of the brave France resisting the Nazi occupier. In reality the bulk of the French resistance had been communist, and remembering this, a great many French were inclined to vote communist. De Gaulle offered an alternative and continued insisting for the rest of his life that he was the only alternative to a communist-run France. In the late 1940s the French had decided to take that chance and drove him from power. Though he managed to challenge the socialist governments with a contentious opposition, by 1955, at age sixty-five, he had officially retired from politics, ending a distinguished career.

But in 1958 plots and counterplots were whispered in France and Algeria, and France was faced with the real possibility that the socialist government would be overthrown by a right-wing military coup. The army, commanded in Algeria by General Raoul Salan, would not back a French government that would let go of Algeria, and the socialists could not be trusted. How much de Gaulle was behind all of this plotting remains a mystery. A number of his known associates were clearly involved, but de Gaulle managed to stay removed from the intrigue. As head of one of several French factions during World War II, he had become skilled at this kind of international maneuvering. Now the retired general simply let it be known that if France were to need him, he would be available. There was enough suspicion of de Gaulle that the legislature openly questioned him on whether his intentions were democratic. "Do you think that, at the age of sixty-seven, I am going to begin a career as a dictator?" de Gaulle responded.

Even when the government had decided to step down and turn over the reins to the General, it was difficult to convince the National Assembly, the powerful lower house of legislature, to approve the deal. André Le Troquer, the socialist president of the National Assembly, would not accept de Gaulle's terms—adjournment of the parliament and the writing of a new constitution—and instead demanded that the General appear before the assembly. De Gaulle refused, replying, "I shall have nothing else to do but to leave you to have it out with the parachutists and return to the seclusion of my home to shut myself up with grief." With that he returned to his retirement home in Colombey-les-Deux-Églises. But it was clear that only a de Gaulle government could prevent a military coup attempt. The legislators agreed to his terms, including the power to write a new constitution.

France had turned to him to end the Algerian crisis, not to reform the French state. Few modern monarchs and no democratic heads of state have enjoyed the degree of absolute power that de Gaulle granted by constitution to the president of the Fifth Republic, who, for the foreseeable future, would be himself. The president has the right to override parliament either by calling for a referendum or by dissolving parliament. The president also sets the agenda for the legislature, decides what bills are to be discussed and what version of them. He can block proposals to reduce taxes or increase spending. If a budget is not passed in seventy days, the president has the right to decree one.

On September 4, 1958, the General had officially launched his new constitution, standing in front of an enormous twelve-foot-high V. It was the Roman numeral five for the Fifth Republic that he was launching, but it was also the old World War II symbol for victory. De Gaulle never missed a chance to refer to his favorite myth, that he had single-handedly saved France from the fascists. Of course, to a new generation the V was the peace symbol, which stood for nuclear disarmament. De Gaulle, dreaming of a French hydrogen bomb, didn't know about antinuclear youth, nor did he want to know about the young people on the streets of Paris protesting his constitution with signs denouncing it as "fascism." The police attacked the youths, who fought off several police assaults by erecting makeshift barricades.

But one of the reasons de Gaulle could step into office on his terms was that he was walking into a situation few would want, one even worse than that in which Lyndon Johnson would find himself in 1968. France was in the midst of a bitter and hated colonial war. The torture and other atrocities with which the ruthless and determined independence movement was fought tarnished the reputation of France, a nation still struggling to recover its good name from German occupation. In 1968 Lyndon Johnson knew that if he chose to end the Vietnam War, the war's supporters and the military would accept his decision. But for de Gaulle to end the Algerian war, he would have to face a possible rebellion. Not ending it could produce a similar result.

France had a growing antiwar movement capable of mounting sizable demonstrations, many of which met with brutal police response. A wide range of French people opposed the war, including some veterans. Servan-Schreiber was an outspoken opponent of the Algerian war. After serving there, he wrote a book, *Lieutenant in Algeria,* for which he was unsuccessfully court-martialed.

Alain Geismar, a French Jew, was nineteen years old when de Gaulle came to power. His father had died fighting the Germans, and his grandfather had been deported to a concentration camp. He had spent the first years of his life in hiding in France. He was shaped by these experiences. "During the Algerian war I found a number of Nazi characteristics in the army of my country," he recently said. "It was a much smaller scale. There was not mass genocide. But there was torture and there were 'regroupment' camps. In 1945 we had been told that it was over. But in 1956 I found that it was not over."

The Algerian war helped radicalize French youth. In 1960, during the height of the Algerian protest movement, leftist students took over the student organizations that had been dominated for many years by right-wing students. Geismar became active in protesting the Algerian war and was one of the organizers of an October 1961 demonstration in Paris. The police opened fire on Algerian demonstrators. "I saw them shooting Algerians," said Geismar. Afterward bodies were found in the Seine, though it was never determined how many were killed. The incident was not discussed openly in France until the 1990s.

In 1962 de Gaulle finally succeeded in ending the Algerian war. Algeria became independent, and France entered one of its few periods of peace and stability in the twentieth century. In 1963 the French sixties began when Europe 1, a popular radio station, announced a free concert in Paris's Place de la Nation and, to everyone's surprise, thousands of young people showed up. Both records and live music, primarily American and British, played continually for most of the night. France was used to its July 14 balls in which people danced to songs like "Sur Les Ponts de Paris," and "La Vie en Rose," played on an accordion, but an all-night free rock concert in the open air was something very new.

France started experiencing considerable economic growth in the sixties. Between 1963 and 1969 real wages grew by 3.6 percent—enough growth to turn France into a consumer society. Suddenly Frenchmen had automobiles. Indoor toilets were being installed, although by 1968 still only half of Paris homes had them. François Mitterrand spoke of "the consumer society that eats itself."

The French were also buying televisions and telephones, though the installation service on phones was slow and France still lagged behind most of Europe in televisions. Neither of the channels, with their government-managed offerings, was found very interesting, though both had the advantage of being free of commercials. But the French were beginning to learn of the power of television. The first station, black and white only, did not begin broadcasting until 1957. The civil rights movement, the American war in Vietnam, and protests against that war were all seen in a large number of French living rooms where the French war in Indochina had never been seen. De Gaulle used this new tool, completely in his hands as president, fairly well, not only in controlling the coverage of his presidency, but in stage-managing and timing personal appearances. "De Gaulle is in love with television," said Servan-Schreiber. "He understands the medium better than anyone else." Owners of print media were furious that de Gaulle was threatening to allow commercials on television, which they saw as a ploy to drain advertising away from the print that could criticize him and into state-owned television.

In 1965 France had its first presidential election by direct ballot—presidents had been appointed by the elected majority in the old system. This first direct ballot contest was also the first television election and the first French election to be tracked by pollsters as well. De Gaulle, to avoid the appearance of complete unfairness, allowed each of the candidates two hours of time on his television channels in the last two weeks of the campaign. The effect of seeing François Mitterrand and Jean Lecanuet on television was tremendous. Most French people had never actually seen a presidential candidate in motion before, except for de Gaulle, who was always on television. The fact that Mitterrand and Lecanuet were on television at all gave them the stature of a de Gaulle. And it was difficult not to notice how young and vigorous the two seemed compared to the General. De Gaulle won the election, but only after being forced to a second-ballot runoff with Mitterrand to gain the required absolute majority. He was not the untouchable monarch he had thought.

In the mid-sixties, prices were rising in France and the government believed inflation threatened the economy. The sudden population growth from the immigration of about one million North Africans, mostly Christians and Jews, contributed to price increases. Unemployment also began to increase.

In 1967 the government decreed a series of measures aimed at redressing economic problems. But to the working class these measures seemed aimed at them. Wages were held down, and the workers' contribution to Social Security was raised because of the added cost of bringing farmworkers under the system. On a rainy May 1, after fifteen years' absence, the traditional leftist Communist Party–sponsored May Day demonstration at the Place de la Bastille, where workers with raised fists sang "The Internationale," was again observed.

With a better standard of living, more French were getting higher education, but they were not happy in their crowded halls of learning. In 1966 students at the University of Strasbourg published a paper, "On the Poverty of Student Life," which stated:

> The student is the most universally despised creature in France, apart from the priest and the policeman. . . . Once upon a time, universities were respected: the student persists in the belief that he is lucky to be there. But he arrived too late. . . . A mechanically produced specialist is now the goal of the "educational system." A modern economic system demands mass production of students who are not educated and have been rendered incapable of thinking.

In 1958 there were 175,000 university students in France, and by 1968 there were 530,000—twice as many students as Britain had. But France granted only half as many degrees as British universities, because three-fourths of French students failed their courses and left. This was the reason de Gaulle dismissed the student movement at first; he assumed the students involved were simply afraid of facing exams. The universities were horribly overcrowded, with 160,000 students in the University of Paris system alone, which was why, once they started demonstrating, student causes were able to attract such enormous numbers of marchers. Added to these ranks were high school students in the college preparatory lycées, who had the same issues as the university students.

At most of the universities, and especially Nanterre, the physical campus was not a comfortable place to live and study. But also, even more than the American Ivy League, the French university was an absolute autocracy. At a time when the future of France, the future of Europe, new sciences and new technologies, provoked far-reaching debates—which explained the popularity of books such as *The Ameri-*

can Challenge—students had no opportunity to talk about any of this. There was no dialogue, inside or outside classrooms, between professors and students. Decisions were handed down without any discussion. In May the walls of the Sorbonne were scrawled with the message "Professors, you are as old as your culture." To laugh about the age of French culture was a new kind of iconoclasm.

But the teachers and professor were not given a voice, either. Alain Geismar, who had become a young physics professor and director of le Syndicat National de l'Enseignement Supérieur, the National Union of Professors of Higher Education, the SNE.Sup., recently said, "The young generation had a sense that they did not want to live like the generations before. I reproached the generation of the Liberation for having missed the opportunity to modernize society. They just wanted to put things back the way they were. De Gaulle had done the resistance, he had done the liberation, he had ended the war in Algeria, and he did not understand anything about the young people. He was a great man who had grown too old."

In chemistry it is found that some very stable elements placed in proximity to other seemingly moribund elements can spontaneously produce explosions. Hidden within this bored, overstuffed, complacent society were barely noticeable elements—a radicalized youth with a hopelessly old-fashioned geriatric leader, overpopulated universities, angry workers, a sudden consumerism enthralling some and sickening others, sharp differences between generations, and perhaps even boredom itself—that when put together could be explosive.

It began with sex, back in January when France was still bored. Students at the University of Nanterre, an exceptionally ugly four-year-old concrete campus where eleven thousand students were crowded on the edge of Paris, raised the issue of coeducational dormitories, and the government ignored them. François Missoffe, the government minister of youth, was visiting Nanterre when a small red-haired student asked him for a light for his cigarette. Cigarette lit and smoke exhaled, the student, Daniel Cohn-Bendit, one of the more outspoken and articulate students at Nanterre, said, "*Monsieur le Ministre,* I read your white paper on youth. In three hundred pages there is not one word on the sexual issues of youth."

The minister responded that he was there to promote sports programs, which was something he suggested the students should take more advantage of. To his surprise, this did not brush off the redheaded student, who instead repeated his question about sexual issues.

"No wonder, with a face like yours, you have these problems: I suggest you take a dip in the pool."

"Now there's an answer," said the student, "worthy of Hitler's youth minister."

That exchange alone made Cohn-Bendit known to almost every student in Paris simply as "Dany." The brief nondialogue between student and government was a formula that was to be repeated over and over on an ever escalating scale until all of France was shut down and Dany was famous around the world as Dany le Rouge—Dany the Red.

He had been born in newly liberated France in 1945 to German Jewish parents who had survived the war hiding in France. His father had fled when Hitler came to power, because he was not only a Jew, but an attorney known for defending leftist dissidents. After the war he returned to his work in Frankfurt. Being a surviving Jew returning to Germany was a strange and isolating experience. Dany stayed for a while in France with his mother, an educator. But they were not particularly comfortable in France, with its history of collaboration and deportations. Every few years they switched from one country to the other. Dany was brought up to identify with the radical Left. He has said that the first time he felt Jewish was in 1953, when Julius and Ethel Rosenberg, accused of spying for the Soviets, were executed in the United States. In Germany he and his brother would guess the age of passersby and speculate on what they had been doing during the war. He was horrified when he visited his dying father in a deluxe sanitarium and heard businessmen loudly clicking heels in the old German style of obedience.

In 1964 he went to America, the dreaded land of the Rosenberg execution, and attended a memorial service in New York City for SNCC volunteers killed in Mississippi. Andrew Goodman and Michael Schwerner had both been from New York City. "I was very impressed with the atmosphere," Cohn-Bendit said. "These two white Jewish guys who went to Mississippi. How dangerous. That was something different than what I was prepared to do."

It was in March 1968, while France was still bored, that Nanterre began to heat up. According to the Ministry of the Interior, small extremist groups were agitating in order to imitate radical students in Berlin, Rome, and Berkeley. This point of view was often repeated by Alain Peyrefitte, the minister of education. There was an element of truth to this. The minuscule Trotskyite group JCR, la Jeunesse Communiste Révolutionnaire—the Revolutionary Communist Youth—

had become suddenly influential, and its twenty-seven-year-old leader, Alain Krivine, had not only worked with Rudi Dutschke in Berlin, but had also closely followed events on American campuses through the American Socialist Workers Party, a fellow Trotskyite organization.

It is significant that what was to emerge as the most important group was the least ideological. It was called le Mouvement du 22 Mars—the March 22 Movement. Its leader was Cohn-Bendit. Its cause was unclear. As in other countries, the people who emerged in France in 1968 were not joiners, were suspicious of political organizations on the Right and the Left, and tried to live by an antiauthoritarian code that rejected leadership. They rejected the cold war, which had always said that everyone had to choose one or the other, and they rejected de Gaulle, who always said "Stay with me or the communists will come to power." They agreed with what had been expressed in the Port Huron Statement: They wanted alternatives to the cold war choices that were always presented to them.

"The Liberation missed a great opportunity, and soon the cold war froze everything," said Geismar. "You had to choose your side. 1968 was an attempt to create a space between those sides, which is why the communists opposed these 1968 movements."

In the mid-sixties the Paris métro stop at Nanterre still said "*Nanterre à la folie,*" which indicated that Nanterre was the country home of a Paris aristocrat. From that beginning it had gone on to become a comfortable middle-class Parisian suburb with houses on cobblestone streets. Then factories moved in, and in the middle of the factories, almost indistinguishable from them, the University of Nanterre was built, surrounded by the barrackslike homes of North African and Portuguese immigrants. The sterile dormitory rooms had large glass windows that, like a good window at Columbia, looked out on the slum. While Sorbonne students lived and studied in the heart of the beautiful city, in a medieval neighborhood of monuments, cafés, and restaurants, Nanterre students had no cafés and nowhere to go. Their only space was a dormitory room in which they were not allowed to change furniture, cook, or discuss politics, and nonstudents were not allowed. Women were allowed in men's rooms only with parental permission or if they were over twenty-one. Men were never allowed in women's rooms. Habitually, women visited men's rooms by sneaking underneath a counter.

Nanterre was supposed to be one of the more progressive schools, where students were encouraged to experiment. But in reality the autocratic university system made reform no more possible at Nanterre than at any other university. The only difference was that at Nanterre heightened expectations made for a particularly disappointed and embittered student body. Attempts to reform the university in 1967 further frustrated students, leading a few with political activist backgrounds to form a group called the *enragés*—a name that originated in the French Revolution and literally means "angry people." There were only about twenty-five *enragés,* but they forced lectures to stop in the name of Che Guevara and created whatever mayhem they could dream up. Like Tom Hayden, they believed that the problems of the universities could be solved not by reforming the school system, but only by completely changing society.

They were not a very well liked group. How twenty-five mischief makers were turned into a force of one thousand during the course of the month of March, how this in a matter of weeks became fifty thousand and by the end of May ten million, paralyzing the entire nation, is a testament to the consequences of overzealous government. Had the government from the beginning ignored the *enragés,* France might never have had a 1968. Looking back, Cohn-Bendit shook his head. "If the government had not thought they had to crush the movement," he asserted, "we never would have reached this point of a fight for liberation. There would have been a few demonstrations and that would have been it."

On January 26, 1968, the police came on campus to break up a rally of perhaps three dozen *enragés.* The students and faculty were angered by the presence of police on the campus. As other protesters around the world would discover that year, the *enragés* realized, seeing this anger, that they only needed to start a demonstration and the government and their police force would do the rest. By March they were doing this regularly. The dean of Nanterre helped build the tension by refusing to provide larger spaces as their numbers grew. He also further provoked the students by refusing to speak up for four Nanterre students arrested at an anti–Vietnam War demonstration near the Paris Opéra. On March 22, with now about five hundred militants, the *enragés* in a sudden inspiration borrowed an American tactic and siezed the forbidden eighth-floor faculty lounge, occupying it all night in the name of freedom of expression. The March 22 Movement was born.

On April 17 Laurent Schwartz, one of the world's most renowned physicists, went to Nanterre on behalf of the government to explain its 1967 university reform program. The students shouted him down, declaring that he was an antirevolutionary and should not be allowed to speak. Suddenly Cohn-Bendit, the affable redhead with a smile so bright it was featured on revolutionary posters, took a microphone. "Let him speak," said Cohn-Bendit. "And afterwards, if we think he is rotten, we will say, 'Monsieur Laurent Schwartz, we think you are rotten.' "

It was a typical Cohn-Bendit moment, spoken with charm and a minimum of authority at exactly the right moment.

The critical day that would escalate everything, May 2, was one of pure farce. The University of Paris decided on the exact same mistaken tactic as the administrators at Columbia, attempting to deflate the student movement by disciplining its leader. Cohn-Bendit was ordered to appear before a disciplinary board in Paris. This angered the Nanterre students, who decided they would disrupt classes by protesting with loudspeakers. But they had no such equipment, and Pierre Grappin, the increasingly helpless and frustrated dean of Nanterre, refused to give them access to the school's loudspeakers. The students, believing themselves to be "direct action revolutionaries," a concept popularized by Debray among others, simply went into his office and took the equipment. The dean, seeing the opportunity for some direct action of his own, locked his office doors, incarcerating the students inside. But it was a short-lived triumph because the windows were open and the students escaped with the equipment.

De Gaulle was growing anxious about law and order on the streets of Paris because the Paris peace talks on resolving the Vietnam conflict were due to begin. He had ordered extra contingents of the special antiriot police, the Compagnies Républicaines de Sécurité, the CRS, to Paris. At the request of Grappin, the Ministry of Education shut down Nanterre, an extraordinary decision that shifted the action from an obscure suburb to the heart of Paris.

At the time, the city was glutted with international news media trying to cover the Vietnam peace talks, whose delegations, after agreeing on where and with whom, settled down on May 14 to begin arguing about how many doors to the main room—North Vietnam insisted on two—and to continue their discussion on whether to have a square, rectangular, round, or diamond-shaped table—each option affecting the seating arrangements. But just the fact that they were talking sent the markets, especially the New York Stock Exchange, on a sharp rise.

The Nanterre crowd moved into Paris, to the Sorbonne. Cohn-Bendit had found a megaphone, which was to become his trademark. But the rector of the Sorbonne, against the advice of the police chief, had gotten the police to enter the Sorbonne and arrest students. A police invasion of the Sorbonne was without precedent. Also without precedent was the administration's reaction to the outrage of the students: They closed the Sorbonne for the first time in its seven-hundred-year history. Six hundred students were arrested, including Cohn-Bendit and Jacques Sauvageot, the head of the national student union. Alain Geismar called for a nationwide teachers strike on Monday. This was when de Gaulle, himself enraged, came up with the theory that the movement was led by second-rate students who wanted the schools closed because they couldn't pass their exams. "These are the ones who follow Cohn-Bendit. These abusive students terrorize the others: one percent of *enragés* to 99 percent sheep who are waiting for the government to protect them." An informal leadership was established: Cohn-Bendit, Sauvageot, Geismar. The three seemed inseparable. But they later said that they had had no plan and not even a common ideology. "We had nothing in common," said Cohn-Bendit. "They had more in common with each other. I had nothing in common with them, not the same history. I was a libertarian; they were from a socialist tradition."

The official communists, the French Communist Party, were against all of them from the start. "These false revolutionaries ought to be unmasked," Communist Party chief Georges Marchais wrote. But Jean-Paul Sartre, the most famous French communist, sided with the students, giving them a mature, calm, and respected voice at critical junctures. The French government had thought of arresting him, but according to legend, de Gaulle rejected the idea, saying, "One doesn't arrest Voltaire."

Cohn-Bendit, unlike his co-leaders, had little discernible ideology, which may be why he was the most popular. His appeal was personal. A stocky little man who smiled unexpectedly and broadly, his red hair sticking out in unkempt tufts, he was at ease with himself. He liked to have fun and had a light sense of humor, but when he spoke, that humor had a sharp, ironic edge and his voice grew as he became impassioned. In a political culture given to pompous rhetoric, he seemed natural, sincere, and fervent.

The government made much of Cohn-Bendit's German nationality. The Germans were the most noted student radicals of Europe. Cohn-Bendit had had some contact with them, as had other French radicals. He had gone to their February anti-Vietnam rally, and he had even met Rudi Dutschke. In May, when he became widely known as Dany the Red, it was a reference not only to his hair color, but to Dutschke, who was known as Rudi the Red.

But Dany did not see himself as a Rudi, nor was the March 22 Movement anything like the German SDS, which was a highly motivated and organized national movement. The March 22 Movement had no agenda or organization. In 1968 nobody wanted to be called a leader, but Cohn-Bendit made a distinction. "SDS had antiauthoritarian rhetoric," he said. "But in truth Dutschke was the leader. I was a type of leader. I slowly stepped in because I was saying something at the right moment and the right place."

He was not unlike other 1968 leaders, like Mark Rudd, who said, "I was the leader because I was willing to take the heat."

To Cohn-Bendit there was a connection among the movements of the world, among the student leaders, but it did not come from meetings or exchanges of ideas. Most of these leaders had never met. "We met through television," he said, "through seeing pictures of each other on television. We were the first television generation. We did not have relationships with each other, but we had a relationship with what our imagination produced from seeing the pictures of each other on television."

De Gaulle by late May became convinced that there was an international plot against France, and there were rumors of foreign financing. The CIA and the Israelis were among the suspects. De Gaulle said, "It is not possible that all of these movements could be unleashed at the same time, in so many different countries, without orchestration."

But there was no orchestration, not internationally, not even within France. Cohn-Bendit said of the events of May, "It all happened so fast. I didn't have time to work. The situation provoked decisions." All Dany the Red or the thousands of others on the streets of Paris were doing was reacting spontaneously to events. Geismar, Cohn-Bendit, Krivine—all the leading figures as well as rank-and-file participants have remained consistent on this point. There were no plans.

The way things were happening recalled the early 1960s situationist movement that began in poetry and turned political. They called themselves situationists, after the belief that one had only to create a situation and step back and things would happen. This was the situationists' dream come true.

Cohn-Bendit admitted, "I was surprised by the intensity of the student movement. It was absolutely exciting. Every day it changed. Our personas changed. There I was, the leader of a little university, and in three weeks I was famous all over the world as Dany the Red."

Every day the movement got bigger and bigger by an exact formula. Each time the government took a punitive step—arresting students, closing schools—it added to the list of student demands and the number of angry students. Each time the students demonstrated more people came, which brought more police, which created more anger and ever larger demonstrations. No one had any idea where it was going. Some of the more orthodox radicals, such as Geismar, were convinced that this was the beginning of a revolution that would change French or European society by pulling up the old ways by the roots. But Cohn-Bendit, with his big smile and easy manner, had no idea of the future. "Everyone asked me, 'How will this end?' " Cohn-Bendit recalled. "And I would say, 'I don't know.' "

On Monday, May 6, one thousand students turned out to see Cohn-Bendit report to the disciplinary board at the Sorbonne. In almost equal numbers, a contingent of the CRS was present, wearing dark combat helmets, dark goggles, and the occasional long black trench coat and carrying large shields. When they attacked, nightsticks raised in the air, they looked like a menacing invasion by extraterrestrials.

Cohn-Bendit and several friends walked by them and through the crowd of a thousand demonstrators, who seemed to be parted by Dany's smile. He waved and chatted, always a jovial radical.

The government, repeating its same mistakes, banned demonstrations for the day, which of course caused many. The students swept through the Latin Quarter and across the Seine and back and arrived hours later at the Sorbonne to confront the CRS. Finding an impressively large contingent waiting for them, they passed behind the school and started up the medieval rue Saint-Jacques when suddenly a club-whirling mass of CRS charged them. The demonstrators backed off in silence.

Between them and the CRS was an open no-man's-land on the wide street, where about two dozen bodies of injured demonstrators lay writhing on the cobblestones. For a moment it seemed no one knew exactly what to do. Suddenly, consumed with anger, the demonstrators attacked the CRS, lining up, some digging up cobblestones, others passing them bucket-brigade style to the front line, where others ran into clouds of tear gas and threw the stones at the CRS. They then retreated, overturning cars to throw up barricades. Charge after charge by the incredulous CRS, who were used to ruling the streets, was driven back. Some of these determined and orderly combatants may have wanted for years to see these shock troops of the government forced into retreat.

François Cerutti, a draft dodger from the Algerian war who ran a popular leftist bookstore frequented by Cohn-Bendit and other radicals, said, "I was completely surprised by 1968. I had an idea of the revolutionary process, and it was nothing like this. I saw students building barricades, but these were people who knew nothing of revolution. They were high school kids. They were not even political. There was no organization, no planning."

The fighting drew in thousands of demonstrators, and by the end of the day the government reported 600 wounded protesters and 345 wounded policemen. As another week wore on, there were more demonstrations, with protesters carrying the red flag of communism and the black flag of anarchy. Sixty barricades had been erected. Neighborhood people who viewed from their windows these young French people bravely fending off an army of police went to the barricades to give food, blankets, and supplies.

The prefect of police, Maurice Grimaud, was beginning to lose control of his force. Generally credited with trying to restrain the police, Grimaud had been appointed to his position six months earlier. He had never wanted the job. Having been director of national security for four years, he felt that he had done all the police work he wanted in his career. He was a bureaucrat, not a policeman. He saw his force completely shocked by the violence and insistence of these people. "Fights would begin which continued until very late at night," said Grimaud, "and were especially severe, not just because of the number of demonstrators, but because of a degree of violence that was completely surprising and which astonished the police officials." To the police, the 1968 movement had grown directly out of the anti–Vietnam War movement, which they had been confronting for a number of years. But this was different. Not only were the police becoming frustrated, they were getting hit on the head by cobblestones the size of large bricks. Every day they grew angrier and more brutal. *Le Monde* printed this protester's description from May 12 in the Latin Quarter: "They lined us up back to the wall, hands over our heads. They started beating us. One by one we collapsed. But they continued brutally clubbing us. Finally they stopped and made us stand up. Many of us were covered with blood." The more brutal the police became, the more people joined the demonstrators. However, unlike in the Algerian demonstrations earlier in the decade, the government was resolved not to open fire on these children of the middle class, so miraculously there were no deaths from night after night of furious combat.

Cohn-Bendit was as surprised as the police by the students. But he could not control it. "Violent revolt is in the French culture," he said. "We tried to avoid an escalation. I thought that violence as a dynamic was destroying the movement. The message was getting lost in the violence, the way it always does. The way it did with the Black Panthers." This was said by a mature Cohn-Bendit in reflection, but he was by no means a clear voice of nonviolence at the time. He admitted under police questioning to having been involved in the printing and distribution of a diagram explaining how to make a Molotov cocktail, but he explained to them that the flyers had been intended as a joke, which may have been true. 1968 humor.

French television, expressing the state's viewpoint, emphasized the violence. But so did foreign television. Nothing made for better television than club-wielding CRS battling stone-throwing teenagers. Radio and print were drawn to the violence, too. Radio's Europe 1 had its correspondent on the street breathlessly reporting, "It's absolutely extraordinary what's happening here, right in the middle of Saint Germain, three times the demonstrators charged and three times the CRS retreated, and now—this is extraordinary—live, the CRS is charging!" It was a tonic for a population that had grown bored. Today, most photographs and film footage available from that time are of the violence. To the average French participants, however, it wasn't about violence at all, and that is not what they most remember. It was about a pastime for which the French have a rare passion: talking.

Eleanor Bakhtadze, who had been a student at Nanterre in 1968, said, "Paris was wonderful then. Everyone was talking." Ask anyone in Paris with fond memories of the spring of 1968, and that is what they will say: People talked. They talked at the barricades, they talked in the métro; when they occupied the Odéon theater it became the site of a round-the-clock orgy of French verbiage. Someone would stand up and start discussing the true nature of revolution or the merits of Bakuninism and how anarchism applied to Che Guevara. Others would refute the thesis at length. Students on the street found themselves in conversation with teachers and professors for the first time. Workers and students talked to one another. For the first time in this rigid, formal, nineteenth-century society, everyone was talking to everyone. "Talk to your neighbor" were words written on the walls. Radith Geismar, then the wife of Alain, said, "The real sense of '68 was a tremendous sense of liberation, of freedom, of people talking, talking on the street, in the universities, in theaters. It was much more than throwing stones. That was just a moment. A whole system of order and authority and tradition was swept aside. Much of the freedom of today began in '68."

In a frenzy of free expression, new proverbs were created and written or posted on walls and gates all over the city. A sampling from out of hundreds:

Dreams are reality

The walls are ears, your ears are walls

Exaggeration is the beginning of inventions

I don't like to write on walls

The aggressor is not the person who revolts but the one who conforms

We want a music that is wild and ephemeral

I decree a permanent state of happiness

A barricade closes the street but opens a path

Politics happens on the street

The Sorbonne will be the Stalingrad of the Sorbonne

The tears of philistines are nectar of the Gods

Neither a robot nor a slave

Rape your alma mater

Imagination takes power

The more I make love, the more I want to make revolution. The more I make revolution, the more I want to make love.

Sex is good, Mao has said, but not too often

I am a Marxist of the Groucho faction

There were occasional, though not many, references to other movements such as "Black Power gets the attention of whites" and "Long live the Warsaw students."

Or one statement, written on a wall at Censier, may have expressed the feelings of many that spring: "I have something to say but I am not sure what."

For those who had some additional thoughts, too wordy to write on a wall—though some did write whole paragraphs on buildings—if they had access to a mimeograph machine, they could print one-page tracts and pass them out at demonstrations. Once the symbol of radical politics, the mimeograph machine—with its awkward stencils to type up—had its last hurrah in 1968, soon to be taken over by photocopy machines. There were also the French movement newspapers—a large tabloid of a few pages called *Action* and another, smaller tabloid, *Enragé,* which for its special June 10 issue on Gaullism ran an illustration of a floor toilet, the kind most in use in France at the time, with the cross of Lorraine, the symbol of Gaullism, for the hole and the tricolored French flag for the toilet paper. Demonstrators quickly found themselves with piles of paper to read or browse.

The art schools, the École des Beaux-Arts and École des Arts Décoratif at the Sorbonne, established the *atelier populaire*, producing in May or June more than 350 different silk-screen poster designs a day with simple, powerful graphics and concise slogans in the same vein as those on the walls. It remains one of the most impressive outpourings of political graphic art ever accomplished. A fist with a club accompanies Louis XVI's famous line often used to characterize Gaullist rule, "*L'état, c'est moi*"—I am the state. The shadow of de Gaulle gags a young man, with the caption "Be young and shut up."

The police peeled the posters off the walls. Soon collectors were peeling them off the walls also, and pirated editions were being sold, which angered the art students. "The revolution is not for sale," said Jean-Claude Leveque, one of the art students. The atelier turned down an offer of $70,000 from two major European publishers. In the fall both the Museum of Modern Art and the Jewish Museum in New York had shows of the atelier's work. The Jewish Museum's show was entitled *Up Against the Wall*, once more using the ubiquitous LeRoi Jones quote.

They not only talked, they sang. The students sang "The Internationale," which is the anthem of world communism, the Soviet Union, the Communist Party, and many things they did not support. It would have seemed strange to the students of Poland and Czechoslovakia, but to the French this song—written in the 1871 Commune, an uprising against French authoritarianism—is simply a song of antiauthoritarian revolt. The Right retaliated by singing the French national anthem, "The Marseillaise." Since these are two of the best anthems ever written, having huge crowds singing them through the wide boulevards of Paris was always stirring and having each group identify itself by anthem was ideal for television.

Cohn-Bendit, Sauvageot, and Geismar were invited for a debate with three television—and therefore state-employed—journalists. In a prerecorded message, Prime Minister Georges Pompidou, an aging Gaullist with the practiced political skills and soon-this-could-all-be-mine hunger of a Hubert Humphrey, explained that viewers were about to meet three of the horrible revolutionaries. The journalists were intense, the frightening revolutionaries were relaxed and pleasant. Cohn-Bendit smiled.

"We destroyed them," Cohn-Bendit said. "I started to realize that I had a special relation with the media. I am a media product. After that they just came after me. For a long time I was the media's darling."

Though state television did cover what was happening, there were glaring omissions, major events that did not make it on the air. But the journalists were growing tired of having their shows canceled, and caught up in the spirit of the time; on May 16, television reporters, cameramen, and drivers went out on strike.

By then something had happened that was only dreamed about in other student movements, which often failed because the students had no other groups joining them. On May 13, the anniversary of de Gaulle's return to power, all of the major trade unions called for a general strike. France was shut down. There was no gasoline for cars, and Parisians walked the empty streets talking, debating, having a wonderful time that they would always remember.

In Morningside Heights, Columbia students were thrilled, as were students at the University of Warsaw, in Rome, in Berlin, at the Autonomous National University of Mexico, at Berkeley. The French had done it—students and workers hand in hand.

In reality, nothing of the sort had happened. Though some of the younger workers, in disagreement with the unions, were sympathetic to the students, their unions, especially those backed by the Communist Party, were not. Perhaps the students had created the opening for a long overdue explosion, because the workers too had become increasingly angry with the Gaullist regime. The workers did not want revolution, they did not care about the students' issues, other than the overthrow of de Gaulle. They wanted better working conditions, higher salaries, more paid time off.

"The workers and the students were never together," said Cohn-Bendit. ". . . They were two autonomous movements. The workers wanted a radical reform of the factories—wages, etc. Students wanted a radical change in life."

De Gaulle, faced with a nationwide crisis, left for a four-day trip to Romania. It seemed strange that with Paris closed down by student revolutionaries, de Gaulle would disappear to Romania. Christian Fouchet, the minister of the interior, had questioned him on the choice, and de Gaulle had said that the Romanians would not understand if he canceled. Fouchet respectfully argued that the French would not understand if he didn't. The next morning, as the ministers saw him off and his country's situation was being reported on the front page of most major newspapers in the world, de Gaulle declared, "This trip is extremely important for French foreign policy and for détente in the world. As far as the student agitation is concerned, we aren't going to accord it more importance than it deserves."

De Gaulle tended to focus on the things he was good at. The student problem was something he did not understand at all. On the other hand, Romania had showed an increasing independence from the Soviet bloc, and de Gaulle, who dreamed of leading a third movement between the two superpowers—"a Europe stretching from the Atlantic to the Urals," he liked to say—was, for good reasons, very interested in Romania. Even with the nation in a crisis, foreign policy took precedent over domestic. While he was gone, Pompidou was in charge. The prime minister prided himself on his formidable negotiating skills, and he worked out an accord in which most of the student demands were met. He freed those who had been arrested, reopened the Sorbonne, and withdrew the police. This simply allowed the students to reoccupy the Sorbonne in the same way they had been holding the Odéon theater, with an endless French deluge of words. But while the students were having their wonderful debates, ten million workers were on strike, food shops were becoming empty, traffic had stopped, and garbage was piling up.

Both Pompidou and de Gaulle understood that the student problem was separate from the worker problem. To them, the student problem was a perplexing phenomenon, but the worker problem was familiar ground. The Gaullists completely abandoned their economic policy, offering the workers a 10 percent pay increase, a raise in the minimum wage, a decrease in work hours, and an increase in benefits. The minister of finance and architect of economic policy, Michel Debré, was not consulted on the offer and resigned when it was announced. But the strikers quickly rejected the offer anyway.

De Gaulle, looking older than he ever had before and completely confused, cut short his Romania trip and returned to France, saying unfathomably, *"La réforme, oui. La chienlit, non." Chienlit* is an untranslatable French word referring to defecating on a bed—a big mess. This led to Beaux Arts posters with a silhouette of de Gaulle and the caption *"La chienlit, c'est lui"*—The *chienlit*, it is he.

The French government decided to deport Cohn-Bendit, who was a German national. Grimaud, the prefect of police, was not in favor of the move because he recognized that Cohn-Bendit was a stabilizing force among the students. It was late enough in the game that the government should have realized that their provocations kept the movement alive. But they did not see that.

Another issue was that the image of deporting a Jew back to Germany stirred ugly memories. During Nazi occupation, seventy-six thousand Jews had been delivered by the French police to the Germans for deportation to death camps. The France of the 1960s had still not made peace with its 1940s, was still caught between the facts of disgraceful collaboration and de Gaulle's myth of heroic resistance. May 1968 was filled with Nazi imagery, most of it unfair. The CRS was called the CR SS. One Beaux Arts poster showed de Gaulle removing his mask and revealing himself to be Adolf Hitler, another showed the cross of Lorraine twisted into a swastika. On Cohn-Bendit's expulsion, the slogan of the student movement instantly became "We Are All German Jews"—chanted even by Muslim students. The phrase appeared on posters for a demonstration protesting his deportation at which tens of thousands marched.

Throughout de Gaulle's long career, at the most difficult moments, he had shown a knack for just the right move and just the right words. But this time he was silent. He disappeared completely from public view to his country home, where he wrote, "If the French don't see where their own interests lie, too bad for them. The French are tired of a strong state. Basically this is it: The French remain by nature drawn to factionalism, argumentativeness, impotence. I tried to help them through this. . . . If I have failed, there is nothing more I can do. That's just the way it is."

At last, on May 24, le Grand Charles spoke. Looking tired and old and sounding uncertain, he called for a referendum on his continued leadership. No one wanted the referendum seen as an extralegal invention of the wily old general. While he spoke, rioting began anew in Paris and started up in several other major French cities. In Paris the students from the Latin Quarter had crossed the Seine and were attempting to set the stock exchange building, the Bourse, on fire.

In all the weeks of street violence in France, amazingly, only three people died. Two of them died that night, including one among the hundreds wounded in Paris and a police commissioner in Lyons. Later, a protester chased by the police would jump into the Seine and drown.

The referendum seemed impossible to hold and unwinnable if held. Once again de Gaulle himself seemed to vanish. Improbable as it was, the revolutionaries started to sense victory. At the very least, they were going to overthrow the government. It might already be gone. Both Mitterrand and Mendès-France made themselves available for a provisional government. Then it was discovered that de Gaulle had flown to Germany to the French military command there. Why he did this was uncertain, but many feared he was preparing to bring in the French army. When he returned to France he was the old de Gaulle—domineering and sure of himself, as he had once called Jews. The referendum was to be dropped, the National Assembly dissolved, and new legislative elections called. The nation, he contended, was on the edge

"We are all Jews and Germans." Daniel Cohn-Bendit and
his famous smile. 1968 Paris student silk-screen poster.
(Galerie Beaubourg, Vence)

of falling into a totalitarian communism, and he was the one alternative who could once again save France. The Gaullists organized a demonstration on the Champs-Élysées as a show of support. The public responded to rebuilding through fresh elections, to de Gaulle once again saving France from disaster. An estimated one million people showed up to march in support of de Gaulle's call for an end to chaos. The marchers sang the national anthem and in between chanted slogans, among them "Send Cohn-Bendit to Dachau."

Cohn-Bendit had heard it before. When he had been arrested, a policeman had pointed a finger at him and said, "My little friend, you are going to pay. Too bad you didn't die at Auschwitz with your parents because that would have spared us the trouble of what we are going to do today."

His parents had not been at Auschwitz, but the fact that he was Jewish was never totally forgotten. Only within his own movement did he feel it had never been an issue. Of course, Geismar, Krivine, and so many others were Jewish. Marginal leftist movements in France were accustomed to sizable Jewish participation. A popular French joke asks the question: If the Maoists wanted to have a dialogue with the Trotskyites, what language would they speak? The answer: Yiddish.

The government finally came up with a package satisfying all labor demands, including a two-step 35 percent wage increase. The unions and workers took it happily. Only a handful of younger workers gave a second thought to abandoning the students.

But then de Gaulle did something odd and unexplained: He freed from prison fourteen members of the Secret Army Organization, the OAS, the fanatic group that had tried to stop Algerian independence by murdering numerous Algerians, French officers, and French officials. Some of these men, including Raoul Salan and Antoine Argoud, both French army officers, had been involved in numerous plots to assassinate de Gaulle between 1961 and 1964. Why were these men out? Had de Gaulle made some kind of deal in Germany to maintain the backing of the military? The answer has never been uncovered, but at the time of this uncelebrated tenth anniversary of de Gaulle's Fifth Republic, his act reminded the French public of the clandestine deals with Salan and the Algerian officers that had brought him back to power in 1958.

Still, it seemed a great many French were even more suspicious of the alternatives on the Left. On June 23 the Gaullists won 43 percent of the vote, and after the second round a week later they won an absolute majority in the assembly. The Gaullists had outperformed their most optimistic predictions. The Left had lost half their assembly seats, and the students with their New Left remained, as before, unrepresented.

Demonstrations at Berkeley to support French students and oppose de Gaulle turned into two nights of rioting until police enforced a curfew and state of emergency on the entire city of Berkeley. Annette Giacometti, widow of the sculptor Alberto, stopped plans for an extensive retrospective of her husband's work at Paris's Orangerie in the fall. She said she was protesting "police repression of students and workers, expulsion of foreigners and foreign artists." Several other artists also sent letters to the Ministry of Culture canceling shows.

Alain Krivine said, "De Gaulle was the smartest politician France ever produced. De Gaulle understood the communists. He understood Stalin. Mitterrand was a de Gaulle with little feet. Pompidou, Giscard, Mitterrand, Chirac—they are all little de Gaulles—they all try to copy him. In '68 he knew the communists would accept having the elections. Not the referendum. The referendum was a little tactical error. No one wanted it. But once he proposed elections, it was over. He never understood the students, but in the end that wasn't important. He saved the Right in 1945, and he could do it again in '68."

De Gaulle had shown that he was still a brilliant politician. But he would never again have the same prestige and would simply fade away. He later admitted, "Everything slipped through my fingers. I no longer had any hold over my own government." His role as the enfant terrible of world affairs was greatly diminished by his domestic crisis. His dream of dictating solutions to everything from Vietnam to Quebec independence to the Middle East, once a bit overambitious, now appeared completely improbable. The foreign editor of *Le Monde*, André Fontaine, wrote that the General was "no longer in a position to give everyone advice."

Never above spite, de Gaulle took his revenge on both the print media, which had been critical of him, and the state television, which had gone on strike. With increased support in the assembly, he decided to allow commercials on one of his two television stations. On October 1, before the evening news, viewers learned about a garlic cheese, a stretch-proof sweater, and the pleasures of powdered milk. At first, only two minutes a day of commercials would be allowed, always before the evening news, but gradually this was to be expanded. He also cut more than a third of the television news positions.

By late summer de Gaulle had found a way to disarm the next leftist uprising. As far back as the year 1185, the cobblestone pavement in the Latin Quarter had proved an effective weapon—at that time against royalists. In 1830 cobblestones were used again, and again in the revolution of 1848, and then by the Commune in 1871 when they first sang "The Internationale." The students who hurled them in 1968 had learned their history. One of the Beaux Arts posters of 1968 showed a paving stone and was captioned "Under 21 years old, here is your ballot." But this was to happen no more. In August de Gaulle ordered the cobblestone streets of the Latin Quarter paved over in asphalt.

On June 17 the last of the students who had been occupying the Sorbonne for more than a month left. They were faced with offers for book contracts. At least thirty-five books on the student uprising were signed up by the day the last rebel left the Sorbonne. Typically, the first one published was a collection of photographs of street violence. Cohn-Bendit had been right—when there is violence the message gets lost. But many other books followed, including books by and about Cohn-Bendit. In his book *Le Gauchisme—Leftism*—with the subtitle *Remedy for the Senile Illness of Communism,* he began with an apology: "This book has been written in five weeks. It has the blemishes of such speed, but the publisher had to get the book out before the market was completely flooded." With typically edged Cohn-Bendit humor he also wrote,

> In the market system, *capitalists* are ready to prepare their own deaths (as capitalists, naturally, and not as individuals) in divulging revolutionary ideas that could in the short term earn them money. For this, they pay us handsomely (50,000 DM in the account of Dany Cohn-Bendit before having written a single line), even though they know that this money will be used to make Molotov cocktails, because they believe that revolution is impossible. Here's to their readers to fool them!

Revolution may be possible, but it didn't happen in France in 1968. Classic Marxists insist that revolutionaries have to slowly build their bases and develop their ideology. None of this happened that year. There was simply an explosion against a suffocatingly stagnant society. The result was reform, not revolution. It was only the students who had wanted revolution. They had not sold the idea to the workers or the larger society, which, to paraphrase Camus's comment in the early 1950s, so longed for peace that they were willing to accept inequities. The universities became slightly more democratic; teachers and students could talk. The society left the nineteenth century and entered the late twentieth century, but for Europe this turned out to be a time of tremendous materialism and little of the spiritualism for which the young students had hoped.

Cohn-Bendit thought he would be able to return to France in a few weeks, but it was ten years before he was allowed back in. "It saved me," Cohn-Bendit said of his expulsion. "Becoming so famous so quickly, it is difficult to find yourself. In Germany I had to reconstruct myself."

In September, while the Frankfurt Book Fair was honoring Léopold S. Senghor, president of Senegal, to the strings of a Mozart quartet inside a Frankfurt church, thousands were outside being pushed away by police water cannons while shouting, "*Freidenspreis macht Senghor Weiss*"—The freedom prize makes Senghor white, it whitewashes him. The students were protesting this peace award going to a leader whose regime was extremely repressive to students. While bottles and rocks flew and the police tried to contain the crowd, a small redheaded man, the reconstructed Dany the Red, leaped over the metal police barricades and was beaten a few times with a rubber truncheon on the way to being arrested.

When it was time for Cohn-Bendit to appear before a judge, he realized that by coincidence, it was the same week as the scheduled trial in

Warsaw of the Polish student movement leaders Jacek Kuroń and Karol Modzelewski. Such things had been watched closely back in Paris, especially championed by Alain Krivine and the JCR, who would frequently chant in demonstrations, "Free Kuroń and Modzelewski." Back in the days when police breaking onto a campus was unthinkable in France, the Trotskyites used to circulate this joke: Who are the best-educated police in the world? The answer: The Polish, because they are always going to the university.

When Cohn-Bendit went before the judge in a Frankfurt courtroom crowded with his young followers and the judge asked his name, Cohn-Bendit sensed that he had the moment and the audience. He answered in a clear, loud voice, "Kuroń and Modzelewski."

"What?" said the judge. "Who?" he demanded, looking as if he were trying to decide if Cohn-Bendit was a lunatic.

"What?" muttered his young supporters. "Who? What did he say?"

Cohn-Bendit realized that no one in the courtroom, including the judge, knew who Kuroń and Modzelewski were. He had to explain that they were Polish dissidents, about the open letter and the student movement, and that their trial was this week. By the time it was all clear, the moment had been lost. Nothing kills drama like a thorough explanation, as Abbie Hoffman had pointed out.

"May '68: the beginning of a long struggle."
1968 Paris student silk-screen poster.
(Galerie Beaubourg, Vence)

CHAPTER 13

THE PLACE TO BE

Springtime will be beautiful; when the rapeseed is in blossom, truth will have had its victory.

— *Czech student slogan, 1968*

As the cold, wet days grew longer and warmer, and the sun returned to dark, old Prague, the city's young people became infected with a sense of optimism that could be found in few places that spring. The Paris talks showed no signs of bringing the Vietnam War to an end; the war in Biafra was starving children; there seemed no hope for peace in the Middle East; the student movement had been crushed in Poland, France, and Germany—but in Prague there was optimism or, at least, determination. New clubs opened, though it took a few demonstrations to get them open, with young men in long hair, women in miniskirts and velvet boots and fishnet stockings as in Paris, and jukeboxes playing American music.

Thousands of people in Prague, especially the young, had taken to the streets on February 15 to celebrate the Czechoslovakian hockey team's victory over the undefeated Soviet team five to four in the winter Olympics in Grenoble, France—and it seemed they hadn't left the streets since. They discussed the game for weeks. It was a widespread belief that if Novotný had stayed in power, somehow the Czechoslovakian team would not have been allowed to win. No one could explain how Novotný would have stopped it. It was simply that with Novotný nothing was possible, while without him everything seemed possible. And while the news from neighboring Poland was depressing, the Czechoslovakian press was covering the student movement there with a candor and openness that was exciting, even shocking, to its audience.

The news media—print, radio, and television—were still controlled almost entirely by the government, but to the utter amazement of their readers, listeners, and viewers, the government was using the press to promote the idea of democracy—communist democracy, it was always careful to emphasize. The independent and reform-minded Writers Union, once considered a dissident group, was given permission to start its own magazine, *Literarni Listy—Literary Journal*—though it did have to struggle to get a sufficient allotment of paper for the weekly. That was often the way things now worked. The top officials would open the way, but lesser bureaucrats would still try to obstruct. As time went on and Dubček purged more and more of the old guard, fewer of these incidents occurred.

The protocol officials paid a visit to the new leader and suggested that Dubček's shabby hotel room was not an appropriate residence. They showed him a number of houses, which he said were "too big for my family's needs and my taste." Finally he accepted a four-bedroom house in a suburb.

For a man of communist training, schooled in a foggy rhetoric left to interpretation, Dubček was turning out to have a startling directness and simplicity to his message. People were finding him not only clear but even likable. He said, "Democracy is not only the right and chance to pronounce one's own views, but also the way in which people's views are handled, whether they have a real feeling of co-responsibility, co-decision, whether they really feel they are participating in making decisions and solving important problems."

The people took him at his word. Meetings became lengthy debates. The Congress of Agricultural Cooperatives, normally a dull, pre-dictable event, turned into a rowdy affair with farmers actually voicing their grievances to the government—demanding more democratic collectives, lobbyists to represent peasant interests, and benefits comparable to those for industry. The sixty-six-district Party meetings around the country in March were equally frank and raucous. Thousands of youth cross-examined government officials and stamped their feet and booed what they thought were unacceptable responses.

Many inside and outside the country wondered, as did Brezhnev, if Dubček had gone further than he meant to and was now losing control. "Freedom," wrote *Paris Match,* "is too strong an alcohol to be used pure after a generation of a dry regime. Dubček is from the elite of the Soviet Union—a Communist, after all. Is it possible that he has gotten carried away with the forces he has liberated? And that he will try, too late, to put the brakes on?"

Having been raised in its hinterlands, Dubček thought he had a deep understanding of the Soviet Union. But he could only guess at the inner workings of the Brezhnev government. He had never been close to Brezhnev and had never felt a rapport with him. Dubček wrote in his memoirs, "It is Brezhnev who always brings to mind the not entirely welcome Russian custom of male kissing."

The Czechoslovakian people pushed to get as much as quickly as possible, so that it would be too late to go back. But Dubček knew that he had to be clearly in charge of events. He would complain to colleagues that the people were pushing too hard. "Why do they do this to me?" he said more than once to Central Committee secretary Zdeněk Mlynář. "They would have been afraid to do it under Novotný. Don't they realize how much harm they are causing me?" The government continually warned the people that reform must not go too quickly. Dubček's mistake, as he later admitted, was not understanding that he had a limited time. He thought that by going gradually, he could bring his allies, the Soviets, with him. Dubček was careful, in almost every speech he made, to once again declare the loyalty of Czechoslovakia to the Soviet Union, its contempt for the pro-Nazi West Germans, and its admiration and friendship with East Germany. If true, this last was an unreciprocated friendship. East Germany's Walter Ulbricht was one of Dubček's harshest critics.

It was difficult to go far with reforms while Novotný was still president. But a series of outrageous corruption scandals involving him and his son made it possible to remove him from his second post only months after he was ousted as Party chairman. At the last moment he tried to develop a following, by suddenly becoming a "regular guy," being seen having beers with the boys in working-class bars. But he was a deeply disliked figure. On March 22, with no other possible choice, he resigned from the presidency.

Dubček did not have a free hand in naming Novotný's replacement because it was critical that the new president be someone who would not only work with him, but also please, or at least not enrage, Brezhnev. Various groups wrote letters suggesting different candidates. It was the only open discussion of an appointment for head of government in the history of the Soviet bloc. The students favored forty-seven-year-old Čestmír Cisař, a known reformer and somewhat charismatic television personality whose liberal ideas had met with disfavor in the Novotný regime. He was exactly the kind of candidate who would not ease Moscow's fears.

The intelligentsia and some of the students also liked Josef

Smrkovsky, age fifty-seven, whose popularity was enhanced by an attack on him from the East German government. In the end, Dubček chose the least popular of the three top candidates, seventy-two-year-old retired general Ludvik Svoboda, a hero of World War II who had fought with the Soviets. The other contenders were given important but lesser positions. The students in the new Czechoslovakia let their disappointment be known by demonstrating for Cisař. The demonstration, in itself something unheard of, went on for hours undisturbed, and at midnight the students moved to Communist Party headquarters and shouted their demand to speak with Dubček.

This was in March, when in neighboring Poland students were being clubbed to the ground for demanding freedom of speech. Dubček was at home when he was told of the student demonstration. He reacted as though this were the normal way things were done here in the Communist People's Republic: He went over to Party headquarters to talk to the students. He tried to explain his choice to them, saying the other candidates were needed in other places in government, and he assured them that Cisař would have an important role in the Central Committee. One student asked Dubček, "What are the guarantees that the old days will not be back?"

Dubček responded, "You yourselves are the guarantee. You, the young."

Was it possible to have a communist democracy in the Soviet bloc? Some were daring to hope. But the students took Dubček at his word, that they were the guarantors, so when Svoboda was installed as president, as protest, and perhaps also just to say that the students of Czechoslovakia could have a sit-in, too, they staged one that lasted for hours.

When spring, with all its promise, came to Prague, not everyone was happy. In the month of April there was an average of a suicide a day among politicians, starting with Jozef Brestansky, the vice president of the Supreme Court, who was found hanging from a tree in the woods outside of the capital. He had been working on a massive new project attempting to undo miscarriages of justice from the 1950s. It was believed the judge feared that his role in the sentencing of several innocent people was about to be revealed. Such revelations were surfacing every day, and television was playing a prominent role. Victims were being interviewed on television. Even more shocking, some of the perpetrators were interviewed on television, with viewers across the country watching them squirm as they gave their evasive answers.

Camera crews also traveled throughout the country, filming the points of view of ordinary people. What resulted was a national debate about the injustices of the past two decades under communist rule.

The mass rallies and public meetings that began in the winter became widespread in the spring, and many were shown on television. Students and workers were seen challenging government officials with tough, even hostile, questions. In a country where most officials were gray bureaucrats little known to the public, the officials who played best to cameras and spoke best to microphones—like Josef Smrkovsky—were now becoming national media stars.

If, as some suspected, Dubček hoped to satisfy the public with a small taste of democracy, that was not what was happening. The more they got, the more they wanted. Increasingly the demand was heard for opposition political parties. The *Literarni Listy* frequently championed this idea, as did playwright Václav Havel and philosopher Ivan Svitak, who wrote an article contending that there had been no reforms, just a few measures that had slipped by because of a power struggle. According to Svitak, the entire Party apparatus had to be uprooted. "We must liquidate it or it will liquidate us." The press, both print and broadcast, were in the vanguard of political reform. They were well aware that although the state censors were not censoring anymore, they still had their positions. The press wanted a law that banned censorship. One radio editor said, "We have press freedom only on the promise of the Party, and that is democracy on recall." Dubček warned of excesses. Though he did not say so, he must have understood that Brezhnev would never tolerate relinquishing the Communist Party's monopoly on power.

In April Dubček issued the Action Program of the Czechoslovakian Communist Party, which spoke of a "new model of socialist democracy." At last the official positions of the Dubček regime were stated, declaring the equality of Czechs and Slovaks, that the aim of government was socialism, and that personal and political beliefs could not be subject to secret police investigations. It denounced abuses of the past and the monopoly of power by the Communist Party.

Articles in *Pravda* in Moscow made it clear that the Soviets were not pleased. *Pravda* wrote of "bourgeois elements" undermining socialism and by summer was writing of anti-Soviet propaganda on Czech television. One of the problems was that efforts to investigate crimes of the past kept ending up on trails that led to Moscow. There was the mystery of Jan Masaryk, for example. Masaryk had been the Czech foreign minister and son of the founding father, who two days after the communist coup in 1948 jumped, fell, or was thrown from a window to his death. The subject had been untouchable for twenty years, but the Czechs wanted at last to resolve what had happened. On April 2 the Prague weekly student paper carried an article by Ivan Svitak demanding the case be reopened. He noted evidence connecting a Major Franz Schramm to the case. Schramm had gone on to become a liaison officer between Czechoslovakian and Soviet security police. Both Czechoslovakian and foreign press discussed the hypothesis that Masaryk was murdered on the direct orders of Stalin. In some stories, Soviet agents had pulled Masaryk from his bed, dragged him to the window, and thrown him out. Investigations into injustices of the 1950s also led to the Soviets. But this was not a time when the Soviet Union was prepared to review the crimes of Stalin, since the two top figures, Brezhnev and Premier Aleksei Kosygin, had been not insignificant figures in his regime.

May Day in most of the communist world was the occasion for a very long military parade displaying very expensive weapons and even longer speeches. But in Prague a touch of the ancient rite of spring had always remained. Three years earlier Allen Ginsberg had been crowned King of May in Prague, shortly before being expelled. This May Day people poured into the streets and passed before the official reviewing stand carrying signs and flags. Some carried American flags. Some carried Israeli flags. If it was forbidden last year, it was fashionable this year. Among the signs:

Fewer monuments more thoughts

Make love, not war

Democracy at all costs

Let Israel live

I would like to increase our population but I have no apartment

The official guests on the reviewing stand were becoming uncomfortable. The Bulgarian ambassador left in anger after seeing a sign stating that Macedonia, which Bulgaria claimed, belonged to Yugoslavia. The crowd surrounded Dubček. Hundreds of people tried to shake the hand of the tall, smiling leader. The police stepped in to rescue him, and then, remembering that police force had been used the year before, a Prague Party official went to the microphone to apologize and explain that too many people had crowded the first secretary. The police had not been violent, and the crowd seemed to understand. But the representatives of other Soviet bloc countries were shocked by how things were done here. That night demonstrators marched to the Polish embassy to protest Poland's treatment of students and the anti-Zionist campaign that was continuing to drive Jews from their Polish homeland. Two nights later there were more protests against Poland. Then, abruptly, Dubček left for Moscow.

The lack of explanation produced considerable anxiety in Czechoslovakia. Nor were the Czechs calmed by a communiqué from Dubček saying that it was "customary among good friends not to hide behind diplomatic politeness" and so the Soviets had been forthright in expressing concern that "the democratization process in Czechoslovakia" was not an attack on socialism. He seemed to be saying that their concern was a reasonable one, and he added that the Czechoslovakian Communist Party had often warned against such "excesses." The statement did not in the least reassure his people, and the trip did not appear to calm the Soviets.

It was not easy to grab world attention on May 9, 1968. Columbia and the Sorbonne had been closed. Students were building barricades in the streets of Paris. Bobby Kennedy won the Indiana primary, securing his place as a contender for the nomination. Peace talks opened in Paris. Investors went on a buying spree. Competing with these stories was a rumor that huge numbers of Soviet troops stationed in East Germany and Poland were heading for the Czechoslovakian border. Reporters who attempted to go to the border region to confirm this were stopped by Polish roadblocks. The day before, Bulgaria's Zhivkov, East Germany's Ulbricht, Hungary's Kádár, and Poland's Gomułka had met in Moscow and issued a communiqué on Czechoslovakia that was so intricately worded and evasive, even by communist standards, that no one could interpret what it was attempting to convey. Had they decided on invasion?

The following day the Czech news agency reported that these were normal Warsaw Pact military maneuvers about which they had been forewarned. No one inside or outside the country completely believed this, but at least the crisis seemed to be over—for now.

With the new freedom in Czechoslovakia came an explosion of culture. Thin young men in blue jeans with long hair sold tabloids with listings of rock, jazz, and theater. Prague, which had always been a theater city, had twenty-two theaters offering plays in the spring of 1968. Tad Szulc of *The New York Times* asserted enthusiastically, "Prague is essentially a Western-minded city in all things from the type and quality of its cultural life to the recent mania for turtleneck sweaters." He observed that not only artists and intellectuals but

May Day parade in Prague, 1968.
(Photo by Josef Koudelka/Magnum Photos)

bureaucrats in the ministries and even taxi drivers were wearing turtle-necks in a wide range of colors.

It is true that Prague, with its blend of Slavic and German culture, has always seemed more Western than other central European cities. It is the city of Kafka and Rilke, where German is a common second language. This has always been one of its profound differences with Slovakia, whose capital, Bratislava, is not German speaking and is clearly central European.

The leading jazz club in Prague that spring was the Reduta, near the sprawling green mall known as Wenceslas Square. The Reduta was a small room that could comfortably seat fewer than one hundred but always had more crammed into it. Before the Dubček era, this club had been known for the first Czech rock band, Akord Klub. Havel used to go there and wrote, "I didn't understand the music very well, but it didn't take much expertise to understand that what they were playing and singing here was fundamentally different from 'Krystynka' or 'Prague Is a Golden Ship,' both official hits of the time." When Szulc went there in the spring of 1968, he reported a group doing variations on Dave Brubeck "with a touch of bossa nova."

Among the theater offered that spring was *Who's Afraid of Franz Kafka?*, which had first opened in 1963 when the works of Kafka, previously banned as bourgeois, had become permissible again. The title was intended to resemble that of Edward Albee's *Who's Afraid of Virginia Woolf?* Another theater presented František Langer's long-banned work, *The Horseback Patrol*, about Czech counterrevolutionaries fighting Bolsheviks in 1918. Another drama appearing that spring was *Last Stop* by Jiri Sextr and Jiri Suchy, considered two of the best playwrights of this 1968 renaissance. Their play is about the fear that the Dubček reforms could be undone and Czechoslovakia could go back to the way it had been before January.

There was a great deal of excitement about the international film festival at the spa of Karlovy Vary because the Cannes Film Festival, three weeks earlier, had been closed by directors Jean-Luc Godard, François Truffaut, Claude Lelouch, Louis Malle, and Roman Polanski to show sympathy for the students and strikers. It was hoped that some of the Cannes films, including Alain Resnais's *Je t'aime, je t'aime,* would be shown at Karlovy Vary. When Cannes had attempted to show *Je t'aime, je t'aime* against Resnais's wishes, actor Jean-Pierre Léaud had physically held the curtains shut to keep it from being projected. Léaud was starring in *La Chinoise,* Godard's new film about the New Left. The Karlovy Vary Festival also showed three Czech films that could not be shown at Cannes, including Jiri Menzel's *Closely Watched Trains,* which went on to win the 1968 Oscar for best foreign film.

Václav Havel was not among the literati in Prague that spring because he was in New York, one of five hundred thousand Czechoslovakians who traveled abroad in 1968, since travel for the first time in many years was open to anyone. Havel, thirty-one years old, spent six weeks of the Prague Spring working with Joseph Papp's Shakespeare Festival in the East Village, where *The Memorandum,* his absurdist comedy about a new language for offices, was produced to reviews that instantly made Havel a recognized name in Western theater. "Wittily thought provoking" and "strangely touching" were among the descriptions in Clive Barnes's review for *The New York Times.* The play went on to win an Obie Award. Meanwhile, Havel may have had one of the more interesting glimpses of democracy in America since Tocqueville, frequenting the Fillmore East and other institutions of the East Village and talking to students at riot-torn Columbia University. He returned to Czechoslovakia with psychedelic rock band posters.

A poll was taken from June 30 to July 10 asking people if they wanted the nation to continue with communism or turn to capitalism. The Czechoslovakian population responded unequivocally—89 percent wanted to stay with communism. Only 5 percent said they wanted capitalism. Asked if they were satisfied with the work of the current government, a third of the respondents, 33 percent, said they were satisfied, and 54 percent said they were partially satisfied. Only 7 percent said they were dissatisfied. Dubček, walking a precarious line with Moscow, was leading a happy, hopeful communist country at home.

But the Soviets were not happy and by July had settled on a choice of three possible solutions. Either they would somehow get the wily Dubček to commit to their program, or the leaders still loyal to Moscow within Czechoslovakia—and they seem to have overestimated how many remained—would take back the country by force, or they would invade. Invasion was by far the least appealing of the three options. It had taken twelve years of difficult diplomacy to recover from the hostility and anger from the West caused by the 1956 invasion of Hungary. An invasion of Czechoslovakia would be even more difficult to explain, because Dubček had gone to great lengths to show that he was not opposing the Soviet Union. Also, the two nations had a long history of friendship, going back to the 1930s, whereas Hungary had been a Nazi ally and an enemy of the Soviets. The Soviets liberated Czechoslovakia, and the Czechs were the one people who voluntarily voted in communism and welcomed an alliance with the Soviets. As the July poll showed, Czechoslovakia was a nation still committed to communism.

Now at last, just as the faltering economy needed it most, Soviet relations with the West were warming. It was called détente. The Johnson administration had worked hard at improved Soviet relations. After long negotiations, the nuclear proliferation treaty had been achieved. In late July, after ten years of on-again, off-again cold war negotiations, a deal between Pan Am and Aeroflot would establish the first direct air service between the Soviet Union and the United States. These were good beginnings to more important openings.

Still, the Soviets had decided that the one thing they could not risk was letting Czechoslovakia drift out of their orbit, to be followed—they imagined—by Romania and Yugoslavia, with the students then taking over in Poland—and after twelve years, how pacified were the Hungarians? Ironically, in all of Dubček's statements and writings there is no indication that he ever contemplated leaving the Soviet bloc. He clearly recognized that as a line not to be crossed. But the Soviets did not trust him because he would not run his country the way they wanted him to.

Alternative number two, the internal coup, showed little sign of being possible. The Soviets would try solution one, trying one last time to bring Comrade Dubček around before resorting to invasion. There was clearly great disagreement about what to do. Kosygin, for one, appeared to oppose invasion. And the two largest Western Communist Parties, the French and the Italian, sent their leaders to Moscow to argue against invasion.

The Soviets nevertheless began putting the option of an invasion in place so that were it to be decided on, it could roll at the wave of a hand. A huge circle of Warsaw Pact troops, most of them Soviet, backed by massive armored divisions, encircled Czechoslovakia from East Germany across Poland and the Ukraine and arching through Hungary. There may have been hundreds of thousands of troops ready for an order. The only perimeter not facing tanks was the small Austrian border. A media campaign on the terrible antisocialist crimes being carried out in Czechoslovakia was intended to prepare the Soviet people for the idea of an invasion. The East German and Polish leaders were already prepared. In July the Soviets met with Hungary's Kádár to pressure him. After a July 3 meeting, both Kádár and Brezhnev issued strong statements about "defending socialism."

Then, as the one last attempt to persuade Dubček, he was ordered to Moscow to discuss the Czech program. Dubček considered this an obnoxious and illegal interference with internal affairs of his country. He put it to the Czechoslovakian presidium, which voted overwhelmingly to turn down the Moscow invitation. How unfortunate that no chronicler was present to record Brezhnev's reaction to the polite message from Prague, the first time ever that a head of the Czechoslovakian Communist Party had turned down an order from Moscow to attend a meeting.

Dubček was absolutely confident that he could manage the Soviets. To him it was unimaginable that they would invade. They were friends. It was as far-fetched as the United States invading Canada. He believed that he knew how to reassure them. When he spoke with Brezhnev and the senior Soviet leaders, he knew the words to avoid. He would never say "reform," "reformist," or especially "revision." These were terms certain to enrage the true Marxist-Leninist.

In June thousands of Soviet troops had been allowed into Czechoslovakia for "staff maneuvers." This was normal, but the quantity, tens of thousands of troops and thousands of vehicles, including tanks, was not. The maneuvers were supposed to end on June 30, and as each July day passed with the troops still there, the population was growing angrier. Clearly stalling, the Soviets presented a steady stream of ridiculous excuses: They needed repairs and so additional "repair troops" began entering, problems with spare parts, the troops needed rest, they were concerned about blocking traffic, the bridges and roads on which they had entered seemed shaky and in need of repairs.

Rumors spread through Czechoslovakia that the trespassing Soviet troops had brought with them printing presses and broadcast-jamming equipment, files on Czechoslovakian political leaders, and lists of people to be arrested.

The Czechoslovakian government demanded the removal of the Soviet troops. The Soviets demanded that the entire Czechoslovakian presidium come to Moscow and meet with the entire Soviet presidium. Prague responded that they thought the meeting was a good idea and "invited" the Soviet presidium to Czechoslovakia. The entire Soviet presidium had never traveled outside the Soviet Union.

Dubček knew he was playing a dangerous game. But he had his own people to answer to, and they clearly would not accept capitulation. In retrospect, one of the deciding factors that kept the Soviets from giving the invasion order that July was the tremendous unity of the Czechoslovakian people. There had never before really been a Czechoslovakian people. There were Czechs and there were Slovaks, and even among Czechs there were Moravians and Bohemians. But for one moment in July 1968 there were only Czechoslovakians. Even with troops around and within their border, with the Soviet press vilifying them daily, they spoke with one voice. And Dubček was careful to be that voice.

At almost 3:00 in the morning on July 31, a rail worker and a small group of Slovak steel workers recognized a man out for a walk as First Secretary Comrade Dubček. Dubček invited them to a small restaurant that was open at that hour. "He spent about an hour with us and explained the situation," one of the workers later told the Slovak press. When they asked why he was out so late, he told them that for the last few weeks he had been sleeping only between 3:00 A.M. and 7:00 A.M.

Czech television interviewed Soviet tourists and asked them if they had seen counterrevolutionary activity and if they had been treated well. They all spoke highly of the country and the people and saluted Soviet-Czechoslovak friendship. For four days, the two presidiums met in Čierna nad Tisou, a Slovak town near the Hungarian-Ukrainian border. On August 2, when the meeting had ended, Dubček gave a television address in which he assured the Czechoslovakian people that their sovereignty as a nation was not threatened. He also told them that good relations with the Soviet Union were essential to that sovereignty, and he warned against verbal attacks on the Soviets or socialism.

The message was that there would be no invasion if the Czechoslovakians refrained from provoking the Soviets. The following day, the last of the Soviet troops left Czechoslovakia.

Dubček appeared to be reining in free speech. Still, he seemed to have won the confrontation. Sometimes survival alone is the great victory. The new Czechoslovakia had made it through the Prague Spring into Prague summer. Articles were being written around the world on why the Soviets were backing down.

Young people from Eastern and Western Europe and North America began packing into Prague to see what this new kind of liberty was about. The city's dark medieval walls were being covered with graffiti in several languages. With only seven thousand hotel rooms in Prague, there was often nothing available anywhere in the city, although sometimes a bribe would help. A table at one of the few Prague restaurants was getting hard to come by, and a taxi without a fare was a rare sight. In August *The New York Times* wrote, "For those under 30, Prague seems the right place to be this summer."

PART III

THE SUMMER OLYMPICS

The longing for rest and peace must itself be thrust aside; it coincides with the acceptance of iniquity. Those who weep for the happy periods they encountered in history acknowledge what they want: not the alleviation but the silencing of misery.

—ALBERT CAMUS, L'Homme révolté—The Rebel, *1951*

CHAPTER 14

PLACES NOT TO BE

In the colonies the truth stood naked, but the citizens of the mother country preferred it with clothes on.
— JEAN-PAUL SARTRE, *Introduction to Frantz Fanon's* The Wretched of the Earth, *1961*

EVERYTHING SEEMED to get worse in the summer of 1968. The academic year had ended disastrously, with hundreds walking out on Columbia graduation—even though President Kirk did not attend in order to avoid provoking demonstrations. Universities in French, Italian, German, and Spanish cities were barely functioning. In June violent confrontations between students and police erupted in Rio de Janeiro, Buenos Aires, and Montevideo and in Ecuador and Chile. On August 6 a student demonstration in Rio was canceled when 1,500 infantrymen and police with thirteen light tanks, forty armored vehicles, and eight jeeps mounted with machine guns appeared. Often the demonstrations began over very basic issues. In Uruguay and Ecuador the original issue had been bus fares to school.

Even relatively quiet England was at last having its 1968, with students ending the year occupying universities. It had begun in May at the Hornsey College of Art and Design, a Victorian building in affluent north London, where students had a meeting about issues such as a full-time student president and a sports program and ended by taking over the building and demanding fundamental changes in art education. Their demands spread to art schools throughout the country and became a thirty-three-art-college movement. Students at Birmingham College of Art refused to take final examinations. By the end of June students still held Hornsey College.

So little progress was seen in the stalemated Paris peace talks that on the first day of summer *The New York Times* offered Americans a sad crumb of hope in the carefully worded headline CLIFFORD DETECTS SLIGHT GAIN IN TALKS ON VIETNAM. On June 23 the Vietnam War edged out the American Revolution as the longest-running war in American history, having lasted 2,376 days since the first support troops were sent in 1961. On June 27 the Viet Cong, attacking nearby American and South Vietnamese forces, either accidentally or intentionally set fire to the nearby fishing village of Sontra along the South China Sea, killing eighty-eight civilians and wounding more than one hundred. In the United States on the same day, David Dellinger, head of the National Mobilization Committee to End the War in Vietnam, said that one hundred organizations were working together to organize a series of demonstrations urging an end to the war, all scheduled to take place in Chicago that summer during the Democratic National Convention. On August 8 American forces on nighttime river patrol in the Mekong Delta, attempting to fight the Viet Cong with flamethrowers, killed seventy-two civilians from the village of Cairang, which had been friendly to American forces.

A new generation of Spaniards, after submitting passively to decades of Franco's brutality, was beginning to confront the violent regime with violence. In 1952 five young Basques, dissatisfied with the passivity of their parents' generation, formed an organization later called *Euskadi Ta Askatasuna,* which in their ancient language meant "Basqueland and Liberty." Until 1968, the activities of the organization, known as ETA, consisted primarily of promoting the Basque language, which had been banned by Franco. Later, ETA members began burning Spanish flags and defacing Spanish monuments. In 1968 Basque linguists created a unified language in place of eight dialects. An example of the linguistic difficulties prior to 1968: The original name for ETA used the word *Aberri* instead of *Euskadi,* so that the acronym was ATA. But after six years of clandestine operations as ATA, they discovered that in some dialects, their name, *ata,* means "duck," so the name was changed to ETA. The unified language of 1968 cleared the way for a renaissance of the Basque language.

But in 1968 ETA became violent. On June 7 a Civil Guard stopped a car that had two armed ETA members in it. They opened fire and killed the guard. One of the ETA killers, Txabi Etxebarrieta, was then tracked down and killed by the Spanish. On August 2, in revenge for the killing of Etxebarrieta, a much disliked San Sebastian police captain was shot dead by ETA in front of his home with his wife listening on the other side of the door. In response to the attack, the Spanish virtually declared war on the Basques. A state of siege was established that lasted for most of the rest of the year, with thousands arrested and tortured and some sentenced to years in prison, despite angry protests from Europe. Worse, a pattern of action and reaction, violence for violence, between ETA and the Spanish was established and has remained to this day.

In the Caribbean nation of Haiti it was the eleventh year of rule by François Duvalier, the little country doctor, friend of the poor black man, who had become a mass murderer. In a midyear press conference he lectured American journalists, "I hope the evolution of democracy you've observed in Haiti will be an example for the people of the world, in particular in the United States, in relation to the civil and political rights of Negroes."

But there were no rights for Negroes or anyone else under the rule of the sly but mad Dr. Duvalier. One of the cruelest and most brutal dictatorships in the world, Duvalier's government had driven so many middle- and upper-class Haitians into exile that there were more Haitian doctors in Canada than in Haiti. On May 20, 1968, the eighth coup d'état attempt against Dr. Duvalier began with a B-25 flying over the capital, Port-au-Prince, and dropping an explosive, which blew one more hole in an eroded road. Then a package of leaflets was dropped, which did not scatter because the invaders had not untied the bundle before dropping it. Then another explosive was dropped in the direction of the gleaming white National Palace, but it failed to explode. Port-au-Prince supposedly thus secured, the invasion began in the northern city of Cap Haïtien, where a Cessna landed with men opening tommy-gun fire at the unmanned control tower. The invaders were quickly killed or captured by Haitian army troops. On August 7 the ten surviving invaders were sentenced to death.

Walter Laqueur, a Brandeis historian who had written several books on the Middle East, wrote an article in May arguing that the region was potentially more dangerous than Vietnam. Later in the year Nixon would make the same point in his campaign speeches. What frightened the world about the Middle East was that the two superpowers had chosen sides and there was an obvious risk that the regional conflict would become a global one. The Israelis and the Arabs were in an arms race, with the Arabs buying Soviet weapons and Israelis buying American, while the Israelis, whose allies were not supplying them as quickly as the Soviets were the Arabs, also built up a homegrown arms industry.

"Gradually," Laqueur wrote, "the world has reconciled itself to the fact that there will be a fourth Arab-Israeli War in the near future." In July a poll showed that 62 percent of Americans expected another Arab-Israeli war within five years. The Egyptian government insisted on referring to its complete military rout in the Six Day War as the "setback." Israel's plan to offer the land it had seized in that war in exchange for peace was not working. There was a great deal of interest in land, but not in peace. The president of Egypt, Gamal Abdel Nasser, refused even to enter into negotiations with Israel. Mohammed Heykal, an Egyptian spokesman, insisted that another war was "inevitable"—perhaps because demonstrating Egyptian students were furious about the Egyptian performance in the last war. While the age of student movements had given birth to antiwar protests on campuses all over the world, Cairo students were protesting that their war hadn't been fought well enough. Because Saudi Arabia considered itself a religious state, King Faisal was calling for a "holy war," whereas Syria, considering itself to be a socialist state, had opted to call for a "people's war." The Palestinian organizations staged murderous little raids known as "terrorist attacks," and the Israelis responded with massive firepower, often making incursions into Jordan.

The Arabs all agreed not to talk to the Israelis, because this would give the Israeli seizures some form of recognition. However, according to Laqueur, some were beginning to think they had made a mistake, since "in negotiation, the Zionists would have settled for much less than they eventually got." A poll conducted in France showed that 49 percent of the French thought Israel should keep all or part of the new territories it gained in the 1967 war. Only 19 percent thought it should give it all back. The same poll conducted in Great Britain showed 66 percent thought Israel should keep at least some of the new territory and only 13 percent thought it should give it all back.

That land was the reason observers were giving as long as five years until the next war. If the Arabs had taken a beating in 1967, the next time would be even worse, now that the Israelis controlled the high ground at the Suez and the Golan. Many were already predicting Nasser's overthrow from the last failure. But this situation subtly created a shift in the Middle East that was not clearly seen at the time. In the Arab world, the new policy was called "neither peace nor war." Its aim was to wear down the Israelis. If the big armies were no longer in a position to lead conventional warfare, the alternative was small terrorist operations, which meant the Palestinians. Originally, such raids by Palestinians had been an Egyptian idea, sponsored by Nasser in the 1950s. The attacks were inexpensive and popular with the Arab public. Syria started sponsoring them in the mid-1960s. Now hundreds of guerrilla fighters were being trained in Jordan and Syria. This would greatly strengthen the hand of Palestinian leaders and facilitate the evolution of the "Arabs of occupied Jordan" into "the Palestinian people." The Arab nations, especially Syria, were scrambling to assert control over these guerrilla organizations. But by the summer of 1968 Al Fatah had established itself as a separate power in Jordan beyond King Hussein's control. The group had come a long way from its first operation—a disastrous attempt to blow up a water pump—only four years earlier.

Before the 1967 war, the Israelis refused to describe any of their actions as either a "reprisal" or a "retaliation." Government censors would even cut these two words from correspondents' dispatches. But by 1968 both of these terms were in common usage as Israelis struck beyond Jordan's and Lebanon's borders to reach the Palestinian guerrillas.

By summer, with the Israeli government having given the concept of land for peace a year's effort, Israelis, if not their government, were giving up and settling in to Jerusalem and the Golan Heights, into a larger and different Israel from the one they had dreamed of. Amnon Rubenstein of the Tel Aviv daily *Ha'aretz* wrote, "The Israelis, on the other hand, will have to learn the art of living in an indefinite state of non-peace."

In the tropical, oil-rich delta of the Niger River, it was not nonpeace but open warfare that people were living with indefinitely. An estimated fifty thousand people had already died in combat. In May, when Nigerian troops took and destroyed the once prosperous city of Port Harcourt and put up a naval blockade and encircled Biafra with eighty-five thousand soldiers, the rebel Biafrans lost all connection to the outside world. It was reported that the Nigerian force had massacred several hundred wounded Biafran soldiers in two hospitals. The small breakaway state that did not want to be part of Nigeria was fighting on with an army of twenty-five thousand against the one-hundred-thousand-soldier Nigerian army. It had no heavy weaponry, a shortage of ammunition, and not even enough hand weapons to arm each soldier. The Nigerian air force with Soviet planes and Egyptian pilots bombed and strafed towns and villages, leaving them littered with corpses and writhing wounded. The Biafrans said that the Nigerians, whom they usually referred to by the name of the dominant tribe, the Hausa, intended to carry out genocide and that they specifically targeted schools, hospitals, and churches in their air attacks. But what

Biafran soldier in 1968
(Photo by Don McCullin/Contact Press Images)

finally started to get the world's attention after a year of fighting was the shortage not of weapons but of food.

Pictures of skeletal children staring with sad, unnaturally large eyes—children who looked unlikely to live through the week—began showing up in newspapers and magazines all over the world. The pictures ran in news articles and in advertisements that were desperate pleas for help. But most attempts at help were not getting through. The Biafrans maintained a secret and dangerous airstrip—a narrow, cleared path lit with kerosene lamps to receive the few relief planes. Those who attempted to find this strip had to first fly through a zone of radar-guided Nigerian antiaircraft fire.

The West learned a new word, "kwashiorkor," the fatal lack of protein from which thousands of children were dying. Queen Elizabeth Hospital in Umuahia had treated 18 cases of kwashiorkor in all of 1963, but, visited by reporters in August 1968, the same hospital was treating 1,800 cases a day. It was estimated that between 1,500 and 40,000 Biafrans were dying of starvation every week. Even those who managed to get to refugee camps often starved. What food there was had become unaffordable. A chicken worth 70 cents in 1967 cost $5.50 in 1968. People were being advised to eat rats, dogs, lizards, and white ants for protein. Hospitals filled with children who had no food, medicine, or doctors. The small, bony bodies rested on straw mats; as they died they were wrapped in the mats and placed in a hole. Every night the holes were covered and a new one dug for the next day.

The Nigerians would not allow in relief flights, including Red Cross, to help Biafra's ten million people, one-tenth of whom were living in refugee camps. They said that such flights inhibited the ability of the Nigerian air force to carry out its mission. The only food getting through arrived on a few night flights by daredevil pilots sponsored by international relief organizations.

Most of the world, preoccupied with the year's busy agenda, regarded this war with a fair amount of indifference, not supporting the Biafran claim to nationhood but urging the Nigerians to let relief planes get through. But on July 31 the French government, despite predictions that de Gaulle's days of foreign policy initiatives were over, departed from its allies and its own foreign policy by stating that it supported Biafra's claim to self-determination. Aside from France, only Zambia, Ivory Coast, Tanzania, and Gabon officially recognized Biafra. On August 2 the war became a U.S. political issue when Senator Eugene McCarthy criticized President Johnson for doing little to help and demanded that he go to the United Nations and insist on an airlift of food and medicine to Biafra.

Americans responded by creating numerous aid groups. The Committee for Nigeria/Biafra Relief, which included former Peace Corps volunteers, was looking for a way to get relief into Biafra. Twenty-one leading Jewish organizations, Catholic Relief Services, and the American Committee to Keep Biafra Alive were all looking for ways to help. The Red Cross hired a DC-6 from a Swiss charter company to fly in at night, but on August 10, after ten flights, the flights were suspended because of Nigerian antiaircraft fire.

Then, on August 13, Carl Gustav von Rosen, a Swedish count and legendary aviator, landed a four-engine DC-7 on a little dirt runway in Biafra. The plane, carrying ten tons of food and medicine, had come in on a new route free from Nigerian radar-guided antiaircraft guns.

Von Rosen had first become famous in a similar role in 1935 when he defied the Italian air force and managed to fly the first Red Cross air ambulance into besieged Ethiopia. In 1939, as a volunteer for the Finnish air force in the Finnish-Soviet war, he flew many bombing missions over Russia. And during World War II he flew a weekly courier plane between Stockholm and Berlin.

After successfully landing in Biafra, von Rosen then went to São Tomé, the small Portuguese island off the coast of Nigeria, where warehouses of food, medicine, and ammunition were stacked up ready for Biafra. There he briefed the pilots on the air corridor he had discovered. He had flown this corridor into Biafra twice to make sure it was safe. The first time he did it in daylight, even though daylight runs were unheard of because of the risk of interception by the Nigerian air force. But von Rosen said he had to be able to examine the terrain before attempting a night run. He said that he didn't care whether the pilots used the corridor for food or guns. "The Biafrans need both if they are to survive." The tall Scandinavian with blue eyes and gray hair called what was happening there "a crime against humanity. . . . If the Nigerians go on shooting at relief planes, then the airlift should be shielded with an umbrella of fighter planes. Meanwhile we are going to continue flying and other airlines will join in."

Correspondents who managed to get into Biafra reported extremely high morale from the Biafrans, who usually said to them, "Help us win." The Nigerians launched ever more deadly assaults led by heavy shelling, and the Biafrans continued to hold their ground, training with sticks and fighting with an assortment of weapons acquired on the European market. But by August Biafran-held territory was only a third the size of what it had been when the people had declared their independence the year before. With hundreds of children starving to death every day, eleven thousand tons of food had piled up ready for shipment from various points.

Odumegwu Ojukwu, the thirty-four-year-old head of state, a British-educated former colonel in the Nigerian army, said, "All I really ask is that the outside world look at us as human beings and not as Negroes bashing heads. If three Russian writers are imprisoned the whole world is outraged, but when thousands of Negroes are massacred . . ."

The U.S. government told reporters that it was helpless to aid Biafra because it could not afford to give the undeveloped world the appearance that it was interfering in an African civil war. It was not clear if this decision took into account the impression it had given the world that it was already interfering in an Asian civil war. But it did seem true that there was a growing resentment in Africa of Western aid for Biafra. This, not surprisingly, was particularly true of Nigerians. One Nigerian officer said to a Swiss relief worker, "We don't want your custard and your wheat. The people here need fish and *garri*. We can give them that, so why don't you find some starving white people to feed."

CHAPTER 15

THE CRAFT OF
DULL POLITICS

Yes, Nixon was still the spirit of television. Mass communication was still his disease—he thought he could use it to communicate with masses.
—NORMAN MAILER, Miami and the Siege of Chicago, *1968*

1968 WAS AN AMERICAN election year, and election years in America tend to display a peculiar kind of frontier campaigning so brash that the other democracies study the spectacle with bemused fascination. But beyond the power plays, the unbridled ambition, and the unconscionably phony posturing are voters who are allowed to hope once every four years. In 1968 hope ended in the late spring on a kitchen floor in California. After the killing of Robert Kennedy, novelist John Updike said that God may have withdrawn His blessing for America.

The world had watched Bobby growing a little every day in 1968 — the muttering family runt who became a little more clear-spoken, a little more inspired, with every interview, each appearance, campaigning with an energy and determination rare even in American politics, through crowds with signs that said "Kiss Me Bobby" and who ripped off his shoes and clothing as though he were a rock star. He became so good at television that Abbie Hoffman enviously called him "Hollywood Bobby." Hoffman said with frustration, "Gene wasn't much. One could secretly cheer for him the way you cheer for the Mets. It's easy knowing he can never win. But Bobby . . . Every night we would turn on the TV set and there was the young knight with long hair, holding out his hand. . . . When young longhairs told you how they heard that Bobby turned on, you knew Yippie! was really in trouble." Tom

Hayden, not given to admiring candidates from the political establishment, wrote, "And yet, in that year of turmoil, I found that the only intriguing politician in America was the younger brother of John F. Kennedy."

Yevtushenko had described Kennedy's eyes as "two blue clots of will and anxiety." When Kennedy met the Russian poet, Yevtushenko proposed a toast and wanted to smash the glasses. Kennedy, being not at all Russian, wanted to substitute some cheaper glasses. But cheap glasses are thick, and those, slammed to the floor, did not break, which the Russian poet took as a frightening bad omen.

Everyone could see the doom that Lowell wrote was "woven in" his nerves. So could he. When he learned of his brother's assassination, he said that he had expected it to be himself. His brother's widow, Jackie, had feared that he would be next and told historian Arthur Schlesinger at a dinner party, "Do you know what I think will happen to Bobby? The same thing that happened to Jack." Only two weeks before he was shot, he had a conversation with French writer Romain Gary in which, according to Gary, Kennedy said, "I know that there will be an attempt on my life sooner or later. Not so much for political reasons, but through contagion, through emulation."

First was the political question, could he win? It was often said that he would be shot if it looked as if he would win. On June 4 he won the California primary, defeating McCarthy 45 to 42 percent, with Humphrey drawing only 12 percent of the vote. At that moment he had finally overcome McCarthy's considerable lead. He had only to outmaneuver Hubert Humphrey at the Chicago convention. "And now it's on to Chicago, and let's win there," he said. Minutes later he was shot in the head, strangely while taking an unplanned shortcut through the kitchen because admirers had blocked the planned exit path. And there in the kitchen, on the unplanned route, was a man waiting with a handgun.

He had been shot by someone named Sirhan Sirhan, an odd appellation that made no sense to American ears. Who was Sirhan Sirhan? Unsatisfactory answers started coming. A Jordanian, an Arab from occupied Jordan, a Palestinian, but not in the old sense of a militant. Not an Arab with an agenda—no agenda. A displaced person who seemed mentally unstable. We learned who killed him, but we have never found out why.

Now that Kennedy was gone, who would be the next front-runner, and would he too be killed? "There is no God but death," Ferlinghetti wrote in a poem to Kennedy that he read the day he was buried. All the candidates, Democrats and Republicans, none so much as McCarthy, who seemed to have withdrawn from the race, knew that they could be next. Norman Mailer, who covered both party conventions, observed that all of the candidates had become uneasy-looking when in crowds. The most likely victim already dead, the federal government decided it had to do more to protect the other seven. Robert Kennedy's assassination would have failed if the Secret Service had been guarding him, because they would have cleared the kitchen before he entered. One hundred and fifty Secret Service agents were attached to the remaining candidates, which had little impact on Hubert Humphrey or George Wallace because they were already heavily guarded. But it was a huge change for Eugene McCarthy, who had never even had a bodyguard.

With politics dead and seven candidates still alive, the political conventions were empty, like a sporting event in which the star athlete had been scratched from the competition. Republicans and Democrats are different, and so the Republican convention was controlled emptiness, whereas the Democratic one was empty chaos.

National political conventions were invented for political bosses from around the country to meet and pick their candidate for president. The first president to be nominated by a convention had been Andrew Jackson in his second term. Originally, candidates were chosen by a few top party cronies in private. Not only did this seem undemocratic, but as the country got larger it became unwieldy, because all American political parties have always been a confederation of local bosses—state bosses, city bosses, people like Mayor Richard J. Daley of Chicago. As the country got bigger, the parties had more bosses.

The conventions were always bad theater, full of grandiose and foolish stunts. In 1948, the first year they were televised, they became bad television. That was the year the Democrats unleashed a flock of recalcitrant pigeons who attempted to perch everywhere, including on chairman Sam Rayburn's head while he was trying to call the meeting back to order with a gavel. He swatted it away, but the persistent bird landed in front of him on the podium. In front of a platoon of photographers with flashbulbs and television cameras, he grabbed the bird and flung it out of the way.

In 1952 the summer event became air-conditioned, which eliminated wilted suits and hand-flapping fans and made it look less backroom. Air-conditioning also opened up new venues. There could have been no August convention in Miami before air-conditioning. In 1960 John Kennedy made conventions more interesting by inventing the tactic of monitoring every delegation and courting every delegate. He spent four years on them before the convention met and then placed spies in each delegation to detect shifts so that prevaricating delegates could be massaged. Barry Goldwater adopted the same technique in 1964, and it became the way conventions were worked, adding a note of intrigue. 1968 would be the end of the drama, the year the parties learned that if it was going to be on television, the bosses had to work out the nomination in advance and then choreograph it for the cameras like the Miss America pageant or the Oscars—no more stubborn pigeons or any other surprises.

But in 1968 the future of the party was actually decided in front of live television over the course of a week. It was the biggest story in television—bigger than wars, famine, or invasions. Most of the network organization moved to the convention city, and the network stars were made there. Huntley, Brinkley, and Cronkite had all secured their starring roles anchoring convention coverage. When CBS pulled Daniel Schorr off the Chicago convention to cover the Soviet tanks rolling into Czechoslovakia, he complained that he was being pulled from the big story.

Up until 1968, the differences between Republicans and Democrats were more a matter of style than ideology. The Democrats had carried out the Vietnam War, yet the most prominent antiwar candidates were Democrats. The Republicans had their own antiwar candidates, such as New York senator Jacob Javits, who kicked off his 1968 campaign for a third term by calling for an end to the war, and New York City mayor John Lindsay, a long-shot bid for the Republican presidential nomination who was also vociferously antiwar.

The most popular Republican candidate was New York governor Nelson Rockefeller, who was not exactly antiwar—he had supported the war "to protect the rights of self-determination" of the people of South Vietnam. But in 1968 he changed his tone, calling the war effort a "commitment looking for a justification," and called for a unilateral withdrawal of U.S. troops. He was a social liberal with notable support among black voters. As governor, he had been pushing the New York State Legislature to legalize abortion. The eighty-five-year-old state law allowed abortion only to save the mother's life. He called for the Republican Party to become "the voice of the poor and oppressed." He even paid homage to Eugene McCarthy for bringing youth into politics and promised to lower the voting age to eighteen.

He was a candidate of tremendous appeal—much liked by the press, a brilliant television performer with an almost believable common touch with his gravelly-voiced "Hi ya," despite the fact that he was obviously "rich as Rockefeller." In August he went to the Republican convention with polls showing him as a favorite who could comfortably beat Hubert Humphrey or Eugene McCarthy, whereas the same polls showed that his rival, Richard Nixon, could beat neither. Rockefeller was well liked even by Democrats, and his only problem with Republicans was the extreme Right, which was bitter in the belief that in 1964 he had failed to help their martyred conservative, Barry Goldwater.

But he did have a problem. Nominees were picked at conventions by delegates, and most of the delegates were lined up for Richard Nixon, whom it seemed nobody liked. Very few were there for "Rocky," whom it seemed everyone liked. How had this happened?

Some pivotal moments in history get forgotten. Sometimes they don't look significant at the time. On March 22 Rockefeller had announced that he was not a candidate. The statement shocked and mystified the political world. Most concluded it was some kind of tactic. Perhaps he intended to prove his popularity with a landslide of write-in votes. A *New York Times* editorial openly asked him to reconsider, saying, "The Rockefeller refusal to run means the nomination of Richard M. Nixon by default." The editorial also said, "His decision leaves moderate Republicans leaderless and impotent." In the hindsight of history, both statements have been proven correct. Though it did turn out to be an ill-conceived strategy and Rockefeller did get back into the race—he had never really left it the move left Nixon, far more popular in the Republican Party than in the nation, free to rack up an unbeatable lead in delegates. Rockefeller spent an unprecedented $10 million to get back in the race, but Mailer quipped that he would have done better to buy four hundred delegates at $25,000 each.

His mishandling of the 1968 campaign when he had everything in his favor meant the undoing of Rockefeller's career, which in turn meant the orphaning of the liberal wing of the Republican Party. With the exception of one desperate hour when Rockefeller himself served as unelected president Gerald Ford's vice president after Nixon resigned in disgrace, the Republican Party has never again turned to a politician from its moderate wing for president or vice president. 1968 was the year in which the Republican Party became a far more ideological party—a conservative party in which promising moderates have been marginalized.

The only other Republican candidate was Ronald Reagan, the new governor of California in his second year, who had distinguished himself for unleashing police brutality on the California State campuses and for cutting spending for education, heath, and other social programs. This had impressed any number of conservatives. But Reagan appeared so unelectable, was the butt of so many jokes, that he

made Nixon, a favorite comic subject in his own right, look like a serious contender. At least Nixon seemed smart, even if his intelligence was
used to seamlessly shift positions with dizzying frequency.

Later during his own presidency, Reagan's apparent confusion was
often blamed on his age. But even in 1968, only fifty-seven, Reagan
often seemed lost. On May 21 he appeared on NBC's *Meet the Press*
and was asked to explain how he differed from Barry Goldwater.
"There are a lot of specific issues, I was trying to recall," he said.
"Frankly, my memory is failing me. Just a short time ago I found he
had made a statement. I was asked it and I disagreed on that particular
statement." By June a petition drive to put a referendum on the state
ballot about Reagan's competence had five hundred thousand signatures. California polls showed only 30 percent of the population believing he was doing a "good job." Comedians always loved to do Nixon
jokes, but Reagan jokes were increasingly coming into their own.
Comedian Dick Gregory, who was running for president on his own
party ticket as a write-in candidate, said, "Reagan is nigger spelled
backwards. Imagine, we got a backwards nigger running California."

And there was Eisenhower, a ghost from the 1950s, who had consistently insisted that U.S. strategy in Vietnam was working and should be
continued to protect the world from communist domination. Typical
of Eisenhower's fascinating contradictions, as president he had spoken
grandly about the people's demand for peace, but in the sixties, when
they finally were demanding it, he accused the antiwar movement of
"rebellion" and "giving aid and comfort to the enemy." Like de Gaulle,
he frequently referred to his World War II experiences. Yes, he admitted, we appeared to be losing in Vietnam, but he recalled reading the
newspapers after the Battle of the Bulge and feeling the same way. After
yet another heart attack he appeared on the front pages from his bed at
Walter Reed Hospital in pajamas and a bathrobe that said on it "Feeling Great Again." He warned of the communists, and, live from his
bed, he was broadcasting to Miami to endorse his former vice president, Nixon. It was as though the 1950s would not go away. Ten hours
later Eisenhower had a sixth heart attack, which he also survived.

Conventions chose candidates by a series of ballots—delegate
counts, state by state. These ballots would go into the night, ignoring
the broadcast needs of prime-time television, until a single candidate
had an absolute majority of delegates. Usually the more ballots that
took place, the more the front-runner's support would erode. Rockefeller imagined the delegates turning to him after a few rounds. Reagan
fantasized that Rockfeller and Nixon would be deadlocked ballot after

ballot until the delegates finally turned to him as a way out. Lindsay, though no one believed it, harbored a similar fantasy about himself.

Nixon won on the first ballot.

The only drama was Nixon's struggle with Nixon. His political career had been considered over in 1948, when he attacked former State Department official Alger Hiss. It was supposed to be over again in 1952, when he was caught in a fund-raising scandal. And in 1962, when he was defeated for governor of California only two years after losing the presidency to Kennedy, he gave his own farewell to politics. Now he was back. "The greatest comeback since Lazarus," wrote James Reston in *The New York Times*.

Then something weird happened: Nixon, in his acceptance speech, started talking like Martin Luther King. Mailer was the first to notice it, but this was not just one of his famously eccentric imaginings. Nixon, who also adopted the SDS's two-fingered peace salute, never put limits on what he could co-opt. Martin Luther King in the four months since his death had journeyed from rebel agitator to the heart of the American establishment. His organization was picketing outside the convention hall. Six miles away, Miami was having its first race riot. The governor of Florida was talking about responding with necessary force, and black men were being shot. Richard Nixon was delivering a speech.

"I see a day," he repeated nine different times in the unmistakably familiar cadence of "I have a dream." Then, further on in the speech, seemingly enraptured with his own or whomever's rhetoric, he declared, "To the top of the mountain so that we may see the glory of a new day for America. . . ."

The Republican convention in Miami the second week of August 1968 was a bore that according to pollsters alienated youth, alienated blacks, and excited almost no one. Even the one possibility for drama—the complaints of black groups that black representation was unfairly excluded from the delegations of Florida, Louisiana, Mississippi, and Tennessee failed to produce drama because it was quickly glossed over. Norman Mailer wrote, "The complaints were unanimous that this was the dullest convention anyone could remember." One television critic said the coverage was so long and dull that it constituted "cruel and unusual punishment." But the boredom helped the Republicans. It kept people from paying attention and consequently kept them from noticing the rioting in the street. A poll taken in segregated white Florida public schools in 1968 had found 59 percent of white students were either elated or indifferent to the news of Martin Luther King's assassination. While Nixon was being crowned in Miami Beach, Ralph Abernathy, head of the late Martin Luther King's Southern Christian Leadership Conference, was leading daily black demonstrations outside, and across the bay in the black ghetto called Liberty City, a violent confrontation erupted between police and blacks, with cars overturned and set on fire. National Guard troops were called in. While Nixon was selecting his running mate, three blacks were killed in the Liberty City riot.

There was only the question of vice president left, and logic seemed to dictate a liberal who could pick up the Rockefeller votes—either Rockefeller himself or New York City mayor John Lindsay, who was campaigning hard for the nomination, or Illinois senator Charles Percy. Rockefeller, who had declined to be Nixon's running mate in 1960, seemed unlikely to accept now.

In the end Nixon surprised everyone—at last a surprise—and picked the governor of Maryland, Spiro T. Agnew. He said he did this to unify the party, but the party could not conceal its unhappiness. The entire moderate half of the party had been ignored. The Republican Party had a ticket that would greatly appeal to white southerners who felt embattled by years of civil rights and to some northern reactionary "law and order" voters who had been angered by the rioting and disorder of the past two years, but to no one else. The Republicans were leaving most of the country to the Democrats. Alabama renegade Democrat George Wallace, an old-time segregationist running on his own ticket, could not only siphon off Democrats, he could also deny the Republicans enough votes to cost them southern states and their whole southern strategy. There was a move to try to force Nixon to pick someone else that was stopped only because Mayor Lindsay, the leading liberal candidate for the job, performed Nixon the service of seconding the Agnew nomination.

Nixon defensively said that Agnew was "one of the most underrated political men in America." The following day, the National Association for the Advancement of Colored People, the NAACP, one of the most moderate black groups, denounced the ticket, which they termed "white backlash candidates." Was that bad news for Nixon? Was that even news? Richard Nixon, with few people noticing, had reshaped the Republican Party.

Then on to Chicago—for a convention that would not be boring.

CHAPTER 16

PHANTOM FUZZ DOWN BY THE STOCKYARDS

> Jean Genet, who has considerable police experience, says he never saw such expressions before on allegedly human faces. And what is the phantom fuzz screaming from Chicago to Berlin, from Mexico City to Paris? "We are REAL REAL REAL!!! as this NIGHTSTICK!" As they feel, in their dim animal way, that reality is slipping away from them.
> —WILLIAM BURROUGHS, *"The Coming of the Purple Better One,"* Esquire, *November 1968*

> There's nothing unreal about Chicago. It's quite real. The mayor who runs the city is a real person. He's an old time hack. I might chastise the Eastern establishment for romanticizing him. The whole "Last Hurrah" aspect. He's a hack. A neighborhood bully. You have to see him to believe him.
> —STUDS TERKEL, *interviewed by* The New York Times, *August 18, 1968*

> People coming to Chicago should begin preparations for five days of energy-exchange.
> —ABBIE HOFFMAN, Revolution for the Hell of It, *1968*

EVERYTHING SEEMED inauspicious for the Democratic National Convention in Chicago at the end of August. The convention center had burned down, the most exciting candidate had been murdered, leaving mostly a void filled with anger, and the mayor had become notorious for his use of police violence.

Chicago's McCormick Place Convention Center was what Studs Terkel might have a called "a real Chicago story." It had been built a few years earlier at a cost of $35 million and named after the notorious right-wing publisher of the *Chicago Tribune*, one of the few backers of the project besides Mayor Daley. Environmentalists fought it as a degradation of the lakefront, and most Chicagoans regarded it as abysmally ugly. Then, mysteriously or, according to some, miraculously, it burned down in 1967, leaving the Democrats without a location and Chicagoans wondering exactly how the $35 million had been spent.

Mayor Richard Daley, who in his 1967 reelection faced what was close to a serious challenge because of the McCormick Place scandal, was not going to let fire or scandal rob his city of a major convention. By the old Union Stockyards, the beef center of America until it was closed down in 1957, stood the Amphitheatre. Miles from downtown, since the closing of the stockyards this had become an out-of-the-way part of Chicago where such events as wrestling and the occasional car or boat show took place. The convention could take place in the Chicago Amphitheatre once Daley had it wrapped in barbed wire and surrounded by armed guards. The delegates could stay, as planned, in the Conrad Hilton Hotel, about six miles away, by the handsomely landscaped downtown Grant Park.

For almost a year, Tom Hayden, Rennie Davis, and other New Left leaders had been planning to bring people to Chicago to protest. In March they had met in secret in a wooded campground outside Chicago near the Wisconsin border. About two hundred invited activists attended the meeting sponsored by Hayden—among them Davis, David Dellinger, and the Reverend Daniel Berrigan, Catholic chaplain at Cornell. Unfortunately, the "secret meeting" was written about in major newspapers. Davis and others had talked about "closing down the city," but Mayor Richard J. Daley dismissed such comments as boastfulness. Now they were coming to Chicago: Hayden and Davis and the SDS, Abbie Hoffman and Jerry Rubin and the Yippies. David Dellinger and the Mobe vowed to bring in hundreds of thousands of antiwar protesters. The Black Panthers were to have a contingent, too. Dellinger had been born in 1915, and the World War I armistice was one of his earliest memories. Jailed for refusing the draft in World War II, he had almost thirty years of experience demonstrating against wars and was the oldest leader in Chicago. Everyone was going to Chicago, which may have been why Mayor Daley had made such a show of brutality in the riots after King's shooting in April.

1968 was a hard year to keep up with. Originally the movements were going to Chicago to protest the coronation of incumbent president Lyndon Johnson. McCarthy and whatever delegates he had would protest inside the convention, and the demonstrators would be outside, before the television cameras, reminding America that there were a lot

Silk-screen poster protesting the attempt by federal prosecutors to
prosecute the leaders of the Chicago convention protesters
(Center for the Study of Political Graphics)

of people who were not supporting Johnson and his war. But with Johnson not running, they were coming to Chicago to support McCarthy and the antiwar plank. Then Bobby Kennedy was running, and when for a moment it looked as though he might be winning, some, including Hayden, began to wonder if they would be protesting at all in Chicago. But while Kennedy and McCarthy had been fighting it out in the primaries, Hubert Humphrey—without McCarthy and Kennedy's armies of devoted volunteers, but with a skilled professional organization—was picking up delegates at the caucuses and meetings of nonprimary states. Once Kennedy was killed, plans turned to bitterness and fatalism. Go to Chicago to stop Humphrey from stealing the convention, to make sure the Democratic platform was antiwar, or . . . go to Chicago because there was nothing else that could be done.

Even by national political convention standards, the media had high expectations for Chicago. Not only were hordes of television and print media planning to be there, but writers were coming, too. Playwright Arthur Miller was a Connecticut delegate for McCarthy. *Esquire* magazine commissioned articles from William Burroughs, Norman Mailer, and Jean Genet. Terry Southern, who had written the screenplay of the antinuclear classic *Dr. Strangelove*, was there, as was poet and pacifist Robert Lowell. And of course Allen Ginsberg was there, half as poet, half as activist, mostly trying to spread inner peace and spirituality through the repetition of long, deep tones: "Om . . ."

A mayor other than Daley might have recognized that bottled pressure explodes and made provisions for a demonstration that some said might involve as many as a million people. It was not necessarily going to be violent, but given the way the year was going, the absence of violence was unlikely. There might have been some tear gas and a few clunked heads, which he could hope to keep off television while the networks were preoccupied by what was certain to be a bitter and emotional fight within the convention.

But Daley was a short, jowly, truculent man, a "boss" from the old school of politics. Chicago was his town, and like a great many Americans with working-class roots, he hated hippies. The first and insurmountable problem: He refused a demonstration permit. The demonstrators wanted to march from Grant Park to the Amphitheatre, a logical choice as the route from the hotel where the delegates were staying to the convention. Daley could not allow this; he could not allow a demonstration from anywhere in downtown to the Amphitheatre. The reason for this was that getting from downtown to the Amphitheatre required passing through a middle-class neighborhood of trim brick houses and small yards called Bridgeport. Bridgeport was Daley's neighborhood. He had lived there all his life. Many of his neighbors were city workers who got the patronage jobs on which a local Chicago politician built his political base. Nobody was ever able to tabulate how many patronage jobs Daley had handed out. Chicago politics was all about turf. There was absolutely no circumstance, no deal, no arrangement, by which Daley was going to allow a bunch of hippies to march through *his* neighborhood.

The argument that everything that happened in Chicago during that disastrous August convention was planned and under orders from the mayor gains some credibility considering an April antiwar march with an almost identical fate. That time also, no amount of cajoling or imploring could get the marchers a permit from city hall. And that time also, the police suddenly, without warning, attacked with clubs and beat the demonstrators mercilessly.

The demonstrators were not what Daley and the police feared most. They were worried about another race riot, having already had a number of them. Relations between the black community and the city government were hostile; it was summer, the riot season, and the weather was hot and humid. Even Miami, which never had ghetto riots, had one during its convention that year. The Chicago police were ready and they were nervous.

At first, refusing the demonstration permit seemed to work. Far fewer hippies, Yippies, and activists came to Chicago than were expected—only a few thousand. Participants estimated that about half their ranks were local Chicago youth. For the Mobe, it was the worst turnout they had ever had. Gene McCarthy had advised supporters not to come. Black leaders, including Dick Gregory, who went himself, and Jesse Jackson, had advised black people to stay away. According to his testimony in the Chicago Eight conspiracy trial the following year, Jackson, who was already familiar with the Chicago police, had told Rennie Davis, "Probably Blacks shouldn't participate. . . . If Blacks got whipped nobody would pay attention. It would just be history. But if whites got whipped, it would make the newspapers."

Abbie Hoffman and the Yippies arrived with a plan, which they called A Festival of Life—in contrast with the convention in the Amphitheatre, which they called A Festival of Death. On the weeklong schedule of events listed on their Festival of Life handout flyers were included the following:

August 20–24 (AM) Training in snake dancing, karate, nonviolent self-defense
August 25 (PM) MUSIC FESTIVAL—Lincoln Park
August 26 (AM) Workshop in drug problems, underground communications, how to live free, guerrilla theatre, self-defense, draft resistance, communes, etc.
August 26 (PM) Beach party on the Lake across from Lincoln Park.
Folksinging, barbecues, swimming, lovemaking
August 27 (Dawn) Poetry, mantras, religious ceremony

August 28 (AM) Yippie Olympics, Miss Yippie Contest, Catch
the Candidate, Pin the Tail on the Candidate, Pin the Rubber
on the Pope and other normal, healthy games

Many of the items were classic Abbie Hoffman put-ons. Others were
not. An actual festival had been planned, bringing in music stars such
as Arlo Guthrie and Judy Collins. The Yippies had been working on it
for months, but the music stars could not be brought in without
permits, which the city had been declining to give for months. A meeting between Abbie Hoffman and Deputy Mayor David Stahl was
predictably disastrous. Hoffman lit a joint and Stahl asked him not to
smoke pot in his office. "I don't smoke pot," Hoffman answered,
straight-faced. "That's a myth." Stahl wrote a memo that the Yippies
were revolutionaries who had come to Chicago to start "a revolution
along the lines of the recent Berkeley and Paris incidents."

On the Yippie agenda was an August 28 afternoon Mobe march
from Grant Park to the convention. It was the only event for which
they had listed a specific time—4:00 P.M. But the entire program was in
conflict with the Chicago police because it was based on the premise
that everyone would sleep in Lincoln Park, an idea ruled out by the
city. Lincoln Park is a sprawling urban space of rolling hills and shady,
sloping lawns, where Boy Scouts and other youth organizations are
frequently allowed to hold sleep-outs. The park is a few miles long, but
it's a very quick drive from Grant Park to the Conrad Hilton or, as
Abbie Hoffman kept calling it, the Conrad Hitler. Even before the
convention began, the police posted signs in Lincoln Park: "Park
Closes at 11 P.M." When all city avenues were exhausted, the demonstrators turned to federal court to seek permission to use the park.
Judge William Lynch, Daley's former law partner who had been put on
the bench by the mayor himself, turned them down.

The events the Yippies did go ahead with were those that would
attract television. The snake dance was a martial arts technique
supposedly perfected by the Zengakuren, the Japanese student movement, for breaking through police lines. The Yippies in headbands and
beads continually practiced against their own lines and failed consistently. But it looked exotic on television, and few crews catching their
martial arts practice in the park could resist filming what was reported
as hippies practicing martial arts to prepare for combat with the
Chicago police. One crew even caught Abbie Hoffman himself participating; he identified himself as "an actor for TV."

Another event that they did intend to carry out was the nomination
of the Yippie candidate for president, Mr. Pigasus, who happened to be

a pig on a leash. "The concept of pig as our leader was truer than reality," Hoffman wrote in an essay titled "Creating a Perfect Mess." Pig was the common pejorative for police at the time, but Hoffman insisted that in the case of Chicago, the "pigs" actually looked like pigs, "with their big beer bellies, triple chins, red faces, and little squinty eyes." It was a kind of silliness that was infectious. He pointed out the resemblance of both Hubert Humphrey and Daley to pigs, and the more he explained, the more it seemed that everyone was starting to look like a pig.

But there was a problem: There were two pigs. Abbie Hoffman had gotten one and Jerry Rubin had gotten one, and a conflict arose over which one to nominate. Typical of their differences in style, Rubin had picked a very ugly pig and Hoffman a cute one. The argument between them over the pig selection almost became physically violent. Rubin accused Hoffman of trying to make the Yippies his own personality cult. Hoffman said that Rubin always wanted to show a fist, whereas "I want to show the clenched fist and the smile."

The arguing continued for some time before it was decided that the official candidate of the Youth International Party would be Rubin's very ugly pig. Hoffman, still angry from the dispute, stood in the Chicago Civic Center as Jerry Rubin said, "We are proud to announce the declaration of candidacy for president of the United States by a pig." The police then arrested Rubin, Hoffman, the pig, and singer Phil Ochs for disorderly conduct but held them only briefly. The next day another pig was loose in Lincoln Park, apparently a female, supposedly Mrs. Pigasus, the candidate's wife. As the police pursued the animal, Yippies shouted, "Pig! Pig!" for the fun of it, because it was unclear whether they were shouting at the pursuers or the pursued. When the police finally grabbed the pig, someone shouted, "Be careful how you treat the next First Lady." Some of the police laughed; others glared. They threw the little pig into the back of a paddy wagon and threateningly asked if anyone wanted to go with the pig. A few Yippies said yes and jumped into the wagon. They closed the door and drove off. Some journalists took the bait and started interviewing Yippies. The Yippies said that they were unstoppable because they had a whole farm full of pigs just outside Chicago. A journalist wanted to know how they felt about losing their pig, and one of the Yippies demanded Secret Service protection for both their candidate and his First Lady. A radio reporter asked with great earnestness just what the pig symbolized. Answers were hurled back: Food! Ham! Parks belong to pigs.

The Yippies quickly found that there was so much media and they were so hungry that any put-on at all could get coverage. Their threat to put LSD in the Chicago water system and send the entire city on a "trip" was widely reported. Other threats included painting cars to look like independent taxis that would kidnap delegates and take them to Wisconsin, dressing up as Viet Cong and walking through town handing out rice, bombarding the Amphitheatre with mortar rounds from several miles away, having ten thousand naked bodies float on Lake Michigan. The city government seemed to understand that these threats were not real but followed through on them as though they were. Unfortunately, there is no record of the police response to Abbie Hoffman's threat to pull down Hubert Humphrey's pants. Each Yippie threat, no matter how bizarre, was reported to the press by the police. The *Sun-Times* and *Daily News* talked to the New Left leaders and knew the threats were put-ons, but the *Tribune* papers, after having spent years uncovering communist plots, reported each plan with menacing headlines that only scared the police. The Yippies were gleeful about the media attention that police precautions drew. In truth, of the few thousand demonstrators who were in town, with probably fewer than two thousand from outside the Chicago area, most were not affiliated with the Yippies or anyone else, so that the Yippie presence itself was somewhat mythical. The law enforcement presence, however, was not. Twelve thousand Chicago policemen were being backed up by five thousand soldiers from the army and six thousand National Guard. The military were closer in age to the demonstrators and many were black, and the demonstrators expected them to be more sympathetic. In fact, forty-three soldiers were court-martialed for refusing to be sent to Chicago for riot duty. Generally the military had a calming effect, as opposed to the Chicago police, who from the beginning were prepared for war. Had it not been for the police response, the Chicago demonstrations would have been noted as a failure, if noticed at all.

Chicago Sun-Times columnist Mike Royko wrote, "Never before had so many feared so much from so few."

The convention had not yet begun, and already the talk and the reporting was of the clash, the violence, the showdown. This language was used to refer to the convention itself, where the Humphrey forces were meeting McCarthy and the peace delegates, but also to the thousands of demonstrators and police in downtown Chicago, kept miles away from the convention.

At 11:00 P.M. Tuesday night, August 20, Soviet tanks made their move across the Czech border. By Wednesday morning Czechoslovakia had been invaded. Television images of Soviet tanks in Czech towns were being broadcast.

In Chicago, the Soviet invasion was immediately seized as a metaphor. Abbie Hoffman gave a press conference in which he called Chicago "Czechago" and said that it was a police state. It looked like one, with police everywhere and the barbed-wire-ringed Amphitheatre awaiting the delegates. Hoffman invited the press to film the day's "Czechoslovakian demonstrations." John Connally of Texas argued that the Soviet invasion showed that the party should support the Vietnam War effort, but Senator Ralph Yarborough, also of Texas, argued to the credentials committee that political power should not be misused by them to crush "the idealism of the young" the way the Soviets were using military power. The demonstrators had started referring to Chicago as Prague West, and when they heard that Czechoslovakian protesters were walking up to Soviet tanks and asking, "Why are you here?" they began walking up to Chicago police with the same question. Incredibly, the police gave the same answer: "It's my job."

The New Left was so parochially fixated on the fight in Chicago that some even argued that the Russians had deliberately timed the invasion of Czechoslovakia to ruin the McCarthy campaign, because what the Soviets really feared was a United States that was truly progressive. Few Moscow decisions have ever been dissected more carefully and no evidence of a wish to sabotage McCarthy has ever been unearthed, but the invasion was bad for the antiwar movement in the same way it ruined de Gaulle's idea of a Europe "to the Urals." It reinforced the cold war view of hegemonic communists bent on world domination, which was in fact the justification for the Vietnam War. This did not stop David Dellinger and a handful of other antiwar activists from picketing the Polish tourism office, it being the only office in Chicago they could find that represented the Warsaw Pact. But McCarthy made it worse for himself by attempting to defuse the crisis with his classically tin ear for political orchestration. He insisted that the Soviet invasion of Czechoslovakia was no big thing, which only served to reinforce the suspicion that the senator was a strange one.

On Saturday night the demonstrators seemed particularly reluctant to leave Lincoln Park and chanted, "Revolution now!" and, "The park belongs to the people!" The police amassed their troops, and just as they seemed ready to attack, Allen Ginsberg mystically appeared and led the demonstrators out of the park, loudly humming a single note: "Om."

On Sunday the convention began and Hubert Humphrey arrived in town. Humphrey had a progressive record on social issues, but he was associated with Johnson's Vietnam policy and refused to break away from it. Even without the Vietnam issue, Humphrey, at fifty-seven, would have been a victim of the generation gap. He seemed almost cartoonish with his vibratoed, tinny voice, his corny midwestern wholesomeness, and his halfhearted good cheer; with the way he could in all seriousness use expressions like "Good grief"; and with his perpetual smile that looked as if he had just bitten something. This is how his biographer, Carl Solberg, described the politician nicknamed the Happy Warrior as he left for the Chicago convention:

> On the elevator to the street he kissed his wife, danced a little two step, and punched his friend Dr. Berman on the arm. "Off we go into battle—and I can hardly wait," he said.

This was not a candidate whom McCarthy and Robert Kennedy supporters could turn to, not a personality to calm the young demonstrators who had come to Chicago.

The Happy Warrior frowned, and not for the last time, when his plane landed in Chicago. Daley had sent a bagpipe band to meet him. There is no lonelier sound than bagpipes without a crowd. Few supporters were there to greet him, and even more upsetting, the mayor himself wasn't there. McCarthy had been met by an energized crowd. "Five thousand supporters," according to Humphrey, who was muttering about the contrast. An even bigger disappointment was that Daley was holding off on endorsing Humphrey. Daley found it hard to believe that Humphrey was a man who would attract all the voters who had gone for Robert Kennedy in California. Daley and a few other party bosses were last-minute shopping for another candidate, especially the last brother, Senator Edward Kennedy of Massachusetts. Humphrey was as terrified of taking on a Kennedy as was Nixon.

Sunday night the police started forcibly to clear Lincoln Park at 9:00. Abbie Hoffman went up to them and in a mock scolding tone of voice said, "Can't you wait two hours? Where the hell's the law and order in this town?" The police actually backed off until their posted 11:00 curfew.

Remembering the Paris students of May, the Yippies built a barricade of trash baskets and picnic tables. The police squared off with the demonstrators and ordered them and the media to leave the park. In a long line three men deep, the police looked ready to attack, so the television crews turned on their camera lights, making the flimsy barricade look more substantial by giving it deep black shadows. The newsmen had started wearing helmets. There were flags, the Viet Cong flag, the red flag of revolution, and the black flag of anarchy. The police were beginning to appear. The Yippies, though visibly afraid, held their ground. Suddenly a strange humming sound was heard, and Allen Ginsberg once again appeared leading a group in "Om."

But the om, designed to render both sides peaceful, didn't work this time. The police started pushing back the crowd, the crowd shouted, "Pigs!" and, "Oink-oink!" and the police began swinging clubs. As the police attacked they were heard shouting, "Kill, kill, kill the motherfuckers!" "Motherfucker" was everybody's word that year. The police swung at everyone in sight. After driving the crowd out of the park, they beat them in the streets. They yanked bystanders off their steps and beat them. They beat journalists and smashed cameras. They roamed a several-block area around the park, clubbing anyone they could find. After that night's battle, the police went to the Lincoln Park parking lot and slashed the tires of every car that had a McCarthy campaign sticker on it.

Playboy entrepreneur Hugh Hefner emerged from his Chicago mansion and received a smack from a club. He was so angered that he financed the publication of a book on police violence during the convention, *Law and Disorder.*

The police later claimed that they had been provoked by the obscenities being shouted at them, though Chicago police are not likely to be taken aback by obscenities. They also said that as soon as they were blinded by television lights, the demonstrators started throwing objects at them. But most nonpolice eyewitnesses do not back this up. Twenty reporters needed hospital treatment that night. When Daley was questioned about this, he said that the police were unable to distinguish reporters from demonstrators. But Daley often attacked the press verbally, and now his police force was clearly and deliberately doing it physically. Local Chicago reporters were becoming increasingly frustrated. They were being beaten and their cameras were being smashed, but these important details were being deleted from their copy just as the fact that the police had singled out McCarthy cars was deleted. In response, a group of Chicago reporters started its own monthly, the *Chicago Journalism Review,* which has gone on to become a noted critical review of the news media. Its first issue was a critique of the coverage of the Chicago convention.

The convention had to share the front page of newspapers with the invasion of Czechoslovakia, and added to this, the fights within the convention had to compete with the fights on the street. Every night for the next four nights, the duration of the convention, the police cleared Lincoln Park and went on a clubbing rampage in the neighborhood. The demonstrators began to feel that they were doing something truly dangerous, that these Chicago police were methodically brutal and no

Demonstrators in Grant Park, Chicago,
during the August 1968 Democratic convention
(Photo by Roger Malloch/Magnum Photos)

one knew how far they would go. The odd thing was that they would pass beautiful summer days together in the park. The sky had turned clear and the temperature dropped to the seventies. The police would sometimes bring lawn chairs and park their blue riot helmets on the grass. They would read the pamphlets about free love and drugs and the antiwar movement and revolution with amusement, or bemusement. Sometimes they even threw around a softball and Yippies would join in the game of catch. But when they left, the cops would ominously say, "See you at eleven o'clock, kid."

By Tuesday McCarthy was saying that he would lose, which was an odd stance to take while Kennedy votes were still in play and while his young, dedicated campaigners were still working hard in their headquarters in the Hilton. He couldn't possibly lose until Wednesday. Was McCarthy trying to make it clear that he wasn't about to win because it had been demonstrated in California what happened to peace candidates who were about to win? Guessing was always an important part of trying to follow Senator McCarthy's campaigning. On Wednesday downtown Chicago was full of demonstrators—hippies, Yippies, the Mobe, and a mule train of Poor People marchers, the foundering orphaned spring plan of the late Martin Luther King. David Dellinger was pleading with the demonstrators to stay nonviolent while pleading with the city for a permit to march to the Amphitheatre. The city did not understand why he was pursuing this already resolved issue. But the demonstrators were filling Grant Park opposite the Hilton and ready to march, and there was really no one in charge of them unless it was to lead them to the Amphitheatre. They were listening to the events on the convention floor on small transistor radios when the platform committee announced a prowar stance—meaning that the Democratic Party was not going to go into the campaign opposed to continuing the war. After everything that had happened this year, after Tet, Johnson's resignation, McCarthy's campaign, Martin Luther King's death, Bobby Kennedy's campaign and death, and four months of futile Paris peace talks—after all that, both parties were to have prowar stances.

Johnson announced that he intended to go to Chicago and address the convention now that they had adopted his stand on the war. Daley had even arranged a celebration at the Stockyards Inn next to the Amphitheatre for the president's sixtieth birthday. Back when he had assumed the convention would be his coronation, Johnson had insisted it take place the week of his birthday. Now some insiders still suspected he wanted to burst into town and use the birthday bash to announce his candidacy. Humphrey could be counted on to step aside, and Johnson would easily have the votes for a first ballot victory. But party leaders advised Johnson not to show up because the war plank was so unpopular among delegates that he might be booed on the convention floor, not to mention the streets, where Abbie Hoffman and the Yippies had already announced plans for their own Johnson birthday celebration.

Ted Kennedy refused to run, and Humphrey at last got the endorsement of Daley, which came with the votes of the Illinois delegation. Humphrey was looking happy again at a convention where no one else was. "I feel like jumping!" he said when the Pennsylvania delegation's votes clinched his first ballot victory. Humphrey, who had told *Meet the Press* the day he flew to Chicago, "I think the policies the president has pursued are basically sound," was to be the nominee. The Democratic Party was going to offer a continuation of the Johnson presidency.

Perhaps it was a bad omen that by Wednesday night, Allen Ginsberg—after omming, reciting mystical passages from Blake, and getting gassed in riots every night and then getting up to lead a Hindu sunrise service at the Lake Michigan beach—had little voice left for omming or even speaking.

In Grant Park, facing the Hilton, leaders were struggling that evening to control the demonstrators, but no one was restraining the police. The police later claimed that demonstrators were filling balloons with urine and bags with excrement to throw at the police. Some demonstrators denied this, but it was clear that after four nights of being beaten up by the police, they were tired and losing patience. Rennie Davis tried to calm one group of demonstrators, but the police, recognizing Davis, began clubbing him, hitting him so soundly on the head that he had to be hospitalized.

The police began clubbing everyone, and the demonstrators started fighting back in what turned into a pitched battle of hand-to-hand combat. City hospitals were warning demonstrators not to bring in injured demonstrators because the police were waiting outside and stuffing them into paddy wagons. Grant Park filled with tear gas and the wounded. A sit-in began in front of the Hilton and overflowed into the park. The white lights of television cameras were nearly blinding. The police said that objects were being thrown at them, but none of the numerous films of that evening's events show this. They do show the police and National Guardsmen wading into the crowd with clubs and rifle butts, beating children and elderly people and those who watched behind police lines, beating even those who had fallen, where they lay on the ground. They dragged women through the streets. A crowd was pressed so hard against the windows of a hotel restaurant—middle-aged women and children, according to *The New York Times*—that the windows caved in and the crowd escaped inside. The police pursued them through the windows into the restaurant, clubbing anyone they could find, even in the hotel lobby. "Demonstrators, reporters, McCarthy workers, doctors, all began to stagger into the Hilton lobby, blood streaming from head and face wounds," Mailer reported. The police had run amok in front of the hotel, and the television cameras that had been mounted on the entrance awning had caught all of it. Seventeen minutes of police mayhem could be bounced off a satellite called Telstar to show the world. The police smashed cameras, seemingly not realizing—or not caring—that other cameras were documenting the assault. They also went beyond the cameras' range, pursuing the crowd into the streets of downtown Chicago, clubbing whomever they could find.

It was one of those moments of 1968 television magic, something ordinary enough today but so new and startling at the time that no one who had their television sets on has ever forgotten. Rather than taking the time to edit, process, analyze, and package the film for tomorrow night's news—what people were used to television doing—the networks just ran it. Dellinger had urged the demonstrators not to fight back, saying that "the whole world could see" who was committing the violence. While the cameras recorded the police violence, they also picked up the crowd chanting—absolutely right—"The whole world is watching! The whole world is watching!"

In the Amphitheatre, the convention stopped to see what was happening. When Wisconsin was called for voting, the head of the delegation, Donald Peterson, said that young people by the thousands were being beaten in the streets and the convention should be adjourned and reconvened in another city. A priest then rose to lead the convention in prayer, and it seemed to Allen Ginsberg, who was in the convention hall, that the priest was blessing the proceedings and the system it represented. He jumped to his feet and, though no one had heard more than a raspy whisper from his tired voice that day, he blasted out an "omm" so loud that it drowned out the priest, and he continued without stopping for five minutes. According to Ginsberg, he did this to drive out hypocrisy.

Daley was now glaring out at the convention floor, looking as if he were ready to call in his police and take care of these delegates. Then Abraham Ribicoff, senator and former governor of Connecticut, went to the podium to nominate George McGovern, a last-minute alternative peace candidate. "With George McGovern as president of the United States, we wouldn't have those Gestapo tactics in the streets of Chicago."

The convention seemed to freeze for only a second, but it was the most memorable second of the convention. Television cameras sought out and found the neckless, fleshy face of boss Richard Daley, and Daley, perhaps oblivious to the cameras but it seemed almost playing to them, shouted something across the hall to Ribicoff, something not picked up by the microphones. Millions of viewers tried their lip-reading skills. It seemed to involve a pejorative for Jewish people and a sexual relationship. According to most observers who studied the film, he said, "Fuck you, you Jew son of a bitch." Many thought he also added, "You lousy motherfucker! Go home!" In 1968 even Abe Ribicoff was a motherfucker.

Daley, however, insisted that he had said none of these things. George Dunne, president of the Cook County Board, explained that they were all yelling—the Chicago people surrounding Daley. They had all been shouting, "Faker!" Ribicoff was a faker. It was not their fault if it sounded like the other F-word.

The violence continued Thursday into early Friday morning, when the police went to McCarthy headquarters on the fifteenth floor of the Hilton and dragged campaign workers out of bed to beat them. Senator McCarthy used his private plane to fly his workers safely out of Chicago.

Chicago was, along with Tet, one of the seminal events in the coming of age of television, and the star was not Hubert Humphrey. It was the seventeen-minute film in front of the Hilton. The *Chicago Sun-Times, The New York Times,* and most of the other print media wrote about the historic significance of the television coverage. This was the Yippie dream, or Abbie Hoffman's dream. Later he explained to the Walker Commission, the government-appointed task force to study the violence in Chicago, "We want to fuck up their image on TV. It's all in terms of disrupting the image, the image of a democratic society being run very peacefully and orderly and everything according to business."

Hoffman and many of the journalists who covered the event believed that tens of millions of viewers seeing the Chicago police out of control and beating up kids would change the country and radicalize youth. Perhaps it did. A minority of the country cheered and said, "That's how to treat those hippies," and according to Mike Royko, Daley's popularity in Chicago increased. In 1976, the day after Daley died, Royko wrote of the mayor's anti-Semitic cursing at Ribicoff, "Tens of millions of TV viewers were shocked. But it didn't offend most Chicagoans. That's part of the Chicago style. . . ." Daley angrily insisted that the police had done a fine job and the fault lay in the "distorted and twisted" reporting. But it was a different age now; people saw unedited film, and most were appalled by what they saw. Bizarrely, Humphrey claimed he had never seen the film. "I was busy receiving guests," he said.

There was an irony waiting in the wings. If the events in Chicago were to produce disenchantment with the political establishment and a low voter turnout among Democrats, no one stood to gain more from this than Richard M. Nixon, the Republican candidate for president.

When Humphrey started realizing this, he became angry at the television networks for airing the violence outside instead of the convention inside. "I'm going to be president someday," the candidate said, already sounding uncertain when that day might be. "I'm going to appoint the FCC. We are going to look into all this."

Where did you stand on Chicago? It became another one of those 1968 divides. You were either on the side of Daley and the police, who were severely criticized even by the Walker Report, or you were on the side of the demonstrators, the hippies, the Yippies, the antiwar movement, the McCarthy workers. Humphrey, coming out of the convention as the new Democratic candidate, said, "Rioting, burning, sniping, mugging, traffic in narcotic, and disregard for the law are the advance guard of anarchy." Whatever else that might mean, it meant that he was on the side of Daley and the police, on the side of "law and order," which was the new code phrase for what others called "white backlash." Humphrey was going after George Wallace and Richard Nixon voters. The Left, he assumed, would have no choice other than himself. Wallace had already said that the Chicago police had "probably used too much restraint."

Before leaving Chicago, Humphrey gave an interview to CBS's Roger Mudd in which he backed off of "too busy receiving guests" and said:

> Goodness me, anybody who sees this sort of thing is sick at heart and I was. But I think the blame ought to be put where it belongs. I think we ought to quit pretending that Mayor Daley did anything wrong. He didn't. . . .
>
> I know what caused these demonstrations. They were planned, premeditated by certain people in this country that feel that all they have to do is riot and they'll get their way. They don't want to work through the peaceful process. I have no time for them. The obscenity, the profanity, the filth that was uttered night after night in front of the hotels was an insult to every woman, every mother, every daughter, indeed, every human being, the kind of language that no one would tolerate at all. . . . Is it any wonder police had to take action?

It seems a surprising degree of shock about obscene language for a man who had just spent several years working with Lyndon Johnson. But Johnson did not talk that way in front of women, which was the old code. It might have shocked Humphrey to know that a psychiatrist who taught at Columbia during the spring upheavals wrote that a Barnard woman was more likely than a Columbia man to "curse a cop" during a riot. "They were aware that cursing was a weapon, one of the few they had." William Zinsser, writing about this in *Life* magazine, said, "Feminism finds its ultimate tool—the four letter word"— but then Zinsser referred in his article to "Barnard girls" and "Columbia men."

The majority of people on the other side of the generation gap from Humphrey were not likely to empathize with his horror of naughty words in front of the fairer sex. Why didn't Daley's anti-Semitism shock Humphrey, not to mention that trendy word about carnal relations with a female parent? In any event, he had probably lost most of those voters on "Goodness me." By 1968 not many people were still saying "Goodness me."

In later hearings, Abbie Hoffman agreed with Mayor Daley that it was the television cameras that had brought the protesters to Chicago. In September Hoffman boasted, "Because of our actions in Chicago, Richard Nixon will be elected President." Many were inclined to agree with that assessment. But it could still come down to the campaigns the two candidates would run. Strangely, for the first time in 1968, the war in Vietnam was not the deciding issue.

Miraculously, the clubbings in Chicago killed no one, though one man was shot while fleeing. The police claimed he was armed. At the same time, Vietnam had its worst week of the summer, with 308 Americans killed, 1,134 wounded, and an estimated 4,755 enemy soldiers killed.

CHAPTER 17

THE SORROW OF PRAGUE EAST

> I think that in the long run, our non-violent approach and the moral supremacy of the Czechoslovak people over the aggressor had, and still has moral significance. In retrospect it could be said that the peaceful approach may have contributed to the breakup of the "aggressive" bloc. . . . My conviction that moral considerations have their place in politics does not follow simply from the fact that small countries must be moral because they do not have the ability to strike back at bigger powers. Without morality it is not possible to speak of international law. To disregard moral principles in the realm of politics would be a return to the law of the jungle.
> —ALEXANDER DUBČEK, *August 1990*

ON TUESDAY, AUGUST 20, Anton Tazky, a secretary of the Slovak Communist Party Central Committee and a personal friend of Dubček's, was driving back to Bratislava from an outlying Slovak district. He saw odd, bright lights, and as he drove closer, realizing that these were the headlights of tanks and military trucks, and that these vehicles were accompanied by soldiers in foreign uniforms, he concluded that he had driven by a movie shoot. He went to bed.

August 20 was a hazy summer day. Dubček's wife, Anna, had been up much of the night before with intense pain from a gallbladder problem. On Tuesday morning Dubček took her to the hospital and explained to her that he had an afternoon presidium meeting that would run late and he might not be able to visit her until Wednesday morning. It was the last time the presidium would meet before the Fourteenth Party Congress three weeks later, and Dubček and his colleagues wanted to use the congress to solidify in law the achievements of the Prague Spring.

Over the weekend, when protesters were just beginning to settle into Lincoln Park and the Chicago police hadn't yet taken their first good swing, the fate of Prague East, as they called it in Chicago, had already been decided by Brezhnev and Kosygin in Moscow. The Soviets believed that once the Czechoslovakian presidium, already in session, saw the tanks coming, they would oust Dubček and his team. According to some scenarios, Dubček and other key figures would quickly be put on trial and executed. The official East German newspaper, *Neues Deutschland,* believing the Soviet plan would work, ran a story the night of the invasion about the uprising and the new revolutionary government that had asked for Soviet military support.

But no new government had been formed, and no one had asked for Soviet intervention. The presidium session, as predicted, went late into the evening. A working supper was served. Two of the members frustrated the others by presenting a proposed text that went back on the progress they had made. But it received little support. At 11:30, without any shift in power, the premier, Oldřich Černík, called the defense minister and returned to announce, "The armies of the five countries have crossed the Republic's borders and are occupying us."

Dubček, as though alone with his family, said softly, "It is a tragedy. I did not expect this to happen. I had no suspicion, not even the slightest hint that such a step could be taken against us." Tears began to slide down his cheeks. "I have devoted my entire life to cooperation with the Soviet Union and they have done this to me. It is my personal tragedy." In another account he was heard to say, "So they did it after all—and to *me!*" It was as though at that moment, for the first time in his life, he had let go of his father's dream of the Soviet Union as the future's great promise. The initial response of many officials, including Dubček, was to resign, but quickly Dubček and the others realized that they could make it far more difficult for the Soviets by refusing to resign and insisting that they were the sole legitimate government. After that, it took only a day for leaders in Moscow to start understanding the terrible mistake the Soviet Union had made.

Three days earlier, on August 17, Dubček had had a secret meeting with Hungary's Kádár. The Dubček generation in Prague had little regard for Ulbricht and Gomułka. Zdeněk Mlynář, one of the Party Central Committee secretaries, called them "hostile, vain, and senile old men." Bulgaria's Todor Zhivkov was closer to Dubček in age but was considered dull and possibly stupid. János Kádár, on the other

Lenin weeps in a poster taped to a window in Prague after the invasion
(Photo by Josef Koudelka/Magnum Photos)

hand, was regarded as an intelligent and like-minded communist who wanted reform to succeed in Czechoslovakia for the same reason Gomułka opposed it: He thought it might spread to his own country. But he had come to realize that he was out of step with the rest of the Hungarian leadership and that he risked bringing Hungary out of step with Moscow. Hungary, having experienced invasion twelve years earlier, was not going to become a rebel state again. Kádár probably knew the decision to invade had already been made or was about to be

when he met with Dubček to warn him and convince him to back away
from his positions. He even cautioned Dubček that the Soviets were not
the men he imagined them to be and that he did not understand with
whom he was dealing. It was probably too late, but in any event,
Dubček did not understand Kádár's subtle but desperate warning.

In the beginning of July, after the Cierna meeting had appeared to
resolve the crisis, the Soviet Union had genuinely decided against invasion and it is still not completely clear what changed its mind. In 1989
Vasil Bilak, who had been one of the pro-Soviet officials in the Czechoslovakian government, revealed in his memoirs that on August 3, two
days after the Cierna meeting, he and eighteen other pro-Soviet
Czechoslovakian officials had given a letter to Brezhnev. The nineteen
secretly renounced Dubček and asked for Soviet military assistance for
a coup d'état. They wanted a decision before August 19, because on
August 20 the presidium was going to meet for the last time before the
Slovak Party Congress on August 23, which the pro-Soviet conspirators insisted would be "counterrevolutionary."

So the Soviets after all, as they had claimed, had been asked to
invade by pro-Soviet elements who wanted to take over the government and then welcome the troops. But this faction was small, and the
conspirators did not have enough support to act on their plan. When
the troops arrived, the pro-Soviet plotters had failed to take control of
anything, including the television station they had conspired to seize.

Also contributing to the Soviet decision to invade, possibly, were
extravagant KGB reports about counterrevolutionary plots in Czechoslovakia. Soviet sources in Washington reported that contrary to what
some in Moscow believed, the CIA was not involved in events in
Prague and, in fact, had been caught completely by surprise by the
Prague Spring. But these reports were destroyed by KGB chief Yuri
Andropov, who reportedly said, "We cannot show such things to our
leadership."

At 11:00 P.M. central European time, August 20, the summer night air
was suddenly filled with sound, the earth rumbled, and the invasion
code-named Operation Danube had begun. This was not a film shoot.
That night 4,600 tanks and 165,000 soldiers of the Warsaw Pact
invaded Czechoslovakia across twenty crossing points, rolling west
from East Germany, south from Poland, west from the Soviet Union,
and north from Hungary into the undefended nation of Czechoslovakia. Five countries participated in the invasion, including token forces
from Hungary and Bulgaria. East Germany and Poland sent a division
each; the Soviets sent thirteen divisions. In seven hours 250 aircraft

delivered an entire airborne division, including small armored vehicles, fuel, and supplies. The operation was the largest airlift ever carried out by the Soviet military outside of its borders. Militarily it was magnificent, except that no army was fighting back.

Dubček and the other leaders waited in the Central Committee building. Dubček kept staring at the telephone, half expecting the call that would explain it had all been a misunderstanding. At 4:00 A.M., a black limousine led a tank column toward the Central Committee building. Faced with an angry crowd, the Soviet column opened fire with machine guns and one young man was shot to death while Dubček and the other leaders, angry but helpless, watched from their window.

Though Czechoslovakia was thought to have the best-trained and best-equipped fighting force in the Warsaw Pact, it was under orders from Dubček not to resist. Dubček and his government had quickly discussed and rejected the possibility of armed resistance. The Czechoslovakian army, like all the Warsaw Pact armies, had no independent chain of command and would function poorly without Soviet leadership. They all agreed without argument that armed resistance was impossible and would not only cost too many lives but would aid the Soviet claim that it was putting down a counterrevolution, as it did in Hungary in 1956. Better to have the world see peaceful Czechoslovakia crushed by a brutish foreign military. As far as is known, not a single border guard fired a shot or in any way tried to impede the armored columns. Nor was there an effort to stop troops and equipment arriving at Czechoslovakian airports. But by the end of the first day, twenty-three Czechoslovaks were dead.

Paratroopers surrounded the Central Committee building, and all the phones inside went dead. It was not until 9:00 in the morning that paratroopers burst into Dubček's office. They blocked the windows and doors, and when Dubček reached to pick up a phone, forgetting that they no longer functioned, one of the soldiers menaced him with an automatic weapon as he tore the phone out of the wall. Half a dozen high officials were with Dubček watching this when a very short KGB colonel festooned with decorations burst into the office, accompanied by several other KGB officers and an interpreter. After listing the members of government present, he announced that they were all being taken "under his protection." They were then all seated at a long table, and behind each of them was a soldier pointing a weapon. Then Dubček was taken away. As he passed his office manager, he whispered for him to secure his briefcase, which contained papers he hoped to keep from the Soviets. A week later, when he got back to Prague and found his briefcase empty, Dubček finally understood that his office manager had been a Soviet agent.

The Warsaw Pact soldiers had orders not to respond to provocations and to fire their weapons only if fired upon. But the invading soldiers did not always have the prerequisite discipline for the sensitive work of invading an ally. For the most part, these heavily armed troops were facing unarmed teenagers. At first, young people tried to block the oncoming tank columns by sitting in front of them—a sit-in. Like good '68 students, they threw up barricades of cars, buses, and anything else they could scrape together. But they quickly discovered that the Soviet tanks would not stop—not for them or anything else put in their path. These tanks could run over people, cars, walls. Occasionally a tank was stopped. A legless World War II veteran stopped a tank in Prague by daring it to run over him. On Wednesday morning, the same day that many hours later the Chicago police would be filmed in a violent rampage, angry young people had filled the streets of Prague, ready to resist, though not exactly sure how. Reasoning that the Radio Center, home of Radio Prague, was a critical target, many had gone there to defend it. They got there ahead of the tanks and blocked off the street with their bodies. The tanks stopped, uncertain what to do, and watched the young Czechs build a roadblock with cars and overturned buses. Radio Prague was covering the confrontation on the air. Through loudspeakers they were giving the young resisters the same instructions the invaders had received: Don't use weapons, don't be provoked.

The Czechs started speaking Russian to the tank crews, asking them why they were there, why they didn't leave. The young tank crews became flustered and, against their orders, opened fire over the heads of the crowd and then directly at the Czechs. Rather than flee, the Czechs produced Molotov cocktails and threw them at the tanks while the people around them were falling dead or wounded. Some of the tanks caught fire, producing black smoke, and a few of the tank crews were wounded. Some may even have been killed. But a huge T-55 tank moved into firing position, and Radio Prague broadcast the message, "Sad brothers, when you hear the national anthem you will know that it is over." Then the first bars of the national anthem were heard as the tank opened fire and Radio Prague went silent.

In Bratislava young girls in miniskirts hiked them up, and while the Russian farm boys on the Soviet tank crews stopped to admire their young thighs, boys ran up and smashed their headlights with rocks and even managed to set some oil drums on fire. A tank column from

August 21, 1968, outside the radio station in Prague
(Photo by Josef Koudelka/Magnum Photos)

Hungary noisily rumbled and creaked across the Danube bridge in Bratislava while university students threw bricks and shouted obscenities at them. A Soviet soldier dropped to firing position on the back of a tank and shot into the crowd, killing a fifteen-year-old nursing student. This further enraged the students, but the Soviets responded with more gunfire, killing another four students while their shower of stones and bricks clanked dully off the Soviet armor. Throughout the country, students threw Molotov cocktails. If they didn't know how to make them, they threw burning rags. Sometimes a tank would catch fire. Young men wrapped themselves in Czech flags and charged at the tanks armed only with cans to stuff in gun barrels.

Soon the tanks controlled the country, but defiant graffiti such as "Ivan Go Home!" still appeared on the walls. Direction signs throughout the country were twisted north and replaced with "Moscow— 2,000 km." The walls were covered with posters denouncing the invasion and graffiti with messages such as "Socialism, Yes; Occupation, No," "The Russian National State Circus has arrived, complete with performing gorillas," "This is not Vietnam!," "Lenin awake!

Brezhnev has gone mad!"—or simply huge letters spelling out Dubček's and Svoboda's names or the initials USSR with the two Ss in lightning bolts like the Nazi SS insignia.

The angry people of Czechoslovakia would walk up to the invaders on their tanks and try to persuade them that they were wrong and should leave, a dialogue as futile as the one demonstrators in Chicago were attempting by shouting at young National Guardsmen, "Join us!" The Czechs, at last using the book-primer Russian they had been required to learn in school, would ask the men on the tanks why they were in this country where they didn't belong. The men of the Soviet tank crews, typically uneducated eighteen-year-old peasants, would look at them hopelessly and explain that they had received orders to come. Tanks surrounded by such citizen interrogators were a common sight. Nor were foreigners an unusual sight in Prague, which until that summer night had been "the place to be." Within days they all left without incident, including five thousand American tourists.

Before Czechoslovakian Television was put off the air, it managed to smuggle film of the invasion out of the country. One particularly striking scene showed youths sitting, refusing to move, in front of a Soviet tank whose gun turret seemed to be swiveling furiously. A BBC executive had arranged for the European Broadcast Union, a network of Western European stations, to have its Vienna station, just across the Danube from Bratislava, record everything it could pick up from across the river. Ironically, Czechoslovakia was set up for this because it was the communist bloc's broadcast center for sending transmissions to the West. In the past it had been used primarily for transmitting sports events. The Czechoslovakians managed to get out about forty-five minutes of film showing resistance, along with a plea to UN secretary-general U Thant. In just a few minutes of pictures, the film completely refuted all Soviet claims about being welcomed in Czechoslovakia. Parts of the film were broadcast on the evening news in the United States, in Western Europe, and around the world.

This in turn led to an American experiment. The evening television news now had half an hour to air several minutes of commercials plus coverage of the Chicago convention in the hall and on the street, the invasion of Czechoslovakia, the UN debate on the invasion, the worst week in Vietnam, and a few other stories. Ever since the autumn of 1963, when the networks successfully expanded from fifteen minutes to a half-hour news program, which gave them more space for civil rights footage, Walter Cronkite had been pushing CBS to go to one hour. The argument against it was the same one that had been used against the half-hour format: The affiliates would not want to buy it.

After the Czech invasion story broke on August 21 in mid-convention/riot, *New York Times* television critic Jack Gould wrote congratulating public television on its flexibility, which allowed it to expand its news time for the day's extraordinary glut of breaking stories. He contrasted this with the networks, locked in their half-hour format and unable to air sufficient coverage. Finally Walter Cronkite got his wish, and on the evening of August 22 CBS expanded his show to an hour. Gould hailed the "experiment" and particularly complimented the time given to film footage smuggled out of Czechoslovakia. But the television industry argued that most people were unwilling to sit through an entire hour of news and, more important, the affiliates— using the same argument that had blocked the expansion to a half hour for a number of years—did not want to lose a half hour of valuable programming in which their own highly profitable local ads aired. The experiment was over. Cronkite had won the battle, but he lost the war. In September, however, CBS launched a one-hour news "magazine" program twice monthly—*60 Minutes*.

A popular Czech singer, Karel Cernoch, recorded a new song: "I Hope This Is Just a Bad Dream."

But for Moscow, too, this was a bad dream. Images had been instantly relayed around the world to every television station, the front page of every newspaper, and the cover of every magazine, and instead of being pictures of the new pro-Soviet government greeting the liberating forces, as had been planned, they were of unarmed young Czechoslovakians waving bloody Czech flags, defiantly running in front of huge Soviet tanks, throwing stones and lighted gas-soaked rags, sometimes just engaging in debate—longhaired, bearded Prague students and thickset, blond, frightened Russian country boys.

When in the past some had argued in Moscow against invasion, this must have been what their worst fears looked like. Their official story, that they had come to the aid of Czechoslovakia, was demonstrably untrue. Dubček had put out a radio broadcast saying that the country had been invaded without the knowledge of the president, the chairman of the National Assembly, or himself. The Soviets quickly learned that the Czechoslovakian people trusted their government and believed what their leaders said, especially Dubček, Černík, and Smrkovsky. It was useless for the Soviets to contradict them. A brief moment of intrigue ensued when a Soviet agent in the government tried to sideline the broadcast, but he was caught. That Soviet plan A had failed and the presidium had not overthrown Dubček surprised no one, but that pro-Soviet elements were not able to take control even after the troops arrived was more of a surprise. That an unarmed population was not complying with the heavily armed might of five nations was infuriating. That it was being recorded and had already been broadcast and printed around the world was an unimagined calamity.

The Soviets had one card left to play: Ludvik Svoboda, the septuagenarian military officer who had, to the disappointment of the youth, been placed in the presidency. Party secretary Zdeněk Mlynář said of Svoboda, "Not only was he not a part of the political reform, he was not a politician at all. He was a soldier. Already an officer in the army of the first Czechoslovakian Republic between the two world wars, by a quirk of fate, he became commander in chief of the Czechoslovakian forces that fought in World War II in the USSR alongside the Soviet army. It was clear that from this moment during the war, he embraced the notion that Czechoslovakia should unconditionally support the Soviet Union."

But when a pro-Soviet group visited the president in Hradčany Castle, where he was being held under armed Soviet guard, and asked him to sign a document endorsing the Soviet presence, the seventy-two-year-old soldier shouted, "Get out!"

Nothing seemed to be going according to Soviet plans. Normally an invading army or even coup plotters would have seized radio and television stations as a first order of business. But this had not been part of the Soviet plan because they had expected to be in control of the country by the time they arrived in Prague. When they finally did shut down Radio Prague, underground radio stations in secret locations began broadcasting news of the Soviet repression and the Czechoslovakian resistance. These stations also undercut Soviet propaganda. When the Soviets announced that Slovakia had defected, underground radio stations were broadcasting that it was a lie. They also reported on Soviet movements, whom the Soviets were trying to arrest, whom they had arrested. And as long as the Czechoslovakians were broadcasting, there was a sense that the Soviets did not completely control the country. The underground radio's slogan was, "We are with you. Be with us." Jan Zaruba, an official in the Czechoslovakian Ministry of the Interior, killed himself rather than reveal the location of the radio transmitters. Soviet efforts to counter underground radio were disastrous. They started their own radio station but could not find an announcer who spoke fluent Czech and Slovak. They tried dropping leaflets, but the leaflets scattered over the Czech lands turned out to be the ones written in Slovak.

The static-covered voice of playwright Václav Havel seemingly miraculously was heard on the radio saying, "I happened to be one of the few Czech citizens who can still use a free transmitter in this country. Therefore I presume to address you in the name of the Czech and Slovak writers in an urgent plea for support." He asked Western writers to speak up condemning the Soviet invasion.

Yugoslavia's Tito and Romania's Ceauşescu openly denounced the invasion, and the streets of Belgrade and Bucharest filled with protesters. Ceauşescu called the invasion "a great mistake." Poland's Gomułka, on the other hand, declared Czechoslovakia a counterrevolutionary state, outside the Warsaw bloc, that was plotting to overthrow Poland. And of course it was only a matter of days before the Poles and East Germans discovered that the "Zionists" were behind the counterrevolutionary plotting in Czechoslovakia.

The Italian and French Communist Parties denounced the Soviet action, as did the Japanese Communist Party. In Tokyo, where the university was immobilized in its third month of occupation, students for the first time ever marched on the Soviet embassy. Fidel Castro approved of the invasion, saying it was painful but necessary. The Cubans, North Vietnamese, and North Koreans were the only Communist Parties not in Eastern Europe to support the invasion. Of the eighty-eight Communist Parties in the world, only ten approved of the invasion. Marxist philosopher Herbert Marcuse called the invasion "the most tragic event of the post-war era."

A few young people in East Germany passed out leaflets of protest. And many hundreds of East German workers refused to sign a petition supporting the invasion. The few Polish dissidents who were not in prison wrote letters protesting the invasion. Jerzy Andrzejewski, a leading Polish novelist, wrote a letter to the Czechoslovakian Writers Union denouncing the Polish part in the invasion and asserting that "Polish colleagues are with you, although deprived of free speech in our country." He added, "I realize that my voice of political and moral protest does not and cannot counterbalance the discredit with which Poland has been covered in the opinion of progressives of the entire world." Worse still, there were reports of gunfire exchanged in Czechoslovakia between Russian and Bulgarian units, and between Hungarian and Russian units.

Even in Russia seven protesters sat in Red Square with a banner that said "Hands Off the CSSR"—the Czechoslovak Socialist Republic. The group included Pavel Litvinov, grandson of a deceased Soviet foreign minister, the wife of Yuli Daniel, an imprisoned poet, and Natalya Gorbanevskaya, a well-known poet. They were arrested briefly, and according to a letter Gorbanevskaya wrote to foreign correspondents, some were beaten, but "my comrades and I were happy that we were able, even briefly, to break the sludge of unbridled lies and cowardly silence and thereby demonstrate that not all the citizens of our country are in agreement with the violence carried out in the name of the Soviet people." The day after the invasion, poet Yevgeny Yevtushenko sent a telegram to Premier Kosygin and Party chief Brezhnev and distributed it to the Western press:

> I don't know how to sleep. I don't know how to continue living. All I know is that I have a moral duty to express to you the feelings that overpower me.
>
> I am deeply convinced that our action in Czechoslovakia is a tragic mistake and a bitter blow to Soviet-Czechoslovak friendship and the world Communist movement.
>
> It lowers our prestige in the world and in our own eyes.
>
> It is a setback for all progressive forces, for peace in the world and for humanity's dreams of future brotherhood.
>
> Also it is a personal tragedy for me because I have many personal friends in Czechoslovakia and I don't know how I will be able to look into their eyes if I should ever meet them again.
>
> And it seems to me that it is a great gift for all reactionary forces in the world and we cannot foresee the consequences of this action.
>
> I love my country and my people and I am a modest inheritor of the traditions of Russian literature of such writers as Pushkin, Tolstoy, Dostoyevsky, and Solzhenitsyn. These traditions have taught me that silence is sometimes a disgrace.
>
> Please place on record my opinion about this action as the opinion of an honest son of his country and the poet who once wrote the song "Do the Russians Want War?"

De Gaulle and Britain's Harold Wilson were among the first of many world leaders to condemn the invasion—one of the first times all year when the two were in complete agreement. De Gaulle went on to liken the Soviet invasion to the U.S. invasion of the Dominican Republic in April 1965. The General was trying once again to assert his policy between the two superpowers. It was an idea that would be widely rejected as a direct result of the Soviet invasion, which made many Europeans feel that Moscow was a far more imminent danger than Washington. But on August 24 de Gaulle had a good day—he announced that France had exploded a hydrogen bomb in the Pacific. De Gaulle called the blast "a magnificent scientific, technical, and industrial success, which has been achieved for the independence and security of France, by an elite of her children."

Senators Eugene McCarthy and George McGovern both, like de Gaulle politically damaged by the Soviet invasion, also compared it to the U.S. invasion of the Dominican Republic and Vietnam. The invasion was also proving awkward for Richard Nixon, who only a few weeks before had softened his career-long anticommunist posture to say that the Soviets were not the menace they had once been and now was the time to be open and negotiate. The problem for many Western politicians was that the invasion had come at a time when it was thought that the Soviet Union didn't do things like that anymore.

Oddly, one of the mildest condemnations came from Washington. The Soviet ambassador to the United States, Anatoly F. Dobrynin, met with President Johnson shortly after the invasion had begun. Johnson called an emergency meeting of the National Security Council, for which Eugene McCarthy, trying to play down the invasion, criticized him. In Chicago, it seemed what little chance was left for a peace plank in the party platform had vanished with the invasion. The cold war was back. But Johnson clearly was not willing to take any measures other than a strong denunciation in the UN. He said that the progress that was being made in U.S.-Soviet negotiations was too important to be abandoned. In fact, while the tanks were still crossing the borders, Secretary of State Dean Rusk was giving a speech to the Democratic Party platform committee on the progress being made in negotiations with the Soviets.

The UN did condemn the Soviet action, but the Soviets simply used their veto to override the condemnation.

Moscow was focused on Czech president Svoboda, who they had never imagined would be much of a problem. If Svoboda did not agree to the Soviets changing the regime, there was no possibility of a claim of legitimacy for the Soviet invasion. But Svoboda, who had always shown his first loyalty to the Soviet Union, still refused to sign anything. The Soviets threatened him and he countered by threatening suicide, which would have been a disaster for the Soviets. The stick having failed, the carrot came, in the form of promises of unprecedented Soviet aid to Czechoslovakia. The septuagenarian was unmoved by this and by offers of a high position for himself and a hand in choosing other high-level Czech leaders. Nothing the Soviets tried worked with Svoboda. To the aging general, the only acceptable course for Moscow was to release Dubček, Černík, Smrkovsky, and the other constitutionally installed Czechoslovakian leaders from imprisonment in KGB barracks in the Ukraine and bring them to Moscow for a negotiated settlement. Once the Soviets had worked out an agreement with

*Student silk-screen poster in Czechoslovakia after the invasion,
contrasting the reception of Soviet troops in 1945 with 1968*

these leaders, in Svoboda's view, whatever the terms of that agreement
were, it could be considered a legitimate resolution. He believed that
once he had everyone sitting around the same table, he could resolve
the problem. "And when the Soviet soldiers finally do leave here," he
stated calmly, "you'll see, the people will throw flowers at them again
just as they did in 1945."

Svoboda was not a supporter of Prague Spring and in fact following
the invasion gave his backing to years of repression. But at that critical
moment he stopped the Soviets from completely plowing his country
under their tanks. He denied their invasion legitimacy. But he was also
concerned about the strong feelings of the Czechoslovakian people and
thought their devotion dangerous. An unknown woman had somehow
gotten through to his telephone and suggested that the general shoot
himself in protest. He explained to her that this was not a useful
approach, that it was up to him to resolve the crisis. The woman
insisted, "Ah, Mr. President, but how beautiful it would be if you were
to shoot yourself."

When the imprisoned leaders arrived in Moscow, their appearance
made clear that they had been through an ordeal. They were pale and
sick-looking, their nerves on edge. Dubček seemed to be completely
exhausted and had a wound on his forehead said to have been caused
by slipping in a bathroom. Throughout the Moscow negotiations,
Dubček, sometimes stammering, was on medication for his unsettled
nerves.

In Havel's play *The Memorandum*, written more than a year before
the invasion, there is a scene in which the men who drove Kraus from
his position as director with a scheme to impose an artificial language
realize that the entire scheme, language included, is an unmitigated

disaster. They dust off Kraus, ask him to come back, and for the first time start calling him Jo, as though they are old friends. That is exactly what Brezhnev did to Dubček.

Brezhnev referred to Dubček as "our Sacha" and spoke to him in the Russian familiar *-ty* form, which struck Dubček as peculiar since they had never been familiar before. Dubček continued to address Brezhnev in the more formal *-vy* form.

For four days the Czechoslovak leadership met with the Soviets, sometimes with Brezhnev, sometimes with ranking Politburo members, sometimes with the entire Politburo, at a long table, with Czechs and Slovaks on one side and Soviets on the other. There was no discussion of table shape here. They fought across the table and with their own sides. Svoboda was eager to get an accord, believing that the longer they went without one, the more irrevocable would be the damage in relations. He also feared that the tension would be too great for the Soviet troops and discipline might break down. By September 2, 72 Czechoslovakians had been killed and 702 wounded. Increasingly, the deaths and injuries were caused by drunken Soviet troops, sometimes on shooting sprees and sometimes just in vehicle accidents. Loggers were afraid to go to work because of camps of drunken troops in the woods. While the meeting was going on in Moscow, on Jan Opletal Street in Prague, a street named for a student executed by the Nazis, a young apprentice named Miroslav Baranek was shot at close range by a drunken Soviet soldier.

Svoboda angrily pushed his government to quickly come to almost any settlement. He exploded at Dubček, "You don't do anything but babble and more babble. Isn't it enough that you have provoked the occupation of your country with your babble? Learn from the lessons of the past and act on them!"

But Dubček was not in the same hurry. He seemed more uncertain and more careful, and as always, it was difficult to understand his position. According to Mlynář, most of them besides Dubček felt that they did not have much time or leeway "because the Soviet Politburo was acting like a bunch of gangsters." As an exasperated Kádár had warned Dubček in that last meeting before the invasion, "Do you really not know the kind of people with whom you are dealing?"

Even while the Soviets were pushing from their side of the table, there was a wide range of viewpoints from the Czechoslovakian side, reflecting the nature of the Dubček regime. Svoboda was a dominant voice, rarely silenced, always urging resolution. František Kriegel, the sixty-year-old doctor elected by the Central Committee to the presidium as one of three liberals in a compromise government, was more volatile. He was a Jew from the Galicia region of southern Poland. Kriegel had been arrested and imprisoned with Dubček, and when he arrived in Moscow with Dubček an angry Brezhnev said, "What is this Jew from Galicia doing here?" The Soviets banned him from the negotiating table, and the Czechoslovakians got him back only by refusing to negotiate without him. Kriegel had always been one of the radicals of the regime, pushing for relations with China as an alternative to the Soviet Union. Now the Soviets tried to keep Kriegel, a diabetic, reined in at negotiations by cutting back on his insulin supply. One of the few times Svoboda was silenced was when Kriegel turned to him and said, "What can they make me do? I have two choices, either they are going to send me to Siberia or they will shoot me." Kriegel was the only member of the delegation who never signed the accord, saying in the end, "No! Kill me if you want."

The Soviets made numerous anti-Semitic references to not only Kriegel but Deputy Prime Minister Ota Šik and Prague first secretary Bohumil Šimon. Actually Šimon was not Jewish, but his name sounded Jewish to Slavic ears.

When the meeting was opened by Brezhnev, Dubček seemed so depressed, so heavily sedated, that Černík had to make the opening remarks for the Czechoslovakian side. He spoke very directly and frankly, not emphasizing the standard line about friendship with the Soviet Union, but instead defending the Prague Spring and the actions of the Czechoslovakian Communist Party and insisting that a military intervention by the Soviets was not a good thing for socialism. He was interrupted and contradicted several times by Brezhnev. When he had finished, Dubček asked for the floor. This was contrary to the rules of procedure, but he insisted, at first awkwardly, then after a few minutes in fluent Russian. Mlynář described his speech as "a moving and enthusiastic defense" of the Czechoslovakian reforms and a denunciation of the intervention. It was an improvised speech and Brezhnev gave an improvised response, insisting that the Prague Spring was damaging to Moscow and explaining his views on sovereignty and the Soviet bloc. Turning to Dubček, he said, "I tried to help you against Novotný in the beginning." He seemed personally hurt that Dubček never took him into his confidence. "I believed in you and I defended you against others," he told Dubček. "I said our Sacha is nevertheless a good comrade, but you let us down."

Brezhnev made it clear that Dubček's greatest sin was in not consulting Moscow—his failure to send his speeches to Moscow for approval, his failure to consult on personnel changes. "Here, even I myself give my speeches to all the members of the Politburo in advance for their

comments. Isn't that right, comrades?" He turned to the entire Politburo sitting in a row behind him, and they all eagerly and dutifully
nodded agreement. But there were other sins: "Underlying antisocialist
tendencies, letting the press write whatever they wanted, a constant
pressure from counterrevolutionary organizations . . ." And, eventually, as always happened when conferring with Soviet officialdom at
any level, Brezhnev brought up the Soviet Union's "sacrifices of World
War II." Neither side ever forgot the 145,000 Soviet lives lost in the
liberation of Czechoslovakia.

Dubček never hesitated to point out his disagreements with Brezhnev. Finally, Brezhnev's face reddened and he shouted that it was
useless to negotiate with such people. He walked slowly out of the
room, obediently followed at a ceremoniously slow pace by the entire
Politburo.

It was a threat. When Dubček was first taken away, he was told that
he would face a tribunal. While the Soviets thought they had a quisling
Czechoslovakian government to replace him and his colleagues, the
possibility of executions was real. But when Svoboda held out and
events turned more and more unfavorable for the Soviets, the imprisoned leaders were treated with increasing politeness. Both sides needed
an agreement. Without it the Soviets would have no legitimacy, but the
Prague Spring reformers would have no possibility of influencing the
future of their country, and their lives might be in danger. By storming
out, Brezhnev reminded them of the fate of their country as well as
themselves if no agreement occurred.

Eventually the two sides hammered out a document that both sides
could sign. The document represented almost nothing of the Prague
point of view. It recognized neither the legality nor the value of
anything the Dubček government had accomplished. But in truth the
Czechoslovakians were holding a very weak hand. The Soviets could
be ruthless enough to rule even without legitimacy if they had to. When
the document was almost ready to be signed, Dubček appeared to sink
so deeply into despondency, his body shaking, that it was feared he
would not be able to participate in the final ceremony. More shots were
ordered for him. The nature of these sedatives is not clear from the
accounts, but he suddenly horrified all the negotiators by refusing to
have any more shots "or else I won't sign. They can do what they will,
I won't sign." During a long night of negotiation he finally did get a
shot.

At last the "Moscow Protocol," forced down the throats of captive
leaders while their country was occupied by tanks, was ready for the
official signing. Suddenly massive double doors were swung open, and

on cue every member of the Soviet Politburo rose to their feet, placed smiles on their faces, stuck out their arms, and crossed the room to embrace their exhausted and defeated Czechoslovakian prisoners.

The delegation went to the airport to return to Prague and suddenly realized that they had left Kriegel behind. Some argued that they would be better off without having him in the returning delegation, but others, including Svoboda and Dubček, insisted that the Soviet authorities turn him over. After a final two hours of negotiation, the Soviets brought him to the airport.

The delegation returned to Prague with a document offering almost nothing. The Soviets agreed to give the Czechoslovakian Party "understanding and support with the goal of perfecting the methods of directing society." The troops would be withdrawn from their territory on a schedule that depended on progress toward "normalization." The Czechoslovakian people were fluent in Soviet doublespeak. Normalization was a new word, but they knew what it meant—a return to the old dictatorship. The demands of the Soviets had been solidly declared in the Moscow Protocol, whereas those of the Czechoslovakians, such as withdrawal of troops, were for the future and depended on Moscow's whim. By now, a week after the invasion, half a million foreign troops and six thousand tanks occupied the country.

On August 27, Dubček, looking as though he could barely stand, gave a speech asking the people to once more show confidence in him and asserting that these were "temporary measures." He could barely pronounce a fluid sentence. But he and some of the other leaders believed that they would find opportunities for reform. At first the government, with Dubček back in power, showed independence. The National Assembly even passed a resolution declaring Soviet occupation illegal and a violation of the United Nations charter. The leaders were able to fire the pro-Soviet officials within their ranks.

In September measures were forced on the country to curb its free press, though by Soviet bloc standards it remained surprisingly rebellious and independent. Dubček pursued a schizophrenic rule, caving in to the Soviets at one moment, standing by his principles the next. In October, meeting with the leaders of the five invading countries, Brezhnev declared Operation Danube a great success, but everything that followed, he said, was disastrous. Gomułka was even more harsh, insisting that Czechoslovakia was still a hotbed of dangerous counterrevolutionaries. Having so efficiently taken care of counterrevolutionaries in his own country, he had little patience for Czechoslovakia, where students were still fighting with police.

Thousands fled the country, and many who were outside decided not to return. Černík encouraged immigration. Soon the borders would be closed, and he explained that he could not guarantee even his own safety, let alone anyone else's. A month after the invasion, fifty thousand Czechoslovaks were out of the country out of a population of about fourteen million. About ten thousand of them had already applied for refugee status in other countries. A number of Czechoslovakians were caught out of the country on their first summer vacation abroad. Many had to wait more than twenty years before they could enter or leave again.

Meanwhile the Czechoslovakian Writers Union, one of the institutions that pushed Dubček hard for reform when he first came to power in January, was urging its members not to go into exile and if they were outside of the country to come back before the borders closed. Pavel Kohout, playwright and novelist, had been shuttling back and forth between Prague and Frankfurt, where his new novel was being published, seeking out Czech writers and persuading them to return to rebuild the writers union as a dissident center. Kohout contacted several members at the Frankfurt Book Fair that was attacked by Daniel Cohn-Bendit. The book fair in 1968 had an unusually high number of Czech writers for the same reason the Lincoln Center Film Festival was suddenly packed with Czechoslovakian directors. Supporting Czech art became an act of political defiance, and many of the artists were still—no one was sure for how much longer—available for travel.

Youth were joining the Communist Party at an unprecedented rate with the intention of taking it over and directing it. In the month following the invasion, 7,199 people joined, and according to official figures, 63.8 percent, two out of three, were less than thirty years old. This seemed certain to have an impact on a Party that had been largely middle-aged and elderly.

The Soviet troops were tucked quietly out of sight, but they were there. When Czech youth staged a demonstration in late September, the Soviets had only to threaten the Czech police that if they did not break up the march, the Soviet troops would be brought out. The police stopped the march.

Youth were also forming Dubček clubs around the country, most of which attracted hundreds of members who collected and discussed his speeches.

In the fall of 1968 Dubček sent a letter to the Czechoslovakian Olympic team in Mexico City. He said that if the team was not as successful as they hoped, "don't hang your heads: What will not succeed today, may succeed tomorrow."

CHAPTER 18

THE GHASTLY STRAIN
OF A SMILE

One is not born, but rather becomes a woman. No biological, psychological or economic fate determines the figure that the human female presents in society; it is civilization as a whole that produces this creature.

—SIMONE DE BEAUVOIR, The Second Sex, *1949*

I think this has been the unknown heart of a woman's problem in America for a long time, this lack of a private image. Public images that defy reason and have very little to do with women themselves have the power to shape too much of their lives. These images would not have such power, if women were not suffering a crisis of identity.

—BETTY FRIEDAN, The Feminine Mystique, *1963*

Take a memo, Mr. Smith: Like every other oppressed people rising up today, we're out for our freedom—by any means necessary.

—ROBIN MORGAN, *"Take a Memo, Mr. Smith,"*
Win *magazine, November 1968*

IT WOULD HAVE MADE little sense for the Miss America pageant to have gone off without a problem. This was, after all, 1968. Television viewers, after watching the Chicago riots, could take time out from the Soviet subjugation of Czechoslovakia, in between reports of burning villages in the Mekong, to see Bert Parks, the make-believe celebrity, explode onto the stage in white tie and tails like a flat-footed Fred Astaire, to shoo on the young, white, preferably blond, handpicked last virgins of America's college campuses, competing for the crown of what was purportedly the ideal of American womanhood.

To measure up, they would need to display such skills as answering questions without controversy and looking shapely, though not *too* shapely, in a swimsuit, all the while gleaming with a smile so wide it had gone rectangular—a carnivorous smile not unlike that of Hubert Humphrey. The pageant might have been challenged on race alone. Is the American feminine ideal always white? Would being black or brown or red or yellow be in itself less than ideal?

But that was not the thrust of the attack. In the best tradition of Yippie theater, on September 7 a group of one hundred women, possibly more, met on the boardwalk outside the pageant and crowned a sheep. When the press rushed to them—normally there are not many breaking stories at a Miss America pageant—the protesters insisted on speaking to women reporters only, who in 1968 were not commonplace.

Having gotten the media's attention, the group, declaring itself the New York Radical Women, started throwing items into a trash bin labeled the "freedom trash can"—language, not by chance, from the civil rights movement. Into the freedom trash can went girdles, bras, false eyelashes, hair curlers, and other "beauty products." About twenty of the Radical Women managed to stop the competition inside the convention hall for twenty minutes by gurgling the high-pitched Arab women's cheer, which they had learned from the film *The Battle of Algiers,* and shouting, "Freedom for women!" while hoisting a banner that read "Women's Liberation."

For years after this watershed incident, radical feminists were labeled "bra burners," although nowhere did they actually burn bras. The original bra burners said they were protesting "the degrading, mindless boob-girlie symbol" of Miss America.

The New York Radical Women who debuted with this action were largely experienced in the New Left or the civil rights movement, and most had worked on the organization of numerous demonstrations. But this was the first time any of them had been pivotal organizers in a protest. Robin Morgan, their leader, said, "We also all felt, well, grown up; we were doing this one for ourselves, not for our men. . . ."

There had been other women's marches in 1968. In January five thousand women had marched on Washington to protest the war. The demonstration had been organized by the Jeanette Rankin Brigade, named after the first congresswoman, who at the age of eighty-seven was still a fiery activist. Despite turning out five thousand marchers dressed in mourner's black, which should have been effective for television, the demonstration received very little press coverage. The *New*

York Times managing editor Clifton Daniel explained in a television interview that the reason for the lack of coverage was that violence seemed unlikely. Those who worked in the civil rights movement had learned years earlier that the presence of women reduces the risk of violence and that a reduced risk of violence diminishes media coverage.

Morgan regarded the greatest success of the event at the Miss America pageant to have been their decision to speak only to women reporters. The idea, like so many protest ideas, came from SNCC. The Radical Women were more successful at sticking to this, perhaps because their movement was a new beat that newspapers had not been covering. Within a few years this became standard feminist practice, and news media automatically sent women reporters to feminist events. At a time when feminism was becoming a growing story, and women journalists were struggling to get beyond the fashion, culture, and food pages, this had an important effect on newsrooms.

But Morgan had her regrets. The demonstrators appeared to be attacking the contestants instead of the contest, and in retrospect she thought it was a mistake to have protesters saying, "Miss America goes down!" and singing the altered lyrics, "Ain't she sweet / Making profit off her meat. . . ." The contestants were supposed to be viewed as victims.

September 7, 1968, is often given as the date that modern feminism was launched. Feminists had been campaigning for numerous years, but like the New Left in the early 1960s when Tom Hayden first began writing about it, only a few had noticed until it got onto television. For millions of Americans, "women's liberation" began in Atlantic City on September 7 with a sheep and a trash bin. Not far away, another group of protesters was holding a black Miss America contest to protest the racist nature of Miss America. But by then, black movements were old news.

It was not that Miss America was a revered institution. By the late sixties it had lost its luster and was widely thought to be racist or empty-headed and as faded as Atlantic City itself. Shana Alexander wrote in *Life*:

> Talent being rarer than beauty in 18-year-old girls, the talent contest places the Smile under a ghastly strain. One girl, a trampolinist, smiled madly upside down. A ballerina smiled her way through "the dying swan," somehow suggesting death in a frozen poultry locker. A third girl's talent was to synchronize bubble gum chewing and the Charleston. At rhythmic intervals her smile was wiped out by a large, wet pink splat.

So many things seem wrong and boring and silly about the Miss America Pageant as it comes across on TV that one struggles to rank the offenses in order of importance. It is dull and pretentious and racist and exploitive and icky and sad. . . .

Morgan, who led New York Radical Women, was a child actress turned political activist. For her and everyone in her group, Atlantic City was their first act of radical feminism. Their thinking had clear roots in the New Left. Morgan said of the choice of targets, "Where else could one find such a perfect combination of American values—racism, materialism, capitalism—all packaged in one ideal symbol, a woman." As for Miss America of 1968, which of course had to be the winning Miss Illinois, Morgan said she had a "smile still blood-flecked from Mayor Daley's kiss." To top it off, the contestant winner went on a tour of the troops in Vietnam.

But not all the passersby were sympathetic. Men heckled and denounced the demonstrators and suggested that they should throw themselves in the freedom trash can and strangely yelled, "Go home and wash your bras!"—once again buying into the idea that nonconformists are dirty. One outraged former Miss America contestant from Wisconsin quickly appeared with her own freshly painted sign that read, "There's only one thing wrong with Miss America—She's beautiful." The former contestant, Terry Meewsen, surprised no one by wearing a "Nixon for President" button.

Before September 7 the common image of feminism was that it was a movement of long-skirted women in bonnets who fought from 1848 until 1920 to get women the right to vote. In 1920, with the passage of the Nineteenth Amendment, feminism, according to popular belief, had served its purpose, achieved its goal, and ceased to exist. In a 1956 special issue of *Life* magazine on women, Cornelia Otis Skinner said of feminism, "We have won our case, but for heaven's sake let's stop trying to prove it over and over again." This idea was so entrenched that in 1968, when the press and the public realized that there was a growing contemporary feminist movement, they often referred to it as "the second wave."

One of the first surprises of the second wave was when *The Feminine Mystique*, a book by Betty Friedan, a suburban mother of three and graduate fellow in psychology, became one of the most read books of the early 1960s. Friedan was a graduate of Smith College class of 1942, and at the beginning of the sixties the college had asked her to conduct a survey of her classmates. Two hundred women answered her questionnaire. Eighty-nine percent had become housewives, and most of the housewives said that their one regret in life was that they hadn't used their education in a meaningful way. Friedan rejected the usual concept that educated women were unhappy because education made them "restless." Instead she believed that they had been trapped by a series of beliefs that she called "the feminine mystique"—that women and men were very different, that it was masculine to want a career and feminine to find happiness in being dominated by a husband and his career and to be busy raising children. A woman who did not want these things had something wrong with her, was against nature and unfeminine, and therefore such unnatural urges should be suppressed. *Life* magazine in its profile of her called her "nonhousewife Betty." Television talk shows wanted her for a guest. The media seemed fascinated by the apparent contradiction that a mother of three who was living "a normal life" would be denouncing it. While the media wanted her, the suburban community in which she lived didn't and began ostracizing her and her husband. But women around the country were fascinated. They read and discussed the book and formed women's groups that asked Friedan to come speak.

Friedan came to realize that not only had women's groups been organized all over the country, but active feminists like Catherine East in Washington were fighting for women's legal rights. In 1966, two years before radical feminism's television debut, East's political savvy combined with Friedan's national reputation to form the National Organization for Women, NOW.

One of the earliest fights had been over airline stewardesses. Stewardesses were required to be attractive females, could be fired for gaining weight, and were fired as too old at the age of thirty-two. The age requirement had not been questioned by many women because most women agreed that a woman should be married and raising children by thirty-two. In fact, thirty-two was considered very late. Stewardesses were expected to leave their job when they married, but many married secretly and kept working until they reached the young age of retirement. The generation of women who were born in the 1940s married younger than any other twentieth-century generation, no doubt in part because there was no war to stop them. The average age of matrimony was twenty. Many couples got married in college, and certainly after graduation there was no time to lose. Those who didn't go to college were free to marry after high school.

In the meantime, if a woman was extremely attractive and wanted a little career before getting married, she could be a stewardess for a few years. It was considered a glamour job. Stewardesses were told how to wear hair and makeup and were required to wear girdles. Supervisors did "touch checks" to make sure they were complying.

A group of stewardesses led by Dusty Roads and Nancy Collins organized a union and fought for almost ten years to force airlines to stop age and marital discrimination. New guidelines and contracts were not won until 1968, only three weeks before television viewers discovered feminists in Atlantic City.

Slowly women were beginning to take their place in the job market. In 1968, when Muriel Siebert became the first woman with a seat on the New York Stock Exchange, she still had to convince clients that market advice from a woman could be as worthy as that from a man, despite the fact that by 1968 the United States had more female stock-holders than male. But when the year ended she reported "an incredible year." Before she bought her seat she was grossing half a million dollars, and with her seat in 1968 she grossed more than a million dollars, specializing in aviation and aeronautics stocks. Several large New York banks and all twenty-five of the largest mutual funds were among her clients.

For the first time, women won the right to serve on juries in the state of Mississippi. For the first time, two women were licensed as professional jockeys, although one of them, Kathy Kusner, then broke her leg and was out for the season. The North Vietnamese National Liberation Front taught the West a lesson by sending a woman, Nguyen Thi Binh, as their chief negotiator in the Paris peace talks. And First Lieutenant Jane A. Lombardi, a nurse, became the first woman ever to win a combat decoration.

But progress was slow and long overdue, which was why the feminist organization was called NOW. Already by 1960, 40 percent of American women over the age of sixteen were working. The idea of women as solely housewives was becoming more myth than reality. What was true was that most working women did not have good jobs and were not paid well for their work. In 1965, when the federal government made it illegal to discriminate in employment by race, religion, or national origin, despite rigorous lobbying gender was left out.

NOW made a priority of changing the practice of listing help wanted ads by gender in newspapers. It was now illegal for newspapers to separately list jobs for whites and jobs for "colored." But it was still common practice to single out women for low-paying jobs by separating "Male Help Wanted" and "Female Help Wanted" listings. NOW fought hard, using such tactics as invading the hearings by the Equal Employment Opportunities Commission with huge signs bearing telegenic messages such as "A chicken in every pot, a whore in every home." The leading New York City newspapers dropped separate listings in 1967. But many newspapers around the country continued the practice until the U.S. Supreme Court ruled against it in a 1973 case against the *Pittsburgh Press*.

In 1968 NOW took on a variety of issues, including a key battle in New York over changing state law to legalize abortion. At the same time, they wanted Congress to produce an amendment to the Constitution guaranteeing equal rights for women. Such an amendment, the ERA, had been proposed and rejected by every Congress since 1923.

The feminist movement, like all the great movements of 1968, was rooted in the civil rights movement. Laws that enforced separate female status, a principle repeatedly upheld in the courts, were referred to as "Jane Crow laws." Many feminists referred to NOW as the women's NAACP, leading others to insist it was more radical—the women's CORE or SNCC. Betty Friedan referred to women who pandered to male sexism as Aunt Toms.

Demonstration for abortion rights, New York, 1968
(Photo by Elliott Landy/Magnum Photos)

"There are striking parallels," insisted Florence Henderson, a New York lawyer best known at the time for her defense of SNCC leader H. Rap Brown. "In court you often get a more patronizing attitude to blacks and women than white men: 'Your Honor, I've known this boy since he was a child, his mother worked for my family. . . .' 'Your Honor, she is just a woman, she has three small children. . . .' And I think white male society often takes the same attitude toward both: 'If we want to give power to you O.K. But don't act as if you are entitled to it.' That's too manly, too . . . white."

The second wave of feminism might have broken sooner except that in the late 1950s and early 1960s the most talented, courageous, and idealistic women had joined the civil rights movement. Later in the sixties, the New Left was focused on ending the war, while white women in the civil rights movement for a long time felt it unseemly to raise issues of women's rights, in the face of the far more serious abuse of blacks. Women, after all, were not being lynched or shot.

Among those white women from church backgrounds who went south and risked their lives with SNCC were Mary King and Sandra Cason—later to marry and divorce Tom Hayden and become Casey Hayden. Some of the older female SNCC workers, notably Ella Baker, were tremendous influences on the younger women. Baker, an important inspiration for Mary King and others, had started with the Southern Christian Leadership Conference as an adviser to Martin Luther King. But in 1960 she switched to SNCC. She said this about the SCLC:

> I was difficult. I wasn't an easy pushover. Because I could talk back a lot—not only could but did. And so that was frustrating to those who never had certain kinds of experience. And it's a strange thing with men who were supposed to be "men about town"; if they had never known a woman who knew how to say No, and No in no uncertain terms, they didn't know what to do sometimes. Especially if you could talk loud and had a voice like mine. You could hear me a mile away sometimes, if necessary.

In fact, Martin Luther King had a number of important issues in his own marriage completely aside from his womanizing. Coretta complained bitterly of being kept out of the movement. "I wish I was more a part of it," she said in an interview. She envisioned a significant role for herself in the civil rights movement, and he had denied her that. This was a source of continual anger in their marriage and, according to some aides, often led to his being unable to go home at the end of a day. Dorothy Cotton, who worked closely with Martin Luther King in the SCLC, said, "Martin . . . was absolutely a male chauvinist. He believed that the wife should stay home and take care of the babies while he'd be out there in the streets. He would have a lot to learn and a lot of growing to do. I'm always asked to take the notes. I'm always asked to go fix Dr. King some coffee. I did it too." To her it was the times. "They were sexist male preachers and grew up in a sexist world. . . . I loved Dr. King but I know that that streak was in him also." Only after King's death was Coretta Scott King free to emerge as an important voice for civil rights.

All of the 1960s movements—until NOW and other feminist groups became active—were run by men. Women in the SDS talked of how intimidating Tom Hayden and other male leaders were. An SDS brochure read, "The system is like a woman. You've got to fuck it to make it change." Hayden in a recent interview said that part of the problem had been that "the women's movement was dormant at the time SDS was started." But he attributed the problem largely to his own "ignorance" and that of other leaders. Suzanne Goldberg, a leader in the Free Speech Movement and later Mario Savio's first wife, said:

> I was on the executive committee and the steering committee of the FSM. I would make a suggestion and no one would react. Thirty minutes later Mario or Jack Weinberg would make the same suggestion and everyone would react. Interesting idea. I thought maybe I'm not saying it well enough. I thought that for years. But then at the twenty-fifth anniversary of FSM, I ran into Jackie Goldberg and she said, "No, you were fine. It was classic. I used to use it in my street theater. Suzanne being ignored."

Bettina Aptheker, another leader in the Free Speech Movement, said, "Women did most of the clerical work and fund-raising and provided food. None of this was particularly recognized as work, and I never questioned this division of labor or even saw it as an issue!"

Probably no group had a more equal distribution of labor than SNCC. SNCC work was physically arduous and always dangerous, and though it was sometimes argued that the leaders who got the media attention were all men, the work and the danger were equally divided. By 1968 SNCC's problem was no longer attracting violence and media attention, it was surviving the violence. Once SNCC members realized, as did the Janet Rankin Brigade later, that less violence was used against them if they had women present, they wanted a strong female presence. Though they were constantly scared, beaten, arrested, intimidated, shot at, and attacked by snarling dogs— the women had to acknowledge that they were in less danger than the men, and the white women in less danger than the black women. The black men were in the most danger always. In October 1964 in the state of Mississippi, the civil rights movement suffered fifteen killings, four woundings, thirty-seven churches bombed or burned, and more than one thousand arrests.

In this one aspect, at least, SNCC was less sexist than the antiwar movement. David Dellinger was shocked, when organizing peace marches in 1967 and 1968, to find that pediatrician-turned–antiwar activist Benjamin Spock, and even Women's Strike for Peace, one of the early women's antiwar groups, urged that women and children not participate in demonstrations because of the threat of violence.

Among the books that were passed around SNCC, along with works by Frantz Fanon and Camus, one book that grew dog-eared, wilted, and coverless was Simone de Beauvoir's condemnation of marriage and critique of women's role in society, *The Second Sex*. Feminist ideas were slowly drifting into the movement. As Bettina Aptheker pointed out, before exposure to de Beauvoir and Friedan and a few others, a woman did not have the vocabulary to articulate her vague feelings of injustice.

In 1964 Mary King and Casey Hayden coauthored a memo to SNCC workers on women's status in the movement. It was the SNCC style to float ideas in this way and later have meetings and talk them through. The memo consisted of a list of meetings from which women were excluded and projects in which eminently qualified women were overlooked for leadership roles.

> Undoubtedly this list will seem strange to some, petty to others, laughable to most. The list could continue as far as there are women in the movement. Except that most women don't talk about these kinds of incidents, because the whole subject is not discussable. . . .

The memo was anonymous because they feared ridicule. Bob Moses and a few others expressed admiration for it. Julian Bond smiled wryly about it, "non committal with his sidelong glance." But by and large it was ridiculed. Mary King said that some who had figured out that she authored it "mocked and taunted" her. Late one moonlit night, King, Hayden, and a few others were sitting around with Stokely Carmichael. A compulsive entertainer, Carmichael was on, delivering a monologue ridiculing everyone and everything, keeping his audience laughing. Then he got to that day's meeting and then to the memo, and staring at Mary King, he said, "What is the position of women in SNCC?" He paused as though waiting for an answer and said, "The position of women in SNCC is prone." Mary King and the others doubled over with laughter.

In the decades since, the Carmichael quote is often cited as evidence of the sexist attitude in the radical civil rights movement. But the women who first heard it insist that it was intended and was received as a joke.

In 1965 they wrote another memo:

> There seem to be many parallels that can be drawn between treat-ment of Negroes and treatment of women in our society as a whole. But in particular, women we've talked to who work in the movement seem to be caught up in a common-law caste system that operates, sometimes subtly, forcing them to work around or outside hierarchical structures of power which may exclude them. Women seem to be placed in the same position of assumed subor-dination in personal situations too. It is a caste system which, at its worst, uses and exploits women.

This second one that they signed became an influential document in the feminist movement, but of the forty black women, civil rights activists, friends, and colleagues to whom they sent it, not one responded.

The founding members of NOW—such as Friedan; East; Dr. Kathryn Clarenbach, a Wisconsin educator; Eileen Hernandez, a prominent lawyer; Caroline Davis, a Detroit United Auto Workers executive—were women with successful careers. Of their 1,200 members in 1968, many were lawyers, sociologists, and educators. There were also one hundred men, almost all of them lawyers. They hoped to reach out to women who did not have careers, to housewives and women working at low-status, underpaid jobs. But the new wave, much like the antiwar movement, was starting among a well-educated elite who had shed the conventional prejudice of society.

In 1968 a feminist was still denigrated, a woman with a problem, something wrong with her, probably unattractive. Feminists—bra burners—it was believed, were bitter women who opposed beauty because they didn't have it. Disturbing that stereotype was the head of the New York chapter of NOW, Ti-Grace Atkinson, a twenty-nine-year-old unmarried woman from Louisiana who, it was unfailingly pointed out in every newspaper account, was "attractive," "good-looking," or, in the words of *The New York Times,* "softly sexy."

In 1968 the least attempts at reforming marriage were considered radical by the general population. It was still considered a radical feminist act for a married woman not to take her husband's name. Like Simone de Beauvoir, the tremendously influential French feminist who lived with, but never married Sartre, many of the sixties feminists were at best distrustful of the institution of marriage. Atkinson said, "The institution of marriage has the same effect the institution of slavery had. It separates people in the same category. It disperses them, keeps them from identifying as a class. The masses of slaves didn't recognize their condition either. To say that a woman is really 'happy' with her home and kids is as irrelevant as saying that the blacks were 'happy' being taken care of by the ol' Massa. She is defined by her maintenance role. Her husband is defined by his productive role. We're saying that all human beings should have a productive role in society." Her own views on marriage were shaped by having been married at seventeen. She divorced, got an arts degree at the University of Pennsylvania, became the first director of the Philadelphia Institute of Contemporary Art, got a graduate degree at Columbia in philosophy. She said de Beauvoir's *The Second Sex* "changed my life." She wrote to de Beauvoir, who suggested she get involved with an American group. That was when Atkinson found the nascent NOW.

In France, land of de Beauvoir, the feminist movement is also said to have been born in 1968. Yet de Beauvoir's *The Second Sex* was first published in France in 1949 and by 1968 had influenced a large part of an entire generation of women whose daughters were now reading it. The year 1968 was when activists formed groups pressuring the government to legalize abortion and widen access to the pill, which was available only by prescription. Women were refused prescriptions by doctors for a variety of reasons, including the arbitrary verdict that they were too young.

In Germany, too, the feminist movement can be traced to 1968, to a Frankfurt conference of the German SDS, when Helke Sander declared the equality of the sexes and demanded that future planning take into account the concerns of women. When the conference refused to have an in-depth discussion of Sander's proposal, angry women began pelting men with tomatoes. But in fact women's groups had been founded in several cities before this incident, the first one in Berlin in January 1968.

De Beauvoir, with her famously long and deep relation with Sartre, said that people should be joined by love and not legal sanctions. Atkinson and many other American feminists in 1968 were saying that in order for women and men to have equal status, children would have to be raised communally. The commune was becoming a popular solution. Communes were springing up all over the United States. Some child development experts who had studied the kibbutz system in Israel were unimpressed. Dr. Selma Fraiberg at the University of Michigan's Child Psychiatric Hospital told *The New York Times* in a 1968 interview that her studies of children raised on a kibbutz produced what she called "a bunch of cool cookies"—cold, unfriendly people. But women in communes began to complain that there was a gender-based caste system there as well, that the women would do the cleaning while the men meditated.

The American feminists of 1968 subdivided into two groups: the politicos and the radicals. The politicos were sophisticated activists, many with long experience in the civil rights movement and the New Left. NOW was a politico group. The radicals included groups such as the New York Radical Women and a similar Chicago group. The New York Radical Women were responsible not only for the Miss America action, but also for even more important innovation: C-R, or consciousness-raising. In 1968, when the New York Radicals came up with this concept for recruiting feminists, the politicos, including NOW, thought it was a counterproductive idea that would alienate men. In consciousness-raising, women talked to other women about all the false things they did to please men such as acting stupid, pretending to agree, and wearing shoes, clothes, and undergarments that were so unnatural they inflicted pain. Women, through C-R sessions, would realize the extent to which they distorted themselves because of the fear that men would not find their true selves attractive. It was out of this C-R process that the Miss America protest was born. Frantz Fanon in *The Wretched of the Earth* wrote about how colonized people had colonized minds—they accepted the place the mother country had put them in, but they were not aware that they were accepting this role. The New York Radical Women believed that men had done the same thing to women and that making them aware of this was the key to turning feminism into a mass movement, that this process that appeared to be merely a form of self-therapy would recruit thousands of women for the feminist cause. They were clearly right, and in a few years most feminists embraced consciousness-raising as a way to bring women around to their cause. An example of this was the speakout, where women publicly described the nightmares of their illegal abortions, which had a major impact on changing abortion laws.

    In 1968, when consciousness-raising began, people had had a heightened consciousness of race issues from more than ten years of civil rights but very little consciousness of gender issues. In *Soul on Ice*

Eldridge Cleaver described in detail the pleasure he took in what he termed "an insurrectionary act," the rape of a white woman: "It delighted me that I was defying and trampling upon the white man's law, upon his system of values, and that I was defiling his women." Indicative of the times, this was seen as a confession of racial hatred to be later recanted, and little was said of the sexist implication of a white woman simply being *his* appendage. Charlayne Hunter, a Russell Sage fellow who reviewed the book for *The New York Times,* emphasized Cleaver's ability to articulate the bitterness of "a black man in this country" but said nothing about his attitudes toward women.

By 1968 a level of sexism that seems shocking to contemporary sensibilities was still generally acceptable even among New Left youth. The 1968 film *Barbarella* starring Jane Fonda featured Amazons in erotic little outfits conquering through sex. In *Planet of the Apes* the women don't speak, and have no character, and are scantily clad, with the exception of the ape women, probably because no one is interested in a scantily clad ape. The following year, Robert Altman's *M*A*S*H,* extremely popular with college students because it appeared to be anti-war, starred Elliott Gould and Donald Sutherland as martini-drinking army doctors who are contemptuous of any woman who even hesitates to bed down with them. Rock culture was even more sexist. In Ed Sanders's book that claims to be a novel, *Shards of God,* women, never with names or faces, appear only to offer for sex one orifice or another to the male characters who have such names as Abbie Hoffman and Jerry Rubin.

By the end of the year, women's fashions were indicating that the times were "a-changin' " again. It was only back in March that New York had the "Down with Dirndl" movement against "those fat, gathering balloon skirts and dirndls, dresses with old-fashioned waistlines. . . . Big ugly belts in the middle of dresses and coats make women look like mastodons in full retreat," read a petition with sixty-six signatures, of which seventeen were men. The movement was led by Dona Fowler Kaminsky, a twenty-eight-year-old Berkeley graduate who went to department stores to protest the new fashion that had turned from miniskirts toward the long-skirted "maxi." They threatened to picket department stores with signs that read, "Maxis Are Monstrous." In the early spring, *Time* magazine fashion writers were predicting the summer season to be "the barest in memory"—with see-through blouses with nothing underneath, bare midriffs, wide and plunging necklines, and backs open, as *Time* put it, "right down to the coccyx." Rudi Gernreich, who in 1964 came out with the topless bathing suit, which the Soviets called "barbarous" and was even banned in the south of France, now predicted that "the bare bosom look" would gain complete acceptance in the next five years. Chicago designer Walter Holmes came out with the miniskirted nun's habit, also a miniskirted monk's cowl, both with removable hoods to show plunging necklines, with neither design intended for nuns.

But by the end of the year, to the consternation of many men, the pantsuit had become the "in" look. Women wanted to be taken seriously and compete with men, and that is more difficult to do in a miniskirt. Few noticed that in society something new and exciting was about to happen for women even if it translated badly into fashion. Somehow it seemed that both the unfairness and the fun were going to be over, that the sixties were drawing to a close. William Zinsser wrote in *Life* magazine, "The city pantsuit is the Richard Nixon of high fashion. Send it away once, unwanted. Send it away twice, unloved. No matter: it will return in slightly different form, to beg approval still another time. Nixonlike, the pantsuit knows that it's now or never, and I'm very much afraid it's now."

CHAPTER 19

IN AN AZTEC PLACE

All the history of every people is symbolic. This is to say: history
and its events and its protagonists allude to another concealed
history, are the visible manifestation of a hidden reality.
—OCTAVIO PAZ, Posdata, *1970*

G USTAVO DÍAZ ORDAZ was a very ugly man. Mexicans were
divided into two camps about their president: those who
thought he resembled a bat and those who thought he was more like a
monkey. His small frame, little snipped nose, long teeth, and thick-
lensed glasses that magnified his irises to a primordial size all
contributed to this debate. The monkey side gave him his nickname,
El Chango, a Mexican word for a monkey, though his long, flapping
arm gestures were suggestive of bat wings. But he was credited with a
good sense of humor and reputedly once responded to the accusation
of being "two-faced" by saying, "Ridiculous, if I had another one don't
you think I would use it?" And though not especially skilled with
language, he had a powerful, booming speaking voice. His voice was
the only physical attribute in his favor. But a good voice is an important attribute for a president of Mexico. The Mexican poet Octavio
Paz wrote, "Accustomed as they are to delivering only monologues,
intoxicated by a lofty rhetoric that envelops them like a cloud, our
presidents and leaders find it well-nigh impossible to believe that aspirations and opinions that are different than their own even exist."

In 1968 the president of Mexico was worried. Some of the things
that worried him were in his own mind and some were real. He had
reason to worry about the Olympics. So far this year, almost every
cultural and sporting event had been disrupted. The winter games in
Grenoble, France, had gone well, though perhaps too much attention

"Let's demand to know who is responsible." 1968 Mexican
student silk-screen poster depicting President Díaz Ordaz
as a monkey.
(Amigos de la Unidad de Postgrado de la Escuela de Diseño A.C.)

had been paid to Soviet-Czech competition. But the games had taken place before April, when the French were still bored. The April Academy Awards were postponed two days to mourn the death of Martin Luther King and then were overshadowed by politics. Bob Hope, not well liked on the Left for his girlie shows for the troops in Vietnam, appalled the audience with jokes about the postponement. Two films about race relations, albeit simplistic stories almost silly with didacticism—*In the Heat of the Night* and *Guess Who's Coming to Dinner*—won awards. In a positive touch of the times, Czech director Jirí Menzel won the Oscar for best foreign language film for *Closely Watched Trains,* and he was free to travel to receive it. It was a completely politicized event.

Disruption would be even worse than politicization. Protesters had closed the annual Venice Biennale art show and the Cannes Film Festival, attacked the Frankfurt Book Fair, and even disrupted the Miss

America pageant. Even the winner of the Kentucky Derby was disqualified for drug use. And of course there was the Chicago convention. Nothing like that was to happen in Mexico.

Díaz Ordaz, as president of Mexico, the appointed leader of the PRI, the Institutional Revolutionary Party, was heir to the revolution and guardian of the stated contradiction in the ruling party's carefully worded name. In 1910 Mexico had been a labyrinth of political chaos and social injustice. Centuries of inept colonial rule followed by corrupt dictatorships and foreign occupations then culminated in thirty years of one-man rule. It was a familiar pattern. After years of chaos, the dictator Porfirio Díaz offered stability. But in 1910 he was eighty years old and had arranged for no successor or any institutions to outlast him. There were no political parties, and he represented no ideology. Mexico was divided by different cultures, ethnic groups, and social classes, all with dramatically different needs and demands. When the country erupted into what was called the Mexican revolution that year, it was an endless series of highly destructive civil wars, most of them fought on a regional basis. There were many leaders and many armies. But this was the Mexico Hernán Cortés had found in the early sixteenth century. The Aztecs had ruled by managing a coalition of leaders from different groups. Cortés had defeated the Aztecs by dividing his coalition, gaining the loyalty of some of the leaders. That was how politics was played in Mexico.

Francisco Madero, a bourgeois from the north, led one faction. He attracted upper-class, middle-class, and working-class Mexicans of moderate politics. Also in the north were tough, mounted guerrilla fighters—bandits who took up the cause of the revolution, in some cases as paid mercenaries. The most brilliant of these was Pancho Villa. Villa was the only revolutionary leader to get good American press. Even Madero was criticized bitterly for suggesting a minuscule tax on the Mexican oil that was controlled and imported to the United States by American oil companies. But Pancho Villa had little of the "anti-Americanism" of which Washington suspected all the others. He did personally rape hundreds of women and murder according to whim, and he was a racist who killed Chinese people whenever he found them working in mining camps. His lieutenants were even more murderous and sadistic, devising hideous tortures. But General Villa was not anti-American. The Americans supplied his weapons and ammunition. Ten thousand men rode with Villa, mostly in the northern state of Chihuahua. They robbed and raided, did as they wanted, and once even won a spectacular military victory for the revolution at Zacatecas.

In the central area, in Morelos, was Emiliano Zapata, who did not fit in with any of the others, aside from the fact that they were all *mestizo*—of mixed European and indigenous blood. Zapata with his big, sad eyes was leading a peasant revolt in the central highlands. His followers were agrarian Mexicans, either *mestizo* or from indigenous non-Spanish-speaking tribes, of which there are still many in Mexico, fighting for land. His goal was to have the arable land of Mexico taken away from wealthy landowners and distributed equally among the peasants. He and his followers intended to go on fighting regardless of what the others did, until the farmers got their land.

Fighting continued after Madero became president in 1911, and he was helpless to stop it. Madero, for whom Zapata had a great fondness, was from the wrong class. He was a landowner with a large ranch in the north, and he was surrounded by other figures such as Venustiano Carranza, who had interests in the moneyed classes and were disturbed at the way this Zapata was trying to turn the Revolution into a revolution. Madero could not give Zapata his land, and he could not bribe the bandits, the "generals" in the north, enough to make peace seem profitable to them. Like many revolutionary figures, Madero was murdered by supporters of the Revolution.

By the end of 1914 the combined forces of the revolutionary armies of Carranza and Pancho Villa and Zapata had secured control of Mexico and defeated the federal army that Porfirio Díaz had left behind. Zapata and Villa moved their armies into the capital as a new revolutionary government was formed. Carranza declared himself president and reluctantly and under great pressure adopted Zapata's land reform program, though he did little to put it into action.

Álvaro Obregón, who, like most leading figures of the period, held the title of general, was a schoolteacher from the northern state of Sonora who had started out with a guerrilla army but had learned the modern warfare of machine guns and trenches. He had military advisers from Europe's "Great War." His temperament and politics, which had a huge influence on the shaping of modern Mexico, were resolutely moderate. He had sympathy for workers and peasants but was not about to do anything too revolutionary. He had considerable worker support and enlisted them in his army as "Red Battalions." In April 1915 Villa had a showdown with Obregón, who surrounded the mounted bandits with barbed wire and trenches with machine-gun emplacements. Villa used his field artillery effectively and fought furiously, but he never understood modern tactics. His men were cut down by the machine guns and cut up by the barbed wire. Obregón himself had an arm blown off, and the partial limb in a pickling jar became the emblem of Obregón's Red Battalions, which was later fashioned into the Revolutionary Army of Mexico, supposedly an "Army of the People" that embodied the ideals of the revolution.

Zapata stuck to his land reform goals. Such stubborn local chieftains could usually be bought off. But Zapata would not take money or accept compromise. His organization was infiltrated by an army double agent who was allowed to carry out several sneak attacks, killing large numbers of soldiers, to prove his authenticity to Zapata. Once Zapata trusted him, the agent led Zapata, looking splendid as always in his dark riding clothes on his sorrel horse, into six hundred army rifles that opened fire. Upon his death in 1919, the murdered revolutionary became the Che of his day, the youthful poster boy for a new revolutionary government that had killed him rather than carry out his revolution.

There was a lot of killing going on in Mexico—so much so that from 1910 to 1920 the total population of the country declined by several hundred thousand. In November 1920 the one-armed Obregón became president. He legalized all the land confiscations that had taken place, something Carranza had refused to do. By this act, along with having the man who set up Zapata's murder shot, he finally obtained a peace settlement with Zapata's fighters in Morelos, even though most of the land was getting distributed to generals and only small patches to the poor. Villa was bought off and agreed to spend the rest of his days as a comfortable rancher. But in 1923, friends and family of people he had murdered and raped over the years shot him as he passed by in his new automobile.

Some can be bought off, and some have to be shot. That became the Mexican way. "No general can withstand a cannonade of a hundred thousand pesos," Obregón once said. By 1924 a fourth of the national budget went to paying off generals. But many other "generals," local chieftains with their bands of armed followers, were shot.

Starting with the 1917 constitution, a system of government was established whose primary goal was not democracy but stability. In 1928 Mexico almost slid back into revolution. Obregón ran for president without an opponent and was elected. He might have been on his way to dictatorship were it not for the artist who, while sketching him as president, took out a pistol and shot him to death. The assassin was immediately killed.

It seemed the changing of presidents was forever threatening the national stability. The Mexican solution was the PNR—the National

Revolutionary Party—formed in 1929. Through this institution, a qualified president could be chosen and presented to the public. For six years this president would have almost absolute power. There were only three things he could not do—give territory to a foreign power, confiscate land from indigenous people, and succeed himself as president. During World War II, in an attempt to appear more stable and democratic, the PNR changed its name to that uniquely Mexican paradox, the Institutional Revolution Party.

That is what Mexico had become, not a democracy but an institutional revolution—the Revolution that feared revolution. The PRI bought out or killed agrarian leaders, all the while paying verbal homage to Zapata and carrying out as little land reform as possible. It bought out the labor unions until they became part of the PRI. It bought out the press, one newspaper at a time, until it completely controlled them. The PRI was not violent. It tried to co-opt. Only in those rare situations where that did not work would it resort to killing.

In 1964 the PRI chose the former minister of the interior, Gustavo Díaz Ordaz, as the next president. Of all possible candidates, he was the most conservative. As minister of the interior, he had managed unusually good relations with the United States. He seemed the right choice to lead Mexico in the dangerous 1960s.

Díaz Ordaz was eager to put Mexico on display. It was at one of its best moments of economic expansion, with annual growth rates between 5 and 6 percent, up to 7 percent for 1967. In January 1968 *The New York Times* reported, "Steady economic growth within a framework of political and financial stability has distinguished Mexico among the major Latin American countries." Octavio Paz wrote with a tone of incredulity about this period, "The economy of the country had made such progress that economists and sociologists cited the case of Mexico as an example for other underdeveloped countries."

The 1968 summer Olympics was the first large international event hosted by Mexico since 1910, when as three decades of dictatorship was crumbling, Porfirio Díaz attempted an international celebration of the centennial of the beginning of the independence movement. The 1968 Olympics was the first time the Mexican Revolution was to show itself to the world with all its accomplishments, including an emerging middle class, the modernity of Mexico City, and the efficiency with which Mexico could run a huge international event. It would be televised to the world that Mexico was no longer backward and strife-torn but had become an emerging, successful modern country.

But Díaz Ordaz also understood that the world was having its 1968 and there would be troubles. The most apparent controversy on the horizon, the U.S. race conflicts, had the potential to politicize the games the same way the King assassination had politicized the Oscars. The idea of a black boycott of the Olympics first emerged in a meeting of Black Power leaders in Newark after that city's riots during the summer of 1967. In November, Harry Edwards, an amiable and popular black sociology instructor at San Jose State College in California, again raised the idea at a black youth conference. Most athletes and black leaders did not think a black boycott would be effective, but one of Edwards's first adherents to the idea was Tommie Smith, a student at San Jose State College and an extraordinary athlete who already held two world records in track and field events. Lee Evans, another champion sprinter at San Jose State, also said he would boycott. In February fresh life was breathed into the boycott idea by the International Olympic Committee, which in exchange for a few token gestures readmitted the apartheid team of South Africa.

Harry Edwards, a six-foot-eight, bearded twenty-five-year-old in sunglasses and black beret, was a former college athlete who insisted on referring to the U.S. president as "Lynchin' Baines Johnson." From his sports boycott office in San Jose, he was interested not only in the Olympics, but also in boycotts of college and professional programs. In 1968, though, the big target was in Mexico City. A poster on his wall said, "Rather than run and jump for medals, we are standing up for humanity." His wall also featured the "Negro traitor of the week," a prominent black athlete who opposed the boycott. Among those so honored were baseball's Willie Mays, track's Jesse Owens, and decathlon champion Rafer Johnson. A boycott of the 1960 Olympics had been suggested to Johnson, and Dick Gregory had called for a boycott in 1964. But this year, with the help of Harry Edwards's office, the idea seemed to be gathering force.

In March, *Life* magazine published a survey of top black college athletes and was surprised to discover a widely held conviction that it would be worth giving up a chance at an Olympic medal to better conditions for their race. *Life* also found that black athletes were angry about their treatment at American universities. They would be promised housing but would get no help when confronted with housing discrimination. At San Jose State, white athletes were entertained by the athletic department in fraternities that did not accept black members. In the top 150 college athletic programs, there were only seven black coaches. White coaches bunched the black athletes together in locker rooms or on road trips. Academic advisers were constantly counseling them to take special easy courses so they could pass. And they would find that no one on the faculty or the student body ever talked to them about anything other than sports.

The International Olympic Committee had made the decision to let South Africa back early in the year, after a successful winter Olympics. It did not yet understand what 1968 was going to be like. In the spring, the Mexicans, sensing disaster, asked the committee to reconsider after at least forty teams threatened to boycott the games. The committee reversed itself, once again banning South Africa. This made a number of black American athletes, including Smith and Evans, say that they would reconsider competing in Mexico. The Americans were trying desperately to avoid a black boycott because they were putting together a track and field team that had the potential of being the best in American history and perhaps in the history of the modern sport. At the end of the summer, Edwards told a Black Panther meeting that the Olympic boycott had been called off but that athletes would wear black armbands and decline to participate in medals ceremonies. By September the Mexican government had every reason to hope for an extremely successful Olympics.

The Mexican government did not see itself as a dictatorship, since the president, in spite of his absolute power, had to step down at the end of his term. There would be no Porfiriato, as the three decades of Porfirio Díaz's rule was known. The government responded to the needs of the people. If workers wanted unions, the PRI would provide them with unions. Mexicans who wanted to change things, improve things, make life better, needed to join the PRI. Only PRI members could be players. Even Emiliano Zapata's three sons, one of whom inherited his father's spectacular face, worked for the PRI. In Mexico the PRI still encountered Villa-like people who could be bought off, as well as a few Zapatas, people too stubborn to be co-opted, people who had to be either locked away indefinitely in prisons or killed. When the peasants kept noticing that the revolution was not delivering on its promise of land, they turned to peasant organizations, which were all controlled by the PRI. Sometimes a new organization emerged to represent the peasant. Its leaders too had to be bought out or killed, just as did new labor organizers and new journalists.

As the economy experienced its seemingly miraculous growth, year after year, there was an increasing suspicion that the distribution of this new wealth was grossly unfair. In 1960 Ifigenia Martínez, a researcher at the economics school, conducted a study that showed that about 78 percent of disposable income in Mexico went to only the upper 10 percent of Mexican society. No one had ever scientifically researched this before, and the results seemed hard to believe, so others, such as the Bank of Mexico, repeated the study but got the same results.

Such research was just the statistical explanation for an observable phenomenon: In fast-growing, rapidly developing Mexico, there were a lot of unhappy people. Starting in the late 1950s a series of protest movements emerged—peasant movements, a teachers union protest, a Social Security doctors' strike, and, in 1958, a bitter railroad workers strike. They were quickly crushed, with everyone either co-opted, imprisoned, or killed. Ten years after the railroad strike, its leader, Demetrio Vallejo Martínez, was still in prison.

Yet in 1968, as the Olympics approached, there was only one group that the PRI did not have under its control, and that was students. The reason for this was that students as a political force was a new concept in Mexico. The students were a product of Mexico's new economic expansion. After World War II, the growth rate in Mexico City began accelerating. By 1968 Mexico City was one of the fastest-growing cities in the world, its population increasing at about 3 percent each year. Typical of the pyramid-shaped demographics of rapidly developing countries, a very large percentage of the Mexican population, especially the Mexico City population, was young. And with a growing middle class, Mexico had more students than ever before, many of them crammed into the National Autonomous University of Mexico, UNAM, and the National Polytechnic Institute, on vast, sprawling new campuses in the newer parts of a capital city that swallowed miles of new area every year.

These students, like those in France, Germany, Italy, Japan, the United States, and so many other places, were acutely aware that they had more economic comfort than their parents. But in the case of Mexico, they were also aware that they had been the recipients of a growing economy that had not benefited many of the people around them.

Roberto Escudero, who became one of the student leaders in 1968, said, "There was a big difference between our generation and our parents'. They were very traditional. They had received benefits from the Mexican revolution, and Zapata and others from the revolution were their heroes. We had those heroes, too, but we also had Che and Fidel. We saw the PRI more as authoritarian, where they saw it as revolutionary liberators."

Salvador Martínez de la Roca, a small, scrappy-looking blond man known to everyone as Pino, also was a student leader in 1968. Born in

1945, he was studying nuclear physics at UNAM in 1968. Pino was a *norteño*, a Mexican from the northern states, where the United States is much closer and its cultural impact far greater. "In the 1950s we loved Marlon Brando in *The Wild One* and James Dean in *Rebel Without a Cause*," he recalled. "We were more interested in American culture than our parents. In the fifties students wore shirts and ties. We wore jeans and indigenous-style shirts."

To him UNAM also showed him more of the world. "The Cine Club at UNAM showed films that were not available anywhere else in Mexico—French films, the first film I ever saw about lesbians, *Easy Rider*. There was a cultural rebellion. We loved Eldridge Cleaver and Muhammad Ali and Angela Davis, Joan Baez, Pete Seeger," he said. Songs of the civil rights movement such as "We Shall Overcome" were well known, and Martin Luther King, especially after his death, had a place in the UNAM student pantheon of heroes in proximity to Che and Zapata. The Black Panthers also enjoyed some popularity at UNAM. Norman Mailer was widely read by students, as were Frantz Fanon and Camus. But, as Martínez de la Roca said, "Most important was the Cuban revolution. We all read Régis Debray's *Revolution in the Revolution*."

There were many strikes and marches at UNAM before the famous 1968 events. In 1965 students supported the doctors' strike for better wages. In 1966 UNAM students went on strike for three months against an authoritarian rector, Ignacio Chavez. In March 1968, after the big marches in Europe, Mexico City too had a march against the Vietnam War. But compared with those in the United States, Europe, or Japan, the Mexican student movement was minuscule—a few hundred students.

In 1968, for the first time, the small student movement became a concern of the Mexican government because it did not want *any* problems during the Olympics and because of President Gustavo Díaz Ordaz's particular way of viewing the world. A world in which spontaneous movements spread without organizers across the world on the airwaves of television was something new and, for the Mexican president, very hard to believe. He was convinced there was an international conspiracy of revolutionaries moving from country to country, spreading chaos and upheaval. A key component in this conspiracy was the Cubans. So while the Mexican government defied the U.S. embargo and openly befriended Cuba, in reality the president had a paranoid dread of the Cubans and carefully monitored flights to the island, keeping and studying passenger lists. While publicly refusing to embargo Cuba, he did not let Mexico conduct trade with the island and consulted with American intelligence about "the Cuban threat." While Díaz Ordaz had been minister of the interior, he had cultivated close relations with the CIA and FBI. It was in the nature of Mexican policy toward the United States to have this contradiction between public stance and private communication, the same way that in 1916 Carranza had pretended to oppose U.S. intervention while in reality encouraging U.S. president Woodrow Wilson to send troops to Mexico and attack the troublesome Pancho Villa.

Lecumberri, a black castle in downtown Mexico City, looks like the Bastille and is in fact a French-style prison, with a round central court-yard and cell blocks stretching out in spokes. The cells are about four-teen feet long and six feet wide. In 1968 this was the infamous dungeon into which political prisoners were thrown. Today, the National Archives documents that were state secrets in 1968 are housed in Lecumberri, where the bars have been replaced with large windows and well-polished parquet wooden floors have been installed. The cramped fourteen-by-six-foot cells are filled with files that have clearly been laundered. But they do paint a picture of the kind of state para-noia that was obsessing the Díaz Ordaz government.

The Ministry of the Interior had had a wealth of informants. Every student organization, even if it had only twenty members, had at least one who reported to the government, writing up records in tedious detail of meetings in which nothing happened. Communists of any kind were of particular interest, and of even greater concern were any foreigners who talked to Mexican communists. The government kept detailed reports on who was seen singing Cuban songs, who proposed erecting a Vietnamese statue and who supported the suggestion, and who were on flights to Havana, especially around the time of July 26, when Cuba had its annual celebration of Castro's first uprising. The names of people participating in an homage to José Martí were also noted, even though the writings of the Cuban father of independence were admired by both pro- and anti-Castro elements.

Díaz Ordaz was also obsessively concerned about the French. This may in part have been because Mexican students had a fascination with the French May movement out of all proportion to its conse-quence. Though American and German and numerous other move-ments were older, more durable, better organized, and of greater impact, to many Mexican students, May in Paris was *the* event of 1968.

This was in part because of a nineteenth-century concept that endured in Mexico—that France was the imperialist world power. The

French had briefly ruled Mexico. In 1968 a French graduate degree was still the most prestigious degree in Mexico, and Sartre was considered the leading intellectual. Lorenzo Meyer, a prominent Mexican historian from the Colegio de México, himself a graduate of the University of Chicago, said of this lingering Francophilia, "I think it was caused by inertia . . . something lingering from the past."

But both the students' admiration and the president's fear of the French student movement were also based on the myth that the Paris students were able to join forces with the workers and together shut down the country. On May 31 the Trotskyite Revolutionary Workers Party in Mexico City called for a student and worker meeting "to do what was done in France" and "to apply to Mexico the experience of France." On June 4, in the school of political and social sciences at UNAM, a newspaper had appeared from the Trotskyite Revolutionary Workers Party IV International, Mexican section, with the text "All worker states should support the revolutionary French movement for the formation of a new worker state. The PCF [French Communist Party] and CGT [PCF's trade union] that traditionally are sellouts and traitors to the French revolutionary movement have asked the leadership of the French movement and the workers together with the students and the peasants to confront world capitalism. This French revolutionary movement is a powerful blow to the legacy of the French Communist Party and world bureaucracy." On July 24 UNAM's economics school offered a meeting with two French students, Denis Decreane and Didier Kuesza, both from Nanterre.

All of this was reported to the Ministry of the Interior by government informants within these tiny leftist student groups. The notion of radical students joining forces with workers, as they believed the French students had done—a menacing concept to most political establishments—was particularly threatening to the PRI leadership. It was the PRI that was supposed to bring together diverse elements of society and then control relations between them. That was the way the system was meant to work.

On July 18, the government noted, a communist student group had a meeting about the possibility of a student hunger strike in support of Demetrio Vallejo Martínez, in prison since he led the 1958 railway workers strike. He was one of the best-known political prisoners. In fact, the student strike never happened, but Vallejo Martínez went on a hunger strike by himself, eating nothing but lime water with sugar until he collapsed August 6 and was hospitalized and fed through tubes.

Ironically, the one serious attempt to organize Mexican students in solidarity with the French had fallen apart because of lack of interest.

At the end of May, José Revueltas, a well-known communist writer and winner of Mexico's National Prize for Literature, talked to a group of students about holding a rally in support of the French in the auditorium of the school of philosophy, which was called the auditorium Che Guevara. But the plans drifted into June, and by July the Mexican students felt they had too many problems of their own. "After all," said Roberto Escudero, "they only had one death and that was an accident."

To the president, these were all bits of evidence of a global conspiracy of French and Cuban radicals to spread disorder around the world. They had been doing it effectively all year, and now, with the Olympics coming, it was reaching Mexico! It was repeatedly noted in Interior Ministry files that student tracts often ended with, "*Viva los movimientos estudiantiles de todo el mundo!*"—Long live the student movements around the world!

These small groups of students, together with world events, had set off in the president's mind that distinct strain of Mexican xenophobia that dates to the Aztec experience—the fear of the foreigner conspiring to undermine and take over. The Ministry of the Interior carefully watched American students who came to Mexico for the summer, when Mexican school is still open. They also watched the many Mexicans who attended Berkeley and other California schools and were coming home for the summer. And in fact, these Mexican students from California were influential in the Mexican student movement. Roberto Rodriguez Baños, who in July 1968 was chief of the national desk of AMEX, the first Mexican news agency, which began as an alternative to state-controlled news, said, "In 1968 Mexican students read with fascination about Paris, Czechoslovakia, Berkeley, Columbia, and other U.S. universities. Ever since the Watts riots in the summer of 1965, most Mexicans were convinced that the U.S. was in a state of civil war. They had seen on television a huge American neighborhood in a major city in flames. The government had seen what had happened in France, Czechoslovakia, and the United States and were convinced that the world was destabilizing. It saw in the student movement these same outside forces coming to destabilized Mexico."

Mexico was one of the few countries in the world that did not condemn the Soviet invasion of Czechoslovakia. The Institutional Revolutionary Party did not like revolutions anymore. The government was ready to do whatever was necessary to stop the revolution from coming to Mexico. It was worried about the Cubans and the Soviets. It worried about Guatemala and Belize on the southern border, and worrying about Belize meant it also had to worry about the British, who still had military bases there. Porfirio Díaz had been famous for saying, "Poor Mexico, so far from God and so close to the United States." But now the world was getting smaller. To Díaz Ordaz it was "Poor Mexico, so far from God and so close to everyone else."

What disturbed the PRI was that it was not sure how to control students who were not looking for food, land, work, or money. The PRI could form student organizations, the way it had formed labor unions, journalism groups, and land reform organizations, but the students had no incentive to join a PRI student organization. Student leaders were leaders only because they earned the support of the students every day. If a leader was co-opted by the PRI, he would no longer be a leader. Lorenzo Meyer said, "The students were as free as you could be in this society."

By summer the government's growing anxiety was becoming visible. Allen Ginsberg, on a family vacation before taking on Chicago, was stopped at the border and told that he would have to shave off his beard to enter. Just a few months before, sounding like the peacemaking moderate in a turbulent year, Díaz Ordaz had told the Mexican press, "Everyone is free to let his beard, hair, or sideburns grow if he wants to, to dress well or badly as he sees fit. . . ."

If all the student movements of 1968 had a contest to see which had the most innocuous beginnings, the competition would be stiff, but the Mexican student movement would have an excellent chance of being in first place. Until July 22 it was a small and splintered movement. Plans for the Olympics were proceeding well. Eighteen sculptors from sixteen countries, including Alexander Calder and Henry Moore, were arriving to set up their works. Calder's seventy-ton steel piece was to be placed in front of the new Aztec Stadium. Others were arranged along the "Friendship Route" to the Olympic Village. Oscar Urrutia, who headed the cultural program, in announcing all this to the press quoted an ancient Mexican poem, which ends, "Yet even more do I love my brother man." That was to be the theme of the games.

All that happened on July 22 was that a fight broke out between two rival high schools. No one is certain what caused the fight. The two groups were fighting constantly. Two local gangs, the "Spiders" and the "Ciudadelans," may have been involved. The fight spread into the Plaza de la Ciudadela, an important commercial center in the city. The following day the students were attacked by the two gangs but did not respond. The police and special antiriot military units stood by watching, but then they started to provoke the students and exploded tear gas grenades. As the students retreated to their schools, the military pursued them through the neighborhood, beating them. The rampage lasted three hours, and twenty students were arrested. Numerous students and teachers were beaten. The reason for the attack remains unknown.

Suddenly the student movement had a cause that resonated with the Mexican public—government brutality. The next step happened three days later. A group of students decided to march to demand the release of the arrested students and protest against violence. Up until this point, all of the student protests against political prisoners had been about activists from past movements, such as the one that had led to the railroad strike. Before this, they had never had any of their own in prison. Unlike the other demonstrations, this one drew more than a few students.

Fate likes to tease paranoids. The day of this demonstration happened to be July 26, and the downtown student march ran into the annual march of a handful of Fidel supporters. Combined, this year's July 26 march was the largest the Mexican government had ever seen. The army headed them off and steered them into side streets, where some protesters were throwing rocks at the soldiers. The demonstrators throwing the rocks did not look familiar to the students. And they found the rocks in trash cans, which was curious because downtown Mexico City trash cans did not generally contain rocks. Days of battles followed. Buses were commandeered, the passengers were forced out, and the buses were driven into walls and set on fire.

The students claimed that these and other acts of violence were carried out by military plants to justify the army's brutal response, an accusation that was largely confirmed in documents released in 1999. The government blamed the violence on the youth arm of the Communist Party. By the end of the month at least one student was dead, hundreds injured, and unknown numbers in prison. Each encounter was a recruitment for the next: The more injured and imprisoned, the more students demonstrated against the brutality.

In the beginning of August the students organized a council with representatives from the various schools in Mexico City. It was called the National Strike Council—the CNH. The CNH, unlike Mexico itself, but very much like SDS, SNCC, and so many sixties protest organizations, was scrupulously democratic. Students voted for delegates, and the CNH decided everything by the votes of these three hundred delegates. Roberto Escudero was the oldest delegate, elected by the graduate school of philosophy where he was studying Marxism. He said, "The CNH could debate for ten or twelve hours on ideology. I will give you an example. The government proposed a dialogue. CNH said it had to be a public dialogue—because they controlled all information that was not in the open. It was one of the problems, the government wanted everything secret. So the government called to discuss this idea of a dialogue. The CNH had a ten-hour debate on whether this phone call was a violation of their principle of only having public dialogue."

Like the Polish students four months earlier, Mexican student demonstrators carried signs protesting the press's complete adherence to the government line, but they were left with no way to disseminate to the general public truthful information about what was happening and why they were protesting. So in response to the fact that the PRI controlled all the news media, they invented the Brigades, each of which had between six and fifteen people and each of which was named after a sixties cause or personality. One was called the Brigade Alexander Dubček. The Brigades mounted street theater. They would go to markets and other public places and stage conversations, sometimes arguments, each playing a role, acting out a scene in which current events were discussed; and people overhearing these loud conversations would learn about things they never read in the newspaper. It worked because societies with completely corrupt press learn to pick up news on the street.

In September Díaz Ordaz's nightmare became reality. A French student from the May Paris movement arrived in Mexico to instruct students. But he did not teach about revolution or building barricades or making Molotov cocktails, all of which the Mexican students seemed to have already learned anyway. The architecture student Jean-Claude Leveque had been trained during the French student uprising in silk-screen poster making by Beaux Arts students. Now Mexico City became covered with images printed on cheap Mexican paper of silhouetted soldiers bayoneting and clubbing students, a man with a padlocked mouth, the press with a snaked tongue and dollars over the eyes. There were even Olympic posters with a vicious monkey, who unmistakably resembled a certain president, wearing a combat helmet.

But Mexico was different from France. In Mexico a number of students were shot while trying to put up posters or write graffiti on walls.

By August student demonstrations and the accompanying army violence spread to other states. One student was reported killed in Villahermosa, the capital of Tabasco state. In Mexico City the CNH was able to call out fifty thousand protesters to demonstrate on the

*"Demand the solution to Mexico's problems." A 1968 silk-screen poster
of the Consejo Nacional de Huelga. The figure in the back holding
up the book is taken from posters of the Chinese Cultural Revolution.
(Amigos de la Unidad de Postgrado de la Escuela de Diseño A.C.)*

issue of army violence. *U.S. News & World Report* ran an article in
August that said Mexico was having disturbances "on the eve" of the
Olympics. This was exactly what Díaz Ordaz did not want to see, the
Mexico City Olympics beginning to look like the Chicago convention.
"Before the troops could restore calm about 100 buses were burned or
damaged, shops sacked, four students killed and 100 wounded." The
authorities blamed the violence on "Communist agitators directed
from outside Mexico." According to the Mexican government, among
those arrested were five Frenchmen "identified as veteran agitators" of
the student uprising in May in Paris. No names or further identification
was offered. But the magazine pointed out that there were "other
factors," including discontent over one-party rule.

By the end of August more than one hundred thousand people were
marching in the student demonstrations, sometimes several hundred

thousand, but the students suspected that many of the marchers were actually government agents placed there to provoke violence. Díaz Ordaz decided to play Charles de Gaulle—usually a mistake for any head of state—and stage a huge demonstration in support of the government. But apparently he did not think he could draw the crowds, so he forced government workers to be bused into the center of Mexico City. One of the more memorable scenes involved office workers taking off their high-heeled shoes and furiously whacking them against the armor of tanks to express their fury at being forced to participate.

In addition to his determination to save the Olympics, his fear of destabilization, and his frustration at his inability to control the students, Gustavo Díaz Ordaz must have been shocked by what was taking place. He was an extremely formal man from the nearby state of Puebla, on the other side of the volcanoes from the capital. Puebla was a deeply conservative place. He came from a world in which men, even young men, still wore suits and ties. In his world it was acceptable for the president to be derided with wit at cocktail parties, but not to be ridiculed openly in public, portrayed as a monkey or a bat in public parades. These youth had no respect for authority—no respect for anything, it seemed.

Every year on the first of September the president of Mexico delivers the *Informe,* the State of the Union address. In September 1968 Gustavo Díaz Ordaz said in his *Informe,* "We have been so tolerant that we have been criticized for our excessive leniency, but there is a limit to everything, and the irremediable violations of law and order that have occurred recently before the very eyes of the entire nation cannot be allowed to continue." His speeches often had a threatening quality to them, but this one, in which he assured the world that the Olympics would not be disturbed, sounded especially menacing. The phrase everyone remembered was "We will do what we have to." Like Alexander Dubček with the Soviets, the Mexican students did not know with whom they were dealing. Martínez de la Roca said, "It was a threat, but we didn't really listen."

The demonstrations continued. On September 18 at 10:30 at night the army surrounded the UNAM campus with troops and armored vehicles and, using a pincer movement, closed in and evacuated buildings, rounding up hundreds of students and faculty, ordering them to either stand with hands up or lie on the ground where they were. They were held at gunpoint, bayonet point in many cases, while the army continued their siege of the entire campus, building by building. It is not known how many faculty members and students were arrested, some to be released the next day. More than a thousand were thought to have been held in prison.

On September 23, at the Polytechnic, the police invaded and the students fought them back with sticks. Then the army came— Obregón's Army of the People—and for the first time fired their weapons at students. *The New York Times* reported forty wounded. They also reported exchanges of gunfire and one policeman killed, although there is no evidence of the students ever having possessed firearms. Unidentified "vigilantes," probably soldiers out of uniform, started attacking schools and shooting at students.

The violence was escalating. Finally, on October 2 the government and the National Strike Council had a meeting. According to Raúl Álvarez Garín, one of the CNH delegates, the long-awaited dialogue was a disaster. "There was no dialogue with the government. We didn't say anything." One of the street posters that month showed bayonets and the caption "Dialogue?" "The meeting ended very badly," Roberto Escudero recalled, and the CNH moved on to the rally at which they were to announce a hunger strike for political prisoners for the next ten days until the opening day of the Olympics. Then on that day they would again try to negotiate with the government. The rally to announce the plan was to be at a place called Tlatelolco.

The students did not understand that a decision had already been made. The government had concluded that these students were not Pancho Villas—they were Zapatas.

If this story had been written by an ancient Greek tragedian, it would have played its final scene at Tlatelolco. It is as though it were fated to end in this place. Mexican stories often start out being about the threatening foreigner but always end up being about Mexico, about what Paz called "its hidden face: an Indian, Mestizo face, an angry, blood-splattered face." Martínez de la Roca loved talking about American influences, about the Black Panthers and civil rights. But looking back on the speeches of the CNH, he was surprised to realize how nationalistic they were with their speeches about violating the constitution and the ideals of Zapata. And so their story turns out not to be about Che, or the Sorbonne, or Cohn-Bendit, or even Berkeley; it is about Montezuma and Cortés and Carranza, about Obregón and Villa and Zapata. It was played out in a place the Mexican government called *La Plaza de las Tres Culturas,* the Plaza of Three Cultures—but the event is always identified by the Aztec name for the place, Tlatelolco.

If a single place could tell the history of Mexico, its conquests, its slaughters, its ambitions, defeats, victories, and aspirations, it would be Tlatelolco. When Montezuma ruled an Aztec empire from the island of Tenochtitlán in the high mountain lake that is now the site of Mexico City, one of the small affiliated allies was the nearby kingdom of Tlatelolco, a thriving commercial hub in the empire, a market center, whose last ruler was the young Cauhtemoctzin, who came to power in 1515, four years before the Spanish took control. The Spanish destroyed Tlatelolco, and in the midst of its ruins they built a church, a habit they developed when destroying Muslim areas in Iberia. In 1535 a Franciscan convent was built in the name of Santiago, the patron saint of the newly united Spain.

In the 1960s the Mexican government added its own presence in this spot of conquest and destruction, a high-rise Ministry of Foreign Relations and a huge, sprawling, middle-class housing project made up of long concrete blocks each given the name of a state or an important date in Mexican history. The buildings went on for miles—good apartments at subsidized rents for loyal PRI families, a PRI stronghold in the center of town. Not that there was any opposition. But the buildings stood as proof that PRI delivered. In 1985 this exemplary construction proved not to be of the quality that PRI had claimed, and it was a whispered scandal when most of the buildings tumbled, faltered, or collapsed in an earthquake. The Aztec ruins and the Franciscan church, on the other hand, were barely damaged.

Tlatelolco consists of a flagstone-paved plaza surrounded on two sides by the black stone and white mortar walls of a considerable complex of Aztec ruins. The church also faces the plaza on one of these sides. In the front and on the other side are housing projects. The building in front, the Edificio Chihuahua, has an open-air hallway on the third floor where people can stand in front of a waist-high concrete wall and look out at the plaza.

It is the kind of place an experienced political organizer would not choose. The police had only to block a few passageways between buildings and the plaza would be sealed off. Even the army operation at UNAM allowed a few quick students to slip out. But from Tlatelolco there would be no escape.

The rally was scheduled to begin at 4:00. By 3:00 police were already stopping cars from entering the downtown area. Determined people came on foot—couples, families with small children. Only between five thousand and twelve thousand people went into the plaza, depending on whose estimate is believed—one of the smallest showings

since the troubles started in July. It was a rally to make an announcement and not a mass demonstration.

Myrthokleia González Gallardo, a twenty-two-year-old CNH delegate from the Polytechnic Institute, went despite her parents' pleas not
to; they feared something terrible would happen. But she felt that she
had to go. Progressives in Mexico were just beginning to think about
women's rights, and she was one of only nine women of the three
hundred delegates. "The CNH did not listen as much when a woman
spoke," she recalled. But she had been chosen to introduce the four
speakers, which was an unusually high-profile role for a woman.

"As I approached Tlatelolco with the four speakers I was to introduce," she recalled, choked with tears thinking about it thirty-four
years later to the month, "we were warned to be careful, that the army
had been seen nearby. But I wasn't afraid, though we decided to make
it a short meeting. There were workers, students, families coming into
the plaza, filling it up. We didn't see any army in the plaza."

They went up the elevator to the third-floor balcony of Edificio
Chihuahua, a commanding perch from where they could address the
crowd in the plaza. "We took our place on the third floor and started
the speeches," she said. "Suddenly, off to the left, over the church, were
helicopters with a green light. Suddenly everyone down in the plaza
started falling. And then men with white gloves and weapons
appeared, maybe from the elevator. They ordered us down to the
ground floor, where they began beating us." In the background she
heard the *tap-tap-tap* of automatic weapons fire.

The Mexican army had two chains of command, the regular army,
which reported to the Joint Chiefs of Staff and the Ministry of Defense,
and the Battalion Olympia, which reported directly to the president. It
seemed soldiers from both organizations were there. The soldiers of the
Battalion Olympia were disguised in civilian clothes. But in order to
recognize one another, each wore one white glove, as though this clue
would not be noticed by others. These soldiers went up to the third
floor of the Edificio Chihuahua and mingled with the CNH leaders.
Then, as Myrthokleia Gonzalez Gallardo began speaking, they opened
fire at the crowd below. Many eyewitnesses describe these men as
"snipers," which implies precision marksmen, but in fact they fired
indiscriminately into the crowd, hitting protesters but also the regular
army. One of the first people hit was an army general.

The army fired back furiously at the balcony where the men with
white gloves were shooting, but also where the CNH leaders stood.

The men in white gloves appeared to panic and forget that they were undercover. "Don't fire!" they were heard to shout down. "We are the Battalion Olympia!"

According to witnesses, automatic fire continued in the plaza and many witnesses spoke of "snipers" in the windows of the Edificio Chihuahua. Raúl Álvarez Garín, one of the CNH leaders on the balcony, was taken with many others to the side of the plaza between the Aztec ruins and the ancient Franciscan church and forced to stand with his face to the wall. These prisoners could see nothing. But Álvarez Garín clearly remembers hearing constant automatic gunfire for two and a half hours.

The crowd ran toward the space between the church and the Edificio Chihuahua, but it was blocked by soldiers. Others tried the other side of the church between the ruins, but all escapes were blocked by soldiers. They tried to run into the church, which was supposed to be open at all times to give sanctuary, but the massive sixteenth-century doors were barred and snipers were shooting from the Moorish curves of the scalloped wall along the domed roof. It was a perfect trap. A few of the survivors have stories of soldiers taking pity and helping them out.

The sound of automatic fire for two hours or more is one of the most consistent reports from witnesses. Others, including González Gallardo, remember seeing the army attacking with rifles and bayonets. Bodies were seen being piled up in several downtown locations. Martínez de la Roca, who had already been arrested and locked in a small Lecumberri cell, saw the prison fill up with bleeding prisoners, some with gunshot wounds.

The Mexican government said four students were killed, but the number grew to about a dozen. The government-controlled newspapers also gave small numbers, if any. Television simply reported that there had been a police incident. El Universal on October 3 reported twenty-nine dead and more than eighty wounded. El Sol de México reported snipers firing on the army, resulting in 1 general and 11 soldiers wounded and more than 20 civilians killed. The New York Times also reported "at least 20 dead," whereas The Guardian of London reported 325 dead, a figure then cited by Octavio Paz, who ended his diplomatic career in protest. Some said thousands were dead. And there were thousands missing. Myrthokleia González Gallardo's parents, who had warned her not to go, spent ten miserable days with the Red Cross looking for their daughter among the dead. After ten days they discovered her in prison. Many were in prisons. Álvarez Garín spent two years and seven months in a cramped Lecumberri cell. He was elected head of his cell block. "It was the only election I ever won!" he said. Martínez de la Roca also served three years in prison.

For many years it was difficult to say if a missing person had been killed, was in prison, or had joined the guerrillas. Many did join armed guerrilla groups in rural areas. Families were hesitant to make too much of their son or daughter being missing because it might help the government identify their child with an armed group if that turned out to be the case. Today human rights groups claim five hundred Mexicans allegedly connected to guerrilla groups were killed by the military in the 1970s. But no mass graves have been found from Tlatelolco or any of the later killings. There were cases of whole families being threatened if they persisted in asking about a missing relative from 1968. Martínez de la Roca said, "Families don't come forward about missing children because they have received anonymous phone calls saying, 'If you say anything, all your other children will die.' I understand. When I was a kid someone killed my father and told me if I didn't keep quiet about it, he would kill my older brother. So I didn't say anything."

In the year 2000, Myrthokleia González Gallardo happened across a friend from student times who was amazed to see her. All these years the friend had assumed Myrthokleia had been killed in the plaza.

In 1993, for the twenty-fifth anniversary of the massacre, the government gave permission for a monument to be placed in the plaza. Survivors, historians, and journalists searched for the names of victims but could come up with only twenty names. There was another effort in 1998 that yielded only a few more names. Most Mexicans who have tried to unravel the mystery estimate that between one hundred and two hundred people were killed. Some estimates are higher still. Someone was seen filming from a distance on one of the high floors of the Foreign Ministry, but the film has never been found.

After October 2, the student movement dissolved. The Olympics progressed without any local disturbances. Gustavo Díaz Ordaz's chosen successor was Luis Echeverria, the minister of the interior who worked with him on repressing the student movement. Until he died in 1979, Díaz Ordaz insisted that one of his great accomplishments as president was the way he handled the student movement and averted any embarrassment during the games.

But very much in the same way that the invasion of Czechoslovakia was the end of the Soviet Union, Tlatelolco was the unseen beginning of the end of the PRI. Álvarez Garín said in a remarkably bold 1971 book on the massacre by Mexican journalist Elena Poniatowska, "All of us were reborn on October 2. And on that day we also decided how we are all going to die; fighting for genuine justice and democracy."

In July 2000, for the first time in seventy-one years of existence, the

PRI was voted out of power, and it was done democratically, in a slow process over decades, without the use of violence. Today the press is far more free and Mexico much closer to being a true democracy. But it is significant that even with the PRI out of power, many Mexicans said they were afraid to be interviewed for this book, and some who had agreed, upon reflection, backed out.

The tall rectangular slab erected for the twenty-fifth anniversary lists the ages of the twenty victims. Many were eighteen, nineteen, twenty years old. At the bottom it adds, *"y muchos otros campañeros cuyos nombres y edades aún no conocemos"*—and many more comrades whose names and ages are unknown.

Every year in October, Mexicans of the '68 generation start crying. Mexicans have a very long memory. They still remember how the Aztecs abused other tribes and argue over whether the princess Malinche's collaboration with Cortés, betraying the Aztec alliance, was justifiable. There is still lingering bitterness about Cortés. Nor is it forgotten how the French connived to take over Mexico in 1862. The peasants still remember the unfulfilled promises of Emiliano Zapata. And it is absolutely certain that Mexicans will long remember what happened on October 2, 1968, amid the Aztec ruins of Tlatelolco.

PART IV

THE FALL
OF NIXON

It is not an overstatement to say that the destiny of the entire
human race depends on what is going on in America today. This
is a staggering reality to the rest of the world; they must feel like
passengers in a supersonic jet liner who are forced to watch
helplessly while a passel of drunks, hypes, freaks, and madmen
fight for the controls and the pilot's seat.

—ELDRIDGE CLEAVER, Soul on Ice, *1968*

CHAPTER 20

THEORY AND PRACTICE FOR THE FALL SEMESTER

Do you realize the responsibility I carry? I am the only person standing between Nixon and the White House.
—JOHN FITZGERALD KENNEDY, *1960*

I believe that if my judgment and my intuition, my gut feeling, so to speak about America and American political tradition is right, this is the year that I will win.
—RICHARD M. NIXON, *1968*

PRESIDENT GUSTAVO DÍAZ ORDAZ of Mexico formally proclaimed the opening of the games of the XIX Olympiad yesterday in a setting of pageantry, brotherhood and peace before a crowd of 100,000 at the Olympic Stadium in Mexico City." So read the lead on page one of *The New York Times* and in major newspapers around the world. Díaz Ordaz got the coverage he had killed for. The dove of peace was the symbol of the games, decorating the boulevards where students were lately beaten, and billboards proclaimed, "Everything Is Possible with Peace." It was generally agreed that the Mexicans were running a good show, and the opening ceremonies were hailed for pomp as each team presented its flag to the regally perched Díaz Ordaz, *El Presidente,* the former El Chango. And no one could help but be moved as the Czechoslovakian team marched into the stadium to an international standing ovation. For the first time in history, the Olympic torch was lit by a woman, which was deemed considerable progress since the ancient Greek Olympics, where a woman caught at an Olympiad was executed. There was no longer any sign of the student movement in Mexico, and if it was mentioned, the government simply explained in the face of all logic that the movement had been an

¡LIBERTAD
DE EXPRESION!

*"Freedom of expression." 1968 student silk-screen
poster with the logo of the Mexico City
Olympics at the bottom
(Amigos de la Unidad de Postgrado
de la Escuela de Diseño A.C.)*

international communist plot hatched by the CIA. Yet the size of the crowd was disappointing to the Mexican planners. There were even empty hotel rooms in Mexico City.

The United States, as predicted, assembled one of the best track and field teams in history. But then politics began to chip away at it. Tommie Smith and John Carlos, receiving gold and bronze medals for the 200-meter dash, came to the medal presentation shoeless, wearing long black socks. As the U.S. national anthem played, each raised one black gloved hand in the fist that symbolized Black Power. It looked like a spontaneous gesture, but in the political tradition of 1968, the act was actually the result of a series of meetings between the athletes. The black gloves had been bought because they had anticipated receiving the medals from eighty-one-year-old Avery Brundage, the president of the International Olympic Committee, who had spent most of the year trying to get South Africa's segregated team into the games. Certain that they would win medals, they planned to use the gloves to refuse Brundage's hand. But in a change of plans, Brundage was at a different event. Observant fans might have noticed that they had split one pair of gloves, Smith using the right hand and Carlos the left. The other pair of gloves was worn by 400-meter runner Lee Evans, a teammate and fellow student of Harry Edwards's at San Jose State. Evans was in the stands returning the Black Power salute, but no one noticed.

The next day Carlos was interviewed on one of the principal boulevards of Mexico City. He said, "We wanted all the black people in the world—the little grocer, the man with the shoe repair store—to know that when that medal hangs on my chest or Tommie's, it hangs on his also."

The International Olympic Committee, especially Brundage, was furious. The American contingent was divided between those who were outraged and those who wanted to keep their extraordinary team together. But the committee threatened to ban the entire U.S. team. Instead they settled for the team banning Smith and Carlos, who were given forty-eight hours to leave the Olympic Village. Other black athletes also made political gestures, but the Olympic committee seemed to go out of its way to find reasons why these offenses were not as severe. When the American team swept the 400-meter, winners Lee Evans, Larry James, and Ron Freeman appeared at the medal ceremony wearing black berets and also raising their fists. But the International Olympic Committee was quick to point out that they didn't do this while the national anthem was being played and therefore had not insulted the flag. They in fact removed their berets during the anthem. Also, much was made of the fact that they were smiling when they raised their fists. Smith and Carlos had been somber. And so, as in the days of slavery, the smiling Negro with a nonthreatening posture was not to be punished. Nor did bronze medal–winning long jumper Ralph Boston, going barefoot in the ceremonies, achieve condemnation for his protest. Long jumper Bob Beamon, who on his first attempt jumped 29 feet 2.5 inches, breaking the world record by almost 2 feet, received his long jump gold medal with his sweat pants rolled up to show black socks, which was also accepted.

The original incident at the medal presentations of Smith and Carlos attracted almost no attention in the packed Olympic stadium. It was only the television coverage, the camera zooming in on the two as though everyone in the stadium were doing the same, that made this one of the most remembered moments of the 1968 games. Smith, who had broken all records running 200 meters in 19.83 seconds, had his career in sports overshadowed by the incident, but whenever asked he has always said, "I have no regrets." He told the Associated Press in 1998, "We were there to stand up for human rights and to stand up for black Americans."

On the other hand, an unknown nineteen-year-old black boxer from Houston had his career shadowed by the Olympics for doing the reverse of Smith. After George Foreman won the heavyweight gold medal in 1968 by defeating the Soviet champion Ionas Chepulis, he pulled out from somewhere a tiny American flag. Had he been carrying it during the fight? He began waving it around his head. Nixon liked the performance and contrasted him favorably with those other anti-war young Americans who were always criticizing America. Hubert Humphrey pointed out that the young man with the flag when interviewed in the ring had saluted the Job Corps that Nixon was threatening to disband. But to many boxing fans, especially black ones, it had seemed like a moment of Uncle Tomism, and when Foreman went professional some started referring to him as the Great White Hope, especially when he faced the beloved Muhammad Ali, who beat him in an upset in Zaire, where all of black Africa and much of the world cheered Ali's victory. It was a humiliation from which Foreman did not recover for years.

Yet through this year of upheavals and bloodshed, the baseball season glided eerily, as false and happy as a Norman Rockwell painting. Names like Mickey Mantle and Roger Maris, Maris now traded to the St. Louis Cardinals, were still popping up, names that belonged to another age, before there were the sixties, before the Gulf of Tonkin Resolution, when most Americans had never heard of a place called Vietnam. On April 27, less than a mile from besieged Columbia University, Mickey Mantle hit his 521st home run against the Detroit Tigers, tying Ted Williams for fourth place in career home runs. The night Bobby Kennedy was shot in Los Angeles, the Dodgers were playing in town and thirty-one-year-old right-handed pitcher Don Drysdale threw his sixth consecutive shutout, this time against the Pittsburgh Pirates. This broke Doc White's sixty-four-year-old record for consecutive shutouts. On September 19, the day before the Mexican army seized UNAM, Mickey Mantle hit his 535th home run, breaking Jimmie Foxx's record, to become the third-biggest career home run producer in history, behind only Willie Mays and Babe Ruth. The massacre at Tlatelolco shared front pages with the Cardinals' Bob Gibson, who, while the massacre was unfolding, struck out seventeen Detroit Tigers in the opening game of the World Series, beating Sandy Koufax's memorable fifteen strikeouts against the Yankees in 1963.

Baseball was having a great season, but it was getting difficult to care. Attendance was low in almost every stadium except Detroit, where the Tigers had their first good team in memory. Some of the stadiums were in neighborhoods associated with black rioting. Some fans thought that the pitching had gotten too good at the expense of hitting. Some thought that football, with its fast-growing audience, was more violent and therefore better suited to the times. The 1968 World Series was expected to be one of history's finest pitching duels, between Detroit's Denny McLain and St. Louis's Bob Gibson. It was a seven-game series in which the Tigers, after losing three out of four games, came back to win the next three, thanks to the unexpectedly brilliant pitching of Mickey Lolich. For baseball fans it was a seven-game break from the year 1968. For the rest, Gene McCarthy—who was said to have been a respectable semiprofessional first baseman—said that the best ball players were men who "were smart enough to understand the game and not smart enough to lose interest in it."

The only thing as out of step with the times as baseball was Canada, which was in the strange embrace of something called Trudeaumania. This country that became the home to an estimated fifty to one hundred U.S. military deserters and hundreds more draft dodgers was becoming a weirdly happy place. Pierre Elliott Trudeau became the new Liberal prime minister of Canada. Trudeau was one of the few prime ministers in the history of Canada to have been described as flashy. At forty-six and unmarried, he was the kind of politician whom people wanted to meet, touch, kiss. He was known for his unusual dress, sandals, a green leather coat, and for other unpredictable whimsy. He even once slid down the bannister of the House of Commons while holding piles of legislation. He practiced yoga, loved skin diving, and had a brown belt in karate. He had a stack of prestigious graduate degrees from Harvard, London, and Paris and until 1968 was known more as an intellectual than a politician. In fact, one of the few things he was not known to have experienced very much of was politics.

As Americans faced the bleak choice of Humphrey or Nixon, *Time* magazine captured the thinking of many Americans when it wrote:

The U.S. has seldom had occasion to look north to Canada for political excitement. Yet last week, Americans could envy Canadians the exuberant dash of their new Prime Minister Pierre Elliot Trudeau who, along with intellect and political skill, exhibits a swinger's panache, a lively style, an imaginative approach to its nation's problems. A great many U.S. voters yearn for a fresh political experience. . . .

In a time of extremism, he was a moderate with a lefty style, but his exact positions were almost impossible to establish. He was from Quebec and of French origin, but he spoke both languages beautifully and it was so uncertain whose side he was on that many hoped he might be able to resolve the French-English squabble that consumed much of Canada's political debate. While most Canadians were against the war in Vietnam, he said he thought the bombing should halt but that he was not going to tell the United States what to do. A classic Trudeauism: "We Canadians have to remember that the United States is kind of a sovereign state too." He was once apprehended in Moscow for throwing snowballs at a statue of Stalin. But he was sometimes accused of communism. Once, when asked flat out if he was a communist, he answered: "Actually I am a canoeist. I've canoed down the Mackenzie, the Coppermine, the Saguenay rivers. I wanted to prove that a canoe was the most seaworthy vessel around. In 1960 I set out from Florida to Cuba—very treacherous waters down there. Some people thought I was trying to smuggle arms to Cuba. But I ask you, how much arms can you smuggle in a canoe?"

It is a rare politician who can get away with answers like that, but in 1968, with the rest of the world turned so earnest, Canadians were laughing. Trudeau, with his lack of political experience, would say that the voters had put him up to running as a kind of joke. And now they "are stuck with me." Fellow Canadian Marshall McLuhan described Trudeau's face as a "corporate tribal mask." "Nobody can penetrate it," McLuhan said. "He has no personal point of view on anything."

On social issues, however, his position was clear. Despite a reputation for womanizing, he took strong stands on women's issues, including liberalizing abortion laws, and he was also an outspoken advocate of rights for homosexuals. Prior to the April election, Trudeau had always been seen in a Mercedes sports car. A reporter asked him, now that he was prime minister, whether he was going to give up the Mercedes. Trudeau answered, "Mercedes the car or Mercedes the girl?"

When Trudeau died in 2000 at the age of eighty, both former president Jimmy Carter and Cuban leader Fidel Castro were honorary pallbearers.

The Beatles also surprised everyone with their lack of stridency, or lack of commitment, depending on the point of view. In the fall of 1968 they released their first self-produced record—a single with "Revolution" on one side and "Hey, Jude" on the other. "Revolution" carried the message "We all want to change the world"—but we should do it moderately and slowly. The Beatles were attacked for the stance in many places, including the official Soviet press, but by the end of 1968 many people agreed. By the fall, when there is usually a sense of renewal, there was instead a feeling of weariness.

Not everyone felt it. Student activists returned to school hoping to resume where they had left off in the spring, while the schools hoped to go back to the way things were before. When the Free University of Berlin opened in mid-October, the women's dormitories had been occupied by men for most of the summer. The university gave in and announced that the dormitories would henceforth be coeducational.

At Columbia, the radical students hoped to continue and even internationalize the movement. In June the London School of Economics and the BBC had invited New Left leaders from ten countries to a debate it called "Students in Revolt." Student movements seized on this opportunity. Opponents such as de Gaulle talked of an international conspiracy, and the students thought this might be a good idea. The fact was, they had mostly never met one another, except those who had gone to Berlin for the spring anti-Vietnam march.

Columbia SDS had decided to send Lewis Cole, as Rudd said impatiently, "because he chain-smoked *Gauloises*." In truth, Cole was the group intellectual most fluent in Marxist theory. Cole and Rudd were being regularly invited on the better talk shows such as David Susskind and William Buckley.

At Columbia, SDS students felt the need for an ideology that fit their action program. Martin Luther King had had his moral imperative, but since these students hadn't come from religious backgrounds, this approach did not suit most of them. The communist approach of being part of a great party, the great movement—was too authoritarian. The Cuban approach was too militaristic. "There was an idea in SDS that we have the practice but the Europeans have the theory," said Cole. Cohn-Bendit had the same view. He said, "The Americans have no patience for theory. They just act. I was very impressed with this American Jerry Rubin, just do it." But at Columbia, where the students had been so successful at getting attention, they were feeling the need for an underlying theory that could explain why they were doing the things they did. Cole admitted to a feeling of intimidation at the prospect of debating with skilled European theoreticians.

The London meeting was almost stopped by British immigration, which tried to keep the radicals out. The Tories did not want to let Cohn-Bendit in, but James Callaghan, the home secretary, interceded on his behalf, saying that exposure to British democracy would be good for him. Lewis Cole was stopped at the airport, and the BBC had to contact the government to get him in.

Cohn-Bendit immediately clarified to the press that they were not leaders but rather "megaphones, you know, loudspeakers of the movement," which was an accurate description of himself and many of the others. Cohn-Bendit engaged in a put-on. De Gaulle had first come to prominence in June 1940 when he left France, and in exile in Britain he made a famous broadcast to the French people asking them to keep resisting the Germans and not to follow the collaborationist government of Philippe Pétain. Cohn-Bendit now announced that he was asking for British asylum. "I will ask the BBC to reorganize the Free French radio as they did during the war." He said that he would copy de Gaulle's exact message, except that where he had said "Nazis" he would say "French fascists" and where he had said "Pétain" he would say "de Gaulle."

The debate was dominated by Tariq Ali, the Pakistani-born British leader who had once been president of the famous debating society the Oxford Union. Ali said that students renounced elections as a means for social change.

Afterward they all went to the grave of Karl Marx and had their picture taken.

Cohn-Bendit returned to Germany vowing that he would renounce his leadership and disappear into the movement. He said that he had fallen prey to "the cult of personalities" and that "power corrupts." He told the *Sunday Times* of London, "They don't need me. Whoever heard of Cohn-Bendit five months ago? Or even two months ago?"

Cole found it a confusing experience. He never did understand what Cohn-Bendit's ideology was, and he found Tariq Ali's debating skills offputting. The people he connected with most were from the German SDS, and he toured Germany afterward with "Kaday" Wolf. "In the end," he said, "the ones with the greatest similarities were the Germans. And the Germans had a lot of the same cultural influences—Marcuse and Marx. And an intense feeling of youth being incredibly alienated. A young person in young dress walks down a street in Germany and the older Germans just glared at him."

But by fall Cole was back at Columbia with a theory he had gleaned from the French called "exemplary action." The French had done exactly what the Columbia students were trying to do—analyze what they had done and evolve a theory from their actions. The theory of "exemplary action" was that a small group could take an action that would serve as a model for larger groups. Seizing Nanterre had been such an action.

Traditional Marxist-Leninism is contemptuous of such theories, which it labels "infantilism." In June Giorgio Amendola, a theoretician and member of the steering committee of the Italian Communist Party, the largest Communist Party in the West, attacked the Italian student movement for "extremist infantilism" and scoffed at the idea that they were qualified to lead a revolution without having built their mass base in the traditional Marxist approach. He termed it "revolutionary dilettantism." Lewis Cole said, "Exemplary action gave us our first theory. That was why we had so many meetings. The question was always, what do we do now?"

With their theory now in place, they were ready to be a revolutionary center to prepare, as Hayden had said, "two, three, many Columbias." The theory also helped the national office of the rapidly growing SDS become more of a command center. The first action at

SDS poster announcing a demonstration before election day, 1968
(Center for the Study of Political Graphics)

Columbia was a demonstration against the invasion of Prague. But that was still in August, and few people came. According to Cole, "It wasn't very well done. The slogan was 'Saigon, Prague, the pig is the same all over the world.' "

Columbia SDS, looking for an event to restart the movement, came up with the idea of hosting a student international, but from the outset it was a disaster. Two days before the conference began, the news broke of the student massacre in Mexico. Columbia students, feeling guilty because they had not even known that there was a student movement in Mexico, tried to organize a demonstration at the conference. But they were unable to come up with any consensus. The French situationists spent the second day doing parodies of everyone who spoke. To some, it was a welcome diversion from too much speaking. Cole recalled, "We found that there were huge differences between all of us. All we could agree on was antiauthoritarianism, and alienation from society, these sorts of cultural issues." Increasingly, the other delegations grew irritated at the French, especially the Americans, who felt the French were lecturing them on Vietnam and failing to understand what a burning issue it was in the United States.

In Mark Rudd's assessment, "The Europeans were too pretentious, too intellectual. They only wanted to talk. It was more talk. People made speeches, but I realized nothing would happen."

Rudd had no doubt that he was at a historic moment, that a revolution was slowly unfolding and his job was to help it along. A bit of Che—"The first duty of a revolutionary is to make a revolution"— mixed with the notion called "bringing the war home" and the theory of exemplary action, and in June 1969 he came up with the Weathermen, a violent underground guerrilla group named after the Bob Dylan lyrics "You don't need a weatherman to know which way the wind blows." In March 1970 they changed their name to the Weather Underground because they realized that the original name was sexist. In hindsight, it seems evident that a guerrilla group started by middle-class men and women who name their group from a Bob Dylan song will likely be their own worst enemies. Their only victims were three of their own, who blew themselves up making bombs in a house in Greenwich Village. But others turned to violence as well. The government was violent. The police were violent. The times were violent and revolution was so close. David Gilbert, who had first knocked on Rudd's dormitory door to recruit him for SDS, continued after the mid-1970s when the Weather Underground dissolved and more than twenty years later was still in prison for his part in a fatal 1981 shootout. Many

1968 student radicals became 1970s underground guerrilla fighters in Mexico, Central America, France, Spain, Germany, and Italy.

Politics sometimes has longer tentacles than imagined. That fateful first day of spring when Rockefeller collapsed the earth from under the liberal wing of the Republican Party unleashed a chain of events that the United States has been living with ever since. A new kind of Republican was born in 1968. That became clear at the end of June, when President Johnson appointed Justice Abe Fortas to succeed Earl Warren as chief justice of the U.S. Supreme Court. Warren had resigned before the close of the Johnson administration because he believed Nixon would win and he did not want to see his seat taken over by a Nixon appointee. Fortas was a predictable choice, a friend of Johnson, who had appointed him to replace Arthur Goldberg three years earlier. Fortas had distinguished himself as a leader of the liberal activist judges who had characterized the Court since the mid-1950s. Although he was the fifth Jewish justice on the Court, he would have been the first Jewish chief justice.

At the time, the Senate rarely battled over Court appointments. Both Republican and Democratic senators recognized the right of the president to have his choice. In fact, there had not been a battle since John J. Parker, Herbert Hoover's appointee, was rejected by two votes in 1930.

But when Fortas was named there was an immediate outcry of "cronyism." Fortas was a long-standing friend and adviser to the president, but he was also eminently qualified. The charge of cronyism was more effective against Johnson's other appointment to take Fortas's seat, Homer Thornberry. Thornberry was an old friend of Johnson, who had advised him not to accept the vice presidential nomination and then changed his mind and was at Johnson's side when he was sworn in as president after John Kennedy's death. A congressman for fourteen years, he became an undistinguished circuit court judge. He had been a segregationist until Johnson came to power and then reversed his stance, coming out on the desegregation side of several notable cases.

But cronyism was not the main issue; it was the right of Johnson to appoint Supreme Court justices. Republicans, who had been in the White House only eight of the past thirty-six years, felt they had a good chance of taking over in 1968, and some Republicans wanted their own judges. Robert Griffin, Republican from Michigan, got nineteen Republican senators to sign a petition saying that Johnson, with only seven months left in office, should not get to pick two judges. There was absolutely nothing in law or tradition to back up this position. At that point in the twentieth century, Supreme Court judges had been appointed in election years six times. William Brennan had been named by Eisenhower one month before the election. John Adams picked his friend John Marshall, one of the most respected appointments in history, only weeks before Jefferson was to take office. Griffin simply wished to deny Johnson his appointments. "Of course, a lame duck president has the constitutional power to submit nominations for the Supreme Court," argued Griffin, "but the Senate need not confirm them." But Griffin and his coalition of right-wing Republicans and southern Democrats were not doing this completely on their own. According to John Dean, who later served as special counsel to President Nixon, candidate Nixon kept in regular contact with Griffin through John Ehrlichman, later the president's chief adviser on domestic affairs.

But the Democrats had an almost two-to-one majority and supported the appointments, and a great deal of the Republican leadership, including the minority leader, Everett Dirksen, did as well.

At his hearings Fortas was submitted to a grilling unprecedented in the history of chief justice appointees. He was attacked by a coalition of right-wing Republicans and southern Democrats. Among his chief inquisitors were Strom Thurmond of South Carolina and John Stennis of Mississippi, who denounced him for being a liberal in "decisions by which the Court has asserted its assumed role of rewriting the Constitution." It was a new kind of coalition, and in carefully coded language they were attacking Fortas and the Warren Court in general for desegregation and other pro–civil rights decisions as well as for protection for defendants and rulings tolerating pornography. Fifty-two cases were brought up in which it was claimed that in forty-nine of them Fortas's vote had prevented material from being ruled pornography; this was followed by a private, closed-door session in which the senators reviewed slides of the allegedly offensive material. Strom Thurmond even attacked Fortas for a decision made by the Warren Court before Fortas was on the bench. In October they managed to defeat the nomination with a filibuster, which requires a two-thirds majority to break. The pro-Fortas senators lacked fourteen votes, so the appointment was successfully tied up until the end of the congressional session—the first time in American history that a filibuster was used to try to block a Supreme Court appointment. Since Fortas would not be vacating his associate justice seat, Thornberry's nomination was dead also.

When Nixon came to power, he began to attack the Supreme Court, attempting to destroy liberal judges and replace them with judges, preferably from the South, who had an anti–civil rights record. The first target was Fortas, who was driven from the bench by a White House–created scandal for accepting fees in a manner that was common practice for Supreme Court justices. Fortas resigned. The next target was William O. Douglas, the seventy-year-old Roosevelt-appointed liberal. Gerald Ford spearheaded the impeachment drive for the White House but it failed. The attempt to place southerners with anti–civil rights records in the court failed. The first, Clement Haynsworth, was rejected by the Democratic majority still angry over the attack on Fortas. The second, G. Harrold Carswell, was found embarrassingly incompetent. But the Fortas attack plus bad health of elderly judges did give Nixon the unusual opportunity of appointing four Supreme Court judges in his first term, including the Justice Department's legal expert behind the Supreme Court attacks, William Rehnquist.

To the astute observer, Nixon's strategy, the new Republican strategy, was first presented at the Republican convention in Miami when he chose Maryland governor Spiro T. Agnew. Many thought the choice was a mistake. Given Rockefeller's popularity, Nixon-Rockefeller would have been a dream ticket. Even if Rockefeller wouldn't accept the number two spot, New York mayor John Lindsay, a handsome, well-liked liberal who had helped write the Kerner Commission report on racial violence, had made it clear that he was eager to run as Nixon's vice president. Conservative Nixon with liberal Lindsay would have brought to the Republican Party the full spectrum of American politics. Instead Nixon turned to the Right, picking a little-known and not much loved archconservative, with views, especially on race and law and order, that were so reactionary that to many he seemed an outright bigot.

Agnew, sensitive to the unusually hostile response to his nomination, complained, "It's being made to appear that I'm a little to the right of King Lear." The press took the obvious follow-up question, Why was King Lear a rightist? Agnew replied with a smile, "Well, he reserved to himself the right to behead people, and that's a rightist position." Quickly the smile vanished as he talked about the reception he was getting in the party and press. "If John Lindsay had been the candidate, there would have been the same outburst from the South and accolades from the Northeast." This was exactly the point. Agnew was part of a geographic strategy, what was known in politics as a "southern strategy."

For one hundred years, southern politics had remained frozen in

time. The Democratic Party had been the party of John Caldwell
Calhoun, the Yale-educated South Carolinian who fought in the
decades leading up to the Civil War for the southern plantation/slave-
owning way of life under the banner of states' rights. To white southerners, the Republican Party was the hated Yankee party of Abraham
Lincoln that had forced them to release their Negro property. After
Reconstruction, neither party had much to offer the Negro, so for
another century white southerners stayed true to their party and the
Democrats could count on a solid block of Democratic states in the
South. The point George Wallace was making in his independent runs
for president was that southern Democrats wanted something different
from what the Democratic Party was offering, even though they were
not going to become Republicans. Strom Thurmond of South Carolina
was expressing the same idea as early as 1948 when he ran against
Truman as the candidate for president for a party significantly named
the States' Rights Party.

In 1968 Thurmond, Abe Fortas's harshest interrogator, committed
the once unspeakable act of becoming a Republican. He was an early
supporter of Nixon's and worked hard for him at the Miami convention after getting Nixon's promise that he would not pick a running
mate who was distasteful to the South. So Lindsay had never really
been in the running, though he didn't know this.

In 1964, after Johnson signed the Civil Rights Act, close associates
said he was depressed and talked of his having just signed over the
entire South to the Republican Party. This was why he and Humphrey
had adamantly opposed seating the Mississippi Freedom Party at the
1964 Democratic convention. The inconsistent support from the president, attorney general, and other government agencies that the civil
rights movement experienced was the result of an impossible juggling
act the Democrats wanted to perform—promoting civil rights and
keeping the southern vote.

Many white liberals and blacks, including Martin Luther King, had
always been distrustful of the Kennedys and Johnson because they
knew these were Democrats who wanted to keep the white southern
vote. John Kennedy, in his narrow victory over Nixon, got white southern support. Johnson, as a Texan with a drawling accent, was particularly suspect, but John Kennedy's southern strategy was choosing him
for running mate. Comedian Lenny Bruce, in his not always subtle
satire, had a routine:

Lyndon Johnson—they didn't even let him talk for the first six
months. It took him six months to learn how to say Nee-Grow.

"Nig-ger-a-o . . ."
"O.K., ah, let's hear it one more time, Lyndon now."
"Nig-ger-a-o . . ."

After the Civil Rights Act, white bigots, if not blacks and white liberals, had no doubt about where Johnson stood. In the 1964 election Johnson defeated Goldwater by a landslide. Republicans bitterly blamed northern liberal Republicans, especially Nelson Rockefeller, for not getting behind the ticket. But in the South, for the first time, the Republican candidate got the majority of white votes. In a few states, enough black voters, including newly registered voters, turned out, combined with traditional die-hard southern democrats and liberals who hoped to change the South, to deny Goldwater a regionwide victory. But the only states that Goldwater carried, aside from his home state of Arizona, were Louisiana, Mississippi, Alabama, Georgia, and South Carolina.

Now Nixon was realigning the party. "States' rights" and "law and order," two thinly veiled appeals to racism, were mainstays of his campaign. States' rights, from the time of Calhoun, meant not letting the federal government interfere with the denial of black rights in southern states. "Law and order" had become a big issue because it meant using Daley-type police tactics against not only antiwar demonstrators, but black rioters as well. With each black riot, more white "law and order" voters came along, people who, like Norman Mailer, were "getting tired of Negroes and their rights." The popular term for it was "white backlash," and Nixon was after the backlash vote. Even that most moderate of black groups, the NAACP, recognized this. Philip Savage, NAACP director for Pennsylvania, New Jersey, and Delaware, called Agnew and Nixon "primarily backlash candidates." He said that having Agnew on the ticket "insures the Republican Party that it will not get a significant black vote in November."

In 1968 there were still black Republicans. Edward Brooke of Massachusetts, the only black senator and the first since Reconstruction—a moderate social progressive who served with Lindsay on the Kerner Commission—was a Republican. The Democratic Party had not yet become the black party. It was the nomination of Agnew that changed that. Most of the 78 black delegates to the Miami convention, out of a total of 2,666, went home either unwilling or unable to back the ticket. One black delegate told *The New York Times*, "There is no way in hell I can justify Nixon and Agnew to Negroes." A black Chicago delegate said, "They are telling us they want the white backlash and that they don't give a damn about us." The Republican Party lost its most

famous black supporter when Jackie Robinson, the first black to break
the color line in Major League baseball and one of the country's most
highly respected sports heroes, announced that he was quitting Rockefeller's Republican staff and going to work for the Democrats to help
defeat Nixon, calling the Nixon-Agnew ticket "racist."

Accurately defining the political party division of the future, Robinson said, "I think what the Republican Party has forgotten is that
decent white people are going to take a real look at this election, and
they're going to join with black America, with Jewish America, with
Puerto Ricans, and say that we can't go backward, we can't tolerate a
ticket that is racist in nature and that is inclined to let the South have
veto powers over what is happening."

One of the advantages of Agnew as a running mate was that he could
run a little wildly to the right, while Nixon, statesmanlike, could strike
a restrained pose. Agnew insisted that the antiwar movement was led
by foreign communist conspirators, but when challenged on who these
conspirators might be, he simply said that some SDS leaders had
described themselves as Marxists and he would have more information
on this later. "Civil disobedience," he said in Cleveland, "cannot be
condoned when it interferes with civil rights of others and most of the
time it does." Translation: The civil rights movement has impinged on
the civil rights of white people. He called Hubert Humphrey "soft on
communism" but retracted the statement with apologies after the
Republican congressional leaders, Everett Dirksen and Gerald Ford,
complained. Agnew said, "It is not evil conditions that cause riots but
evil men." Another famous Agnew declaration was, "When you have
seen one slum you've seen them all." And when criticized for using the
words *Jap* and *Polack,* the vice presidential candidate countered that
Americans were "losing their sense of humor."

Liberal Republicans struggled not to show their revulsion at the
ticket. Lindsay, whose city had seen its share of rioting and demonstrating from blacks, students, and antiwar protesters, wrote:

We have heard loud cries this year that we should insure our
safety by placing bayoneted soldiers every five feet, and by
running over nonviolent demonstrators who sit down in the
streets.

You can now see the kind of society that would be. Look to the
streets of Prague, and you will find your bayoneted soldier every
five feet. You will see the blood of young men—with long hair
and strange clothes—who were killed by tanks which crushed
their nonviolent protest against communist tyranny. If we aban-

don our tradition of justice and civil order, they will be *our* tanks and *our* children.

As for the Humphrey campaign that came limping out of Chicago, it was clear to Humphrey that he had to challenge Nixon on the right. His running mate, Senator Edmund Muskie from Maine, was an eastern liberal who helped solidify their natural base. The Left might be unhappy with Humphrey, but they were not going to turn to Nixon. His position on the war was that it was not an issue because North Vietnam "has had it militarily" and a peace would be negotiated before he came to office in January. But in the last weeks before the election, Humphrey started to speak out against the campaign of fear and racism and began to gain ground against Nixon. "If the voices of bigotry and fear prevail, we can lose everything we labored so hard to build. I can offer you no easy solutions. There is none. I can offer you no hiding place. There is none."

Humphrey added a new chapter to the fast-developing television age by campaigning on local TV. Traditionally, a politician would come to a town, arrange a rally, as large as possible, at the airport, and arrange an event at which he made a speech. Humphrey often did this, too, but in many towns he skipped it. The one thing he did everywhere he went was appear on the local television show. As for Nixon, he was probably not the last nontelegenic presidential candidate, but he was the last one to accept that about himself. It was widely believed that his five o'clock shadow on television during the debates had cost him the 1960 election. Significantly, the majority of people who only listened to the debates on radio thought Nixon had won. In 1968 a makeup team had worked out a regimen of pancake foundation and lighteners so that when the lights went on he did not look like the villain in a silent movie. His television coordinator, Roger Ailes, who believed his young age of twenty-eight to be his advantage, said, "Nixon is not a child of TV, and he may be the last candidate who couldn't make it on the Carson show who could make it in an election." In 1968 appearing on television talk shows had become the newest form of campaigning. Ailes said of Nixon, "He's a communicator and a personality on TV, but not at his best when they say on the show, 'Now here he is . . . Dick!' "

With the election only weeks away, the Humphrey-Muskie campaign started running peculiar but effective print ads. Never before had a front-runner been attacked in quite this way. "Eight years ago if anyone told you to consider Dick Nixon, you'd have laughed in his face." It went on to say, "November 5 is Reality Day. If you know, deep down, you cannot vote for Dick Nixon to be President of the United States you'd better stand up now and be counted." The ad included a campaign contribution coupon that read, "It's worth _____ to keep Dick Nixon from becoming President of the United States."

George Wallace was the wild card. Would he draw away enough southern voters to deny Nixon states, thus ruining his southern strategy? Or was he, like the old States' Rights Party, going to draw away traditional southern Democrats still loyal to the old party? Wallace told southern crowds that both Nixon and Humphrey were unfit for office because they supported civil rights legislation, which to cheering crowds he termed "the destruction of the adage that a man's home is his castle." Nixon had called Wallace "unfit" for the presidency. Wallace responded by saying that Nixon "is one of those Eastern moneyed boys that looks down his nose at every Southerner and every Alabamian and calls us rednecks, woolhats, peapickers and peckerwoods." Ironically, Nixon himself always thought he was up against "Eastern moneyed boys" himself.

Out of despair came frivolity. Yetta Brownstein of the Bronx ran as an independent, saying, "I figure we need a Jewish mother in the White House who will take care of things." There was a large bloc of people whose feelings about the election were best expressed by the candidacy of comedian Pat Paulsen, who said with his sad face and droning voice, "I think I'm a pretty good candidate because first I lied about my intention to run. I've been consistently vague on all the issues and I'm continuing to make promises that I'll be unable to fulfill." Paulsen deadpanned, "A good many people feel that our present draft laws are unjust. These people are called soldiers. . . ." His campaign began as a routine on *The Smothers Brothers Comedy Hour,* a popular television show. With Tom Smothers as his official campaign manager, Paulsen on the eve of the election was predicted by pollsters to attract millions of write-in votes.

In the last two weeks of the campaign, polls started to show that Nixon was losing that mystical mandate known in political races and baseball series as "momentum." The fact that Nixon's numbers were stagnant and Humphrey's continuing to grow implied a trend that could propel Humphrey.

The campaigns for the House of Representatives were gaining attention, becoming better financed and more contentious than they had been in many years. The reason was that there was a possibility, if Humphrey and Nixon ended up very close in electoral votes, with Wallace taking a few southern states, that no one would have a majority of state electoral votes, in which case the winner would be picked by the House. The voting public did not find this a very satisfying outcome. In fact, a Gallup poll showed that 81 percent of Americans favored dropping the electoral college and having the president elected by popular vote.

But on election day, Wallace was not an important factor. He took five states, denying them to Nixon, and Nixon swept the rest of the South except Texas. While the popular vote was one of the closest in American history—Nixon's margin of victory was about .7 percent—he had a comfortable margin in the electoral college. The Democrats kept control of both the House and Senate. Only 60 percent of eligible voters bothered to cast votes at all. Two hundred thousand voters wrote in for Pat Paulsen.

The Czechs saw the victory of Nixon, the old-time cold warrior, as a confirmation of U.S. opposition to Soviet occupation. Most Western Europeans worried that the change in the White House would slow down Paris peace talks. Developing nations saw it as a reduction in U.S. aid. Arab states were indifferent because Nixon and Humphrey were equally friendly to Israel.

Shirley Chisholm was elected the first black woman member of the House. Blacks gained seventy offices in the South, including the first black legislators in the twentieth century in Florida and North Carolina and three additional seats in Georgia. But Nixon won a clear majority of southern white votes. The strategy that undid Abe Fortas also elected Nixon, and it became *the* strategy of the Republican Party. The Republicans get the racist vote and the Democrats get the black vote, and it turns out in America there are more racist voters than black ones. No Democrat since John F. Kennedy has won a majority of white southern votes.

This is not to say that all white southern voters are racist, but it is clear what votes the Republicans pursue in the South. Every Republican candidate now talks of states' rights. In 1980 Ronald Reagan kicked off his presidential campaign in an obscure, backwater rural Mississippi town. The only thing this town was known for in the outside world was the 1964 murder of Chaney, Goodman, and Schwerner. But the Republican candidate never mentioned the martyred SNCC workers. What did he talk about in Philadelphia, Mississippi, to launch his campaign? States' rights.

CHAPTER 21

THE LAST HOPE

I am more impervious to minor problems now; when two of my people come to me red-faced and huffing over some petty dispute, I feel like telling them, "Well, the earth continues to turn on its axis, undisturbed by your problem. Take your cue from it. . . ."

— MICHAEL COLLINS, Carrying the Fire, 1974

Tom Hayden later wrote about 1968, "I suppose it was fitting that such a bad year would end with the election of Richard Nixon to the presidency." A Gallup poll showed that 51 percent of Americans expected him to be a good president. Six percent expected him to be "great," and another 6 percent expected him to be "poor." Nixon, looking exactly like the "Eastern moneyed boy" George Wallace accused the Californian of being, formed his cabinet from a thirty-nine-story-high luxury suite with a view of Central Park in New York's Hotel Pierre, conveniently close to his ten-room Fifth Avenue apartment. A hardworking man, he rose at seven, ate a light breakfast, walked the block and a half to the Pierre, passed through the lobby, according to reports, "almost unnoticed," and worked for the next ten hours. Among the visitors who seemed most to delight him was the University of Southern California star O. J. Simpson, the year's Heisman Trophy winner who had run more yards than any other player in history. "Are you going to use that option pass, O.J.?" the president-elect wanted to know.

For the two thousand high-level positions just below the cabinet, he told his staff he wanted as broad a search as possible. Taking his instructions to heart, they had a letter drafted personally from Nixon asking for ideas and sent it to the eighty thousand people in

Who's Who in America, which led to news stories that Nixon was consulting Elvis Presley, who happened to be listed in the book. Though traditionally presidents revealed their cabinet choices gradually, one by one, Nixon, trying to tame that new media that had been troubling his career for a decade, arranged to have his entire cabinet announced at once from a Washington hotel with prime-time coverage on all three television networks.

This was one of his rare television innovations. However, he did show a strange affinity for another piece of technology, which in time was his undoing—the tape recorder. The Johnson administration had been fairly restrictive in the use of wiretapping and eavesdropping devices, but in the spring of 1968 Congress had passed a crime bill that

1968 Yippie poster calling for a demonstration at the Nixon inauguration
(Library of Congress)

greatly liberalized the number of federal agencies that could use such devices and the circumstances under which they could be used. Johnson had signed the bill on June 19 but said he believed that Congress "has taken an unwise and potentially dangerous step by sanctioning eavesdropping and wiretapping by federal, state, and local officials in an almost unlimited variety of situations." Even after the bill passed, he instructed Attorney General Ramsey Clark to continue restricting the use of listening devices. But President-elect Nixon criticized the Johnson administration for not using the powers given by the new crime bill. Nixon called wiretaps and eavesdropping devices "law enforcement's most effective tool against crime."

He also had new ideas for listening devices. In December Nixon aides announced a plan to place listening posts in Birmingham, Alabama, and in Westchester County, New York, so that the president-elect could hear from "the forgotten American." The plan was for volunteers to tape conversations in a variety of neighborhoods, town meetings, schools, and gatherings so the president-elect could hear Americans talking. "Mr. Nixon said that he would find a way for the forgotten man to talk to government," a Westchester volunteer said.

The Chicago convention remained at the heart of one of America's increasingly hot debates, the so-called law and order issue. While revulsion at the comportment of Daley and the Chicago police was the first reaction to the riots, increasing numbers argued that Daley and his police were right to impose "law and order." In early December a government commission headed by Daniel Walker, vice president and general counsel of Montgomery Ward, issued its report on the Chicago riots under the title *Rights in Conflict*. The report concluded that the incident was nothing short of a "police riot" but also that the police were greatly provoked by protesters using obscene language. Not only the Left but the establishment press pointed out that police are quite accustomed to obscene language and wondered if this could really have been the cause for what seemed to be a complete breakdown of discipline. Mayor Daley himself was known to use unpublishable and unbroadcastable language.

The report described victims escaping from the police and the police responding by beating the next person they could find. It never did explore why McCarthy workers and supporters were targeted. *Life* magazine reported that the most corrupt police divisions were the most violent, implying that these were "bad cops" who did not take orders. But many of the demonstrators, including David Dellinger, remained convinced that far from a breakdown in discipline, "organized police violence was part of the plan," as Dellinger testified to Congress.

On the other side, there were still many people who believed the Chicago police were completely justified in their actions. So the Walker Report neither healed, resolved, nor clarified. The House Un-American Activities Committee conducted its own hearings, subpoenaing Tom Hayden and others from the New Left, though they did not hear from Jerry Rubin because he arrived in a rented Santa Claus costume and refused to change out of it. Abbie Hoffman was arrested for wearing a shirt patterned after an American flag. He was charged on a newly passed law making it a federal crime to show "contempt" for the flag. The committee's acting chairman, Missouri Democrat Richard H. Ichord, said that the Walker Report "overreacted," as did newsmen who covered the story. The keen eyes of the House Un-American Activities Committee had, not surprisingly, uncovered that the whole thing was a communist plot. Their evidence: Dellinger and Hayden had met with North Vietnamese and Viet Cong officials in Paris. "Violence follows these gentlemen just as night follows day," Ichord said, waxing nearly Shakespearean.

The Government Printing Office refused to print the Walker Report because the commission refused to delete the obscenities that witnesses accused demonstrators and police of shouting at one another. Walker said that deleting the words would "destroy the important tone of the report." Daley himself praised the report and criticized only the summary. As he walked out of the press conference, reporters shouted, "What about your police riot?" But the mayor had no comment.

The law with which Abbie Hoffman was arrested for his shirt was one of several laws passed by Congress to harass the antiwar movement, as Republicans and Democrats competed for the "law-and-order" vote in an increasingly repressive United States. Another of these 1968 laws made it a crime to cross state lines with the intent to commit violence. Federal prosecutors in Chicago were considering charging the leaders of the Chicago demonstrations with this untested law. But Johnson's attorney general Ramsey Clark had no enthusiasm for such a conspiracy trial. This changed when Nixon took office and appointed New York bonds lawyer John Mitchell attorney general. Mitchell once said that Clark's "problem" was that "he was philosophically concerned with the rights of the individual." He wanted a Chicago conspiracy trial and on March 20, 1969, Tom Hayden, Rennie Davis, David Dellinger, Abbie Hoffman, Jerry Rubin, Bobby Seale, John Froines, and Lee Weiner—who came to be known as the

"Chicago Eight"—were indicted. Hayden, Davis, Dellinger, Hoffman, and Rubin openly admitted organizing the Chicago demonstrations but denied causing the violence that even the government's Walker Report blamed on the police. But they barely knew Black Panther leader Bobby Seale. During the trial, Judge Julius Hoffman ordered Seale bound and gagged for repeatedly calling Hoffman a fascist. None of them understood how SDS activists Froines and Weiner had gotten on the list and in fact the two were the only ones acquitted. The others had their convictions reversed on appeal. But John Mitchell himself later went to prison for perjury in the Watergate investigation.

The Italians for a brief moment in November were gripped by the story of Franca Viola, who married the man she loved, a former schoolmate. Two years earlier she had rejected the son of a wealthy family, Filippo Melodia, so he kidnapped her and raped her. After being raped, a woman had to marry her aggressor because she had been dishonored and no one else would have her. This approach had worked for Sicilian men for about a thousand years. But Franca, to the applause of much of Italy, went into court and said to Melodia, "I do not love you. I will not marry you." This came as a blow to Melodia, not only because he had been rejected, but because under Sicilian law, if the woman doesn't marry the rapist, he is then tried for rape, a crime for which Melodia was sentenced to eleven years in prison.

On December 3 strikes and protests by both workers and students paralyzed Italy after two striking workers were shot and killed in Sicily. An anarchist bomb destroyed a government food office in Genoa. The bombers left flyers that said, "Down with Authority!" By December 5 Rome was closed by a general strike. But by December 6 the workers had ended their strike for higher wages and left tens of thousand of protesting students on their own.

In France, too, the idea of merging the worker and student movements was still alive but still failing. On December 4, Jacques Sauvageot met with union leaders in the hopes of building the unified front that had failed in the spring. De Gaulle had been artificially propping up the franc for more than a year simply because he believed in "the strong franc," and it was now seriously overvalued and declining rapidly in world currency markets. Instead of the normal fiscal maneuver of devaluing, he shocked Europe and the financial world by instituting a series of drastic measures to reduce social spending in order to try to uphold the declining currency. French workers were furious. On December 5 strikes began. But by December 12 the government had negotiated an end to the strikes and the students again found themselves alone when they shut down Nanterre to protest police attempts to interrogate students. The French government threatened to start expelling "student agitators" from the universities.

With each blow, it was predicted that de Gaulle would be tamed— when his prestige declined after the spring riots and strikes, when his foreign policy was shaken by the Soviet invasion of Czechoslovakia, when his economy was undone by the collapse of the franc. Yet at the end of the year, to the utter frustration of his European partners, he blocked British entry into the Common Market for the third time.

On November 7 Beate Klarsfeld, the non-Jewish German wife of French Jewish survivor and celebrated Nazi hunter Serge Klarsfeld, went to the social democrats convention in Berlin, walked up to Chancellor Kiesinger, accused him of being a Nazi, and slapped him in the face. By the end of 1968 the West German state had sent to prison 6,221 Germans for crimes committed during Nazi rule—a considerable number of convictions, but a minuscule percentage of Nazi criminals. In 1968 the West German state convicted a total of only thirty Nazis, almost all minor, obscure figures. Despite the numerous very active and murderous Nazi courts during Hitler's rule, not a single judge had ever been sent to prison. On December 6 a Berlin court acquitted Hans Joachim Rehse, a Nazi judge who had sentenced 230 people to death. The prosecution had chosen to try him on seven of the more arbitrary and flagrant abuses of justice, but the court ruled that the prosecution had shown only abuse of the law, not the intention to do so. The decision was based on an earlier case in which it was ruled that judges were not guilty "if they were blinded by Nazi ideology and the legal philosophy of that time." As Rehse left the courtroom, a crowd chanted, "Shame! Shame!" and an elderly man walked up and slapped him across the face. The following week eight thousand marched through Berlin to the city hall to protest Rehse's release. There was little time left. The federal statute for prosecuting Nazi crimes was to expire in one more year, December 31, 1969.

During the summer of 1968, the Spanish government had placed the Basque province of Guipúzcoa under indefinite martial law. In the village of Lazcano, the village priest denounced the organist for having played the Spanish national anthem during "the elevation of the sacrament." The priest was fined for his criticism, which was easily arranged since the organist also happened to be the mayor of the village. While the mayor was away, his house was burned down. Five young Basques were arrested and held for five days. According to witnesses, they were handcuffed to chairs and kicked and beaten for three of those days. They confessed. The prosecution asked for death sentences in a trial that presented no evidence other than police testimony. In December three were sentenced to forty-eight years in prison, one was sentenced to twelve years, and one was acquitted.

However, on December 16 the Spanish government tried to show its concern for justice by voiding the 476-year-old order by King Ferdinand and Queen Isabella expelling all Jews from Spain who did not convert to Catholicism.

In June, when Tom Hayden had called for "two, three, many Columbias," he had added that the goal was "so that the U.S. must either change or send its troops to occupy American campuses." By December he was getting his second scenario. On December 5, after a week of riots and scuffles between police and students and faculty at San Francisco State College, armed policemen, weapons drawn, tossing canisters of Mace, began to clear the campus. Acting president S. I. Hayakawa, who had made his point of view clear when arriving in office a week before by denouncing the 1964 Free Speech Movement, told a crowd of more than two thousand students, "Police have been instructed to clear the campus. There are no innocent bystanders anymore." The protests had begun with the demands of black students for black studies courses. For the last three weeks of the year the university was kept open only with a large armed police contingent regularly attacking students as they gathered to protest.

The nearby College of San Mateo, which was closed because of violence, reopened December 15, in the words of the school president, "as an armed camp," with riot police stationed throughout the campus.

The most reviled president of a riot-torn campus, Columbia's Grayson Kirk, who resigned in August, in December moved into a twenty-room mansion in the Riverdale section of the Bronx. The mansion had been provided by Columbia University, which owned the property.

In the beginning of December, the British, who had backed the Nigerian federal government, started to change their view of the Biafran war. While before they had been insisting on the imminent victory of Nigeria, they had now come to see the war as a hopeless stalemate. The United States also changed its policy. Johnson ordered contingency plans for a massive $20 million air, land, and sea relief program for Biafra. The French had already been supplying Biafra, which the Nigerians angrily said was the only thing keeping Biafra going. Supply planes for Biafra took off every night at 6:00 P.M. from Libreville,

Gabon. But Biafra was able to continue its fight for only one more year, and by the time it finally surrendered on January 15, 1970, an estimated one million civilians had starved to death.

After eleven months of negotiation, the eighty-two crew members of the U.S. ship *Pueblo* were released from North Korea in exchange for a confession by the U.S. government that it had been caught spying. As soon as the eighty-two Americans were safe, the U.S. government repudiated the statement. Some felt this was a strange way for a nation to conduct its affairs, and others felt it was a small price to pay to get the crew members released without a war. Left unclear was exactly what the *Pueblo* was doing when seized by the North Koreans.

In Vietnam word of the massacre carried out by the Americal Division in My Lai in March continued to spread through the region. In the fall, the letter from Tom Glen of the 11th Brigade reporting the massacre was in division headquarters, and the new deputy operations officer for the Americal Division, Major Colin Powell, was asked to write a response. Without interviewing Glen, he wrote that there was nothing to the accusations—they were simply unfounded rumors. The following September, only nine months later, Lieutenant William Calley was charged with multiple murders, and by November it had

1970 poster, after the My Lai massacre became known. Frazer Dougherty, Jon Hendricks, and Irving Pettin designed the poster from an R. L. Haeberle photograph.
(Collection of Mary Haskell)

become a major story. Yet Powell claimed he never heard about the massacre until two years after it happened. Nothing of Powell's role in the cover-up—he was not even in Vietnam at the time of the massacre—was known by the public until *Newsweek* magazine reported it in September 1995 in connection with rumors of a Powell run for president.

Despite Johnson's November announcement of a unilateral halt to bombing of North Vietnam and the expressed hope that this would lead to intense and productive negotiations, on December 6 the Selective Service announced that the draft call was to be increased by three thousand men a month. By mid-December peace negotiators in Paris were saying that Johnson had "oversold" the prospects for peace as the election approached.

In Paris the year-end peace negotiations had settled down to a tough and determined effort to resolve . . . the table issue. Hanoi was determined to have a square table, and that was completely unacceptable to South Vietnam. Other proposals debated by the different delegations included a round table, two arcs facing each other but not separated, or facing but separated. By the end of the year eleven different configurations were on the metaphoric table, which was still the only one they had. Behind the table issue were thornier realities, such as the North Vietnamese insistence on a Viet Cong presence, while the Viet Cong refused to speak with South Vietnam but were willing to speak with the Americans.

Senator George McGovern, the last-minute peace candidate at the Chicago convention, blurted out what many were trying to avoid saying when he called South Vietnamese vice president Nguyen Cao Ky a "little tinhorn dictator" and accused him and other South Vietnamese officials of holding up peace negotiations. "While Ky is playing around in the plush spots of Paris and haggling over whether he is going to sit at a round table or a rectangular table, American men are dying to prop up his corrupt regime back home." It had been the policy of the antiwar senators to avoid speaking plainly about the South Vietnamese, some out of respect for Johnson, others to avoid upsetting negotiations. With Johnson out of power, they intended to speak more plainly. Some said they wanted to wait until Nixon's inauguration, but McGovern started speaking two weeks early. A Gallup poll showed that a narrow majority of Americans now favored withdrawal and leaving the fighting to the South Vietnamese.

McGovern urged that there be a thoughtful assessment of the lessons of Vietnam. To him one of the great lessons was "the peril of drawing historical analogies." Although there was no parallel between what was happening in Southeast Asia in the early 1960s and Europe in the late 1930s, the World War II generation became mired in a Vietnamese civil war in part because they had witnessed the appeasement of Hitler.

McGovern said, "This is a war of the daily body count, given to us over the years like the football scores." The military understood that this too had been a mistake. They had even exaggerated the body counts. Future wars would appear to be as bloodless as possible, with the military saying as little as possible about enemy dead.

The military was learning its own lessons, not all of which were what McGovern had in mind when he tried to open this discussion. The military concluded that in a television age, journalists would have to be much more tightly controlled. The image of warfare had to be monitored carefully. Generals would have to consider how a battle looked on television and how to control that view.

The idea of a drafted army would be abandoned because it produced too many reluctant soldiers and too much adverse public opinion. It was better to have an all-volunteer military, drawn mostly from a few segments of society, people in need of employment and career opportunities. Wars would cease to be a major issue on campuses when students were no longer asked to fight.

But warfare was also to be used only against relatively defenseless countries, where technological superiority was critical, against enemies that would offer weeks, not years, of resistance.

The year 1968 ended exactly as it began, with the United States accusing the Viet Cong of violating its own Christmas cease-fire. But during the course of this year, 14,589 American servicemen died in Vietnam, doubling the total American casualties. When the United States finally withdrew in 1973, 1968 remained the year with the highest casualties of the entire war.

At the end of the year, Czechoslovakia was still defiant. A nationwide three-day sit-in strike by one hundred thousand students was supported by brief work stoppages by blue-collar workers. Dubček made a speech saying that the government was doing its best to bring back reform but that the population should stop acts of defiance because they only led to repression. In truth, by December, when travel restrictions were put back in place, the last of the reforms had been undone. On December 21 Dubček addressed the Central Committee of the Slovak Communist Party, his last speech of 1968. He was still resolute that the reforms must go through and that they would build a communist democracy. With the exception of a few references to "current difficulties," the speech could have been written when the Prague Spring was in full bloom. He said:

> We must, as a permanent positive feature of the post-January policy, consistently ensure fundamental rights and freedoms, observe Socialist legality, and fully rehabilitate unjustly wronged citizens.

He urged everyone to go home, spend time with their families, and get some rest. In 1969 Dubček was removed from office. In 1970 he was dismissed from the Communist Party. He and the reforms, "socialism with a human face," slowly vanished into history. Mlynář, who resigned his post in November 1968, realizing that he would no longer be able to pursue any of the policies he had wanted, said, "We were really fools. But our folly was the ideology of reform Communism."

In April 1968 Dubček had given an interview to the French communist newspaper *l'Humanité:*

> I do not know why a socialism that is based on the vigorous functioning of all democratic principles and on the people's free right to express their views should be any less solid. On the contrary, I am deeply convinced that the democratic atmosphere in the party and in public life will result in the strengthening of the unity of our socialist society and we shall win over to active collaboration all the capable and talented citizens of our country.

Dubček, the bureaucrat with the pleasant smile, was a confusing blend of contradictions. He spent his entire career as a cog in a totalitarian engine and then, when he emerged on top, declared himself a democrat. He was a pragmatist and a dreamer. He could be a skilled maneuverer in the baroque labyrinth of communist politics. But in the end even he admitted that he could be incredibly naïve.

By the end of 1968 the Soviets were worried, but they had not yet discovered how much they lost when they killed the dream of the Prague Spring. Dubček had tried to come back the way Gomułka had come back in 1956, curbing great ambitions, lowering the people's expectations, getting along with Moscow. But Dubček was not a Gomułka. At least that was what Moscow concluded—while the people of Czechoslovakia were still trying to decide what he was. It is often forgotten that in 1968 Alexander Dubček was the one leader who was unshakably antiwar, who would not contemplate a military solution even to save himself—a leader who refused to be bullied or bought by either communism or capitalism, who never played a cold war game, never turned to the capitalists, never broke a treaty or agreement or even his word—and he stayed in power, true power, for only 220 exciting days. They were days in which impossible things seemed possible, like the slogan written on a Paris wall in May: "Be realistic, ask for the impossible." After he was gone, no one felt that he had ever really known him.

The Soviet invasion of Czechoslovakia on August 20, 1968, marked the beginning of the end of the Soviet Union. When the end finally came more than twenty years later, the West was shocked. They had already forgotten. But at the time of the invasion, even *Time* magazine was predicting the end. It was the end of heroic Russia: a country widely admired because it had bravely dared to stand alone and build the first socialist society, because it was the big protector in the fraternity of socialist countries, because it had sacrificed millions to rid Europe of fascism. It was no longer viewed as benign. It was the bully who crushed small countries. After the fall of the Soviets, Dubček wrote that the Soviet Union had been doomed by one essential flaw: "The system inhibited change."

The downfall took longer than most people predicted. In 2002 Mikhail Gorbachev, the last Soviet leader, told his long-standing friend, former Dubček government official Zdeněk Mlynář:

The suppression of the Prague Spring, which was an attempt to arrive at a new understanding of Socialism, also engendered a very harsh reaction in the Soviet Union, leading to a frontal assault against all forms of free-thinking. The powerful ideological and political apparatus of the State acted decisively and uncompromisingly. This had an effect on all domestic and foreign policy and the entire development of Soviet society, which entered a stage of profound stagnation.

Dubček's dream, a path that was never found, was very different from what happened—the collapse of communism. He and many other communists always believed that the abuses of the Soviet system could be reformed, that communism could be made to work. After the Soviet invasion, no one could believe this, and without that belief, there was little left to believe in.

Without that dream, reform-minded communists had no choice but to turn to capitalism, which they found unacceptably flawed. They made the same mistake that was made in 1968—they now thought capitalism could be reformed and given a human face.

In Poland the students and intellectuals of 1968 finally got the workers to stand with them in the 1980s and drove out communism. Jacek Kuroń, near tears in a 2001 interview, said this about the new system:

I wanted to create a democracy, but the proof that I had not thought it through is that I thought capitalism could reform itself and everything such as self-government by workers could be accomplished later on. But then it appeared to be too late. This is proof of my own blindness. . . .

The problem of Communism is that centralization is the central dictatorship and there is no way to change it. Capitalism is the dictatorship of the rich. I don't know what to do. Central control can't stop it. The one thing I regret is participating in the first government [postcommunist]. My participation helped people accept capitalism.

I thought capitalism was self-reforming. It's not. It's like Russia—controlled by only a small group because capitalism needs capital. Here now [in Poland] half the population is on the edge of hunger and the other half feels successful.

Interviewed at the end of the year, Samuel Eliot Morison, at eighty-one one of the most respected American historians, said, "We have passed through abnormal periods before this, periods of disorder and violence that seemed horrendous and insoluble at the time. Yet we survived as a nation. The genius of our democracy is its room for compromise, our ability to balance liberty with authority. And I am convinced that we will strike a new balance this time, and achieve in the process a new awareness of human relationships among our people."

As Jacek Kuroń discovered in Poland, the changes in the world have been very far from what the people who were out to change the world had wanted. But that is not to say that 1968 did not change the world. Antiwar activists did not end American hegemonic warfare but only changed the way it was pursued and how it was sold to the public. In opposing the draft, the antiwar activists showed the generals what they had to do to continue waging war.

In history it is always imprecise to attribute fundamental shifts to one exact moment. There was 1967 and 1969 and all the earlier years that made 1968 what it was. But 1968 was the epicenter of a shift, of a fundamental change, the birth of our postmodern media-driven world. That is why the popular music of the time, the dominant expression of popular culture in the period, has remained relevant to successive generations of youth.

It was the beginning of the end of the cold war and the dawn of a new geopolitical order. Within that order, the nature of politics and of leaders changed. The Trudeau approach to leadership, where a figure is known by style rather than substance, has become entrenched.

"Back to normal." 1968 *Paris student silk-screen poster.*
(Galerie Beaubourg, Vence)

Marshall McLuhan, that great prophet of the 1960s, predicted, "The politician will be only too happy to abdicate in favor of his image, because the image will be so much more powerful than he could ever be." The political leaders of the 1968 generation who have come to power, such as Bill Clinton in the United States or Tony Blair in the United Kingdom, have shown an intuitive fluency with this concept of leadership.

In 1968 it was often said hopefully by "the establishment" that all of these radical youth were acting the way they were because they were young. When they got older, surely they would "calm down" and busy themselves earning money. The strength of capitalism, like the Mexican PRI, is its limitless belief in its own ability to buy people off. But, in fact, they have remained an activist generation. Pollsters in the United States find that it is the young voters, especially the eighteen-to-twenty-one-year-olds who were enfranchised because of the activism of 1968, who are least likely to participate.

In October 1968 when Hayden testified before the National Commission on the Causes and Prevention of Violence, Judge A. Leon Higginbotham asked him if he believed giving the vote to eighteen-year-olds would decrease the frustration of youth. Hayden warned that if they were not given anyone to vote for it would just increase their frustration. Most of the leaders of 1968 either remained politically active like Daniel Cohn-Bendit and Tom Hayden or became journalists or teachers. Those are the more apparent ways to try to change the world. Adam Michnik, who became the editor of the largest-circulation newspaper in central Europe—a fate he never imagined befalling him—is often visited by what is known in France as "sixty-eighters." "I can recognize a sixty-eighter in a second," he said. "It is not the politics. It is a way of thinking. I met Bill Clinton and I could see he was one."

Of course, one of the great lessons of 1968 was that when people try to change the world, other people who feel a vested interest in keeping the world the way it is will stop at nothing to silence them. In 1970 four antiwar demonstrators at Kent State University were shot and killed.

Yet all over the world people know that they are not powerless, that they can take to the streets the way people did in 1968. And political leaders, particularly those media-genius products of the 1960s, are very aware that popular movements are ignored at their peril. People under twenty-five do not have much influence in the world. But it is amazing what they can do if they are ready to march. Remember 1968? In the mid-1990s, when students began protesting in Paris, the Mitterrand government paid attention in a way the de Gaulle government didn't until whole universities were shut down. Mitterrand remembered 1968, and so did everyone in his government. On November 29–December 3, 1999, when a World Trade Organization conference in Seattle was confronted by huge, angry "antiglobalization" demonstrations, it made such an impression on then president Clinton, a zealous promoter of world trade, that he has regularly discussed the movement ever since.

The year 1968 was a terrible year and yet one for which many people feel nostalgia. Despite the thousands dead in Vietnam, the million starved in Biafra, the crushing of idealism in Poland and Czechoslovakia, the massacre in Mexico, the clubbings and brutalization of dissenters all over the world, the murder of the two Americans who most offered the world hope, to many it was a year of great possibilities and is missed. As Camus wrote in *The Rebel,* those who long for peaceful times are longing for "not the alleviation but the silencing of misery." The thrilling thing about the year 1968 was that it was a time when significant segments of population all over the globe refused to be silent about the many things that were wrong with the world. They could not be silenced. There were too many of them, and if they were given no other opportunity, they would stand in the street and shout about them. And this gave the world a sense of hope that it has rarely had, a sense that where there is wrong, there are always people who will expose it and try to change it.

But by the end of the year 1968, many people felt weary, angry, and longing for a news story that was not abysmally negative. At the very end of the year, the National Aeronautics and Space Administration, NASA, provided that story. Only seven years earlier, when America seemed much younger; when political assassinations seemed to be something that happened in other, poorer, less stable countries; when the generation that was to fight, die, and protest over Vietnam were still schoolchildren—President Kennedy had promised that man would reach the moon by the end of the decade. On May 25, 1961, he had said:

> I believe this nation should commit itself to achieving the goal, before this decade is out, of landing a man on the moon and returning him safely to earth. No single space project in this period will be more impressive to mankind or more important for the long-range exploration of space; and none will be so difficult or expensive to accomplish. In a very real sense, it will not be one man going to the moon—it will be an entire nation.

The new sixties generation thrilled to the early space shots, which were covered by radio and broadcast in the school classrooms. There was a sense of living in a new age of exploration, comparable to that of the fifteenth century. But somehow space exploration seemed to fade away, or at least everyone's focus had shifted. Young men weren't going to the moon, they were going to Vietnam. Occasional articles said the NASA budget had to be cut to divert money to the Vietnam War. Kennedy's prediction that getting to the moon would be expensive was accurate; from the creation of NASA on October 1, 1958, to its tenth anniversary on October 1, 1968, it spent $44 billion on space missions.

Then, in late September, people were allowed to slip back to that more innocent time. As though there had been no Soviet invasion, the space race to the moon was back on. The Soviets had sent *Zond 5* around the moon, and it seemed they would soon send a cosmonaut there. In October the Americans sent three men on the *Apollo 7* mission, in which they orbited the earth for eleven days in a spacecraft designed to eventually go to the moon. The craft had first been tested in January in an unmanned mission. The *Apollo 7* mission went so well, "a perfect mission," according to NASA, that NASA decided to jump ahead. *Apollo 8*, which had been scheduled to repeat *Apollo 7*'s flight, would instead blast out of the earth's orbit and go to the moon. Then, at the end of October the Soviets sent a man in *Soyuz 3*, the closest anyone had ever gotten to the moon.

Less romantic, but of more immediate impact, on December 18, exactly ten years after the first satellite transmission with Eisenhower's Christmas greeting, Intelsat 3 — the first of a new series of communications satellites that would extend live television transmission to the entire world—was launched. The new satellite more than doubled the capacity for television and telephone transmissions through space. The new age of television was now in place.

In time for Christmas, *Apollo 8* was scheduled for December 21. Many predicted that the Soviets would beat the three astronauts to the moon. Sir Bernard Lovell, a leading astronomer and head of the Jodrell Bank Observatory in Britain, said that the mission would not gain scientific information worth enough to justify the risk. NASA was candid that this was a more dangerous mission than usual. The craft was going to orbit the moon, which had not been done before by a manned spacecraft, and if after orbiting the spacecraft engine failed to start, the craft would be stuck in a permanent orbit, like an artificial moon of the moon. NASA also confirmed that the mission was not scientific. Its purpose was to develop and practice the necessary techniques for landing on the moon.

Apollo 8 lifted off on schedule and halfway to the moon broadcast a television program from inside the craft with a clarity that was rare in television. Millions were dazzled. As the craft approached the moon, it turned around and from space sent back to earth the first astonishing photos of our little blue-and-white planet. The pictures ran in black-and-white on the front page of newspapers around the world. The television broadcast and photographs from *Apollo 8* gave a sense in this first global year that this, too, like so many other milestones that year, was an event the whole world was watching. On Christmas Day the three astronauts flew around the moon only seventy miles above its surface, which they found to be gray, desolate, and lumpy. Then they fired their rockets and headed back to this planet of blue seas, rich vegetation, and endless strife.

Just before 1968 was over, there was a moment of tremendous excitement about the future. It was an instant when racism, poverty, the wars in Vietnam, the Middle East, and Biafra—all of it was shoved aside and the public felt what astronaut Michael Collins felt the following summer when he orbited the moon while his teammates landed:

> I really believe that if the political leaders of the world could see their planet from a distance of, let's say, 100,000 miles, their outlook could be fundamentally changed. That all-important border would be invisible, that noisy argument suddenly silenced. The tiny globe would continue to turn, serenely ignoring its

subdivisions, presenting a unified facade that would cry out for unified understanding, for homogeneous treatment. The earth must become as it appears: blue and white, not capitalist or Communist; blue and white, not rich or poor; blue and white, not envious or envied.

And so the year ended like Dante's traveler who at last climbed back from hell and gazed on the stars.

> To get back up to the shining world from there
> My guide and I went into that hidden tunnel:

> And following its path, we took no care
> To rest, but climbed: he first, then I—so far,
> Through a round aperture I saw appear

> Some of the beautiful things that Heaven bears,
> Where we came forth, and once more saw the stars.

> —DANTE, *The Inferno*

The earth in the last week of 1968. Photographed behind the moon by Apollo 8.
(Courtesy of National Space Science Data Center)

NOTES

CHAPTER 1: The Week It Began

3 *with serenity.* French translations, unless otherwise indicated, are by the author.

4 *"unusually mellow, almost avuncular"* The New York Times, January 1, 1968.

4 *"Nguyen who hates the French."* A. J. Langguth, *Our Vietnam: The War 1954–1975* (New York: Simon & Schuster, 2000), 35.

5 *"succeed in provoking a crisis."* Paris Match, January 6, 1968.

6 *"the higher our sales go."* The New York Times, January 8, 1968.

8 *"rescue our wounded officers."* Ibid., March 2, 1968.

8 *the night he was arrested.* Ibid., January 5, 1968.

10 *Gore called "undemocratic."* Ibid.

11 *disagreements on tactics and language.* David Dellinger, *From Yale to Jail: The Life Story of a Moral Dissenter* (New York: Pantheon Books, 1993), 194–199.

11 *April march on Washington.* Maurice Isserman and Michael Kazin, *America Divided: The Civil War of the 1960s* (New York: Oxford University Press, 2000), 170.

13 *in the movement when he was twelve.* The New York Times, January 5, 1968.

14 *"potential problems around the world."* The New York Times, January 1, 1968.

14 *Hoffman later explained to federal investigators.* Jules Witcover, *The Year the Dream Died: Revisiting 1968 in America* (New York: Warner Books, 1997), 43, quoting from the Report of the National Commission on the Causes and Prevention of Violence, 1968.

17 *"catastrophe upon all the people of the region."* The New York Times, January 1, 1968.

17 *Arabs who were removed from the Old City.* Ibid., January 12, 1968.

18 *At least twenty-six such groups were operating before the 1967 war.* Michael B. Oren, *Six Days of War: June 1967 and the Making of the Modern Middle East* (New York: Oxford University Press, 2002), 29.

18 *the PLO under al-Shuqayri,* Paris Match, January 6, 1968.

18 *returned to Lebanon.* Oren, *Six Days of War,* 1.

19 *an official poet was old-fashioned.* The New York Times, January 2, 1968.

19 *" 'I'll be your Baby Tonight.' "* Time, February 9, 1968.

19 *"apparently felt he should return one."* The New York Times, January 11, 1968.

20 *doctors now making godlike decisions?* Life, April 5, 1968.

20 *"I would pick the latter."* Paris Match, January 20, 1968.

22 *blamed the United States for the Vietnam War,* Bratislava Pravda, April 12, 1967, quoted in William Shawcross, *Dubček* (New York: Simon & Schuster, 1990), 94.

23 *Novotný was outmaneuvered again.* Shawcross, *Dubček,* 112.

23 *"but also in progressive culture and art."* The New York Times, January 2, 1968.

23 *"Eto vashe delo"* Shawcroft, *Dubček,* 111.

24 *1,438 enemy soldiers.* The New York Times, January 5, 1968.

CHAPTER 2: He Who Argues With a Mosquito Net

25 *"who happened to immigrate to Chicago,"* Alexander Dubček, *Hope Dies Last: The Autobiography of Alexander Dubček* (New York: Kodansha International, 1993), 1.

26 *"only free country in the world is the Soviet Union."* Shawcross, *Dubček,* 10.

27 *Czech stereotypes of Slovaks.* Tomáš Garrigue Masaryk, *The Making of a State* (London: Allen & Unwin, 1927), 21.

27 *Czecho-Slovak and not Czechoslovakia,* Shawcross, *Dubček,* 12.

28 *raw sparrow eggs in the shell.* Dubček, *Hope Dies Last,* 18–19.

28 *anything to do with politics.* Zdeněk Mlynář, *Nightfrost in Prague: The End of Humane Socialism* (New York: Karz Publishing, 1980), 65.

28 *"love at first sight."* Dubček, *Hope Dies Last,* 35.

29 *porcelain for his wife.* Mlynář, *Nightfrost in Prague,* 66.

29 *"narrow-minded bourgeoisie of Bystrica."* Shawcross, *Dubček,* 50.

30 *"depressing for me."* Dubček, *Hope Dies Last,* 82.

30 *long walks in the forest.* Ibid., 83.

30 *"victims of the 1950s repressions."* Ibid., 82.

31 *meeting of the Slovak Central Committee.* Shawcross, *Dubček,* 76.

34 *"real conditions in the Soviet Union."* Mlynář, *Nightfrost in Prague,* 2.

34 *a habit of listening to others.* Ibid., 122.

CHAPTER 3: A Dread Unfurling of the Bushy Eyebrow

39 *adopted nonviolent law enforcement.* David J. Garrow, *Bearing the Cross: Martin Luther King, Jr., and the Southern Christian Leadership Conference* (New York: William Morrow & Company, 1986), 209.

39 *"and stay in the news."* Gene Roberts, interviewed September 2002.

39 *"Your role is to photograph what is happening to us."* Flip Schulke, *Witness to Our Times: My Life as a Photojournalist* (Chicago: Cricket

Books, 2003), xvi. Also witnessed by Gene Roberts, interviewed September 2002.

39–40 *Sheriff Clark swinging his billy club at a helpless woman.* Garrow, *Bearing the Cross*, 381.

40 *"the pen is still mightier than the sword."* Mary King, *Freedom Song: A Personal Story of the 1960s Civil Rights Movement* (New York: William Morrow, 1987), 248.

40 *"seems to me somebody foreign to me."* Garrow, *Bearing the Cross*, 289.

40 *King statement should be no more than sixty seconds.* David Halberstam, *The Children* (New York: Fawcett Books, 1999), 433.

40 *create fundamental changes—a slow, off-camera process.* Mary King, *Freedom Song*, 480.

41 *"you couldn't shoot two hours."* Daniel Schorr, interviewed April 2001.

41 *"attention by doing that."* Ibid.

41 *"I'm afraid I did."* Daniel Schorr, *Staying Tuned: A Life in Journalism* (New York: Pocket Books, 2001), 205.

42 *enough time to formulate his response.* Ibid., 157.

42 *"a lot of crap! But it was live."* Daniel Schorr, interviewed April 2001.

42 *and playing it that night.* Ibid.

43 *"tides of rage must be loose in America?"* Norman Mailer, *Miami and the Siege of Chicago: An Informal History of the Republican and Democratic Conventions of 1968* (New York: World Publishing Company, 1968), 51.

43 *potential supporters of the antiwar cause.* Dellinger, *From Yale to Jail*, 260–62.

44 *"white people and their attitude."* Garrow, *Bearing the Cross*, 573.

44 *"could really sink us next fall."* *Time* magazine, January 26, 1968.

44 *and economist Milton Friedman.* *The New York Times*, January 12, 1968.

45 *Tet as the next chance for peace.* Ibid., January 2, 1968.

46 *"self-determination in Southeast Asia."* Ibid., January 13, 1968.

47 *McCarthy by a margin of 5 to 1.* Ibid., January 15, 1968.

48 *Time magazine version,* Time magazine, January 26, 1968.

49 *"what people really feel."* United Press International, January 19, 1968, ran in *The New York Times*, January 20, 1968.

50 *IR8 rice story.* Gene Roberts, interviewed September 2002.

51 *film could be quickly shipped.* Don Oberdorfer, *Tet!: The Turning Point in the Vietnam War* (Baltimore: Johns Hopkins University Press, 2001), 5.

52 *killed in an American bombing,* Ibid., 42–44.

52 *to win a public relations victory.* The New York Times, February 1, 1968.

52 *more than ten million homes.* Oberdorfer, *Tet!*, 240.

52 *"could be incomplete."* The New York Times, February 5, 1968.

53 *"stupid," false," and "unspeakable."* Ibid., June 20, 1968.

53 *the good offices of the mass media."* Life magazine, July 7, 1968.

54 *brought the young man back to life.* The New York Times, March 12, 1968.

56 *"the blind, and the female."* Ibid., February 17, 1968.

56 *weekly casualties, with 543 American soldiers killed.* The New York Times, February 23, 1968.

57 *surprise on Christmas Eve 1944.* Oberdorfer, *Tet!*, 71.

57 *"thousands of people around the country."* Ibid., 247.
58 *heads never trusted a word from the generals.* Conversation with David Halberstam, May 2003.
59 *it seemed to Cronkite and Salant,* Walter Cronkite, interviewed June 2002.
60 *Viet Cong attack. The New York Times,* February 12, 1968.
60 *another forty-five wounded.* Ibid., February 16, 1968.
63 *"and for CBS to permit me to do."* Walter Cronkite, interviewed June 2002.

CHAPTER 4: To Breathe in a Polish Ear

66 *"a very large, unlimited ego."* Marian Turski, interviewed July 1992.
67 *he was meeting with Gomułka and other leaders.* Dariusz Stola, historian at Istitut Studiów Politycznych, interviewed June 2001.
70 *"but there was no other."* Jacek Kuroń, interviewed June 2001.
70 *"noble human beings I have met in my life."* Jan Nowak, interviewed May 2002.
71 *"He was boyish . . ."* Ibid.
72 *"anti-Semites call me a Jew,"* Adam Michnik, interviewed June 2001.
75 *"nude and full, as it were, face."* The New York Times, April 30, 1968.
75 *from the bathtub in Brook's production. Paris Match,* June 29, 1968.
76 *"Really stirring,"* Michnik, interviewed May 2002.
76 *"to attack Mickiewicz."* Ibid.
76 *"We decided to lay flowers"* Ibid.
76 *"against students in Poland,"* Ibid.
77 *"an extremely dangerous man."* Ibid.

CHAPTER 5: On the Gears of an Odious Machine

82 *"where most of the seniors are headed." The New York Times,* March 19, 1968.
83 *"It suddenly occurred to me."* Cronkite, interviewed June 2002.
84 *Seeger had turned into a civil rights song when sit-ins began in 1960.* King, *Freedom Song,* 95–96.
84 *at the counter until they were served. Register,* North Carolina A&T, February 5, 1960.
85 *"Tennessee and involved fifteen cities." The New York Times,* February 15, 1960.
85 *"civil rights organizations completely by surprise,"* King, *Freedom Song,* 69.
85 *"identification with their courage and conviction deepened."* Tom Hayden, *Reunion: A Memoir* (New York: Collier, 1988), 32.
87 *completely unaware of it.* Tom Hayden, conversation May 2003.
87 *"the South was beckoning,"* Hayden, *Reunion,* 47.
87 *"beating to beating, jail to jail,"* Ibid., 73.
88 *in green suitcases to the Naked . . .* Allen Ginsberg, "Kral Majales," *Planet News: 1961–1967* (San Francisco: City Lights Books, 1968), 89–91.

88 *"compelled to enforce federal law."* Isserman and Kazin, *America Divided,* 34.
88 *from a bus here Saturday morning.* Montgomery Advertiser, May 21, 1961.
88 *Parchman Penitentiary.* King, *Freedom Song,* 70.
89 *with twenty thousand people arrested.* Todd Gitlin, *The Sixties: Years of Hope, Days of Rage* (New York: Bantam Books, 1987), 129.
89 *North Carolina, South Carolina, and Virginia,* King, *Freedom Song,* 407.
91 *"(I had no idea what that was anyway)?"* Mario Savio, "Thirty Years Later: Reflections on the FSM," 65. In Robert Chen and Reginald E. Zelnik., eds., *The Free Speech Movement: Reflections on Berkeley in the 1960s* (Berkeley: University of California Press, 2002).
95 *their own California party.* King, *Freedom Song,* 490–91.
95 *wearing only bathing suits.* Jonah Raskin, *For the Hell of It: The Life and Times of Abbie Hoffman* (Berkeley: University of California Press, 1998), 64–65.
96 *more than 20 percent white,* King, *Freedom Song,* 502.
97 *"might feel bad if you didn't share it."* Ibid., 406.
97 *"bread by some dark skinned sharpie."* Raskin, *For the Hell of It,* 77.
98 *"wrapped around induction centers,"* Ibid., 96.
98 *"sweep-in" was "a goof."* Ibid., 102.
99 *to say it stood for Youth International Party.* Ibid., 129.
99 *SDS was more than half Jewish.* Paul Berman, *A Tale of Two Utopias: The Political Journey of the Generation of 1968* (New York: W. W. Norton & Co., 1997), 44.
102 *"what a reporter could do to a president, do you?"* Langguth, *Our Vietnam,* 49.
102 *"an epidemic around the world."* Walter Cronkite, interviewed June 2002.

CHAPTER 6: Heroes

103 *had labeled "a conundrum."* Life, February 9, 1968.
105 *"America was falling apart at the seams."* Raskin, *For the Hell of It,* 137.
105 *"should activate the politician within him."* The Times (London), March 14, 1968.
105 *primary inducement.* The New York Times, April 1, 1968.
106 *said British economist John Vaizey.* Time, March 22, 1968.
106 *The houses were all burned.* Neil Sheehan, *A Bright Shining Lie: John Paul Vann and America in Vietnam* (New York: Random House, 1988), 689.
108 *become a student activist.* Hayden, *Reunion,* 76.
108 *"myth is the definitive revolution."* Raskin, *For the Hell of It,* 129.
108 *"the most important philosopher alive."* The New York Times, October 27, 1968.
109 *Marx, Mao, and Marcuse.* Time, March 22, 1968.
109 *to mention "the philosophers of destruction."* Elena Poniatowska, *La Noche de Tlatelolco* (Mexico City: Biblioteca Era, 1993), 38. This and other translations from Spanish, unless otherwise indicated, are by the author.

110 *"the outstanding characteristic of our generation."* David J. Garrow, *Bearing the Cross: Martin Luther King, Jr., and the Southern Christian Leadership Conference* (New York: William Morrow & Co., 1986), 54.
111 *by a ratio of eight to seven did. The New York Times,* July 3, 1968.
111 *who was willing to use them.* Hugh Pearson, *The Shadow of a Panther* (New York: Addison-Wesley, 1994), 149–50.
112 *"shoot to maim" any looters. Time,* April 26, 1968.
112 *"Huey had the good sense to defend himself."* Pearson, *The Shadow of a Panther,* 149.
113 *"find any other in the place." The New York Times,* July 24, 1968.
114 *"de Lawd"* Dellinger, *From Yale to Jail,* 263.
114 *they had gone off to different schools.* Garrow, *Bearing the Cross,* 33.
114 *"intellectual jive."* Ibid., 45.
114 *more mature than he was.* Ibid., 53.
114 *"give them leadership."* Ibid., 84.
115 *"Fucking's a form of anxiety reduction."* Ibid., 375.
115 *said political activist Michael Harrington.* Ibid.
115 *only solution was for him to take his own life.* David J. Garrow, *The FBI and Martin Luther King, Jr.: From "Solo" to Memphis* (New York: W. W. Norton & Co., 1981), 125–26.
115 *"but I'm afraid it will fall on deaf ears."* Garrow, *Bearing the Cross,* 557.
115 *"Maybe it will heed the voice of violence."* Ibid., 612.
116 *"end this nonviolence bullshit."* Isserman and Kazin, *America Divided,* 227.

CHAPTER 7: A Polish Categorical Imperative

119 *"one of the boys. Just like Dad."* Konstanty Gebert, interviewed July 1992.
120 *shouted, "Long live the workers of Poznan," The New York Times,* March 17, 1968.
121 *"children of the elite."* Jacek Kuroń, interviewed June 2001.
121 *"We didn't understand each other."* Eugeniusz Smolar, interviewed June 2001.
121 *"a kind of excitement."* Joanne Szczesna, interviewed June 2001.
123 *"violence was another surprise."* Nina Smolar, interviewed June 2001.
125 *a Jew and a political adversary of Moczar. The New York Times,* March 19, 1968.
128 *"wait for this capital to bear fruit." Trybuna Ludu,* March 26, 1968.

CHAPTER 8: Poetry, Politics, and a Tough Second Act

129 *with new arrivals and he had to read it again. Life,* September 6, 1968.
131 *Louis got him to remove the lines.* Michael Schumacher, *Dharma Lion: A Critical Biography of Allen Ginsberg* (New York: St. Martin's Press, 1992).
131 *safely back in the East Village.* Ibid., xiv–xv.
132 *each Ginsberg had his cheerers. The New York Times,* January 18, 1968.

132 *"I'm a stringer of words."* *Life,* February 9, 1968.
132 *"an amplified poet in black leather pants."* Ibid., April 12, 1968.
133 *"Wallace Stevens. That's poetry."* *The New York Times Magazine,* October 13, 1968.
133 *would have walked out of the room.* Schumacher, *Dharma Lion,* 489.
134 *"no importance here in Russia to us."* Ibid., 434.
134 *"a big man on campus."* *Life,* October 18, 1968.
135 *"So do we."* *The New York Times,* August 31, 1968.
135 *"Robert Lowell is traveling with the candidate."* *Life,* April 12, 1968.
135 *Lowenstein's first choice, one last time.* Witcover, *The Year the Dream Died,* 149.
135 *peasant uprising in 1381.* *Life,* February 9, 1968.
137 *if tongue was the organ to be manifested.* Mailer, *Miami and the Siege of Chicago,* 119.
137 *"That's kind of Greek, isn't it?"* *Life,* April 12, 1968.
137 *had gotten him the job.* Evan Thomas, *Robert Kennedy: His Life and Times* (New York: Simon & Schuster, 2000), 65.
138 *"A paratrooper."* Ibid., 19.
139 *such as Robert Lowell,* Ibid., 304.
139 *"Viva all of you."* *Time,* March 22, 1968.
139 *"Run for the bus."* *Life,* June 21, 1968.
140 *Hayden cited for its similarity to the Port Huron Statement:* Hayden, *Reunion,* 264.

CHAPTER 9: Sons and Daughters of the New Fatherland

145 *two more rounds of appeals.* *Time,* February 2, 1968.
145 *"that is the worst."* *Paris Match,* March 16, 1968.
145 *ruling out retirement or resignation.* *The New York Times,* February 28, 1968.
145 *"every paper I signed."* Ibid., March 2, 1968.
146 *knowing anything about killing Jews.* Ibid., July 5, 1968.
147 *"a relationship to the past."* Barbara Heimannsberg and Christoph J. Schmidt, eds., *The Collective Silence: German Identity and the Legacy of Shame* (San Francisco: Jossey-Bass Publishers, 1993), 67.
147 *West Germans were crossing to East Germany every year.* *The New York Times,* March 21, 1968.
148 *For the last two hundred years.* *Mammon.* Tariq Ali and Susan Watkins, *1968: Marching in the Streets* (New York: Free Press, 1998), 32.
150 *"was new to me and the other French."* Alain Krivine, interviewed June 2002.
150 *chairman for 1968, to speak to students in France.* Ronald Fraser, ed., *1968: A Student Generation in Revolt* (New York: Pantheon Books, 1988), 180.
153 *"the biggest anti-American rally ever staged in the city."* *The New York Times,* February 19, 1968.
153 *Tariq Ali did not believe this was possible.* Fraser, *1968,* 186.
155 *boycott his papers.* *The New York Times,* April 13, 1968.
156 *they opposed the student violence.* Peter Demetz, *After the Fires: Recent*

Writing in the Germanies, Austria and Switzerland (New York: Harcourt
Brace Jovanovich, 1986), 63–64.

156 *students were outspokenly opposed to the violence.* Time, April 26, 1986.
157 *"at the age of twenty will never make a good social democrat." Paris
Match*, April 27, 1968.

CHAPTER 10: Wagnerian Overtones of a Hip and Bearded Revolution

158 *"Then the war will end."* Mark Rudd, interviewed April 2002.
160 *"well born, well-to-do daredevil of 29."* Van Gosse, *Where the Boys Are:
Cuba, Cold War America and the Making of a New Left* (London: Verso,
1993), 68.
161 *SLATE, which was the beginning of activism on that campus.* Ibid., 90.
162 *to charm her into staying.* Hugh Thomas, *Cuba: The Pursuit of Freedom*
(New York: Harper & Row, 1971) 1,202–03.
162 *"on the direct line of the French Revolution of 1789."* Herbert L.
Matthews, *The Cuban Story* (New York: George Braziller, 1961), 89.
163 *lost a great deal of support in the first six months of 1959.* Gosse, *Where
the Boys Are*, 114.
164 *"the foreign menace felt in anguish."* Thomas, *Cuba*, 1,269.
165 *"muscle against a very small country."* Gosse, *Where the Boys Are*, 205.
165 *"wasn't as good as 250,000 Cubans."* Douglas Brinkley, *Dean Acheson:
The Cold War Years 1953–1971* (New Haven: Yale University Press, 1992).
166 *"without understanding its music."* The New York Times, April 22,
1961.
168 *who were in Cuban prisons in the mid-1960s.* Tad Szulc, *Fidel: A Critical
Portrait* (New York: William Morrow & Co., 1986), 54.
169 *his lack of political commitment.* Gosse, *Where the Boys Are*, 185.
170 *the FBI, remained skeptical.* Michael Schumacher, *Dharma Lion*,
419–20.
170 *"to the revolution."* Ibid., 422.
171 *labeled in May 1966 by student radicals at Qinghua University.* J. A. G.
Roberts, *A Concise History of China* (Cambridge: Harvard University
Press, 1999), 279.
171 *and the students from bourgeois backgrounds.* Ibid., 280.
171 *signs of food shortages,* The New York Times, March 5, 1968.
172 *shown much progress since.* Ibid., August 25, 1968.
172 *capable of hitting Los Angeles and Seattle,* The New York Times Magazine, July 14, 1968.
172 *resign from government and move on to another revolution.* Szulc, *Fidel*,
597–98.
173 *950 bars were to be closed.* The New York Times, March 14, 1968.
173 *The crowd shouted and applauded its approval.* Szulc, *Fidel*, 609.
173 *the year of the "new man."* Thomas, *Cuba*, 1,446.
174 *Federal Aviation Administration's recommendation.* Time, March 22,
1968.
175 *"tougher than trying to stop them."* The New York Times, July 21, 1968.
175 *"to fight communism in this manner."* Ibid., December 14, 1968.

175 *"in apologies; it wasn't going to happen to me."* Gitlin, *The Sixties*, 274.
176 *Havana-bound flights to record the Mexicans on board.* Some of these lists of Cubans and American Havana-bound passengers can be found in newly released Mexican government archives in Lecumberri.
176 *"likes and trusts its government."* Ali, *1968*, 24.
177 *"both mobilized and relaxed."* Gitlin, *The Sixties*, 275.

CHAPTER 11: April Motherfuckers

178 *"slightly irrelevant in his presence."* Hayden, *Reunion*, 275.
179 *"changing clothes or engaging in sterile debate."* Ibid.
181 The Bride Got Farblundjet, Bill Graham and Robert Greenfield, *Bill Graham Presents: My Life Inside Rock and Out* (New York: Doubleday, 1992), 227.
181 *70 percent of the professional concert activities*, The New York Times, January 15, 1968.
181 *These trends continued in 1968.* Gitlin, *The Sixties*, 120.
181 *transmits sound waves into nerve impulses.* The New York Times, August 20, 1968.
182 *"age of instant communication."* Life, June 28, 1968.
182 *"music today," said Townshend.* Ibid., June 2, 1968.
182 *"drummer who can really keep time."* Time, August 30, 1968.
183 *"have a good time."* Ibid., August 9, 1968.
184 *"The Know Nothing Bohemians."* Partisan Review (spring 1958).
184 *"Beautify America, Get a Haircut."* Life, May 31, 1968.
185 *"Nobody wants a hippie for President,"* The New York Times, March 16, 1968.
186 *"everything except how to be a man."* Ibid., October 22, 1968.
186 *double between 1968 and 1985.* Ibid., April 7, 1968.
187 *"provides the image for the kids."* Ibid., January 11, 1968.
187 *interrogate someone while under the influence of LSD.* Isserman and Kazan, *America Divided*, 156. Also see Martin A. Lee and Bruce Shlain, *Acid Dreams: The Complete Social History of LSD: The C.I.A., the Sixties and Beyond* (New York: Grove Weidenfeld, 1992).
187 *Nasser and Cuba's Fidel Castro*, Lee and Shlain, *Acid Dreams*, 35.
188 *"found God and discovered the secret of the Universe."* Timothy Leary, *Flashbacks: An Autobiography* (Los Angeles: Tarcher, 1983), 159.
188 *chromosome damage.* Ibid., 154.
188 *an acid-doused sugar cube.* Charles Kaiser, *1968 in America: Music, Politics, Chaos, Counterculture, and the Shaping of a Generation* (New York: Weidenfeld & Nicolson, 1988), 206.
188 *"Beethoven coming to the supermarket."* Raskin, *For the Hell of It*, 110.
189 *"an erotic politician."* David Allyn, *Make Love, Not War—The Sexual Revolution: An Unfettered History* (Boston: Little, Brown & Co., 2000), 131.
189 *"That's what you came for, isn't it."* Ibid. Quoted from James Riordan and Jerry Prochinicky, *Break on Through: The Life and Death of Jim Morrison* (New York: William Morrow & Co., 1991), 186.
189 *"it's supposed to make you fuck."* Isserman and Kazin, *America Divided*,

161. Quoted from Godfrey Hodgson, *America in Our Time* (New York: Random House, 1976), 341.

190 *"the Golden Age of fucking,"* Raskin, *For the Hell of It*, 83.

190 *Anne Bancroft and Dustin Hoffman in bed together.* The *New York Times*, January 9, 1968.

191 *"shook their heads in amusement."* Ibid., February 18, 1968.

191 *"public interest in sex on the college campus is insatiable."* Life, May 30, 1968.

192 *"150 years of American civilization."* Ed Sanders, *Shards of God: A Novel of the Yippies* (New York: Grove Press, 1970), introduction.

198 *"the correct grammatical 'whom.' "* Gitlin, *The Sixties*, 307.

201 *with rice and beans.* Tom Hayden, correspondence with author, June 2003.

201 *"the torment of their campus generation."* Tom Hayden, *Rebel: A Personal History of the 1960s* (Los Angeles: Red Hen Press, 2003), 253.

201 *"turning point of history?"* Hayden, *Reunion*, 275.

202 *underground high school newspapers.* Diane Divoky, *Saturday Review*, February 15, 1969.

203 *with its own steering committee,* The New York Times, April 27, 1968.

203 *"no such justification."* Ibid., April 26, 1968.

204 *to be abandoned by the end of April.* Life, April 19, 1968.

207 *lay about the grass unattended.* The Nation, June 10, 1968.

207 *"that have long festered on campus."* Time, May 3, 1968.

208 *"My son, the revolutionary."* Ibid., May 31, 1968.

208 *president had been forced out by the students.* Ibid., August 30, 1968.

208 " *'Create two, three, many Columbias' "* Ramparts, June 15, 1968.

CHAPTER 12: Monsieur, We Think You Are Rotten

209 *"I shall die sometime."* Life, January 19, 1968.

210 *"France is bored."* Le Monde, March 15, 1968.

210 *"British their financial and economic crisis."* Paris Match, March 23, 1968.

211 *American companies, with $14 billion.* Jean-Jacques Servan-Schreiber, *The American Challenge* (New York: Atheneum, 1968), 3.

211 *"for it defines our future."* Ibid., 32.

212 *"Che Guevara poster on his wall."* Life, May 17, 1968.

214 *"to shut myself up with grief."* Anthony Hartley, *Gaullism: The Rise and Fall of a Political Movement* (New York: Outbridge & Dienstfrey, 1971), 155.

214 *erecting makeshift barricades.* Hervé Hamon and Patrick Rotman, *Génération*, vol. 1: *Les Années de rêve* (Paris: Éditions du Seuil, 1987), 43–44.

215 *"it was not over."* Alain Geismar, interviewed June 2002.

216 *"the consumer society that eats itself."* J. R. Tournoux, *Le Mois de Mai du général* (Paris: Librairie Plon, 1969), 23.

216 *did not begin broadcasting until 1957.* Gérard Filoche, *68–98 Histoire sans fin* (Paris: Flammarion, 1998), 10.

216 *"He understands the medium better than anyone else."* Life, May 17, 1968.

217 *was again observed.* Tournoux, *Le Mois de Mai du général,* 14.
217 *rendered incapable of thinking.* Dark Star, ed., *Beneath the Paving Stones: Situationists and the Beach, May 1968* (Edinburgh: Ak Press, 2001), 9–10.
217 *half as many degrees* Tournoux, *Le Mois de Mai du général,* 48–51, 87.
218 *"who had grown too old."* Alain Geismar, interviewed June 2002.
219 *"worthy of Hitler's youth minister."* Harmon and Rotman, *Génération,* vol. 1, 401.
219 *in the old German style of obedience.* André Harris and Alain Sédouy, *Juif & Français* (Paris: Éditions Grasset & Fasquelle, 1979), 189–91.
221 *"would have been it."* Daniel Cohn-Bendit, interviewed March 2002.
222 *" 'we think you are rotten.' "* Andrew Feenberg and Jim Freedman, *When Poetry Ruled the Streets: The French May Events of 1968* (Albany: State University of New York Press, 2001), 8.
222 *the CRS, to Paris.* Tournoux, *Le Mois de Mai du général,* 25.
223 *"who are waiting for the government to protect them."* Ibid., 30.
223 *Georges Marchais wrote. L'Humanité,* May 3, 1968.
224 *"right moment and the right place."* Daniel Cohn-Bendit, interviewed March 2003.
224 *"pictures of each other on television."* Ibid.
225 *"I would say 'I don't know.' "* Ibid.
226 *"no planning."* François Cerutti, interviewed June 2002.
226 *He was a bureaucrat, not a policeman.* Maurice Grimaud, *En Mai fais ce qu'il te plaît* (Paris: Éditions Stock, 1977), 21.
226 *"astonished the police officials."* Ibid., 18.
226 *". . . covered with blood."* *Le Monde,* May 12–13, 1968.
226 *"The way it did with the Black Panthers."* Daniel Cohn-Bendit, interviewed March 2003.
227 *flyers had been intended as a joke,* Tournoux, *Le Mois de Mai du général,* 33–34.
227 *"Everyone was talking."* Eleanor Bakhtadze, interviewed June 2002.
227 *"freedom of today began in '68."* Radith Gersmar, interviewed June 2002.
229 *The Jewish Museum's show, The New York Times,* December 15, 1968.
229 *"I was the media's darling."* Daniel Cohn-Bendit, interviewed March 2003.
230 *"more importance than it deserves."* Tournoux, *Le Mois de Mai du général,* 94–95.
232 *"That's just the way it is."* Ibid., 246.
233 *"we are going to do today."* Harmon and Rotman, *Génération,* vol. 1, 458.
234 *the entire city of Berkeley. The New York Times,* July 1, 1968.
235 *"do it again in '68."* Alain Krivine, interviewed June 2002.
235 *"I no longer had any hold over my own government."* Hartley, *Gaullism,* 288.
235 *"a position to give everyone advice."* *Le Monde,* June 27, 1968.
236 *readers to fool them!* Daniel Cohn-Bendit, *Le Gauchisme: Remède à la maladie sénile du communisme* (Paris: Éditions du Seuil, 1968), 11.
236 *"reconstruct myself."* Daniel Cohn-Bendit, interviewed March 2002.
237 *are always going to the university.* Harmon and Rotman, *Génération,* vol. 1, 420.

CHAPTER 13: The Place to Be

238 *would not have been allowed to win.* Harry Schwartz, *Prague's 200 Days: The Struggle for Democracy in Czechoslovakia* (London: Pall Mall Press, 1969), 88.
239 *"for my family's needs and my taste."* Dubček, *Hope Dies Last,* 151.
239 *"solving important problems."* Schwartz, *Prague's 200 Days,* 90.
239 *thought were unacceptable responses. Time,* March 22, 1968.
239 *"too late, to put the breaks on?" Paris Match,* March 23, 1968.
240 *"custom of male kissing."* Dubček, *Hope Dies Last,* 101.
240 *"harm they are causing me?"* Mlynář, *Nightfrost in Prague,* 103.
241 *they staged one that lasted for hours.* Schwartz, *Prague's 200 Days,* 120–22.
241 *several innocent people was about to be revealed.* Ibid., 123.
242 *"and that is democracy on recall." The New York Times,* May 6, 1968.
243 *I have no apartment,* Schwartz, *Prague's 200 Days,* 144.
244 *they had been forewarned. The New York Times,* May 11, 1987.
245 *"both official hits of the time."* Berman, *A Tale of Two Utopias,* 230.
246 *Brubeck "with a touch of bossa nova." The New York Times,* May 28, 1968.
246 *Clive Barnes's review.* Ibid., May 6, 1968.
246 *psychedelic rock band posters.* Berman, *A Tale of Two Utopias,* 233.
247 *5 percent said they wanted capitalism.* Jaroslaw A. Piekalkiewicz, *Public Opinion Polling in Czechoslovakia, 1968–69: Results and Analysis of Surveys Conducted During the Dubček Era* (New York: Praeger Publishers, 1972), 4.
247 *7 percent said they were dissatisfied.* Ibid., 34.
248 *to argue against invasion.* Jiri Valenta, *Soviet Intervention in Czechoslovakia 1968: Anatomy of a Decision* (Baltimore: Johns Hopkins University Press, 1991), 66–70.
249 *lists of people to be arrested.* Schwartz, *Prague's 200 Days,* 178.
250 *although sometimes a bribe would help. The New York Times,* May 5, 1968.
250 *"the right place to be this summer."* Ibid., August 12, 1968.

CHAPTER 14: Places Not to Be

255 *"political rights of Negroes."* Bernard Diedrerich and Al Burt, *Papa Doc and the Tonton Macoutes* (Port-au-Prince: Éditions Henri Deschamps, 1986; original McGraw-Hill, 1969), 383.
255 *killed or captured by Haitian army troops.* Ibid., 380.
255 *sentenced to death. The New York Times,* August 8, 1968.
255 *more dangerous than Vietnam. The New York Times Magazine,* May 5, 1968.
255 *Nixon would make the same point, Life,* November 22, 1968.
256 *within five years. The New York Times,* July 24, 1968.
256 *should give it all back. Paris Match,* March 30, 1968.
256 *Originally, such raids by Palestinians,* Oren, *Six Days of War,* 24.
257 *lost all connection to the outside world. Life,* July 12, 1968.

257 *It was reported that the Nigerian force,* The New York Times, May 27, 1968.
259 *white ants for protein.* Time, August 2, 1968.
259 *a new one dug for the next day.* The New York Times, August 1, 1968.
260 *"other airlines will join in."* Ibid., August 14, 1968.
260 *on the European market.* Time, August 9, 1968.
260 *"Negroes are massacred . . ."* Life, July 12, 1968.
260 *"some starving white people to feed."* The New York Times, September 30, 1968.

CHAPTER 15: The Craft of Dull Politics

261 *John Updike said,* Norman Mailer, Miami and the Siege of Chicago, 15.
261 *"Yippie! was really in trouble."* Abbie Hoffman ("Free"), Revolution for the Hell of It (New York: Dial Press, 1968), 104.
261 *not given to admiring,* Hayden, Rebel, 244.
262 *as a frightening bad omen.* Thomas, Robert Kennedy: His Life and Times, 346.
262 *expected it to be himself.* Ibid., 276.
262 *told historian Arthur Schlesinger,* Arthur Schlesinger, Jr., Robert Kennedy and His Times (Boston: Houghton Mifflin, 1978), 895.
262 *Romain Gary,* Le Figaro, June 6, 1968.
265 *"leaderless and impotent."* The New York Times, March 22, 1968.
266 *"on that particular statement."* Ibid., May 22, 1968.
266 *By June a petition drive,* Ibid., June 2, 1968.
266 *"giving aid and comfort to the enemy."* Reader's Digest, April 1968.
267 *"dullest convention anyone could remember."* Mailer, Miami and the Siege of Chicago, 15.
268 *news of Martin Luther King's assassination.* The New York Times, October 6, 1968.
268 *"cruel and unusual punishment."* Jack Gould, The New York Times, August 9, 1968.

CHAPTER 16: Phantom Fuzz Down by the Stockyards

270 *$35 million had been spent.* Mike Royko, Boss: Richard J. Daley of Chicago (New York: Plume, 1988; original 1971), 161.
270 *written about in major newspapers.* The New York Times, March 24, 1968.
273 *local Chicago youth.* John Schultz, No One Was Killed: Documentation and Meditation: Convention Week, Chicago—August 1968 (Chicago: Big Table Publishing Company, 1998; original 1969), 2.
274 *"recent Berkeley and Paris incidents."* Raskin, For the Hell of It, 149.
274 *Judge William Lynch, Daley's former law partner,* Royko, Boss, 179.
274 *"an actor for TV."* Schultz, No One Was Killed, 49.
275 *Food! Ham! Parks belong to pigs.* Ibid., 53.
276 Sun-Times *and* Daily News . . . *only scared the police.* Royko, Boss, 179.

277 *"the idealism of the young,"* Schultz, *No One Was Killed,* 68.

278 *"I can hardly wait,"* he said. Carl Solberg, *Hubert Humphrey: A Biography* (New York: W. W. Norton, 1984), 356–57.

278 *terrified of taking on a Kennedy as was Nixon.* Ibid., 357–58.

278 *backed off until their posted 11:00 curfew.* Raskin, *For the Hell of It,* 159.

279 *a McCarthy campaign sticker on it.* Schultz, *No One Was Killed,* 116.

280 *"See you at eleven o'clock, kid."* Ibid., 103.

281 *"are basically sound,"* Solberg, *Hubert Humphrey,* 356.

282 *stuffing them into paddy wagons.* Schultz, *No One Was killed,* 171–76.

282 *Mailer reported.* Mailer, *Miami and the Siege of Chicago,* 171.

283 *to drive out hypocrisy.* Schumacher, *Dharma Lion,* 516.

284 *"That's part of the Chicago style. . . ."* *Chicago Sun-Times,* December 12, 1976.

284 *Daley angrily insisted,* *The New York Times,* August 30, 1968.

284 *"I was busy receiving guests,"* Solberg, *Hubert Humphrey,* 364.

284 *"We are going to look into all this."* Ibid., 365.

285 *"the advance guard of anarchy."* *The New York Times,* August 30, 1968.

285 *"probably used too much restraint."* Ibid.

285 *Is it any wonder police had to take action?* Solberg, *Hubert Humphrey,* 370.

285 *"Barnard girls" and "Columbia men."* *Life,* November 22, 1968.

286 *"Nixon will be elected President."* Raskin, *For the Hell of It,* 170.

286 *Vietnam had its worst week,* *The New York Times,* August 30, 1968.

CHAPTER 17: The Sorrow of Prague East

287 *Alexander Dubček, August 1990,* Valenta, *Soviet Intervention in Czechoslovakia 1968,* Dubček's introduction, x.

288 *solidify in law the achievements of the Prague Spring.* Dubček, *Hope Dies Last,* 173–78.

288 *Soviet military support.* *The New York Times,* August 22, 1968.

288 *"It is my personal tragedy."* Schwartz, *Prague's 200 Days,* 217.

288 *"So they did it after all—and to me!"* Mlynář, *Nightfrost in Prague,* 146.

289 *spread to his own country.* Ibid., 155–56.

290 *"such things to our leadership."* Valenta, *Soviet Intervention in Czechoslovakia 1968,* 173–75.

290 *4,600 tanks and 165,000 soldiers of the Warsaw Pact,* Kieran Williams, *The Prague Spring and Its Aftermath: Czechoslovak Politics—1968–1970* (Cambridge: Cambridge University Press, 1997), 112.

291 *including small armored vehicles, fuel,* *The New York Times,* September 1, 1968.

291 *it had all been a misunderstanding.* Dubček, *Hope Dies Last,* 182.

292 *manager had been a Soviet agent.* Ibid., 183.

293 *in gun barrels.* Colin Chapman, *August 21st: The Rape of Czechoslovakia* (London: Cassell, 1968), 8.

294 *five thousand American tourists.* Schwartz, *Prague's 200 Days,* 214.

294 *broadcast . . . around the world.* *The New York Times,* August 22, 1968.

295 *Jack Gould wrote,* Ibid., August 22 and 23, 1968.

296 *shouted, "Get out!"* Schwartz, *Prague's 200 Days*, 220.
296 *the leaflets scattered over the Czech lands turned out to be,* Ibid., 220–21.
297 *plotting to overthrow Poland.* Williams, *The Prague Spring and Its Aftermath,* 139.
297 *"progressives of the entire world."* The New York Times, September 28, 1968.
297 *reports of gunfire exchanged,* Ibid., September 1, 1968.
298 *"by an elite of her children."* Ibid., August 25, 1968.
299 *progress that was being made in U.S.-Soviet negotiations,* Ibid., August 22, 1968.
299 *other high-level Czech leaders.* Schwartz, *Prague's 200 Days,* 230.
299 *"as they did in 1945."* Mlynář, *Nightfrost in Prague,* 197.
300 *"Ah, Mr. President, but how beautiful it would be,"* Ibid., 197.
300 *slipping in a bathroom.* Ibid., 277.
301 *Miroslav Beránek was shot,* Williams, *The Prague Spring and Its Aftermath,* 158.
301 *"with whom you are dealing?"* Mlynář, *Nightfrost in Prague,* 232.
302 *refusing to negotiate without him.* Schwartz, *Prague's 200 Days,* 231.
303 *"sacrifices of World War II."* Mlynář, *Nightfrost in Prague,* 237–41.
305 *refugee status in other countries.* Time, October 4, 1968.

CHAPTER 18: The Ghastly Strain of a Smile

307 *"We also all felt, well, grown up;"* Robin Morgan, *Going Too Far: The Personal Chronicle of a Feminist* (New York: Random House, 1977), 62–63.
308 *because violence seemed unlikely.* Todd Gitlin, *The Whole World Is Watching: Mass Media in the Making and Unmaking of the New Left* (Berkeley: University of California Press, 1980), 182.
308 *Morgan had her regrets.* Morgan, *Going Too Far,* 63.
308 *Shana Alexander wrote in Life: Life,* September 20, 1968.
309 *"from Mayor Daley's kiss."* Morgan, *Going Too Far,* 64–65.
309 *a "Nixon for President" button.* The New York Times, September 8, 1968.
309 *"let's stop trying to prove it over and over again."* Sara Evans, *Personal Politics: The Roots of Women's Liberation in the Civil Rights Movement & the New Left* (New York: Vintage Books, 1980), 4.
310 *asked Friedan to come speak.* Davis, *Moving the Mountain,* 50, 52.
310 *The average age of matrimony was twenty.* Ibid., 17.
311 *to make sure they were complying.* Ibid., 18.
311 *United States had more female stockholders than male.* The New York Times, March 10, 1968.
311 *to win a combat decoration.* Ibid., January 1, 1969.
311 *over the age of sixteen were working.* Davis, *Moving the Mountain,* 59.
312 *"A chicken in every pot, a whore in every home."* The New York Times Magazine, March 10, 1968.
312 *rejected by every Congress since 1923.* Ibid.
313 *"That's too manly, too . . . white."* Ibid.
313 *I was difficult . . . if necessary.* King, *Freedom Song,* 43.

314 *"that streak was in him also."* Garrow, *Bearing the Cross,* 374–76, 617.

314 *"You've got to fuck it to make it change."* Allyn, *Make Love, Not War,* 102.

314 *attributed the problem largely to his own "ignorance"* Correspondence with author, July 2003.

314 *"as an issue!"* Chen and Zelnik, *The Free Speech Movement,* 130.

315 *more than one thousand arrests.* Evans, *Personal Politics,* 73.

315 *David Dellinger was shocked,* Dellinger, *From Yale to Jail,* 299.

315 *"non committal with his sidelong glance."* King, *Freedom Song,* 450.

315 *was received as a joke.* Ibid., 451–52.

316 *not one responded.* Ibid., 448–74.

316 *almost all of them lawyers. The New York Times Magazine,* March 10, 1968.

317 *the first one in Berlin in January 1968.* Demetz, *After the Fires,* 73.

318 *"a bunch of cool cookies," The New York Times Magazine,* March 10, 1968.

318 *would do the cleaning while the men meditated.* Allyn, *Make Love, Not War,* 103.

319 *"Maxis Are Monstrous" The New York Times,* March 14, 1968.

319 *would gain complete acceptance in the next five years. Time,* April 19, 1968.

320 *"now or never, and I'm very much afraid it's now." Life,* October 18, 1968.

CHAPTER 19: In an Aztec Place

321 *Octavio Paz, Posdata.* All Spanish translations, unless otherwise indicated, are by the author.

321 *"than their own even exist."* Elena Poniatowska, *Massacre in Mexico* (Columbia, Mo.: University of Missouri Press, 1975), introduction, x.

325 *declined by several hundred thousand.* T. R. Fehrenbach, *Fire and Blood: A History of Mexico* (New York: Macmillan, 1973), 524.

326 *"Steady economic growth within" The New York Times,* January 22, 1968.

326 *"The economy of the country had made such progress"* Octavio Paz, *Posdata* (Mexico City: Siglo XXI, 2002; original ed., 1970), 32.

328 *anything other than sports. Life,* March 15, 1968.

328 *78 percent of disposable income in Mexico went to only the upper 10 percent.* Ifigenia Martinez, interviewed October 2002.

329 *"they saw it as revolutionary liberators."* Roberto Escudero, interviewed October 2002.

330 *"We wore jeans and indigenous-style shirts."* Salvador Martínez de la Roca, interviewed October 2002.

332 *"I think it was caused by inertia"* Lorenzo Meyer, interviewed October 2002.

332 *"French Communist Party and world bureaucracy."* Ministry of the Interior files stored in Lecumberri.

333 *"and that was an accident."* Roberto Escudero, interviewed October 2002.

333 *"coming to destabilized Mexico."* Roberto Rodríguez Baños, interviewed September 2002.

334 *"The students were as free as you could be in this society."* Lorenzo Meyer, interviewed October 2002.

334 *shave off his beard to enter.* Schumacher, *Dharma Lion,* 507.

334 *"to dress well or badly as he sees fit."* *The New York Times,* April 19, 1968.

335 *the attack remains unknown.* Ramón Ramírez, *El Movimiento estudiantil de México (Julio/Diciembre de 1968)* (Mexico City: Ediciones Era, 1998; original ed., 1969), 145–47; and Raúl Álvarez Garín, *La Estela de Tlatelolco: Una Reconstrucción histórica del movimiento estundiantil del 68* (Mexico City: Editorial Ithaca, 1998), 30.

335 *confirmed in documents released in 1999.* *The New York Times,* June 29, 1999.

336 *"their principle of only having public dialogue."* Roberto Escudero, interviewed October 2002.

336 *The architecture student Jean-Claude Leveque,* *The New York Times,* December 15, 1968.

337 *including discontent over one-party rule.* *U.S. News & World Report,* August 12, 1968.

339 *thought to have been held in prison,* *The New York Times,* September 21, 1968.

339 *exchanges of gunfire and one policeman killed,* Ibid., September 24, 1968.

339 *the long-awaited dialogue was a disaster.* Raúl Álvarez Garín, interviewed October 2002.

339 *"The meeting ended very badly"* Roberto Escudero, interviewed October 2002.

339 *"an angry, blood-splattered face."* Poniatowska, *Massacre in Mexico,* introduction, xii.

341 *"listen as much when a woman spoke"* Myrthokleia Gonzalez Gallardo, interviewed October 2002.

343 *were killed by the military in the 1970s.* *The New York Times,* July 16, 2002.

343 *"Families don't come forward"* Martínez de la Roca, interviewed October 2002.

343 *"All of us were reborn on October 2."* Elena Poniatowska, *La Noche de Tlatelolco* (Mexico City: Era, 1971), 267.

CHAPTER 20: Theory and Practice for the Fall Semester

347 *"100,000 at the Olympic Stadium in Mexico City."* *The New York Times,* October 13, 1968.

350 *"stand up for black Americans."* *Augusta Chronicle,* May 20, 1998.

351 *"not smart enough to lose interest in it."* *Life,* October 18, 1968.

351 *The U.S. has seldom . . . a fresh political experience.* *Time,* July 5, 1968.

352 *"a sovereign state too." Life,* April 19, 1968.

352 *"can you smuggle in a canoe."* Ibid.

352 *"no personal point of view on anything."* Philip Marchand, *Marshall McLuhan: The Medium Is the Messenger* (Cambridge: MIT Press, 1998), 219.

352 *"Mercedes the car or Mercedes the girl?" The New York Times,* June 16, 1986.

353 *"the Europeans have the theory"* Lewis Cole, interviewed June 2002.

353 *"Jerry Rubin, just do it."* Daniel Cohn-Bendit, interviewed March 2003.

354 *he would say "de Gaulle." The New York Times,* June 13, 1968.

354 *"Or even two months ago?" Sunday Times* (London), June 16, 1968.

354 *"older Germans just glared at him."* Lewis Cole, interviewed June 2002.

356 *"realized nothing would happen."* Mark Rudd, interviewed April 2002.

358 *"but the Senate need not confirm them." Time,* July 5, 1968.

358 *contact with Griffin through John Ehrlichman,* John W. Dean, *The Rehnquist Choice: The Untold Story of the Nixon Appointment That Redefined the Supreme Court* (New York: Touchstone, 2001), 2 and note 6.

358 *before Fortas was on the bench.* Dean, *The Rehnquist Choice,* and Laura Kalman, *Abe Fortas: A Biography* (New Haven: Yale University Press, 1990), 340.

359 *"South and accolades from the Northeast." The New York Times,* August 10, 1968.

360 *distasteful to the South.* Mailer, *Miami and the Siege of Chicago,* 73.

361 *"Nig-ger-a-o . . ."* John Cohen, *The Essential Lenny Bruce* (New York: Bell Publishing Company, 1970), 59–60.

361 *"getting tired of Negroes and their rights."* Mailer, *Miami and the Siege of Chicago,* 51.

361 *"There is no way in hell . . . give a damn about us." The New York Times,* August 11, 1968.

362 *"veto powers over what is happening."* Ibid., August 12, 1968.

362 *more information on this later.* Ibid., September 9, 1968.

362 *"most of the time it does."* Ibid.

362 *"losing their sense of humor." The New York Times,* September 25, 1968.

363 *our tanks and our children. Life,* September 27, 1968.

363 *"has had it militarily"* Ibid.

363 *"There is none." The New York Times,* October 13, 1968.

364 *"peapickers and peckerwoods."* Ibid., October 29, 1968.

364 *"who will take care of things." The New York Times Magazine,* October 27, 1968.

365 *Nixon and Humphrey were equally friendly to Israel. The New York Times,* November 7, 1968.

365 *three additional seats in Georgia.* Ibid., November 6, 1968.

CHAPTER 21: The Last Hope

366 *"almost unnoticed" Life,* December 13, 1968.
368 *"law enforcement's most effective tool against crime." The New York Times,* November 24, 1968.
368 *a Westchester volunteer said.* Ibid., December 7, 1968.
368 *but the establishment press, Time,* December 6, 1968.
368 *"bad cops" who did not take orders.* Ibid.
369 *"contempt" for the flag. The New York Times,* October 4, 1968.
369 *"as night follows day"* Ibid., December 7, 1968.
369 *But the mayor had no comment.* Ibid., December 2, 1968.
372 *forty-eight years in prison, one was sentenced to twelve years, and one was acquitted.* Ibid., December 13, 1968.
372 *"send its troops to occupy American campuses." Ramparts,* June 15, 1968.
372 *"There are no innocent bystanders anymore." The New York Times,* December 6, 1968.
374 *rumors of a Powell run for president. Newsweek,* September 11, 1995.
374 *"oversold" the prospects for peace as the election approached. The New York Times,* December 14, 1968.
374 *eleven different configurations,* Langguth, *Our Vietnam,* 530.
375 *14,589 American servicemen . . . the highest casualties of the entire war.* Sheehan, *A Bright Shining Lie,* 726.
376 *"the ideology of reform Communism."* Mlynář, *Nightfrost in Prague,* 232.
377 *"The system inhibited change."* Dubček, *Hope Dies Last,* 165.
377 *The suppression . . . profound stagnation.* Mikhail Gorbachev and Zdeněk Mlynář, *Conversations with Gorbachev* (New York: Columbia University Press, 2002), 65.
378 *I wanted to create a democracy . . . the other half feels successful.* Jacek Kuroń, interviewed June 2001.
378 *"We have passed . . . relationships among our people." The New York Times,* December 16, 1968.
379 *"more powerful than he could ever be."* Marchand, *Marshall McLuhan,* 219.
380 *"I can recognize . . . I could see he was one."* Adam Michnik, interviewed June 2001.
381 *$44 billion on space missions. The New York Times,* October 1, 1968.
381 *blast out of the earth's orbit and go to the moon. Time,* October 11, 1968.
382 *I really believe . . . not envious or envied.* Michael Collins, *Carrying the Fire: An Astronaut's Journey* (New York: Cooper Square Press, 2001), 470.
383 *To get back up to the shining world from there,* Closing stanzas of Dante's *Inferno,* translated by Robert Pinsky.

BIBLIOGRAPHY

GENERAL

L'Année dans le monde: Les Faits de 1968, 1969. Paris: Arthaud, 1969.

Les Grands Événements 1968. Paris: Solar et Presses de la Cité, 1969.

Allyn, David. *Make Love, Not War: The Sexual Revolution, an Unfettered History*. Boston: Little, Brown & Co., 2000.

Berman, Paul. *A Tale of Two Utopias: The Political Journey of the Generation of 1968*. New York: W. W. Norton & Co., 1996.

Caute, David. *The Year of the Barricades: A Journey Through 1968*. New York: Harper & Row, 1988.

Charter, Ann, ed. *The Portable Sixties Reader*. New York: Penguin Classics, 2003.

Collins, Michael, *Carrying the Fire: An Astronaut's Journeys*. New York: Farrar, Straus & Giroux, 1974.

Fraser, Ronald, ed. *1968: A Student Generation in Revolt*. New York: Pantheon Books, 1988.

Gitlin, Todd. *The Sixties: Years of Hope, Days of Rage*. Toronto: Bantam Books, 1987.

Goodman, Mitchell, ed. *The Movement Toward a New America: A New Beginning of a Long Revolution*. Philadelphia: Pilgrim Press, 1970.

Hobsbawm, Eric, and Marc Weitzmann. *1968 Magnum Throughout the World*. Paris: Éditions Hazan, 1998.

Katzman, Allen, ed. *Our Time: An Anthology of Interviews from the East Village Other*. New York: Dial Press, 1972.

Kopkind, Andrew. *The Thirty Years War: Dispatches and Diversions of a Radical Journalist*. London: New York, 1995.

Marwick, Arthur. *The Sixties: Cultural Revolution in Britain, France, Italy, and the United States c. 1958–1974*. Oxford: Oxford University Press, 1998.

Schulke, Flip, and Matt Schudel. *Witness to Our Times: My Life as a Photojournalist*. Chicago: Marcato, 2003.

AMERICA

The Kerner Report: The 1968 Report of the National Advisory Commission on Civil Disorders. New York: Pantheon Books, 1988.

Califano, Joseph A., Jr. *The Triumph and Tragedy of Lyndon B. Johnson: The White House Years.* New York: Simon & Schuster, 1991.

Cohen, Robert, and Reginald E. Zelnik, eds. *The Free Speech Movement: Reflections on Berkeley in the 1960s.* Berkeley: University of California Press, 2002.

Dean, John W. *The Rehnquist Choice: The Untold Story of the Nixon Appointment That Redefined the Supreme Court.* New York: Simon & Schuster, 2001.

Dellinger, David. *From Yale to Jail: The Life Story of a Moral Dissenter.* New York: Pantheon Books, 1996.

Goodwin, Richard N. *Remembering America: A Voice from the Sixties.* Boston: Little, Brown & Co., 1988.

Hayden, Tom. *Rebellion and Repression.* New York: Meridian Books, 1969.

———. *Rebel: A Personal History of the 1960s.* Los Angeles: Red Hen Press, 2003.

———. *Reunion: A Memoir.* New York: Collier Books, 1989.

Hoffman, Abbie. *Revolution for the Hell of It.* New York: Dial Press, 1968.

Isserman, Maurice, and Michael Kazin. *America Divided: The Civil War of the 1960s.* New York: Oxford University Press, 2000.

Kaiser, Charles. *1968 in America: Music, Politics, Chaos, Counterculture, and the Shaping of a Generation.* New York: Weidenfeld & Nicolson, 1988.

Lesher, Stephan. *George Wallace: American Populist.* Reading, Pa.: Addison-Wesley Publishing, 1994.

Raskin, Jonah. *For the Hell of It: The Life and Times of Abbie Hoffman.* Berkeley: University of California Press, 1996.

Royko, Mike. *Boss: Richard J. Daley of Chicago.* New York: Plume, 1988.

Schlesinger, Arthur. *Robert Kennedy and His Times,* vols. 1 and 2. Boston: Houghton Mifflin, 1978.

Schultz, John. *No One Was Killed: Documentation and Meditation: Convention Week, Chicago, August 1968.* Chicago: Big Table Publishing Company, 1998.

Servan-Schreiber, Jean-Jacques. *The American Challenge.* New York: Atheneum, 1968.

Solberg, Carl. *Hubert Humphrey: A Biography.* New York: W. W. Norton & Co., 1984.

Steel, Ronald. *In Love with Night: The American Romance with Robert Kennedy.* New York: Touchstone, 2000.

Thomas, Evan. *Robert Kennedy: His Life.* New York: Simon & Schuster, 2000.

Wall, Byron, ed. *Manual for Draft-Age Immigrants to Canada.* Toronto: House of Anansi, 1970.

Witcover, Jules. *The Year the Dream Died: Revisiting 1968 in America.* New York: Warner Books, 1997.

CIVIL RIGHTS MOVEMENT

Carson, Clayborne, David Garrow, Bill Kovach, and Carol Polsgrove, eds. *Reporting Civil Rights: Part One, American Journalism 1941–1963; Part*

Two, *American Journalism 1963–1973*. New York: Library of America, 2003.

Cleaver, Eldridge. *Soul on Ice*. New York: Delta Trade Paperbacks, 1992.

Garrow, David J. *Bearing the Cross: And the Southern Christian Leadership Conference*. New York: William Morrow & Co., 1986.

———. *The FBI and Martin Luther King, Jr.: From "Solo" to Memphis*. New York: W. W. Norton & Co., 1981.

Halberstam, David. *The Children*. New York: Fawcett Books, 1998.

Haley, Alex. *The Autobiography of Malcolm X*. New York: Ballantine Books, 1992.

King, Mary. *Freedom Song: A Personal Story of the 1960s Civil Rights Movement*. New York: William Morrow & Co., 1987.

Lester, Julius. *Look Out, Whitey!: Black Power's Gon' Get Your Mama*. New York: Dial Press, 1968.

Pearson, Hugh. *The Shadow of the Panther: Huey Newton and the Price of Black Power in America*. Reading, Pa.: Addison-Wesley Publishing, 1994.

CUBA

Gosse, Van. *Where the Boys Are: Cuba, Cold War America and the Making of a New Left*. London: Verso, 1993.

Matthews, Herbert L. *Cuba*. New York: Macmillan, 1964.

Mills, C. Wright. *Listen, Yankee: The Revolution in Cuba*. New York: McGraw-Hill, 1960.

Szulc, Tad. *Fidel: A Critical Portrait*. New York: William Morrow & Co., 1986.

Thomas, Hugh. *Cuba: The Pursuit of Freedom*. New York: Harper & Row, 1971.

CULTURE

Cohen, John. *The Essential Lenny Bruce*. New York: Bell Publishing, 1970.

Graham, Bill, and Robert Greenfield. *Bill Graham Presents: My Life Inside Rock and Out*. New York: Doubleday, 1992.

Herbst, Peter, ed. *The Rolling Stone Interviews: Talking with the Legends of Rock & Roll 1967–1980*. New York: St. Martin's Press/Rolling Stone Press, 1981.

Heslam, David, ed. *Rock 'n' Roll Decades: The Sixties*. London: Octopus Illustrated Publishing, 1992.

CZECHOSLOVAKIA

Chapman, Colin. *August 21st: The Rape of Czechoslovakia*. London: Cassell & Company, 1968.

Dubček, Alexander. *Hope Dies Last: The Autobiography of Alexander*

Dubček. Jiri Hochman, ed. and trans. New York: Kodansha International, 1993.

Ello, Hugh, and Hugh Lunghi. *Dubček's Blueprint for Freedom: His Documents on Czechoslovakia Leading to the Soviet Invasion.* London: William Kimber & Co., 1969.

French Communist Party. *Et Les Événements de Tchécoslovaquie.* Paris: Bulletin de Propagande, no. 5, Septembre 1968.

Gorbachev, Mikhail, and Zdeněk Mlynář. *Conversations with Gorbachev: On Perestroika, the Prague Spring, and the Crossroads of Socialism.* George Shriver, trans. New York: Columbia University Press, 2002.

Mlynář, Zdeněk. *Night Frost in Prague: The End of Humane Socialism.* Paul Wilson, ed. New York: Karz Publishers, 1980.

Piekalkiewicz, Jaroslaw A. *Public Opinion Polling in Czechoslovakia, 1968–69: Results and Analysis of Surveys Conducted During the Dubček Era.* New York: Praeger Publishers, 1972.

Salomon, Michel. *Prague: La Révolution étranglée, Janvier–Août 1968.* Paris: Robert Laffront, 1968.

Schwartz, Harry. *Prague's 200 Days: The Struggle for Democracy in Czechoslovakia.* London: Pall Mall Press, 1969.

Shawcross, William. *Dubček.* New York: Simon & Schuster, 1990.

Valenta, Jiri. *Soviet Intervention in Czechoslovakia 1968: Anatomy of a Decision.* Baltimore: Johns Hopkins University Press, 1991.

Williams, Kieran. *The Prague Spring and Its Aftermath: Czechoslovak Politics 1968–1970.* Cambridge: Cambridge University Press, 1997.

Zeman, Z. A. B. *Prague Spring: A Report on Czechoslovakia 1968.* New York: Penguin Books, 1969.

DRUGS

Leary, Timothy. *Flashbacks.* Los Angeles: J. P. Tarcher, 1983.

Lee, Martin A., and Bruce Shalin. *Acid Dreams: The Complete Social History of LSD: The CIA, the Sixties, and Beyond.* New York: Grove Press, 1992.

Wolfe, Tom. *The Electric Kool-Aid Acid Test.* New York: Farrar, Straus & Giroux, 1968.

FEMINISM

Davis, Flora. *Moving the Mountain: The Women's Movement in America Since 1960.* New York: Simon & Schuster, 1991.

de Beauvoir, Simone. *The Second Sex: The Class Manifesto of the Liberated Woman.* New York: Vintage, 1974.

Evans, Sara. *Personal Politics: The Roots of Women's Liberation in the Civil Rights Movement and the New Left.* New York: Vintage Books, 1980.

Friedan, Betty. *The Feminine Mystique.* New York: Laurel, 1983.

Morgan, Robin. *Going Too Far: The Personal Chronicle of a Feminist.* New York: Random House, 1977.

FRANCE

Andro, P., A. Dauvergne, and L. M. Lagoutte. *Le Mai de la révolution*. New York: Julliard, 1968.

Aron, Raymond. *La Révolution introuvable: Réflexions sur les événements de Mai*. Paris: Librairie Arthème Fayard, 1968.

Ayache, Alain, ed. *Les Citations de la révolution de Mai*. Paris: Pauvert, 1968.

Barbey, Bruno. *Mai 68: ou L'imagination au pouvoir*. Paris: Éditions de la Différence/Vence: Galerie Beaubourg, 1998.

Cohn-Bendit, Daniel. *Le Gauchisme: Remède à la madie sénile du communisme*. Paris: Éditions du Seuil, 1968.

Dansette, Adrien. *Mai 1968*. Paris: Librairie Plon, 1971.

Dark Star, ed. *Beneath the Paving Stones: Situationists and the Beach, May 1968*. Edinburgh: AK Press/Dark Star, 2001.

Duprat, François. *Les Journées de Mai 68: Les Dessous une révolution*. Paris: N.E.L. et Défense de l'Occident, 1968.

Fabre-Luce, Alfred. *Le Général en Sorbonne*. Paris: Éditions de la Table Ronde, 1968.

Fauré, Christine. *Mai 68: Jour et nuit*. Paris: Découvertes Gallimard Histoire, 1998.

Feenberg, Andrew, and Jim Freedman. *When Poetry Ruled the Street: The French May Events of 1968*. Albany: State University of New York Press, 2001.

Filouche, Gérard. *68–98, Histoire sans fin*. Paris: Flammarion, 1998.

Grimaud, Maurice. *En Mai fais ce qu'il te plaît: Le Préfet de police de Mai 68 parle*. Paris: Éditions Stock, 1977.

Hamon, Hervé, and Patrick Rotman. *Génération*, vol. 1: *Les Années de rêve*. Paris: Éditions du Seuil, 1987.

Harris, André, and Alain de Sédouy. *Juifs & Français*. Paris: Éditions Grasset-Fasquelle, 1979.

Hartley, Anthony. *Gaullism: The Rise and Fall of a Political Movement*. New York: Outerbridge & Dienstfrey, 1971.

Joffrin, Laurent. *Mai 68: Histoire des événements*. Paris: Éditions du Seuil, 1998.

Karvetz, Marc. *L'Insurrection étudiante 2–13 Mai 1968*. Paris: Union Générale d'Éditions, 1968.

Labro, Philippe. *Les Barricades de Mai*. Paris: Solar & Agence Gamma, 1968.

———. *Ce N'Est qu'un début*. Paris: Éditions et Publications Premières, 1968.

Lacouture, Jean. *Pierre Mendès-France*. George Holoch, trans. New York: Holmes & Meier, 1984.

———. *De Gaulle 3: Le Souverain, 1959–1970*. Paris: Éditions du Seuil, 1986.

Les Murs ont la parole: Journal mural Mai 68. Paris: Claude Tchou, 1968.

Mai 68: À l'Usage des moins de 20 ans. Babel-Actes Sud, 1998.

Nairn, Tom, and Angelo Quattrocchi, *The Beginning of the End*. London: Verso, 1998.

Séguy, Georges. *"Le Mai" de la C.G.T.* Paris: Julliard, 1972.

Tournoux, J. R. *Le mois de Mai du général: Livre blanc des événements*. Paris: Librairie Plon, 1969.

GERMANY

Ardagh, John. *Germany and the Germans: An Anatomy of Society Today.* New York: Harper & Row, New York, 1987.

Craig, Gordon A. *The Germans.* New York: Meridian, 1991.

Demetz, Peter. *After the Fires: Recent Writing in the Germanys, Austria, and Switzerland.* San Diego: Harcourt Brace Jovanovich, 1986.

Heimannsberg, Barbara, and Christoph J. Schmidt, eds. *The Collective Silence: German Identity and the Legacy of Shame.* Cynthia Oudejans Jarris and Gordon Wheeler, trans. San Francisco: Jossey-Bass Publishers, 1993.

Raff, Diether. *A History of Germany: From the Medieval Empire to the Present.* Bruce Little, trans. Oxford: Berg Publishers, 1990.

HAITI

Burt, Al, and Bernard Diederich. *Papa Doc and the Tonton Macoutes.* Port-au-Prince: Éditions Henri Deschamps, 1986.

LITERATURE

Apollinaire, Guillaume. *The Poet Assassinated.* Josephson Matthew, trans. Cambridge: Exact Change, 2000.

Ball, Gordon. *Allen Verbatim: Lectures on Poetry, Politics, Consciousness by Allen Ginsberg.* New York: McGraw-Hill, 1974.

Camus, Albert. *The Plague.* Stuart Gilbert, trans. New York: Alfred A. Knopf, 1971.

———. *The Rebel: An Essay on Man in Revolt.* Anthony Bower, trans. New York: Alfred A. Knopf, 1961.

Ginsberg, Allen. *Planet News, 1961–1967.* San Francisco: City Lights Books, 1968.

———. *Collected Poems 1947–1980.* New York: Harper & Row, 1985.

Harris, William J., ed. *The LeRoi Jones/Amiri Baraka Reader.* New York: Thunder's Mouth Press, 2000.

Havel, Václav. *Selected Plays 1963–83.* London: Faber & Faber, 1992.

———. *Open Letters: Selected Writings, 1965–1990.* Paul Wilson, ed. New York: Vintage Books, 1992.

Jones, LeRoi. *Four Black Revolutionary Plays.* Indianapolis: Bobbs-Merrill, 1969.

———. *Home: Social Essays.* New York: William Morrow & Co., 1966.

Kramer, Jane. *Allen Ginsberg in America.* New York: Fromm International, 1997.

Lowell, Robert. *The Dolphin.* New York: Farrar, Straus & Giroux, 1973.

———. *For the Union Dead.* New York: Farrar, Straus & Giroux, 1964.

Mailer, Norman. *Miami and the Siege of Chicago: An Informal History of the Republican and Democratic Conventions of 1968.* New York: World Publishing Co., 1968.

———. *The Armies of the Night: History as a Novel, the Novel as History.*
New York: New American Library, 1968.
Mickiewicz, Adam. *Dziady (Forefathers' Eve;* Dresden text). Charles S.
Kraszewski, trans. Lehman: Libella Veritatis, 2000.
Sanders, Ed. *Shards of God.* New York: Grove Press, 1970.
Schumacher, Michael. *A Biography of Allen Ginsberg.* New York: St. Martin's
Press, 1992.

MEXICO

Alvarez Garín, Raúl. *La Estela de Tlatelolco: Una Reconstrucción histórica
del movimiento estudiantil del 68.*
Fehrenbach, T. R. *Fire and Blood: A History of Mexico.* New York: Macmillan, 1973.
García, Julio Scherer, and Carlos Monsiváis. *Parte de guerra: Los Rostros del
68.* Col. del Valle: Aguilar, 2002.
Grupo Mira. *La Grafica del 68: Homenaje al Movimiento Estudiantil.* Tercera
edición. Mexico City: Amigos de la Unidad de Postgrado de la Escuela de
Diseño A.C., 1981.
Mora, Juan Miguel de. *T-68, Tlatelolco 68: ¡Por Fin toda la verda!* Col. del
Valle: Edamex, 2000.
Paz, Octavio. *Posdata.* Mexico: Siglo xxi Editores, 2002.
Poniatowska, Elena. *La Noche de Tlatelolco.* Mexico: Ediciones Era, 1993.
Ramírez, Ramón. *El Movimiento estudiantil de México (Julio/Diciembre de
1968).* Mexico: Ediciones Era, 1998.

MIDDLE EAST

Oren, Michael B. *Six Days of War: June 1967 and the Making of the Modern
Middle East.* New York: Oxford University Press, 2002.

NEWS MEDIA

Gans, Herbert J. *Deciding What's News: A Study of CBS Evening News, NBC
Nightly News, Newsweek and Time.* New York: Vintage Books, 1980.
Halberstam, David. *The Powers That Be.* New York: Alfred A. Knopf, 1979.
Schorr, Daniel. *Staying Tuned: A Life in Journalism.* New York: Pocket Books,
2001.

PHILOSOPHY

Fanon, Frantz. *The Wretched of the Earth.* New York: Grove Press, 1963.
Marchand, Philip. *Marshall McLuhan: The Medium and the Messenger.*
Cambridge: MIT Press, 1998.

Marcuse, Herbert. *Reason and Revolution.* New Jersey: Humanities Press, 1997.

————. *One-Dimensional Man.* Boston: Beacon Press, 1991.

McLuhan, Eric, and Frank Zingrone, eds. *Essential McLuhan.* New York: Basic Books, 1995.

McLuhan, Marshall, and Quentin Fiore. *The Medium Is the Massage: An Inventory of Effects.* Corte Madera: Gingko Press, 2001.

POLAND

Abramsky, Chimen, Maciej Jachimczyk, and Antony Polonsky. *The Jews in Poland.* New York: Basil Blackwell, 1988.

Kersten, Krystyna. "The Mass Protests in People's Poland—A Continuous Process or Single Events?" In *Acta Ploniae Historica Sempter,* vol. 83, 165–192. Warszawa: Instytut Historii Pan, 2001.

Tollet, Daniel. *Histoire des Juifs en Pologne: Du XVI siècle à nos jours.* Paris: Presses Universitaires de France, 1992.

THE VIETNAM WAR

Appy, Christian G. *Patriots: The Vietnam War Remembered from All Sides.* New York: Viking, 2003.

Langguth, A. J. *Our Vietnam: The War 1954–1975.* New York: Simon & Schuster, 2000.

Oberdorfer, Don. *Tet!: The Turning Point in the Vietnam War.* Baltimore: Johns Hopkins University Press, 2001.

Prochnau, William. *Once upon a Distant War: Young War Correspondents and the Early Vietnam Battles.* New York: Random House, 1995.

Sheehan, Neil. *A Bright Shining Lie: John Paul Vann and America in Vietnam.* New York: Random House, 1988.

INDEX

university life
  authoritarian culture, 179–80, 208,
    217–18, 220–21, 330
  drug use, 183–84
  job recruitment on campus, 179
  music, 181–82
  See also student activism
University of Bonn, 145
University of California at Berkeley,
    90–93, 161, 234, 314, 372
University of Madrid, 16, 82, 104, 202
University of Michigan, 85–86, 180
University of Nanterre, 202, 217–22,
    355, 371
University of Paris, 217, 222
University of Rome, 82, 104, 109
University of Strasbourg, 217
University of Tennessee, 181–82
University of Warsaw, 68–77, 118–28,
    123, 127
University of Wisconsin, 82
Up Against the Wall exhibit, 229
Updike, John, 261
urban issues, 8, 111–12, 180–83,
    195–96
  See also police brutality; race riots
Urrutia, Oscar, 334

Vaizey, John, 106
Vallejo Martínez, Demetrio, 329, 332
Venice Biennale art show, 322
Viansson-Ponté, Pierre, 209–10
Viet Cong, 9, 374
  Christmas cease-fire, 375
  New Year's truce, 3, 13, 45
  pause in ground combat, January,
    47
  Tet Offensive, 51–52
Vietnam Discourse (Weiss), 152
Vietnamese war against the French, 4,
    60, 165, 211
Vietnam Solidarity Campaign (VSC),
    150, 153
Vietnam War, xviii, 8–11, 45
  American casualties, 9, 24, 56, 60,
    106, 204–5, 286, 375
  Ashau valley assault, 204
  Christmas cease-fire, 375
  costs, 9, 97, 105–6
  Gulf of Tonkin, 9, 95
  Hue, 60–62, 62
  Khe Sanh siege, 60, 204
  lessons gained from, 375
  media coverage, 49–54, 60–61, 179
  Mekong Delta fighting, 254

My Lai massacre, 106, 373, 373–74
napalm, 11–12
New Year's cease-fire, 3, 13, 45
Operation Pegasus, 204
opposition of civil rights leaders,
    43–44
Paris peace talks, 204–5, 222, 254,
    311, 365, 374
potential for use of nuclear
    weapons, 60
radical views, 151–52
Sontra village burning, 254
spin, 60–61
Tet Offensive, 50–60, 149, 151
U.S. Embassy attack, 51
U.S. troop levels, 205
Vietnamese casualties, xviii, 9, 13,
    24, 42, 205, 254
weapons contractors, 180
  See also antiwar movement; draft
    resistance; North Vietnam; South
    Vietnam
Villa, Pancho, 160, 323–25, 331, 339
Village Voice, 96–99
Viola, Franca, 370
violent protest, 116, 195, 307–8
Von Hahn, Fritz Gebhard, 145
von Rosen, Carl Gustav, 259–60
voting rights
  age, 179, 379–80
  registration, 89–91
  suffrage movement, 309
Voznesensky, Andrey, 133

Wagner, Robert F., 163
Wakefield, Dan, 52
Walker, Daniel, 368
Walker, Gordon, 84
Walker, Jerry Jeff, 182
Walker Commission, 284, 368–70
Wallace, George, 174–75, 263, 268,
    285, 360, 364–66
Wallach, Eli, 47
Wall Street, 47
Warren, Earl, 186, 357
War Requiem (Britten), 134
Warsaw Pact invasion of Czechoslo-
    vakia, 244, 248–50, 276–77,
    287–99
Watergate, 370
Watts, Richard, Jr., 74
Watts riot of 1965, 8, 135, 147, 333
Wayne, John, 53
Weather Underground, 356–57
Wein, Lawrence A., 180

PERMISSIONS ACKNOWLEDGMENTS

SDS poster announcing a demonstration before election day, 1968: Center for the Study of Political Graphics.

1968 Yippie poster calling for a demonstration at the Nixon inauguration: Courtesy of The Library of Congress.

1970 poster, after the My Lai massacre became known . . . : From the collection of Mary Haskell.

The earth in the last week of 1968: National Space Science Data Center, *Apollo 8* Photo, 68-118A-01A, The Principal Investigator, Dr. Richard J. Allenby, Jr.

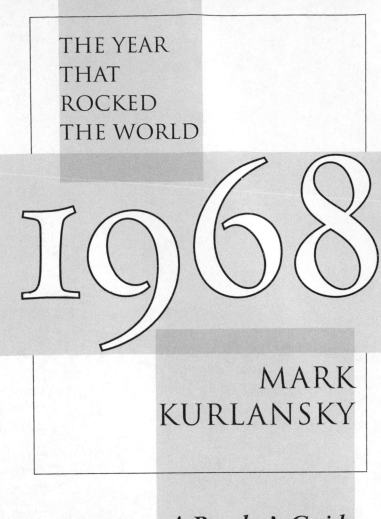

THE YEAR THAT ROCKED THE WORLD

1968

MARK KURLANSKY

A Reader's Guide

READER'S GROUP QUESTIONS

1. How did the explosive worldwide social movements of 1968 make that year unique?

2. What was the international impact of the civil rights movement on the events of 1968?

3. What progress or setbacks have there been in the status of women since that time?

4. How did television influence that year's events?

5. How does the mass media of today differ from 1968's?

6. What was the global significance of the Prague Spring?

7. What events of 1968 would not occur today?

8. How is it that such a tragic year arouses nostalgia in so many people?

9. Was the world a better place before 1968, or do you feel there have been changes for the better since that year?

10. What lessons might we learn from the events of 1968?

ABOUT THE TYPE

This book was set in Sabon, a typeface designed by the well-known German typographer Jan Tschichold (1902–74). Sabon's design is based on the original letterforms of Claude Garamond and was created specifically to be used for three sources: foundry type for hand composition, Linotype, and Monotype. Tschichold named his typeface for the famous Frankfurt typefounder Jacques Sabon, who died in 1580.

Also by
MARK KURLANSKY
THE BIG OYSTER
HISTORY ON THE HALF SHELL

Before New York City was the Big Apple, it could have been called the Big Oyster. When Peter Minuit bought Manhattan for $24 in 1626—the first New York real estate killing—he showed his shrewdness by also buying the oyster beds off nearby Ellis Island. New York became a city world famous for its oysters and their impressive size—until centuries of pollution finally destroyed the beds in the early 1920s. The story of the New York oyster is the story of the city and its place in the world, and the story of centuries of culinary evolution in a city that has always been a gastronomic trend setter.

"A chatty, free-wheeling history of New York City told from the humble perspective of the once copious, eagerly consumed, now decimated eastern oyster (*Crassostrea virginica*) . . . . Kurlansky's history digresses all over the place, and sparkles."
—*Publishers Weekly,* starred review

"Kurlansky takes a fresh look at the tasty, once plentiful mollusk in this stimulating, often fascinating saga. A compelling, highly readable treat." —*Kirkus Reviews,* starred review

A Ballantine Books Hardcover

www.BallantineBooks.com

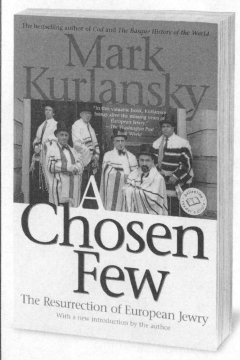